D1563770

Critical Essays on

ALFRED LORD TENNYSON

CRITICAL ESSAYS
ON
BRITISH LITERATURE

Zack Bowen, General Editor
University of Miami

Critical Essays on

ALFRED LORD TENNYSON

edited by

HERBERT F. TUCKER

G. K. Hall & Co. / New York
Maxwell Macmillan Canada / Toronto
Maxwell Macmillan International / New York Oxford Singapore Sydney

Property of
THE HIGH POINT
NEAL F. AUSTIN
PUBLIC LIBRARY

Copyright © 1993 by Herbert F. Tucker

All rights reserved. No part of this book may be reproduced or transmitted
in any form or by any means, electronic or mechanical, including
photocopying, recording, or by any information storage and retrieval
system, without permission in writing from the Publisher.

G. K. Hall & Co.
Macmillan Publishing Company
866 Third Avenue
New York, New York 10022

Maxwell Macmillan Canada, Inc.
1200 Eglinton Avenue East
Suite 200
Don Mills, Ontario M3C 3N1

Library of Congress Cataloging-in-Publication Data

Critical essays on Alfred Lord Tennyson / edited by Herbert F. Tucker.
     p.   cm. — (Critical essays on British literature)
    Includes bibliographical references and index.
    ISBN 0-8161-8864-5
    1. Tennyson, Alfred Tennyson, Baron, 1809–1892—Criticism and
interpretation. I. Tucker, Herbert F. II. Series.
PR5588.C75   1993
821'.8—dc20
                                       92-38699
                                         CIP

The paper used in this publication meets the minimum requirements of
American National Standard for Information Sciences—Permanence of
Paper for Printed Library Materials. ANSI Z3948-1984.∞™

10   9   8   7   6   5   4   3   2   1

Printed in the United States of America

9305681

Contents

◆

General Editor's Note

♦

The Critical Essays on British Literature series provides a variety of approaches to both classical and contemporary writers of Britain and Ireland. The formats of the volumes in the series vary with the thematic designs of individual editors, and with the amount and nature of existing reviews and criticism, augmented, where appropriate, by original essays by recognized authorities. It is hoped that each volume will be unique in developing a new overall perspective on its particular subject. Professor Tucker's brief introduction succinctly covers the history of Tennyson's critical reception from the days of his tremendous popularity and identity with the Empire, through the closer analytical treatment of turn-of-the-century professional scholar/critics of English letters and the decline of public attention following World War I, until the recent revival of interest in the poet-as-public-man by the historical/political criticism of the 1980s. Tucker's selection, all from the 1980s, includes several introductory essays on broad aspects of Tennyson's career, the main section on particular poems in chronological order, and two concluding essays on the poet's later work and general retrospective argument.

ZACK BOWEN
University of Miami

Publisher's Note

◆

Producing a volume that contains both newly commissioned and reprinted material presents the publisher with the challenge of balancing the desire to achieve stylistic consistency with the need to preserve the integrity of works first published elsewhere. In the Critical Essays series, essays commissioned especially for a particular volume are edited to be consistent with Twayne's house style; reprinted essays appear in the style in which they were first published, with only typographical errors corrected. Consequently, shifts in style from one essay to another are the result of our efforts to be faithful to each text as it was originally published.

Editor's Note

◆

The first three essays in this book address broad topics spanning Tennyson's career. The next eight center on particular poems and are arranged to follow the order in which the poet composed them. The last two essays round out the volume with discussions of the poet's later work that illustrate a retrospective argument of more general pertinence. Each contribution, then, may be consulted independently; but the anthology may also be read as an ensemble overview of Tennyson's work from the vantage of the 1980s. The index is organized by proper names and poem titles to facilitate cross-reference.

The place of original publication for each essay is given at the bottom of the page on which it begins. For reasons of space, many of the essays have been abbreviated or assembled from one or more chapters of longer studies; for reasons of legibility, this editorial condensation has been carried out without imposing marks of ellipsis. Endnotes have been renumbered as needed for continuity and reformatted for consistency. Several transitional passages have undergone minor rephrasing, with the authors' consent and in some cases their collaboration—in every case, with the editor's thanks. Thanks are also due to the authors and original publishers for copyright permissions, and to John Appling and Dan Philippon for help in preparing the manuscript.

H. F. T.

Introduction

HERBERT F. TUCKER

This anthology gathers a baker's dozen essays on Tennyson published by North American and British scholars during the 1980s. The choice of such recent criticism makes this book something of an anomaly in the *Critical Essays* series, and also something of a wager: a wager that the following chapters represent the directions likeliest to guide work on the central English poet of the nineteenth century into the twenty-first century. While the contemporaneity of this collection is admittedly a luxury, it is one made affordable in Tennyson's case by the existence of several earlier collections of which the student should be aware. *Tennyson: The Critical Heritage*, ed. John D. Jump (1967), assembles important reviews and commentary published during the poet's lifetime. *Critical Essays on the Poetry of Tennyson*, ed. John Killham (1960), reprints much of the best Tennysonian scholarship and criticism produced during the middle decades of this century. A hundred years of response to Tennyson's most important poem are represented in *Tennyson: In Memoriam: A Casebook*, ed. John Dixon Hunt (1970). Work from the 1960s and 1970s is included in two subsequent anthologies: *Tennyson: A Collection of Critical Essays*, ed. Elizabeth A. Francis (1980), and *Alfred Lord Tennyson*, ed. Harold Bloom (1985). The present anthology resumes the story of Tennyson criticism where its predecessors break off. That story possesses an interest of its own; and some preliminary acquaintance with it will help the reader to situate this book in a continuum of response to Tennyson—as a superbly gifted writer, as a cultural phenomenon without parallel among English poets—and so to appreciate the obligations and urgencies of the essays that follow.

The most interesting thing about the story of Tennyson criticism may be that it gets told so often. It is available in serial installments from the editors' introductions to the anthologies just named, but in Tennyson studies these recapitulations are only the tip of an iceberg. Some version of the story intrudes into most books on the poet, with a regularity that borders on group obsession and that routine academic protocol cannot explain. Tennyson scholars' ritual rehearsal of their critical genealogy suggests that the story they tell stands for something more. And so it does; for Tennyson ranks among those cardinally representative writers whose work and reception hold larger implications for the state of scholarship within literary discourse, and beyond that for the place of literature within modern culture. Partly because of Tennyson's Victorian preeminence, partly because that preeminence and the reaction against it coincided with the establishment of English studies within the modern academy, no claim to neutrality about his poetry and its impact is easy to sustain. The meaning of his work, and the meaning of the meanings given it by readers for a century and a half, concern us nearly. Whether the history of Tennyson's reception arises to vindicate or condemn our work—and no matter how much we mind its capacity for doing both of these things—we come back to it in order to judge ourselves.

This vivid sense of pertinence has charged commentary on Tennyson since the beginning. That the poet's first readers in family and university circles took his writing personally is no surprise, but in the public forum, too, reviewers very quickly did something of the same kind. Tennyson was felt, almost at once, to be exemplary. If his faults epitomized those of the album verse that reigned over British poetry of the 1820s, his virtues promised a way out of the cul-de-sac into which poetry seemed to have turned with the deaths of John Keats, Percy Bysshe Shelley, and Lord Byron—and, more ominously, with the post-Waterloo ascendancy of a commercial society hostile or indifferent to imaginative nurture. During the 1830s, that is, Tennyson became an important focus for questions about poetry, the condition of which mirrored what Victorians were beginning to call the Condition-of-England question. Even where the reviewers treated his first books with reference to poetic tradition and craft, the context of such treatment was current and national.

With the passage of years—and of legislation setting the terms for public life in a reformed England under a young queen newly crowned—issues of national identity yielded to issues of national purpose; and criticism of Tennyson shifted its terms accordingly. What had been matter of debate in the early 1830s became cause for exhortation a decade later. England had a boundless productive energy; that energy wanted consecration as a mission expressed to herself and to the world. Tennyson might be the man for the job if only he could be talked into it. The revised and expanded *Poems* of 1842, critics agreed, had given abundant proof of Tennyson's resourcefulness and invention. And this technical capability in matters poetical bore a striking resemblance to Great Britain's in matters industrial. Both held an inestimable potential, but neither had as yet been harnessed to an end worthy of its promise. The movement in Tennyson criticism from appreciative estimation to optimistic expectancy, and the progress from apprenticeship to mastery that critics in the 1840s encouraged the poet to complete, reflected larger progressivist impulses sweeping the country.

With the appearance of *In Memoriam* in 1850, Tennyson amply fulfilled the national role that critics had forecast for him. At once a personal homage and a public testament, the new poem sounded not only the call of mid-Victorian progressivism but also its suppressed undersong, the burden of anxious disaffection that so manic an era could not help muttering under its breath. Reviewers' accolades, brisk sales, and the award of the poet laureateship consolidated a status that Tennyson would enjoy in the public mind for decades to come. Enjoy, and suffer too: the extraordinary symbiosis between Tennyson's laureate work and Victorian middle-class culture would henceforth condition nearly all that his reviewers found to say, for better or worse, on either topic. During the flush 1850s and 1860s the news was largely good. *Maud* provoked some dissent, to be sure, but that dissent mainly came from a loyal opposition who took the poem's public character for granted and whose reservations had to do with its political implications. After *Maud* the laureate's major work in the domestic and the heroic idyll invited patriotic celebration. Tennyson's eminence on the cultural scene being as much a fait accompli as Britain's on the global scene, critics returned to detailed appreciation that had been dormant since 1842; even the exception they took to occasional blemishes confirmed the general honor of his rule. Commending Tennyson as the representative writer they had said he ought to become, reviewers congratulated themselves, and their readers, on being the models and beneficiaries of the national life his poetry was committed to representing.

The poet who rode to more than fame on the crest of Victorian complacency was destined to totter with the faltering of national confidence. Tennyson knew this very well: he confessed as much to friends; and his principal laureate achievement, *Idylls of the King*, virtually foretold it in the collapse of the consensus upholding King Arthur. Tennyson's decline would be as gradual as Arthur's, and the crumbling of consensual faith would be as incremental and striated in historical London as in mythic Camelot. But the decline may be dated roughly from 1870, or around the time when the Second Reform Bill of 1867 formally altered the electoral basis of political representation from that which had been established under the First Reform Bill in 1832, when Tennyson's reputation was initially being forged. It was also around 1870 that the great Victorian bubble of industrial capitalism was perceived to be bursting, and with it the bourgeois dream of steadily diffusive prosperity. In reaction to the era's incipient malaise, late-Victorian policy makers and spokesmen sought newly explicit grounds for British self-justification. They set about transforming an implicit ideal of rooted nationhood and global outreach into an overt ideology of imperial conquest and dominion.

These changes did much to weaken the attractiveness of a poet who was as fully identified as Tennyson was with the national life, and whose very appeal lay rather in rendering an intuited wholeness than in articulating or defending a consciously held position. As national feeling yielded to national opinion and debate, and as the empire of shared public sentiment gave place to imperialism as a system of rule expressly constructed and enforced, Tennyson the spokesman looked more and more like Tennyson the ideologue. He looked like that especially to a new generation of cosmopolitan aesthetes and literati who were making intellectual headway in the reviewing columns, and on whom the insular therapies of *In Memoriam* no longer cast their old charm. The laureate's popularity had become such that to fault him was to fault the age, and vice versa. And that, for the rising critics of the 1870s and 1880s, was precisely the point.

Tennyson's detractors, however, remained a decided minority during his lifetime. The adoring reportage from the poet's deathbed and the high requiem of his obsequies at Westminster Abbey in 1892 show how firmly he retained a loyal corps of defenders who were also defenders of the old regime, with its old compact between the spheres of private feeling and public mission. But that compact was clearly dissolving, and defenses mounted on its terms were largely reactionary. More significant defenses of Tennyson toward the fin de siècle took up instead the modern stance of that new entrant on the cultural stage, the literature specialist. Not only in periodicals but increasingly in belletristic books and scholarly monographs, professionally certified readers began to focus on such topics as Tennyson's formal technique, his learned allusiveness, his system of ethics, his contribution to the discourse of spirituality—a tapestry of refinements whose common thread was a depoliticizing abstraction of the poet's work from the larger work of culture as formerly conceived. Studies like these, reflecting the specialization and professionalization of late-Victorian intellectual life, cut channels along which critical response to Tennyson has run ever since.

Poets at their death may always become their admirers; but in Tennyson's case the class of admirers soon overlapped with classes of teachers and students, as his poetry became officially what it had been informally for some time: a vehicle of indoctrination. This was due partly to the historical coincidence of the laureate's celebrity with the movement to reground academic humanism on English rather than classical literature and partly to the way the nigh synonymous categories "Victorian" and "Tennysonian" became available in Edwardian days to rearguard and vanguard forces alike. For the rearguard, Tennyson served to focus a nostalgic and doctrinaire reprise of Victorian apologetics for hearth and empire. The cultural vanguard used Tennyson, no less regularly, to sharpen a sense of their own modernity on an establishment icon that could be stigmatized as patently passé, and to hammer that sense into the formulaic manifestos of a Modernist program.

World War I and its aftermath dated Tennyson more decisively than ever in the public mind. Yet the climate of postwar disillusionment did less to change the poet's standing than to accelerate a process of downward revaluation already well underway. The truly decisive change in his reception—one worth highlighting because the enormity of the Great War can obscure it from modern memory—had occurred years before, when men of letters' pronouncements on Tennyson as a topic of commonly shared interest were replaced by experts' lectures converting him into a topic for research and examination. The gains in historical distance and generalizing power that accompanied this change will be self-evident to users of a book like this. Yet to survey the incorporation of Victoria's laureate with her realm's public life is to glimpse the cost entailed by Tennyson's appropriation on the part of a specialist intelligentsia: the loss of a collective stake in a national poet and, in the same stroke, of a belief that poetry might possess a very general pertinence.

These considerations preoccupy the two most significant studies of Tennyson produced after the Great War, each by a writer with Modernist affiliations who stood between academic and publishing worlds. Harold Nicolson's *Tennyson* (1923) set out to save the poet from his success by maintaining, on Bloomsbury premises, that Tennyson's cultural responsiveness and popularity had conspired to corrupt the brooding lyricism that was his authentically native gift. This thesis not only gave expression to a typical twentieth-century ambivalence about Tennyson, but also gave it cogent explanation, and indeed erected it into a principle of critical discrimination. Nicolson's distinction between the reliably enduring Tennyson and the merely timely—and, by extension, between private and public motives for modern poetry—went on to exert wide influence among critics. More influential still was T. S. Eliot's 1936 essay *"In Memoriam,"* the only article to appear in each of the anthologies of twentieth-century criticism recommended above. Pursuing Nicolson's line of argument but treating it in a spirit at once gentler and more vulnerable, Eliot arrived at haunting insights about the relations between Tennysonian surface and depth, faith and doubt, as they register the antithetically conformist and rebellious impulses of modern poetry. (These insights apply of course as fully to Eliot, himself the central figure in a poetic Modernism aggressively astray from social centrality, as to his Victorian forebear.) The staying power of both these Modernist accounts owes much to their having read back into Tennyson the dialectic of incorporation and alienation that has continued to govern his reception, as it has continued to govern twentieth-century intellectual life. The work of Nicolson and Eliot clings to us still, after all theoretical innovation and methodological refinement, by virtue of its admission—and admonition—that Tennyson's dilemma was our own.

It seems impossible to summarize the last fifty years' work without claiming too much or specifying too little about a body of criticism that readers of this book will recognize as typifying either their own training or that of their teachers. Still, that body of criticism may be divided into two main phases that have framed most contemporary interpretations, up to and including the essays selected here. With few exceptions the study of Tennyson's poetry across the middle decades of our century manifested the intensification of textual focus that was heralded by F. R. Leavis' scrutineers in Britain and the formalist New Critics in the United States. Poems came under the microscope for a high-powered analysis of verbal structure and nuance, an analysis keyed to the imaginative framing and refinement of complex psychological states. Students of Victorian literature, it is true, tended more than many others to shun the ascendant textualist fashion, in the name of scholarly responsibility to historical context; yet insofar as by context they usually meant biography, in practice their work on Tennyson followed the psychological bias of the day. Critical and scholarly attention at mid-century thus gravitated toward the melancholic privacy and deep dissent that Nicolson and Eliot had identified in Tennyson, and it concentrated on the more lyrically inward portions of his oeuvre. The other Tennyson, the civic-faced laureate of public mission, received polite or apologetic acknowledgment but comparatively little investigation.

Retrieving this other Tennyson has become the task of a second phase in critical scholarship, a phase belonging to the larger movement currently known as cultural studies. This movement has arisen during the past two decades in conjunction with fresh efforts to theorize the means and ends of literary criticism. Redoubled inquiry into the dynamics of the self, and into the inherently differential character of language, has lately splintered the once sturdy lever of mid-century ego psychology. What is more, rekindled speculation on the social conditioning of subjective desire and expression has all but sent the autonomous Romantic self up in smoke. These developments call into question the psychological premises not only of textual formalism but also of contextual historicism as practiced until quite recently. Positivistic models, according to which a literary work like *Idylls of the King* mirrors a preestablished worldview like Victorian imperialism, are giving way on most sides to suppler, reciprocating models of textual and contextual interaction. The rise of cultural studies has brought with it moreover a new tolerance— in some quarters an expectation—of committed engagement on the part of the critic. Feminism and Marxism, to name just two programs represented among the essays below, conceive the critic's writing to be, no less than the poet's, a value-laden intervention in ongoing struggles for discursive authority.

During the 1980s, then, Tennyson criticism has adopted a mode of inquiry that seeks to preserve the disciplinary legacy of close reading, while locating its practice within an expanded horizon of reference that embraces the social with the human sciences and that carries ethical implications deriving less from psychology than from politics. How well this development bodes for Tennyson criticism emerges from several contributions to this collection, for instance those by Joseph Chadwick, Christopher Craft, Eve Sedgwick, and Alan Sinfield. Cultural-studies approaches are at present ideally suited not just to reviving interest in Tennyson's more obviously public poems, but also to furthering an understanding of the socially representative aspects of all his work. These aspects, though slighted by psychological formalism a generation ago, have always fundamentally oriented Tennyson's reception. As this introduction has tried to show, nineteenth-century criticism first conspired to make the poet a public fixture, then lauded itself and him on the durability of the result, only to seek excuse at century's end from the very alliance it had forged—leaving twentieth-century criticism more or less where it has been ever since, in an uneasy state of truce with Tennyson and what he stands for. Victorianist cultural study has much to tell about the greatest of poet laureates, and will tell more in years to come, because Tennyson himself was from the first such a study in Victorian culture.

The present conjunction of method with subject is propitious: from the vantage point offered by cultural studies, criticism of Tennyson now enjoys an excellent opportunity to recover and assess its own modern origins. Yet this opportunity entails at the same time certain liabilities, among them the tendency of cultural studies to flatten poems into documents and reduce the literary work to an article like any other in the catalogue of historical mentalities. The synoptic ambition of cultural studies risks losing touch, in other words, with the particularity of given poems, which tends to escape notice in proportion to the breadth of compass such studies attempt. Our surest safeguard against such a loss in local attentiveness is probably still the instance of formalism, which survives from mid-century—under correction, and with whatever reservations—in several critical modes represented in this book. Isobel Armstrong's and Matthew Rowlinson's essays, for example, demonstrate the continuing pertinence for Tennyson studies of a deconstructive focus on language and textuality; while the contributions by Daniel Harris and Timothy Peltason exemplify, from different philosophical perspectives, the close reading of tone and mood that Tennyson's strenuous lyricism always requires.

Tennyson's relation to mainstream Victorian ideologies was as subtle as it was steady, and its master key remains his consistent and often devious linguistic finesse. This is why one criterion guiding the choice of essays for the present anthology has been that contributors respect the tact, and the daring, of the poet's language. Only criticism that takes its cue from Tennyson's artfulness will be ready to trace his interweaving of statements with their implications, of a given myth with its specific instance, of ideological reflection with poetic sensation. We have no better means than verbal attentiveness for untangling the webs of complicity and interference that initially gave Tennyson his cultural standing, and that give him his historical significance still. We need to learn more about how his exquisite early poetry emerged from the sweetshop of 1820s verse to shape new Victorian tastes;

about his familiarity with nineteenth-century mythological and philological investigations and how he put them to poetic use; and about the connections between highbrow and middlebrow spheres that made possible, and were in turn reinforced by, his extraordinary popularity. The effectiveness of research into such topics will depend, however, on our ability to turn knowledge into criticism, by returning to the structures of poetic language that constitute Tennyson's chief claim on our time, or on anybody else's.

Literary study in the twenty-first century may add to the innovations of cultural studies a new formalism whose branches include, say, the embodied or materialist prosody advanced here in Eric Griffiths's work on breathing and voice, or in Alan Sinfield's on the poetically compensatory replenishment of the metaphysically hollow signifier. The theory of such a cultural neoformalism has yet to be written; we break ground for it, in the meantime, by writing the most locally alert and historically circumspect criticism we can. Whatever shape it assumes, the criticism of the future will not find a more challenging or rewarding subject than the poetry of Tennyson. The foregoing outline of Tennyson's reception has adduced from recent literary history some general reasons favoring this prophecy; the essays that follow will give it more persuasively specific support. Fulfillment of the prophecy must rest, though, with such readers as these essays may find: readers who approach this anthology as a collective progress report on work in the field, and who are encouraged to go and do likewise—and better.

To this end, Tennyson's future readers will find substantial help from four major aids to research that have appeared during the 1980s. One of them is excerpted below, in the model biographical and bibliographical essay with which Cecil Lang and Edgar Shannon introduce their complete edition of *The Letters of Alfred Lord Tennyson* (3 volumes, 1981–1990). A full-dress critical biography is available in Robert Bernard Martin's *Tennyson: The Unquiet Heart* (1980). The handsome text and discerning annotation of Christopher Ricks' *The Poems of Tennyson* (2nd ed. in 3 volumes, 1987) make that complete edition a scholar's dream come true—a dream without repression, in that the late release of important, hitherto sheltered manuscripts now affords unrestricted access to the record of Tennyson's habits in composition and revision. The great manuscript hoard may itself be consulted, through facsimile reproduction, in *The Tennyson Archive*, ed. Christopher Ricks and Aidan Day, an edition of some thirty volumes still in progress but nearly finished as this anthology goes to press.

The Poet as Man of Letters

CECIL Y. LANG AND EDGAR F. SHANNON, JR.

When the first volume of this edition of letters opens, Alfred Tennyson, third of the eleven surviving children of an obscure, unhappy country parson in mid-Lincolnshire, is a twelve-year-old boy. He composes a letter to one of his aunts showing, or showing off, a self-conscious adolescent familiarity with Milton, Dante, Byron, and Horace. In the second letter, three years later, he adds, ornamentally, Ossian, Milman, Moore, Crabbe, Coleridge, and Cervantes, and includes some of his own compositions.

When the volume closes, three decades later, in December 1850, Alfred Tennyson, aged forty-one, recently married, author of *In Memoriam* (and several other volumes of poems), and newly appointed Poet Laureate, is clearly destined to be, if he is not already, the most famous living English poet. This coincidence of 'life and use and name and fame' all within six months, was not fortuitous—the events depended one upon another. He was appointed Poet Laureate (in his son's words) 'owing chiefly to Prince Albert's admiration for "In Memoriam." ' He finally married, after more than a decade of indecision, uncertainty, self-doubt, poverty, frustration, and actual prohibition, at least partially because of Emily Sellwood's approbation of *In Memoriam*. His own decision to marry, kept secret from most of his friends and relatives, including his mother, was for whatever complex of reasons— emotional, sexual, financial—probably due at least partially to *In Memoriam*.

When this edition concludes, seventy-one years later, Baron Tennyson of Aldworth and Farringford, the style encompassing his two houses, one in Surrey, the other in the Isle of Wight, Poet Laureate to the Queen, wealthy, honoured at home and the world over, friend not only of the intellectual and artistic élite but also of the rich and powerful, beyond all compare the most famous literary figure in the English-speaking world, lies buried in Westminster Abbey, of which the Dean (as his predecessor had been) was a personal friend and where both his sons had been married.

Though the principal events of Tennyson's life are recorded in many places, a review of some of the background will be helpful. Tennyson's grandfather, George Tennyson (1750–1835), son of a surgeon who had

Reprinted from *The Letters of Alfred Lord Tennyson*, vol. 1, ed. Cecil Y. Lang and Edgar F. Shannon, Jr., by permission. © 1981 by Harvard University Press.

married above his station, was a solicitor and attorney in Lincoln and, later, in the village of Market Rasen who, having inherited money, married money, and made money, now set out to acquire the dignity of social standing. He was worldly and secular, and social respectability meant dynastic dignity. Through his mother, Elizabeth Clayton, as Charles Tennyson, the poet's grandson and biographer, has written, he 'claimed descent through the Hildeyards, from two distinct and unrelated holders of the Barony of d'Eyn-court and ultimately from King Edward III'. Having made his pile, he wanted to build one, though in the event the actual accomplishment of this was delayed till the next generation. As early as 1783 he began acquiring property at Tealby, anciently known as the Manor of Beacons (i.e. *Bayons*, fantasied as a corruption of *Bayeux*), an estate that, centuries earlier, had indeed belonged to the D'Eyncourts, though of the olden castle only vague traces now remained of walls, ditches, towers, and a courtyard. Additions to this purchase following, in due course he and his wife, with their two daughters and two sons, moved into Tealby Lodge, which, as early as 1810, they persuaded themselves to refer to as Bayons Manor, a name rescued from title deeds. The country attorney turned country gentleman now aspired to the status of county family.

The older son, born in 1778, the father of Alfred Tennyson, was in the natural course of events named George Clayton; the second son, six years younger, was christened Charles. Within twelve years, their father, perceiv-ing, for whatever reasons, that the elder was not the material out of which dynasties are fashioned, invested his ambitions in the cadet; and during the next four decades he treated the younger as the older, the older as the younger, designating the older for the Church, the younger for public life. Charles was called to the bar in 1806, married money in 1808, became a Member of Parliament in 1818, and in every way justified his father's faith and realized his father's ambitions. George was ordained deacon and priest, presented with several livings, married the daughter of a vicar, and in every way justified his father's lack of faith and (apparently) realized his father's expectations.

Handsome (as his portrait shows), lusty, over six feet tall, learned in languages, literature, music, and other arts, sentenced to a profession for which he had little vocation and less desire, and in which he had no interest, considering himself (not quite accurately) disinherited, he lived and died, as these letters reveal, an embittered, drunken, violent, backwater clergyman.

The grandfather outlived his older son by four years. He persuaded his other son to abandon public office (except the parliamentary seat) in order to start the work of becoming a county family, and he himself quitted his own home and moved into Usselby House, an estate nearby, leaving Bayons Manor to Charles (now with seven children). Charles was not only the heir, he was also the only surviving son—Mr Tennyson, no longer Mr Charles Tennyson. (The distinction had rankled.) Harry Coningsby became Willoughby Patterne. The remains of the old castle, among which he now resided, gleamed in his eyes, and the name of the old barony resounded in his ears. Earlier, with great difficulty, he had persuaded his father to take legal steps to adopt the name of D'Eyncourt (instead of Tennyson), but the petition had been refused by the College of Heralds. Now he persuaded his father to make adoption of the *additional* name a condition of inheriting Usselby. The old man died on 4 July 1835, and three weeks later the Bayons Manor Tennysons 'assumed by Royal License the additional name and arms of D'Eyncourt' (*Landed Gentry*). In the months following, the old manor, Tealby Lodge, was enclosed in a splendidly vulgar 'gewgaw castle' constructed in various styles described as Fake- or Sham- or Pseudo- or Operatic-Gothic, complete with half a moat and a drawbridge not designed to draw.

The history of Tennyson's letters (there *is* a history) must be rehearsed, and it is the story of two men—one his older son, Hallam Tennyson, the other Charles Tennyson, second son of Lionel Tennyson, his younger son.

Hallam Tennyson (1852–1928) attended Marlborough College and in 1872 entered Trinity College, Cambridge. In September 1874, after a supposedly therapeutic tour in France, his mother, Emily Tennyson, who had not only managed the running of two houses, cosseting her husband in every conceivable way, but also handled much of his correspondence, collapsed. In December Hallam Tennyson, home from Trinity, began a fine letter to Edward FitzGerald: 'My father bids me write to you as my mother is not well enough to write' and concluded with 'And now having many letters to write for I have become the family secretary,/With best wishes from us all,/Yours affectionately though unknown/Hallam Tennyson.' Barely an adult, he became—and remained for eighteen years—his father's companion, secretary, and factotum, selfless in his unremitting devotion. In September 1893 about a year after Tennyson's death, the widow wrote to George Lillie Craik, at Macmillan's, desiring him to place at the head of the poem 'De Profundis' the name of Hallam Tennyson (for whom it was composed); 'I should wish our Hallam's name to appear among *His* poems, though of course his Father's entire trust in him is proved by his having left him Sole Literary Executor and by his having desired that if a *Memoir* of him had to be written Hallam should write it' (Arthur Houghton Jr.).

Hallam Tennyson was a hero of filial piety, and all Tennyson scholarship is indebted to his *Memoir*. Until recently all of it *stemmed* from his *Memoir*. Behind this *Memoir*, however, are several stages of preparation, all of which have been described briefly in Philip L. Elliott, *The Making of the Memoir* (Furman University, 1978). Hallam Tennyson must have begun his preparations before his father's death, and the work became his abiding concern within a fortnight of the funeral in Westminster Abbey. In about a year he, together with Henry Sidgwick and Francis Turner Palgrave, had gone through 'upwards of 40,000 letters' for possible use in the biography, consisting largely, of course, of letters written to or about Tennyson. The winnowings from these letters, combined with recollections from Tennyson's friends and Lady Tennyson's journals and cemented with his own considerable personal knowledge, enabled him in an astonishingly short time to assemble the *Ur-Memoiren,* ten massive folio albums, transcripts of documents scissored and pasted or pinned to the thick pages and connected with appropriate narrative. These ten volumes, now in the Tennyson Research Centre, are usually referred to as 'draft *Materials*' or 'MS Materials.' Out of this matter Hallam Tennyson generated *Materials for a Life of A. T.,* the work that Tennysonians know (and always refer to) as *Materials*: four volumes of revised page proofs, of which thirty-two sets were printed, though not all have been traced. (Fifteen copies are in the Tennyson Research Centre; at least six, some imperfect, are in the United States.) The well-loved blameless son, by slow prudence, made mild this rugged matter and subdued it to the useful and the good. He worked his work. The result was *Alfred Lord Tennyson, A Memoir by His Son,* published in two volumes in 1897 and reissued in one volume in 1899 with some corrections, the restoration of a few passages excised from letters, and the addition of a letter written by Gladstone to Hallam Tennyson after reading the *Memoir*.

Tennyson was not Oliver Cromwell, who desired Lely to 'paint my picture truly like me, and not flatter me at all,' and his son's aim was emphatically not to paint all the 'roughnesses, pimples, warts, and everything' as he saw them. Hallam's object, on the contrary, was to fulfil the 'offices of tenderness' and to 'pay meet adoration' to the household gods. 'I have tried to do what he said that I might do,' Hallam Tennyson wrote in the Preface to the *Memoir*, 'and have endeavoured to give briefly something of what people naturally wish to know, something about his birth, homes, school, college, friendships, travels, and the leading events of his life, enough to present the sort of insight into his history and pursuits which one wants, if one desires to make a companion of a man.' In December 1896 revising the *Memoir* for publication, he wrote to James T. Knowles (Yale), who had sent notes and advice: 'You little know how much I have tried to carry out my father's exact wishes. The work has been done with the intensest anxiety on my part; and with the intent to make it as exact and as true as possible: and pardon me if I say that I know better than anyone else what he wished me to do.' But Tennyson himself conceded, in the sonnet first printed at the beginning of the Preface ('Old ghosts whose day was done ere mine began'), that 'The man's life in the letters of the man' is 'half-dream,' not the man as 'he retires into himself and is.'

Whether Hallam Tennyson saw or could not see the 'roughnesses, pimples, warts' is beside the point; he did not regard them as essential. His work is not a *Life and Letters*. It is emphatically a *Memoir*, and it could have appropriately been called *In Memoriam A. T.*, for in it Hallam Tennyson does for his father what his father had done for Arthur Hallam—he shapes a fable transforming Tennyson into a 'noble type . . . who lives in God.' The *Memoir* is not really hagiography (as has been alleged) nor is it quite mythopoeia (though at some points it is close), it is typology—that Victorian version of romantic faith, born of a mystical union of natural history (type as genus or species) and theology (type as prefiguring symbol or emblem), romanticism's last-ditch stand against the inexorability of history. 'From his boyhood,' says the Preface, Tennyson 'had felt the magic of Merlin—that spirit of poetry which bade him know his power and follow throughout his work a pure and high ideal, with a simple and single devotedness and a desire to ennoble the life of the world.' As the father had transmuted Arthur Hallam, his friend, into King Arthur, his ideal, so Hallam, the son, now transfigured Alfred the Great (as he was known to his friends) into Arthur the king, united in holy matrimony to a miraculously pure, and purifying, Guinevere, on whom, in his last words, he pronounced 'a farewell blessing': 'Nothing could have been more striking than the scene during the last few hours. On the bed a figure of breathing marble, flooded and bathed in the light of the full moon streaming through the oriel window; his hand clasping the Shakespeare which he had asked for but recently, and which he had kept by him to the end; the moonlight, the majestic figure as he lay there, "drawing thicker breath," irresistibly brought to our minds his own "Passing of Arthur" ' (Dr Dabbs, the attending physician, quoted in *Memoir*, II. 428–9). 'His last words,' wrote his son to the Duke of Argyll on 24 October, 'were calling out to me "Hallam—Hallam" and to my mother whispering, "God bless you, my joy" ' (Philip L. Elliott, *The Making of the Memoir*, p. 14 n.). If *In Memoriam* is indeed, as Tennyson said, 'a sort of Divine Comedy,' it is tempting to put a different construction on these words, but it is a temptation that scholarship must resist. Two years later Lady Tennyson wrote to G. L. Craik (Arthur Houghton, Jr.): 'It is I need not say a great blessing to us to feel that his influence increases as the years go on and we rely on your reverence for him as abiding.' The matter of *Materials* has been transubstantiated into the spirit which giveth life. The image was sculpted for posterity, and the portrait in the *Memoir* is not likely to be altered in any substantial way. Hallam Tennyson saw to that, for he saw everything. It is thus not an exaggeration to say that with a few exceptions everything we know about Tennyson's life we know by his son's leave.

In his attitude towards textual accuracy and the integrity of letters Hallam Tennyson was less lordly, or indifferent, than many nineteenth-century memoirists. On some matters he was of course reticent, on others silent. Tennyson's inner life, the way of his soul (and heart), memorialized in his verse, is not commemorated in the *Memoir*. Of the actual suppressions, rather than insights withheld, we now know a good deal. Hallam Tennyson kept back all information about his grandfather's drunkenness and violence, about his uncle Frederick's romantic involvements and Oedipal struggles, Charles's romantic escapade with the governess and, more serious, his twice-conquered opium addiction (and his wife's long decade of nervous collapse),

Arthur's alcoholism, Edward's insanity and long half-century of confinement, Septimus's indolence and morbidity, Mary's broken engagement, Emily's marriage to Richard Jesse, Charles Weld's malfeasance (whatever its nature) at the British Institution; he was less than fair about his grandfather's so-called 'disinheritance' and less than candid about the relations between the Somersby Tennysons and the Tennyson d'Eyncourts; and he was discreet to the verge of otherworldliness about his great-uncle Charles Tennyson d'Eyncourt, who in his manorial pretensions and dynastic ambitions became the laughing stock of mid-Lincolnshire. Tennyson himself was frequently unkempt, dirty, gruff, boorish (as late as 1849 he put his feet on the sofa in Mrs Rawnsley's drawing-room), and nearly always hypochondriac, and on these matters his son remained mute.

Tennyson was a great conversationalist, as all witnesses attest, and Hallam mentions his father's gift (and zest) for mimicry, though fastidiously refraining from even a hint as to its range of subject. Satan squatting as a toad at the ear of Eve (Memoir, I. 184) is one thing, an appropriately Victorian thing, and so, no doubt, was the imitation of George IV, 'with a great fluffing up of his hair into full wig, and elevation of cravat and collar'; or 'the sun coming out from a cloud, and returning into one again, with a gradual opening and shutting of eyes and lips, etc.' (*Tennyson and His Friends*, p. 146); or sitting up till one o'clock in the morning amusing his family and friends 'by taking different characters' (p. 160, below); or even, late in life, his enactment of 'a cannibal chief walking up and down to inspect a row of missionaries destined for the pot' (Charles Tennyson, *Six Tennyson Essays*, p. 16). But clearly of a different order was an evening at J. M. Kemble's, in 1832, described by Edward Spedding, when Tennyson 'enacted 1stly a Teutonic deity . . . 3rdly a man on a close stool—and lastly put a pipestopper in his mouth by way of beak, and appeared as a great bird on an opposite branch, and he pecked in my face as I cried haw, haw! with divers other facetiunculae' (*The Letters of Arthur Henry Hallam*, p. 602).

Of Tennyson's sexual life we know *nothing*, and no surviving evidence indicates that (in his own phrase) he took his pastime, that (in prose) he was not a virgin when he married in 1850, aged forty-one. Even if his son had known anything, he would of course not have betrayed it, but he could hardly have been oblivious of his father's 'affair' with Rosa Baring in the early thirties (about which Ralph Rader has written so admirably), though he never alludes to her throughout the *Memoir*. If this discretion implies actual suppression of documentary evidence we do not know it. He did not demur at printing 'The Rosebud', perhaps the most erotic verses surviving by Tennyson, though whether he recognized them as erotic is another matter.

The wonder is not that Hallam Tennyson, whose distinguished public career after the *Memoir* is set forth in *Who Was Who*, told so little but that he told so much and told it so well, for among all the massive nineteenth-century works of comparable scope one could not name many superior to it.

He saw, as we have said, virtually everything written by and to his father and, for better or worse, what we now know is what he chose to reveal. His mother's 'journals,' which would have been an invaluable quarry for the biographer, were of course drawn upon—she herself made an epitome of them for his use. The originals were then destroyed. Thus the *Memoir*, together with *Materials* and 'draft *Materials*', is not merely the best source that we have for certain letters and much information, it is in many cases the only source. No reasonable person, therefore, can help regretting that he destroyed evidence. And finally, though it is no doubt crass to say so, manifestly the death of Hallam Tennyson did as much for Tennyson scholarship as the death of Arthur Henry Hallam did for Tennyson's poetry. The 'meet adoration' that was supposed to preserve and nurture his father's fame would almost certainly have stunted its growth.

Ironically, it was the organic evolution of the Tennyson family that, more than anything else, made it possible for us to see Tennyson plain. The poet's grandson (and Hallam Tennyson's nephew), Charles Bruce Locker Tennyson, second son of a second son, born in 1879, himself a 'wonder of the world', known far and wide and loved and revered by all who knew him, to whose memory these volumes (which he did so much to advance) are dedicated, rescued the poet from the dead hand of Hallam Tennyson and gave him to us as a real person. He breathed life into the marmoreal image. If Hallam Tennyson was a hero of filial piety, Charles Tennyson was a hero of grandfilial candour and honesty.

One does not think of Hallam Tennyson (who died in 1928 at the age of seventy-six) as ever having been young; one does not think of Charles Tennyson (who died in 1977 at the age of ninety-seven) as ever having been old. His own career was a sort of mirror image of his uncle's. He spent the first part of his adult life in business and public service, the second mixed and mingled in his grandfather's. The highlights of his distinguished career before his commandingly influential life of Tennyson are set forth in his charming autobiography, *Stars and Markets* (1957) and conveniently listed in *Who's Who*.

In 1930 when he was fifty-one he edited Tennyson's adolescent drama, *The Devil and the Lady*. In 1931 he published four articles in *The Nineteenth Century and After* called 'Tennyson's Unpublished Poems'. Then, in 1936 in the *Cornhill Magazine* he published a series of four 'Tennyson Papers,' of which the first was called 'Alfred's Father'. In this he discussed what he believed to be the 'disinheritance' and mentioned Dr Tennyson's 'moods of depression and irritability'. 'So intense and violent were these moods . . . .', he wrote, 'that Alfred, as a child, used often to run out into the night in utter misery and cast himself weeping down among the tombstones.' But he went no further. Specifically—though he mentioned the father's 'intermittent bouts of extreme lethargy'—he did not refer to drunkenness.

His biography, '*Alfred Tennyson*, by his grandson Charles Tennyson', was published in 1949, when he was seventy years old, and it was here for the first time that we learned the truth. Charles Tennyson had not been disingenuous. He had in fact come upon a great deal of new documentary evidence, a plenitude that would have been the despair and delight of any scholar—the Tennyson d'Eyncourt papers, 'the vast collection of letters and documents covering the history of the Tennyson [d'Eyncourt] family during the early nineteenth century,' as he described them in the Preface to his biography. 'These', he said, with perfect accuracy, 'have made a detailed study of Alfred Tennyson's childhood and youth possible for the first time.' For the student of Tennyson the value of these papers, now in the Lincolnshire Archives Office, The Castle, Lincoln, is considerable, for not only are they quantitatively massive, they were *new*, in the sense that they had been seen by no earlier writer, in particular and significantly not by Hallam Tennyson. It would be difficult for anyone who was not a student of the poet before the appearance of this biography to appreciate fully what serious investigation of Tennyson was then like.

Even beyond 1949, two decades after his death, however, Hallam Tennyson continued to work his work. In 1924 he had presented to Trinity College, Cambridge, his father's old college, a large collection of poetic manuscripts 'on conditions which the college interprets as forbidding copying or quotation in perpetuity', as Christopher Ricks, editor of *The Poems of Tennyson*, wrote in 1969 (p. xix). Perpetuity in this instance petered out in forty-five years, for by the combined effort of Tennyson's (and Hallam Tennyson's) descendants, primarily the fourth Lord Tennyson and Sir Charles, of Professor Ricks and others, and also (it must be said) with the co-operation of the authorities at Trinity College, the interdiction was finally lifted in 1969—*after* publication of Ricks's great edition of the poetry, which, active, it had shackled, and inactive, rendered obsolete. Hallam Tennyson himself, however, had repeatedly drawn on the Trinity manuscripts for quotation in *Materials for a Life of A. T.*, in the Memoir, in the nine-volume Eversley edition of Tennyson's Works (1907–8), and in the one-volume *Works* (1913). And of the manuscripts in his possession that he did not present to Trinity College he allowed (in his will) Charles Tennyson absolute discretion in the matter of publication.

Something now must be said about various collections of Tennyson materials, which are large and numerous. The four largest—Lincoln, Harvard, Yale, Trinity College—were originally one, Hallam Tennyson's, inherited from his father. Among these the collection at the Tennyson Research Centre occupies a position that may be called matriarchal, for the bulk of it is the family archive (of which the other three are offspring), deposited on indefinite loan by the present Lord Tennyson, Harold, Fourth Baron (born

1919), great-grandson of the poet, in the City Library and Usher Art Gallery, Lincoln. It includes all the books surviving and recoverable that belonged to Tennyson and members of his family—portraits, scrapbooks and press-cuttings, household books, publishers' accounts, manuscripts (among them *In Memoriam, Harold, Becket, Queen Mary*), trial books, corrected proofs, and first editions, not to mention a chair, a cloak and wide-awake hat made about 1840, jewellery, a lock of hair, a pocket microscope, walking sticks, an ointment bottle, a pruning knife, pens, penwipers, a water-colour box, pipes, spectacles, a dog whistle, an umbrella, an unopened packet of Durham Smoking Mixture sent by an American admirer, and many, many other items. It also includes the most extensive Tennyson family correspondence in existence, and other letters from Victorian contemporaries, numbering about 12,000 altogether. A three-volume catalogue called *Tennyson in Lincoln* will describe the collections. Volume one (the Tennyson libraries) appeared in 1971; volume two (works by Tennyson, including trial books and proofs, critical and biographical works on him, music, pictures, prints, photographs, maps, etc.) in 1973; volume three will list the manuscripts and letters.

The Harvard College Library is 'the world's foremost repository of Tennyson manuscripts', among which are included over five dozen letters, and it also has important proofs, in galleys and pages. The collection is described by Edgar F. Shannon, Jr. and William H. Bond in 'Literary Manuscripts of Alfred Tennyson in the Harvard College Library', *Harvard Library Bulletin* (Spring 1956), 254–74, with four plates of facsimiles and copious quotations (on which this account is based). It consists of 72 note-books and 275 folders, all acquired in 1954–5 from Sir Charles Tennyson, to whom it was bequeathed by his uncle, plus '42 additional folders con-taining papers collected by the Rawnsley family and left to Sir Charles':

> The wealth of the collection cannot be overemphasized. Here one indeed sees Tennyson's method of work and quickly touches the human side of a great poet. Here—to mention some instances of the miscellaneous hoard in the notebooks—are school- and college-boy drawings and profiles, none very talented. Here are fragments of prose essays—on fairyland, on genius and national characteristics, and two pages of the one on ghosts that Tennyson was too shy to read to the 'Apostles'. . . . Here are nursery rhymes, observa-tions and jottings on ships' rigging and on astronomy, notes on classical studies, on Greek verse, on the New Testament, on Italian, a German vocabu-lary, a glossary of Old and Middle English, a lengthy complication of rhyming words, a quotation from Layamon, an alphabetical list of books, presumably in his own or his father's library, a diary of the trip to Switzerland with Moxon in 1846. Here . . . are several manuscripts of 'Hail Briton!' previously published only from the Heath Commonplace Book; here is the early manu-script of 'The Two Voices,' entitled 'Thoughts of a Suicide'; here written in a small variety of the tall, thin 'butcher's book,' is an anterior version of the

first section of *The Princess*, called 'The New University' . . . and in another notebook the unused character introductions for the narrators of each of the seven divisions of the poem; here are many parts of *In Memoriam* . . . extensive drafts, partly prose and partly poetry, of most of the *Idylls* . . . entire manuscripts of the plays, and texts, running from manuscript through revised proof, of the fugitive political verses printed in periodicals.

The very valuable Tennyson collection in the Yale University Library runs to over ten dozen letters by Tennyson and a vast number addressed to him. The core of it was purchased from Colonel E. S. M. Prinsep, a relation of Mary Emily Prinsep Hichens, Hallam Tennyson's second wife (m. 1918; d. 1931), widow of Andrew Kinsman Hichens (a latter-day friend of Tennyson and his son) and niece of Tennyson's close friend Thoby Prinsep. (Tennyson attended Hichens's wedding in 1874 and, fond of his wife, expressed the hope that his initials stood for 'a kindly husband'. Hichens's log, as *Materials*, IV. 212–17—abbreviated in *Memoir*, II. 354–6—reveals, is the source of the anecdotes during the cruise of Earl Brassey's yacht, the *Sunbeam*, in May 1889. His name, for reasons not obvious, was dropped from the index of the *Memoir* after 1897.) A fine epitome of the four-volume Tauchnitz edition of the *Memoir*, occasionally with information not easily found elsewhere, annotations in two copies of the *Memoir* and an imperfect copy of *Materials*, all in Mary Hichens's hand, are at Yale. This collection, supplemented by special gifts and purchases, most notably of course the Tinker Collection, includes autograph poems ('Locksley Hall') and many fragments of poems ('The Coach of Death', 'Dora', *In Memoriam*, XXXIX, 'Merlin and Vivien'), proofs with autograph corrections, and the fascinating and useful letters to and from members of the family as well as to Tennyson himself, among them letters from Charlotte Brontë, Brookfield, the Brownings, the Carlyles, Dickens, Dodgson, Emma, Queen Consort of King Kamehameha IV of Hawaii, FitzGerald, Forster, Gladstone, Arthur Henry Hallam and his father, Hugo, Leigh Hunt, Fanny Kemble, Edward Lear, Longfellow, F. D. Maurice, Richard Monckton Milnes, Samuel Rogers, D. G. Rossetti, Ruskin, Thackeray, and many others.

The collection at Trinity College already referred to was generally described by Christopher Ricks in an exuberant article 'The Tennyson MSS at Trinity College, Cambridge', *TLS*, 21 August 1969, as soon as the interdiction was lifted. It consists of a manuscript of *In Memoriam* and of a number of 'manuscript notebooks from Tennyson's first volume, *Poems by Two Brothers* (1827) to his last, *The Death of Œnone* (posthumously published in 1892)', with many verses not published by Tennyson and many drafts of poems—e.g. 'The Lady of Shalott', 'The Two Voices', 'St. Simeon Stylites', 'Tithonus', 'Tiresias', 'Morte d'Arthur', 'Ulysses', 'Ode on the Death of the Duke of Wellington', 'Lucretius', and *Maud*. Trinity's strength in poetic manuscripts, in which it vies with Harvard, is so overwhelming that the letters might be overlooked but for the early letters to J. Jackson, publisher of *Poems by Two Brothers*, and a fine series of a dozen and a half to Richard Monckton Milnes (Lord Houghton, whose descendants presented them to Trinity College) as well as a dozen from Tennyson's sister Emily to Arthur Hallam's sister Ellen. (*The Princess*, also part of the Hallam Tennyson gift, is in the University Library, along with some family correspondence of peripheral interest; the Heath Commonplace Book, containing versions of some early poems, is in the Fitzwilliam Museum.)

In the four decades of Tennyson's life covered by the first volume fewer than 250 letters by him (including fragments) have been traced, and the whole collection from 1821 to his death numbers less than 2,000. He disliked writing letters, and the simple truth is that he avoided writing *prose*. Alone among the major poets, he has left not a single prose essay written for publication, formal or informal, either in the literal or accepted sense. Tennyson was first and last a poet, and only a poet.

Of many letters mere fragments survive, often of one line only, and the sum, from the first letter to the last, from 1821 to 1892, averages out to less than one letter a fortnight—or, in the latter half of his life, about one every ten days. This is a meagre harvest but, though every new bookseller's catalogue, every new auction, brings forth new letters, we see no reason to suppose that the total impression here will be seriously altered. No known letter has been withheld, and two letters only, as far as we know, have been forged, though copies of these two, alas, crop up in the market-place with some frequency.

If we had all the letters Tennyson ever wrote, instead of merely the remnants that survive and have been traced, there is no reason—with two notable exceptions—to suppose that our view of him as a letter-writer or a poet or man would differ in any significant way from what it is now. The exceptions are, of course, the letters to Arthur Henry Hallam, of which not one remains, and the series of letters that he wrote, in the late thirties and forties, to his fiancée Emily Sellwood, who in 1850 became his wife, of which only half a dozen pages of *disjecta membra* survive. These fragments, glowing and pulsing with warmth, tenderness, and radiant affection, suffused perhaps (their tone sometimes suggests) with the marvellous eroticism of 'Ask me no more', 'Now sleeps the crimson petal, now the white', and 'Come down, O maid, from yonder mountain height', allow us to believe that some of the fountains of Tennyson's deepest life boil as visibly in *The Princess* as in *In Memoriam* and *Maud*.

We have described the history of Tennyson's letters, but we have not yet said what they are or are not. Individually or collectively, they are in no sense literary—they do not characteristically discuss his reading, they are not carefully constructed compositions, they do not often deal with poetry.

They reveal no aesthetic creed, no theory of poetry, they conduct no inquiry into the sources of inspiration, they offer no observations or insights that we recognize, gratefully, as the germ of a poem, no speculative delving into the mystery of the creative process, and no hieratic claims for the role of the poet, or of poetry, in society. Nor are his letters egotistical, or even personal, in the sense of expressing emotional overflowings. Nor do they gossip. ('Gossip is my total abhorrence', he wrote.)

Of Hallam Tennyson's *Memoir* Christopher Ricks, editor of Tennyson's poetry as well as the author of a biographical and critical study, remarks, with witty precision, that it breathes 'a sense of what it was like in the immediate vicinity of Tennyson during the second half of his life', an appraisal that recalls Manning's description of Gladstone as a substantive who liked to be surrounded by adjectives. These letters—and this is their virtue, our reason for bringing them together—show us the substantive, they show us Tennyson himself, not merely the 'vicinity of Tennyson'.

Now that we have the substantive, not the qualifying adjectives, his own words not the words of others, *penates* not *vicinitas*, do we indeed see the 'roughnesses, pimples, warts, and everything'? The difficulty lies not in the answer but in the question. About Tennyson, as of every man who ever lived, much remains that we do not know, will never know, and, perhaps, do not care to know. We do not know whether Tennyson read pornography (like Gladstone) or frequented *maisons de supplice* (like Dickens, Houghton, Swinburne, and so many others) or sublimated his erotic fantasies in visual reveries (like Charles Kingsley, Beardsley, Fuseli). We know next to nothing about his *intimate* home life, about his private relations with his wife, little about their conversation. On these matters, as on so many others, one can speculate, but they remain material for imagination, not the man as 'he retires into himself and is'. And if the question seeks such privities as these, it need not be asked.

In these letters, this 'half-dream', we see not the type of the *Memoir*, not the Poet Laureate, not the Voice of the Age, not the Pre-eminent Victorian, but the living, pulsing, breathing, *man*, husband, father, home-owner, house-holder, income-earner, worrier, patient, invalid; selfish, self-indulgent, self-pitying yet generous, egotistical and altruistic, introverted and extroverted, gruffly sentimental, vulnerable and studiously self-protective, anti-social recluse and social lion (and, in the old sense, lionizer). We see a man with a capacity for enduring friendships, loyal to his friends. (Indeed, the 'old boy network', of which so much is seen in the first volume, gives the letters some value in social as well as literary history.) And, finally, we also see a thoroughly professional poet.

These letters, together with those of Arthur Henry Hallam, now available in Jack Kolb's fine edition, and Emily Tennyson's *Journal*, painstakingly transcribed and annotated by James O. Hoge, ought to have been the ideal background for Ricks's magisterial edition of the poetry, which will always occupy the foreground. They are less than ideal only because, as we have said, many of them were destroyed or so mutilated by the son and widow that, in many cases, only pitiful fragments remain. None the less, though much is taken, much abides, and for a man who 'would as soon kill a pig as write a letter' Tennyson does not come off badly. He could turn a phrase as cleanly as an expert carpenter or potter can turn a lathe and his craft is everywhere apparent. He does not often make jokes—though who among us would not willingly have said to a bachelor friend living there, 'We must be married or we must live in Bawtry'—but he is deft, witty, and *honest*.

As Laureate and the most famous English poet alive, he was more vulnerable than most, to a form of harassment that today—organized fund-raising having become a big business, mailing lists a marketable commodity—any middle-class citizen takes for granted. 'I send you a £10 cheque', he writes (February 1865) to one of his oldest and dearest friends: 'You should not be hurt but rather pity us for our worse than Egyptian plague of letters, books, MSS etc. not from England alone but from the colonies, U.S., even France, Germany—nay Liberia and the negroes: and the demands for churches, chapels, hospitals, schools—horseleeches all crying Give, give— are more than the Marquis of Westminster could satisfy. Hurt? when we both dead of pennypost softening of the brain you will have to sprinkle a repentant tear over our ashes and believe in us as of old.' The plague of 'books, MSS etc.' called for special strategies. FitzGerald urged him to 'imitate Charles Lamb and throw them into his neighbour's cucumber frames' (Tennyson, in fact, threw many of them on to his wife's desk), but when personal claims had to be honoured, he could rise to the occasion. 'I have not read it', he wrote to a friend who sent him a play, 'but have cut it open which looks as if I meant to read it.' (To Edmund Gosse, a stranger, he wrote in January 1876: 'I have just received your drama and beg you to accept my thanks.') His guiding principle was to tell the truth and nothing but the truth ('The preface is full of interest. The poems I have not yet looked into'), but he did not always feel compelled to state the whole truth, and in this connection his letters to Robert Browning, from 1864 to 1887, acknowledging new volumes, are a miniature comedy of manners.

'Thanks for yet another of your great imaginative analyses', he wrote, acknowledging *Prince Hohenstiel-Schwangau*, in December 1871, 'and—for perhaps I am one of those who value love more than wit—more than thanks for your kindly inscription'.

Red Cotton Night-Cap Country in May 1873 brought forth this: 'My wife has just cut the leaves—I have yet again to thank you and feel rather ashamed that I have nothing of my own to send you back; but your muse is as prolific as Hecuba and mine by the side of her an old barren cow.' (In a letter to Emily Tennyson several months earlier Browning had referred to Tennyson's 'plumcake' and his own 'black-sausage'.)

Aristophanes' Apology, in April 1875, perhaps a special case, earned its author a credit of 5,705 Tennysonain expressions of gratitude: 'As many thanks for your book as there are lines in it! When will you come my way?' (Matthew Arnold, equally dexterous, wrote that he would keep it 'to read when my summer holiday comes and I can read a poem steadily'.)

On receipt of *The Inn Album*, seven months later, Tennyson wrote: 'Another jet from your full fountain—not yet tasted—but I thank you now before I drink of it, and shall have to thank you more hereafter.' But eleven years—and four letters—later Tennyson, no doubt weary, his invention flagging, is pinnacled dim in the intense inane: 'Thanks for your book just received—a new leaf of your ever new-leafing laurel', he says of *Parleyings with Certain People*, in February 1887. 'I wish I could see you now and then, but I never enter London and you never leave it.'

The art of sidestepping has limitations, however, and other situations called for other techniques, sometimes, indeed, for direct confrontation:

October 21, 1877

Mr. Alfred Tennyson presents his compliments to the Governor of Witley Hospital for Convalescent Lunatics, and requests him to be so kind as to take precautions, that his patients should not pay visits at Aldworth, as two did yesterday (one describing himself as assistant librarian of the British Museum).

Mr. Tennyson is very glad if they in any way enjoy'd themselves here, and hopes that they did not suffer from their long walk.

Like so many of us—and unlike so many poets—he found gardening restorative and loved his flowers—irises, laurels, rhododendrons (which he disbudded, to encourage growth), the wild summer rose, the ferns in the glen. He feared (with a measure of awe) for his ilexes 'rolling and whitening' in the heavy winds, was apprehensive lest a November storm might destroy more of his pines, lest his sons might spoil the lawn. He 'ascertained that weasels *have* a hunting-cry', but altered the concluding lines of 'Aylmer's Field' anyhow. He was fascinated by snakes' eggs, lizards, serpents, dinosaurs, telescopes, microscopes, pink rainbows, the voltaic battery. In the last half-year of his life he observed tartly that 'I am not such a ninny as not to know a crow from a rook' and a week later, thanking a Texan for a gift, wrote: 'It is very kind in you to have thought of sending me nuts from your beautiful Pecan tree and I thank you most sincerely. My Gardener shall try and make them grow here. We consider the Walnut the best among our nuts I think, but to us your Pecan nuts seem better still.' (He loathed the tobacco that American admirers persisted in sending him.)

Before Tennyson was a householder he was, like the rest of us, a househunter, and the story of his houses, after his marriage, conforms to the structure of an incomplete romantic lyric: beginning with an illusion, it modulates to the impossibility of sustaining it, and recognizes then that the only possible consolation is another illusion. For him as for ourselves great expectations led to *illusions perdues*. A bachelor, he (with his family) moved from Somersby to High Beech to Tunbridge Wells to Cheltenham (with London as the saving oasis). Married, he moved from Warninglid to Chapel House, then to Farringford, and then, seasonally, to Aldworth, the house he built. On their first morning at Warninglid Tennyson (according to his wife's journal) 'heard the birds sing as he had never heard them sing since he left Somersby, and he ate a good breakfast', but, as it turned out, the house was draughty, the chimney smoked, and the roof leaked—and, in addition to all else, it was too remote. For these and other reasons they remained there less than a fortnight and, after some searching and some false starts, found another illusion, Chapel House, Twickenham: 'The most lovely house with a beautiful view in every room at top and all over the rooms are so high that you may put up your beds', Tennyson wrote to his wife. 'A large staircase with great statues and carved [bishop?] and all rooms splendidly papered—with a kind gentlemanly old man as proprietor—and all in for 50 guineas.' But, as it turned out, the air was bad and in any case stank of 'the many cabbage marketgardens' (*Memoir*, II. 489), the walks were too short ('Duty walks and alas! without pleasure', according to his wife's journal), the meadows flooded—and, in addition to all else, it was too accessible: a 'continuous stream of visitors', as Charles Tennyson (p. 273) put it, made it impossible to get work done. In less than a year the search commenced once more, and after much 'wretched househunting . . . now in Sussex, now in Gloucestershire, now in Yorkshire', they fled suburban London to the western end of the Isle of Wight, where they leased and then bought Farringford. It was secluded and wooded in 1853; it was on an eminence and the prospects were exhilarating. 'You have a bright view of the sea underneath your windows and a little town close at hand. . . . There is never a house to be let or sold', Tennyson wrote to his wife. They were 'delighted with the snowdrops and primroses in the plantation and by the cooing of the stock-dove and the song of the Redwings', according to his wife's journal, and, later, with the abundance of wild flowers: 'St. John's wort . . . common centaury, common agrimony, campanula, Lawwort, Flea-wort, and the lovely little Lady's tresses.' Lionel, the second son, was born in their new house. Their friends visited them often enough, though none dropped in casually. But, as it turned out, in a few years the island became 'brick-box-dotted'. 'People are seized with a building mania', Emily Tennyson wrote in January 1860. 'Already a bit of our sea is built out from us and we are obliged to buy land at the rate of a thousand pounds an acre merely to prevent more of the bay being hidden by ugly brick houses.' Later, Tennyson wrote that the island is 'getting yearly almost monthly more and more brick-boxed and cockney-villaed'. Like everybody else who settles in the country for the sake of seclusion, they were exasperated by people building near them, and as Tennyson became more famous he was troubled, in the tourist season, 'when the cockneys come tramping over my grounds and staring in the windows'.

He was not deafened by motor-cycles or lawnmowers or power-saws or aeroplanes and helicopters overhead or car horns or faulty silencers or neighbours' radios or record-players, and the 'sound of the cannon practicing for the Crimea', easily audible from their kitchen garden (*Journal*), was a voice that spake out of the skies, the deep calling unto the deep. But new roads threatened his privacy and in less than a decade of residence at Farringford, contemplating the possibility that a railway from Newport to Alum Bay 'would cut right through my grounds', he thought of moving, and in due course bought ninety acres near Haslemere, Surrey, for £1,500, splendid scenery 'on the side of a heathy hill'. This signalled the completion of the 'romantic lyric', for the resolution came (as it had to come) from within. Here, to his own specifications, he built Aldworth ('800 feet above the sea— no roads and no post') in 1869. 'We have got into our new house, which is very charming', he wrote. 'Nothing in it pleases me more than the bath, a perennial stream which falls through the house, and where I take three baths a day'. For the rest of their lives together, they divided their time in the country between Farringford and Aldworth. Two illusions combined led to one consolation.

If the story of Tennyson's homes and haunts can be described as Everyman's romantic lyric, in another aspect of his life he is equally ourselves. He was born, he lived in sickness and in health, and he died. Of his birth we know little; of his death a good deal; of his health we know everything, and here in these letters, for the first time in some detail, we learn much about his ailments. That he was a hypochondriac, at least as a bachelor, seems beyond doubt. Edward FitzGerald, kindest of friends and gruffest of critics, observed in 1848 that 'this really great man thinks more about his bowels and nerves than about the Laureate wreath he was born to inherit'. Tennyson complained of his eyes from the age of twenty until his death. The *muscae volitantes* alluded to so often can be confidently written off as hypochondria—the adult who has not seen 'flying gnats' has not seen anything else, and in associating them with amauresis he may have been thinking of Milton's 'drop serene' (*gutta serena*)—but his optic troubles were not all either imaginary or negligible. He suffered from some form of conjunctivitis, which may have been brought on and was certainly aggravated by hay fever, to which he was so often a victim, and his right eye was particularly troublesome: in March 1854, he noted, it had become 'filled with great masses of floating blackness' and less than two months before his death, after decades of increasing degeneration, perhaps because of a cataract, he had 'entirely lost' the use of it, 'as far as reading is concerned'.

We learn here something about Tennyson's teeth, which (as far as we know) first began to trouble him seriously in the 1850s and continued to plague him for nearly ten years. As a matter of course, he had the best dental care available, being looked after by a dental *surgeon*, Henry John Barrett, of Craigie and Barrett, 42 Finsbury Square, who became a friend with whom he dined in London and who accompanied him on a tour in Norway in August 1858. Barrett filled ('stopt') several teeth in January 1853, and a month later fitted him with some false teeth ('Saw Barrett and since have been eating dinner with new teeth. Queer—seems as if I could never get accustomed to it'). In June 1859 he wrote: 'My lowlying teeth and another old stump were pulled out yesterday and two others cut down, not without pain but not so much as I expected.' And a few days later he was able to report that 'My new teeth serve me much better than the old and he [Barrett] says are almost indestructible'. A good deal is known about Victorian dentistry, which had moved a long way indeed from the threefold tradesman—barber, bloodletter, tooth-drawer—of John Gay, 'who shav'd, drew teeth, and breath'd a vein'. Tennyson's carious cavities were probably filled with gold or gold foil packed in by a spring-hammer, and his artificial teeth were presumably made of porcelain, though they could have been bone, ivory, ox-teeth or, conceivably, natural human teeth. Hordes of ghoulish tooth-drawers (as the *Pall Mall Gazette* reported in a shocking article in 1865) following the battles, from Waterloo to the American Civil War, collected the teeth of the slain soldiers, packed them in boxes, and posted them to London, where they commanded high prices. It is a transcendental conceit, but one cannot resist surmising that the Laureate's substitute teeth might have been extracted from the 'jaws of Death' and the 'mouth of Hell'!

Tennyson had his appointed share of the minor complaints that are our common lot—increasing baldness, a damaged toenail on his honeymoon, for the laceration of which chloroform was necessary, an injured knee, colds, influenza, headaches, eczema, lumbago, hay fever, nervousness ('How should it be otherwise', a friend wrote, 'seeing that he smokes the strongest and most stinking tobacco out of a small blackened old pipe on an average nine hours every day'), palpitation of the heart, and, in the early 1870s, trouble with his gums, which were probably receding—but he had also a far graver condition from which he suffered for more than half a century and which eventually led to his death at eighty-three: cirrhosis of the liver (apparently) and its cursed crew of attendant afflictions, driving him to the hydropathic therapy of which so much is written in this volume and including varicose veins, for which he wore an elastic stocking, what must have been a gastro-intestinal haemorrhage in October 1861, and gout, gout, gout, climaxing, in 1889, in an attack of rheumatic gout, 'nine months of a most painful and depressing illness', as he described it in a letter to the Queen in August.

Three months before his death in October 1892 Tennyson was still walking two miles a day, but over the years his astonishing consumption of port (for him a dinner wine—he hated claret), his genetic heritage, the 'black blood' of the Tennysons, his compulsive smoking, the degenerative nervous uneasiness of the second and third decades of his life, the social rigours of the next two all conspired with the continuum of nature, the needs of evolution, and the nature of protoplasm. So 'the walks dwindled down', the

Memoir (II. 412) tells us, 'and he sat more and more in his summer-houses'. The gout reached his throat and jaw and towards the end of September 'was flying through his knees and jaws'. On the 28th he had 'a gouty attack of some severity', which may well have been a myocardial infarction from a coronary thrombosis, and on the 6th he died.

Like so many poets, Tennyson was given life by the idea of death. Death—nearly all deaths—diminished him, fined him down to the essential condition where he became not a singer but a song. Arthur Hallam obliged him in 1833, a still-born son in 1851, the Duke of Wellington in 1852, Henry Lushington in 1855, Prince Albert in 1861, John Simeon, 'the Prince of courtesy', in 1870, Charles Tennyson Turner, his brother, in 1879, Edward FitzGerald in 1883. *In Memoriam*, 'Ode on the Death of the Duke of Wellington', the 'Dedication' to *Idylls of the King*, 'In the Garden at Swainston', 'Frater Ave atque Vale', and 'To E. FitzGerald' require no comment here, and to the list could be added the lovely, unappreciated 'Prefatory Poem to My Brother's Sonnets'. But death could also be too intimate, too private, too deep, not a diminishment but a dismemberment, the loss not of an objectified yearning but of part of himself. Of the son born dead in 1851 the father's moving commentary speaks for itself: 'He was—not born, I cannot call it born, for he never breathed—but he was released from the prison where he moved for nine months—on Easter Sunday. Awful day. We live close upon an English-church chapel. The organ rolled—the psalm sounded—and the wail of a woman in her travail—of a true and tender nature suffering, as it seemed, intolerable wrong, rose ever and anon.' Concerning the same event, in an extraordinary passage of which only a fragment survives (*Memoir*, I. 340), he said: 'To-day when I write this down, the remembrance of it rather overcomes me; but I am glad that I have seen him, dear little nameless one that hast lived though thou hast never breathed, I thy father, love thee and weep over thee, though thou hast no place in the Universe. Who knows? It may be that thou hast. . . . God's will be done.' In 1886 Lionel, his younger son, returning home from India, died of fever in the Red Sea, and the commemorative poem 'To the Marquis of Dufferin and Ava', though it has effective verses, falls mutely short of the other elegies. The death of his older son or of his wife would perhaps have destroyed him.

The dominating force of the whole man was his quest for Arthur. It is undoubtedly true that Arthur Henry Hallam's name would now be forgotten but for Alfred Tennyson's and it is equally true that Alfred Tennyson's name would be forgotten but for Arthur Hallam's. For Tennyson needed not only an Arthur but a morte d'Arthur. In December 1861, nearly three decades after the death of Arthur Hallam, Tennyson, drafting a letter to Princess Alice on the death of her father, the Prince Consort, attempted to solace her (and himself) with these words: 'When I was some three or four years older than yourself I suffered what seemed to me to shatter all my life so that I desired to die rather than to live.' Arthur Hallam in dying did not betray Alfred Tennyson; Tennyson in living betrayed Arthur Hallam. 'Thou hast betrayed thy nature and thy name,' said the dying king to Bedivere, the last of his knights, whose name signified 'true'.

Tennyson's truth—these letters leave no uncertainty—lay in his persistent (though not unshakable) belief in immortality. Death nourished him because of his conviction that death too would die. T. S. Eliot, in an essay on *In Memoriam* in 1932, calling the faith of that poem 'a poor thing', said it was a religious poem not 'because of the quality of its faith but because of the quality of its doubt'. The terms ought to be reversed. Its doubt now seems old fashioned,—'built in such a logical way/It ran a hundred years to a day'—its faith modern; its doubt quaint, its faith fresh; its doubt (though not the less 'a very intense experience') a historical curiosity, its faith a living force—and not less vivid because not Anglo-Catholic. 'She lives, you know. She is not really gone', he declared on the death of Lady Simeon in September 1860. To Sophia Rawnsley Elmhirst, in June 1871, he averred—'your old friend from your childhood'—that her dead son was 'not really what we call dead, but more actually living than when alive here. You cannot catch the voice or feel the hands or kiss the cheek—that is all—a separation for an hour, not an eternal farewell.' On Brookfield's death in January 1874 he wrote, 'I feel that the *dead* lives whatever the pseudosavants say.' To the widowed Lord Houghton, 'my old college comrade of more than forty years standing', he said, in March 1874, that 'the nobler nature does not pass from its individuality when it passes out of this one life'. 'The dead', he remarked to Cardinal Newman in 1882, 'may be richer in all blessings than ever they were on earth or the friends they leave behind them.' The wife of his older brother Frederick died in January 1884, and Tennyson, himself now in his seventies, began to have a sense of imminent release: 'Neither you nor I can have long to wait before we join those we have lost', he wrote to his brother. 'I myself feel every day as though I stood at the gates of Death and the light of the morning is not always upon them but you have a strong faith to light you through the dark hour.' A few months later, now Lord Tennyson, he said: 'Being now in my 75th year, and having lost almost all my youthful contemporaries, I see myself, as it were, in an extra page of Holbein's "Dance of Death", and standing before the mouth of an open sepulchre while the Queen hands me a coronet, and the skeleton takes it away and points me downward into darkness.'

Tennyson's Breath

ERIC GRIFFITHS

Tennyson on occasion needed not to speak out in order to be the voice of his time. There is an unfinished poem called 'Reticence', which was appropriately not published until after his death, and which begins:

> Not to Silence would I build
> A temple in her naked field;
> Not to her would raise a shrine:
> She no goddess is of mine;
> But to one of finer sense,
> Her half-sister, Reticence.
>
> Latest of her worshippers,
> I would shrine her in my verse!
> Not like silence shall she stand,
> Finger-lipt, but with right hand
> Moving toward her lips, and there
> Hovering, thoughtful, poised in air.[1]

Many of his poems have as their special grace this quality of 'Hovering, thoughtful, poised in air', a suspense in communication which fascinated the poet, as when he once stood by a telegraph pole to listen, as he said, 'to the wail of the wires, the souls of dead messages'.[2] Indeed, this slight poem touches for a moment on a source of its creator's virtues, in particular, on his impassioned expertise with the possible messages of dead souls. Where it does so, Tennyson's rhythmic touch is most secure and delicate, altering the resolute trochaics to the irregular

> Finger-lipt, but with right hand
> Moving toward her lips, and there

so that the return of the trochaics at 'Hovering, thoughtful . . .' has a new poise in its motion given by the small holding of the breath at the line-end,

© 1989 by Eric Griffiths. Reprinted from *The Printed Voice of Victorian Poetry* by Eric Griffiths (1989) by permission of Oxford University Press.

at 'there', a delay of the impetus of 'Hovering' which makes a rhythmic reticence. The popular imagination remembers him, as the popular imagination then received him, mostly as a magniloquent poet, but he was a shy writer as well as a shy man. R. H. Hutton, whom Tennyson considered one of his best critics, put the case more fully: 'No poet ever made the dumb speak so effectually', he wrote, but needed to add that few poets had such a feeling for the 'helplessness with which the deeper emotions break against the hard and rigid element of human speech'.[3] This double aptitude—for vocal skill and for artistic realization of the breaking-points of voice—helped him imagine throughout his career the drama of speaking, the times of successful utterance and those other occasions on which words fail us, or we fail them.

Not all Tennyson's contemporaries managed Hutton's balanced acceptance of such rhythmic half-measures of revelation. F. W. H. Myers, the Spiritualist pioneer, had low hopes for the future of poetry when he read late Tennyson: 'It seems sometimes as though poetry, which has always been half art, half prophecy, must needs abandon her higher mission; must turn only to the bedecking of things that shall wither and the embalming of things that shall decay. She will speak, as in the *Earthly Paradise*, to listeners "laid upon a flowery slope/ 'Twixt inaccessible cliffs and unsailed sea"; and behind all her utterance there will be an awful reticence, an unforgotten image of the end'.[4] He evidently wanted more, but more of what? 'It seems sometimes . . .' cannot make up its mind, tonally, between the expression of a casual mood or of a visionary instant. These tonal indecisions often occur in Tennyson's own work, but he turns them to an inquiring shape whereas here Myers just hedges the question of what he wants. Prophecy is clearly poetry's better half, as far as he is concerned, but he also thrills to the idea of a silenced prophetic voice ('*awful* reticence'—my emphasis), and he even draws his words for the 'unforgotten image of the end' from a poetic drama which partly concerns itself with the seductions of prophecy—'Is this the promis'd end? / Or image of that horror.'[5] Myers's 'disappointed ear',[6] disappointed of full-blooded revelations from poetry, can be guessed at plainly enough from the disarray of his style. Both the disappointment, and the failure of his words quite to grasp it, are representative of the demanding hopes for and against which Tennyson had to write. He wrote for such hopes because they were his hopes too—the hope that there would be an afterlife, the hope that an ideal domesticity was possible, the hope that the poet's calling was to serious human responsibilities—and he wrote against them because, as they were relayed back to him from the reading public, they became corroded parodies of what he held dear, requests for edification that could seem at times no more than a clamour for pap, as if he was being asked to write testimonials for, say, Christianity, as he might have been asked to commend a hair-tonic: 'The Poet Laureate writes, "I have tried it and found it works". '

William Allingham remembered his vexation:

T[ennyson]. '. . . I did lately receive a prose book, *Critical Strictures on Great Authors*, "a first hastily scribbled effusion", the writer said. There was this in it, "We exhort Tennyson to abandon the weeping willow with its fragile and earthward-tending twigs, and adopt the poplar, with its one Heaven-pointing finger." ' 'A pop'lar poet,' says I. . . . I went out to the garden, where were Mrs. Tennyson with Mrs. Patmore and her sister. Returning to the house there was tea, to which Tennyson came in, muttering as he entered the room 'we exhort Tennyson'.—I smiled.[7]

Allingham shows amiable good temper in his bad joke about 'pop'lar' poets and in his smile, but Tennyson shows the temperament of his form of genius in his tenacious grumpiness. He was not one to let things go lightly. He held on to his own past and its roots in the despondent soil of Somersby; he did not want either a popularity or a Heaven out of touch with that dark earth. The two chief subjects of his work—the morbid persistences of the past, and the hope for personal immortality—both lead him to refuse to abandon anything, from the past or for the future.

Where Myers feared an awful reticence *behind* all the utterance of poetry, Tennyson intends to celebrate reticence within the words themselves ('I would shrine her *in* my verse!'—my emphasis). We can begin to see the workings of that reticence in an early masterpiece, 'To J. S.':

> I will not say, 'God's ordinance
>   Of Death is blown in every wind;'
> For that is not a common chance
>   That takes away a noble mind.
>
> His memory long will live alone
>   In all our hearts, as mournful light
> That broods above the fallen sun,
>   And dwells in heaven half the night.
>
> Vain solace! Memory standing near
>   Cast down her eyes, and in her throat
> Her voice seemed distant, and a tear
>   Dropt on the letters as I wrote.[8]

'I will not say' is not only an instance of the rhetorical figure of 'apophasis', 'A kind of irony, a denial or refusal to speak . . . when nevertheless we speak and tell all',[9] for Tennyson does not nevertheless speak and tell all here, but writes to Spedding rather than speaking to him. This poem exists primarily in its written form, any vocalization would create problems of tone which the silent writing indicates but does not suffer from.

Consider how, reading this poem aloud, you would distinguish ' "God's ordinance / Of Death is blown in every wind" ' from the other lines I have quoted. If you are in fact saying all the lines, then these words have to be given a distinct tone to show that they are specially not-said by the poet though many others say such things. Such a tone would tend to emphasize the proverbial quality of these words, make them perhaps a merely formal condolence which conceals behind social propriety something less than kindness, as does Gertrude's 'Thou know'st 'tis common, all that lives must dye, / Passing through Nature, to Eternity.'[10] When Gertrude says that, Hamlet is on stage to rebuke her; in Tennyson's lyric, the drama is within a single person. To give 'God's ordinance . . .' a 'quoting' inflection would tip the balance in weighing up both the help and the insufficiency that may lie in proverbs at such times, as it would also tip the balance if a reader signalled the allusion to Gertrude's ' 'tis common' by an emphasis of indignant rebuttal—'that is NOT a common chance'. (*Hamlet* is diffusely present in these lines, 'noble mind' coming from Ophelia's 'O what a Noble minde is heere o're-thrown?') An utterance of the words need not go in this direction, this is only one obvious pitfall of tone, but the poem, being written, and therefore an utterance of absence as well as an utterance about absence, helps us see what speech has to manage at times of bereavement, helps us listen for a true tone of consolation.

Arthur Hallam had felt that letters let us down when we seek intimacy of converse. He wrote to Emily Tennyson: '. . . how wretched it is to be thrown back into the region of letters after treading the giddy heights of existence, in which your dear presence & converse had placed me. Oh it is sad to think how little a letter gives one! Yours today is all precious sweetness; yet it tells but a few moments of your life, a few thoughts of your mind, and it contains no looks, no tones—that is the great, deplorable, alas irremediable loss . . .'[11] 'No looks, no tones—': the body and the voice are withdrawn from writing. This withdrawal is like death, but, being a model of death, it may then enable us to contemplate actual deaths without being led by our own pain and bewilderment to wish for rapid certainties about what has happened to the dead person. If 'To J. S.' were a treatise, it might have a responsibility to argue that people do or do not survive their deaths, but in the poem what is at issue is not the correctness of a general conclusion but a matter of conduct in the face of particular loss. No metaphysical certitude of itself guarantees tactful and apprehensive behaviour, but Tennyson tries to behave just in this way as he writes. Hallam thought the loss of tone an 'alas irremediable loss'; Tennyson turns the loss to a means of humane delicacy, for the voice in the poem is not withdrawn from writing, but into it, preserved by the lines in sight of resuscitation, poised in air. Tennyson's imagination moves from 'I will not say' to 'I wrote', drawing attention to the physical existence of the printed words, onto which a tear can, after that precisely timed delay at the line-end (the brim of the eye), drop. Out of the death of voice, a new body of significance can be made to arise, a loss perpetuated while a grief is consoled. The written words keep James Spedding

company in his loss, are close to him by taking into themselves a condition
of loss, a Wordsworthian half-absence.

'To J. S.' ends by addressing not James Spedding but his dead brother,
Edward:

> Sleep till the end, true soul and sweet.
> Nothing comes to thee new or strange.
> Sleep full of rest from head to feet;
> Lie still, dry dust, secure of change. [12]

Christopher Ricks brings out the intricacy of thought in this lingering
melody:

> The end of 'To J. S.' is all sleep and no waking. 'Sleep till the end' which
> may be Judgement Day, or the words may simply mean 'till the end'. 'Nothing
> comes to thee new or strange'—nothing? 'Lie still, dry dust, secure of change':
> *still* is delicately dual, and how are we to take 'secure of change'? Does secure
> mean 'assured of'? In which case the after-life does edge into the poem's
> conclusion. And yet the whole feeling of these last lines is set against change,
> is absolute for death. Moreover, the last two lines would seem to recall the
> innocence in Milton: 'asleep secure of harme' (*Paradise Lost*, IV, 791); and in
> that case 'secure of' must mean 'secure against'. Sleep, not heaven, would
> stand as the final solace. For all its mildness, the end of 'To J. S.' is forcefully
> perplexing. It . . . is a poem of which the ending may not be the ultimate
> ending, since we cannot speak of sleeping without wondering about waking. [13]

The comment is completely in tune with the lines, especially so in the
contending impulses of assurance and tentativeness which speak through the
critic's prose as they sing in the verse. The poem closes with 'all sleep and
no waking' and 'the whole feeling of these last lines is set against change'.
On the other hand, 'we cannot speak of sleeping without wondering about
waking' (and the 'we' there must include at least this poet and this critic);
the possible pun on 'secure of' to which Professor Ricks alerts us implies
that 'the after-life does edge into the poem's conclusion'. 'Edge into' is
grudgingly concessive where it should be welcoming. For the stanza, unlike
all others but one in the poem, is divided by a full stop at its mid-point. At
that stressed mid-point, Tennyson changes the sense of the lines though he
does not change their referent. Edward Spedding is both 'true soul and sweet'
and 'dry dust'. These last lines are indeed 'forcefully perplexing' but the force
of their perplexity is that of a religious mystery as well as of a personal
quandary. As a 'true soul and sweet', Edward Spedding sleeps the sleep of
the just until Judgement Day; nothing occurs to the soul in that sleep (it is
not, for example, sentient of the strange processes of physical decomposition).
As an embodied individual whose body awaits its resurrection, he is 'secure

of change' in that whatever changes occur to the matter of his body, it will eventually be recomposed in its integrity—it will be his body still even when it is the body of glory—and he is also 'secure of change' in that, though his body is now become 'dry dust', this is not a dust to which he has finally returned but a dust eventually to be raised and re-united with the 'true soul and sweet'. The stanza is divided as body and soul are for the time divided, but it holds in view, indeed it displays, that resurrection when what has been put asunder will be joined anew. Professor Ricks exactly recognizes what the lines say under their breath about the difficulty of conceiving and desiring what is hoped for in the Christian doctrine of the resurrection of the body. They also speak that doctrine out, plainly and formally. Doing both at once, they are not underhand but open to the stress of living with such a doctrine of the afterlife. It is this unity of faith and tremor which the lines effect in their union of mellifluousness and extreme semantic complexity, something which makes them 'forcefully perplexing' for all their 'mildness', which indeed makes the mildness what is most perplexing about them.

It is possible to say the lines so that the orthodox hope is more evident, and equally possible to voice them so that staying unchanged and not being resurrected is the body's hope, but you cannot have them, vocally, both ways at once. The divergent attitudes would make 'a contradiction on the tongue';[14] the eye can still see the conjunction of meanings in the written words, turn the reciprocal hostility of the opposed senses of hope from bafflement into an authentic richness, a felicitous truth to the complication of our desires for beyond the grave. That is gently intimate, too, with the state of bereavement. It does not belittle loss by making it only temporary (it is not a 'matter of time' before the resurrection of the body at the Last Judgement; 'the end' which the lines mention is the end of time), nor does it bluntly insist that loss is absolute. The whole poem has its attention fixed on James Spedding, though it turns to Edward at the close. Enclosing address to the dead within a letter to the survivor, Tennyson, for the space of the composition, unites all three of them, and not only in memory or imagination.

Memory is abashed in 'To J. S.', and her self-consciousness comes out when she almost loses her voice: 'Memory standing near / Cast down her eyes, and in her throat / Her voice seemed distant'. This self-conscious vocal thwarting is characteristic of Tennyson. In *The Princess*, Lady Psyche, in the all-female precincts of the University, recognizes her brother through his disguise:

> . . . glowing full-faced welcome, she
> Began to address us, and was moving on
> In gratulation, till as when a boat
> Tacks, and the slackened sail flaps, all her voice

Faltering and fluttering in her throat, she cried
'My brother!'[15]

'Full-faced' shows Psyche at ease with her own social competence (the feeling
is that because everything fits for her in her environment she too fits herself
snugly, 'full of it' and so 'full of herself'). When she sees her world's rules
infringed, she shrinks back, the wind taken out of her sails and out of her
voice too, as the rhythmic skewing of the verse away from regular iambics
into 'till as when a boat / Tacks, and the slackened sail flaps, all her voice /
Faltering and fluttering in her throat' makes an effort to convey both by the
jolts of rhythm and by the introduction of internal rhyme and assonance into
blank verse ('Tacks'/'slackened'; 'till'/'sail'/'all'/'Faltering'). This meticulous
effect in the verse presents a hindrance as much as an opportunity for a
reader's delivery. You have to find a way with your voice to preserve the
decorum of the verse even while Tennyson skilfully disturbs its poise, just
as the cry 'My brother!' has to be made both to break the line in which it
occurs and to be contained by that line—you cannot simply cry it aloud,
any more than Psyche can, without drawing unwanted attention to it. The
rules require, in the narrative situation as in the verse, that the emotional
impetus be battened down for the sake of good form. Here Tennyson shows
one of the many dramatic opportunities implicit in Wordsworth's understanding of metre—regular iambics can stand, for a moment, as the embodiment of a social system within which the individual and her voice toil.

The writing is reticent in evoking a cry without voicing it; we attend in
these lines to the desire, and to the dread, of speech, as we do in 'Guinevere':

Then she stretched out her arms and cried aloud
'Oh Arthur!' there her voice brake suddenly,
Then—as a stream that spouting from a cliff
Fails in mid air, but gathering at the base
Re-makes itself, and flashes down the vale—
Went on in passionate utterance:
                          'Gone—my lord!
Gone through my sin to slay and to be slain!
And he forgave me, and I could not speak.
Farewell? I should have answered his farewell.
His mercy choked me. . . .'[16]

The epic simile ('as a stream . . ./. . . flashes down the vale'), an old token
of rhetorical mastery, gains fresh weight in this interim of the constricted
larynx. Tennyson's skill interposes itself in the gaps of Guinevere's utterance,
demonstrating a poet's power with the language but making that power
instinct with a moral imagination about the speechless needs to which only
reticence answers. The lack of strict connection between his composing mind

and her passion makes the movement of the verse respond at every point to the thought of what it is for her to speak in these circumstances, as the rhythms of *The Princess* answer to the situation of Psyche's speech. Such imagination stops Tennyson from 'spouting' himself in these lines because his skill inhabits her broken voice; he finds his way eloquently to the dark truth of a sinner's mute resentment of forgiveness, 'His mercy choked me'.

Arthur Hallam said Tennyson had an 'ear of fairy fineness'.[17] The fineness is particularly that which listens in to the interplay of sound and silence, with dramatic feeling for the charged needs in utterance. Across his career, Tennyson finds words for muffled sounds, creates on the page the vestiges of speech, 'the sound of a voice that is still' as 'Break, break, break' calls it.[18] In early poems we catch 'a stifled moan', 'an ancient melody / Of an inward agony' or 'the phantom of a silent song';[19] Gareth tries to speak in the *Idylls of the King* but '(his voice was all ashamed)'; Geraint bites back his words, 'And there he broke the sentence in his heart / Abruptly, as a man upon his tongue / May break it . . .'; and Merlin's elocution leaves something to be desired: 'He spoke in words part heard, in whispers part, / Half-suffocated in the hoary fell / And many-wintered fleece of throat and chin.'[20]

Tennysonian eloquence leads a double life; it invites and repays voicing, it also asks for constant recognition of the quieter life of the words on the page. The experience of a reader, then, resembles that of the poet listening to Christmas bells in *In Memoriam*:

> Four voices of four hamlets round,
>   From far and near, on mead and moor,
>   Swell out and fail, as if a door
> Were shut between me and the sound . . .[21]

Swelling out and failing are vital motions of the poetry as of Tennyson's life, of anyone's life, the motions of the lungs. Tennyson often said that only he could properly read his own poetry aloud—'the Poet swears no being, existent or possible, can read this but himself' and again 'He will not admit that any one save himself can read aloud his poems properly'[22] The reason he gave for this was that 'Some of the passages are hard to read because they have to be taken in one breath and require good lungs'.[23] He thought nobody had lungs like his. He may have believed that 'poetry looks better, more convincing, in print'[24] but then had to face the fact that it didn't sound better there, that he couldn't count on its good look to secure the right voicing. He worried about 'Boädicea': 'he "feared that no one could read it except himself, and wanted someone to annotate it musically so that people could understand the rhythm". "If they would only read it straight like prose," he said, "just as it is written, it would come all right." '[25] If nobody could read it except himself, who was this 'someone' who would annotate it for him? And if it would come right when read 'just as it is written' why did he need this unknown 'someone' and the musical annotation?

The inconsistency of his claims arises from the centrality of respiration, and other physical motor-rhythms, to Tennyson's poetry, a centrality which was the poet's boast and also his quandary. Every body breathes, and poems written in the rhythm of the breath must be of all others those most patent to any body, but no two bodies breathe alike. Two bodies only rarely and ecstatically breathe in synchronicity (which is a source of the pleasure of duets), and so poems written in the rhythm of breathing are of all others the most personal. Hutton commented on 'the lavish strength of what may be called the bodily element in poetry' in Tennyson's work,[26] and other critics have sometimes taken Hutton's insight as the basis of adverse comment. Tennyson is thought to be preoccupied with word-music, with fondling, as it were, the bodies of words, to the exclusion or detriment of responsible thought; he 'is indolent, over-refining, is in danger of neutralizing his earnestness altogether by the scepticism of thought not too strong, but not strong enough to lead or combine, and he runs, or rather reposes, altogether upon feelings (not to speak it offensively) too sensual'.[27] But Tennyson thought *in* melody, and did so because his preoccupation with self-identity over time and beyond time drew him down repeatedly to an encounter with the human body itself as the crucial location of his thinking. His tunes carry the physique of his intellection, as they must, for what he ponders is the body itself, its grain over the years, the tissues he inherits, and where (and if) he would be without it.

He told W. F. Rawnsley, 'I don't think poetry should be *all thought*: there should be some melody.'[28] Loyal to melody as he remained, he was not therefore deaf or dead to thought; acoustics were for him a form of metaphysics. Thinking about the body involves taking account of the fact that our thinking is itself embodied, our concepts sunk in time like a seal in wax, sunk also in the history of a culture's words. This fact tells on and in Tennyson's melodies with their thought immersed in 'matter-moulded forms of speech'.[29] Hallam had thought the 'highest order' of poetry was 'that which deals with the foundations of our being, and never subordinates the thought to the diction'.[30] Tennyson's poetry does not subordinate thought to diction, but it discovers that the 'foundations of our being' lie a deal lower, though not perhaps 'deeper', than Hallam might have liked to think, and that, at those physical foundations, the distinction between 'thought' and 'diction' does not ring as clearly as it did in Hallam's prose. In the context of concern with self-identity, Tennyson's complaint that 'The worst of folk is that they are so unable to understand the poet's mind'[31] turns out to be at one with an anxiety that people did not hear his rhythm or share his lungs.

In his essay on *In Memoriam,* T. S. Eliot suggested a way to sound out Tennyson's mind:

> . . . I do not think any poet in English has ever had a finer ear for vowel sound, as well as a subtler feeling for some moods of anguish . . . And this technical gift of Tennyson's is no slight thing. Tennyson lived in a time which was already acutely time-conscious: a great many things seemed to be happening, railways were being built, discoveries were being made, the face of the world was changing. That was a time busy in keeping up to date. It had, for the most part, no hold on permanent things, on permanent truths about man and God and life and death. The surface of Tennyson stirred about with his time; and he had nothing to which to hold fast except his unique and unerring feeling for the sounds of words. But in this he had something that no one else had. Tennyson's surface, his technical accomplishment, is intimate with his depths: what we most quickly see about Tennyson is that which moves between the surface and the depths, that which is of slight importance. By looking innocently at the surface we are most likely to come to the depths, to the abyss of sorrow.[32]

Though the poet who looked for the point of intersection of the timeless with time might have been less severe about the Victorians' search for a union of time-consciousness with 'permanent truths', Eliot's repeated bringing-together of 'surface' with 'depths', of 'vowel sound' with 'moods of anguish' finely senses the nature of Tennyson's accomplishment. The metaphysical debates of Tennyson's time did indeed stir the surface of his verse, as I shall show; his musicality is attuned to the time's questioning remote as that music is from the public manners of intellectual exposition. Most particularly, the music asks, 'what is it to be embodied?' even while the proficiency of the writing celebrates such skills of embodied persons as the having of good lungs. Tennyson's verse sounds as if the body thought.

Arthur Hallam in his day had thought 'the doctrine of human immortality . . . [an] excellent . . . theme for the energy of declamation'.[33] Much that Tennyson has to say about immortality cannot be declaimed because it cannot quite be said at all. When 'De Profundis' envisages a future for Tennyson's second Hallam, his son and heir, it does so with vigilance about its own wishes:

> Live, and be happy in thyself, and serve
> This mortal race thy kin so well, that men
> May bless thee as we bless thee, O young life
> Breaking with laughter from the dark; and may
> The fated channel where thy motion lives

> Be prosperously shaped, and sway thy course
> Along the years of haste and random youth
> Unshattered; then full-current through full man;
> And last in kindly curves, with gentlest fall,
> By quiet fields, a slowly-dying power,
> To that last deep where we and thou are still.[34]

Within the plain monosyllables of that last line lies a contrariety of desire. Tennyson may wish for his son and for himself 'That last deep where we and thou *are* still' (where we continue to exist) or 'That last deep where we and thou are *still*' (where we are finally at rest, out of the turmoil of existing). Metrical considerations cannot settle the issue. The line is not definitely a regular iambic pentameter; there may be three consecutive stresses on 'that last deep' (of the other ten lines in the passage I quote, only five are to my ears regular blank verse). A stress on 'are' is not metrically impossible. More importantly, metrical stress and the stress of meaning need not be identical. Stress may fall metrically on 'still' without this fixing the emphasis of thought, for the line can be voiced as an iambic pentameter and yet made to mean, with the intonation contour, 'where we continue to exist'. Begin to allow that a contrariety of desire may speak in this wish for his son, and the accent of Tennyson's doubts about survival and inexistence begins to sound throughout the passage: does the young life break laughingly from the dark (it laughs because it has escaped, broken from, something unpleasant) or is the life itself broken by a laughter which follows it from the dark (compare: 'breaking with fatigue from the strain')—the second possibility would explain why Tennyson has to pray that it will survive 'unshattered'? Are the 'quiet fields' in these lines akin to the 'field' man so happily 'lies beneath', the 'dim fields about the homes / Of happy men that have the power to die' of 'Tithonus'?[35] And does the 'power to die' of the 1860 poem linger on in the 'slowly-dying power' of these lines composed some time between 1852 and 1880? If so, which matters most—that death comes slowly, or that what comes, however slowly, should be death? The lines remarkably absorb these many questions in their steady melody, but, steadily as it goes, the passage stirs with questions.

Human beings sometimes say they want to die but the breath they use to utter that wish is itself a sign of life, so that, as an early Tennyson poem puts it, 'No life that breathes with human breath / Has ever truly longed for death.'[36] But no life that breathes with only *human* breath has ever wholly longed for immortality. It may be, as those lines from 'The Two Voices' imply, that the mechanism of breathing strives, as does any other thing which exists, to preserve itself in existence,[37] and that it is therefore 'life, not death, for which we pant'.[38] If indeed it is our lungs, for example, as much as our selves, which do not want to die, the physical motions wishing on their own account to be a *perpetuum mobile*, then an immortality outside the body will not be quite all which all of a person now desires when he wishes never to die. 'What opposite needs converge to this desire of Immortality!' as another Victorian exclaimed.[39] Tennyson's genius is to do more than merely exclaim about the fact.

The two voices which speak divergent impulses at explicit length, and in alternation, in his early masterpiece, 'The Two Voices', continue their vital debate in simultaneous vocal ambiguities throughout of the style of his mature work. Wilfrid Ward noted of 'Vastness' that, as Tennyson read it aloud to him, it had 'two distinct voices—the last line being placed in the mouth of a separate speaker who answers the rest of the poem'.[40] This is excellently said, but is not quite right. 'Vastness' runs for thirty-five lines of torrential lament over the inane cruelties of human life before coming to rest on 'Peace, let it be! for I loved him, and love him for ever: the dead are not dead but alive.'[41] 'Let it be!' could be an 'amen' to the pointless squandering of creation which the poem details; it may resign to the will of God because, at least, that will has not only permitted the love of Tennyson for Hallam, but assured the eternity such love asks. Or 'let it be!' might decide to leave the whole mess of the world alone, turn from it with a sorrow barely distinguishable from disgust, and concentrate in stead of the world on an exceptional case of decency, so exceptional that it cannot be thought to be part of any scheme which would re-orient all disasters by placing them in the light of a divine plan. The last hemistich also achieves a sublime numbness of tone in print. This is partly because of the logical ambiguity of the colon which introduces it, standing perhaps for a 'because' ('it is because he is an immortal soul that he can be loved as I love him') or perhaps for a 'therefore' ('it is in the perpetuity of love that the dead find their life'). In the former case, the feeling arises from a conviction, in the latter, the conviction is produced by the feeling. The numbness mainly comes from the absence of any indication of attitude in the line, such as might be supplied by 'How frightening!' or 'What joy!'

Imagining such an indicator of attitude is absurd but we need to make such an act of imagination to see why somebody who confidently opted for one of the possible indicators here would have missed the point of the poem. This is not because it does not matter which indicator is supplied, but because it is the absence of an indicator which needs to be precisely imagined. Reading the line in the context of the entire poem does not settle the issue, for 'Vastness' is constructed so that the thirty-five lines which detail human wretchedness are countered by this single last line; it is absolutely clear that a great difference is made but not what the difference is. This seems to me honest. If you were convinced that human beings were immortal, it would clearly make a great difference to how the world struck you, but you could not be clear what the difference was unless you also knew fully what being immortal was like, and human beings do not know this. Properly then, the tone with which 'Vastness' ends remains not unsettled but not settled either.

We cannot say whether the poem concludes with an achieved serenity or whether the poet gets at last a surprise that may not be entirely pleasant. We can *speak* the line so that it will make up Tennyson's mind and voice for him; indeed, it is impossible to say it without either some tonal indication or an evident and deliberate avoidance of such indication, whereas the written line neither drops hints nor maintains a poker-face. All this configuration of feeling is Tennyson's. Ward was right to say that the line sounded as if 'placed in the mouth of a separate speaker', but Tennyson is also that speaker separate from himself, at odds with his own desires and saved from involution only by the managed detachment of his voice onto the page. (The same is true for any sympathetic reader of the poem.)

He frequently punned around the phrase 'let it be' and its cognates;[42] its range of tones, from patience to an angered curtness, could be made to hold an entire temperament as it looked over its past and looked forward with the troubled hope that such a past might have a permanent future. The speaker of *Maud* rebukes himself for spite against Maud's brother, 'Peace, angry spirit, and let him be! / Has not his sister smiled on me?',[43] but the obstinate workings of his mind against his will cannot leave the thought of the brother alone (let him be) and his angry spirit cannot eventually even leave the brother alive (let him be). After the duel, the speaker himself suffers from not being let be, though, and at the same time, he wishes to die, to be let cease to be: 'But the broad light glares and beats, / And the shadow flits and fleets / And will not let me be . . .'[44] The insistent obsession presses in the gruesome echoing of the verse: 'light' becoming 'let' through 'flits', 'beats' and 'fleets' overshadowing 'me' and 'be'. And the echo of 'let me be' back to 'let him be' helps us recognize why the speaker of *Maud* is his own worst enemy—unable to let others be, he cannot himself be let be by himself.

The past maddeningly refuses to die, but then the self obdurately refuses to succumb to death (so that the consciousness in *Maud* seems at once Dracula and his victim). Nor will the past lie down in *The Princess* when Ida repudiates the sentiment of 'Tears, idle tears' with a self-consciously gorgeous tirade of a progressivist colour:

> Wiser to weep a true occasion lost,
> But trim our sails, and let old bygones be,
> While down the streams that float us each and all
> To the issue, goes, like glittering bergs of ice,
> Throne after throne, and molten on the waste
> Becomes a cloud: for all things serve their time
> Toward that great year of equal mights and rights . . .[45]

She wants to speak against what she thinks is the futile nostalgia of 'Tears, idle tears' but it is as if, try as he might to give Ida the words for her projects,

Tennyson's own reluctance to let anything die, even the unpleasantness of the past, makes him put in her mouth the ambiguous sentiment of 'Let old bygones be'—'let them continue to exist, don't interfere with them' / 'let them alone, get on to something else.' The way 'let be' can look at once to the past and to the future shows in the printed voice that if a morbid temperament is to be immortal the immortality will itself be morbid.

In 'To the Marquis of Dufferin and Ava', Tennyson gratefully recalls his son Lionel's last letter:

> But ere he left your fatal shore,
>   And lay on that funeral boat,
>   Dying, 'Unspeakable' he wrote
> 'Their kindness,' and he wrote no more;
>
> And sacred is the latest word;
>   And now the Was, the Might-have-been,
>   And those lone rites I have not seen,
> And one drear sound I have not heard,
>
> Are dreams that scarce will let me be,
>   Not there to bid my boy farewell,
>   When That within the coffin fell,
> Fell—and flashed into the Red Sea,
>
> Beneath a hard Arabian moon
>   And alien stars . . .[46]

Tennyson often read the letters of the dead, from 1833 when Hallam died to Lionel's death in 1886, and took those deaths into his own words. This poem, like *In Memoriam*, XCV, turns on the critical word 'flashed', expressing at once the intensity of an attachment and how its object has disappeared. The dead man's words revive in Tennyson's verse, but do so only because the verse consciously fashions for itself a reduction of living voice to meet the dead half-way. The poems do not impersonate dead voices and so do not insert themselves as substitute satisfactions between Tennyson and what he has lost; they do not take the place of the dead, or of his feelings for the dead, though they can stand for the dead and the feelings with which he survives. *In Memoriam*, XCV, reports Hallam's letters indirectly; 'To the Marquis of Dufferin and Ava' displays how Tennyson's writing has changed what Lionel wrote by the evident poetic inversion of the imaginable prose syntax of his son's letter. That is, Lionel probably wrote something like 'their kindness has been unspeakable' rather than 'Unspeakable . . . / Their kindness'. No reader versed in the conventions of poetry would believe otherwise (Lionel certainly did not write to his father in *In Memoriam* stanzas anyway). But the conventions are very tender here; they allow the last word Lionel leaves Tennyson to be not 'Unspeakable' but 'kindness'—not inarticulacy, then, but gentle attentions, though, as a reader guesses at the prose within the verse, he hears not only the dumb given effectual speech but also the helpless breakage of deep emotions against the rigid element of print. John Bayley captures the delicacy of the relations between the formal and the colloquial in these lines, when he comments of 'Unspeakable': 'Its social sense, applied to the Viceroy's kindness, is also the literal sense applicable to the grief of the bereaved; and it is touchingly right that the father should find how to fit into his poetry the word his son used.'[47] This hovering reticence which touches social decencies into imaginative decorum weighs thoughtfully too on the capital 'T' in 'When That within the coffin fell.' No vocalization of 'That' can do what the written word does—show that Tennyson's loss was great without saying how great, and at the same time abstain from saying what exactly it was within the coffin even while impressing on the reader how dear whatever it was was. 'The simple truth is that we are not in a position to say what is body and what is soul . . .': but it is true that Tennyson was able to write down the complexity of our not being in such a position.

Breathing is the periodical movement he most skilfully frames in his art. The word 'breath' and its cognates mattered to him (there are 197 entries in Baker's 1914 concordance) because breath intimately brings together life and poetry in the fact that it is with the breath that keeps us living that we sing or speak. The root meaning of the word 'spirit' is 'breath', so that breath can be taken as of the essence both of this life and of any other life we imagine. His verse composes breathing so that the bare production of the words becomes significant:

> Ah yet, even yet, if this might be,
>   I, falling on his faithful heart,
>   Would breathing through his lips impart
> The life that almost dies in me;
>
> That dies not, but endures with pain,
>   And slowly forms the firmer mind,
>   Treasuring the look it cannot find,
> The words that are not heard again.[48]

The moral drama of wishing to die and wishing to survive death takes body in the regulated breath we have to take between these stanzas. At the end of the first stanza quoted, at the end of our breath, the impulse of self-sacrifice verges on the suicidal, and the exhaustion of our lungs in speaking the lines endorses that impulse. But the poem is not done, nor done with us, and requires a firmer resolve which makes itself felt as an inhalation: 'The life that almost dies in me' [the reader breathes in] 'That dies not . . .'. Absented from the felicity of death awhile, in this harsh world he draws his breath again in pain to tell Hallam's story. Tennyson discriminates between his desires, knowing that the readiness expressed here to do anything to resuscitate Hallam might, given Tennyson's own desire to die, be only an eagerness to be given the kiss of death himself. The discrimination is made in these lines, and particularly in the breathing space between them. The printed words, of course, do not perform the act of intake they ask a reader to imagine. That abstention from performance guards against fantasy, the fantasy either of suicide or resuscitation; it also permits a self-conscious contemplation of what it is to feel like this, so that, once again, the words survey what at the same time they express. Henry James, magnificently, though with an edge of complaint, described his impression of such Tennysonian self-awareness when it was prolonged throughout one of the poet's readings to his guests: 'the whole thing was yet *still*, with all the long swing of its motion it yet remained where it was—heaving doubtless grandly enough up and down and beautiful to watch as through the superposed veils of its long self-consciousness'.[49] This stillness is the perpetual immobility of print which James acutely managed to hear even when Tennyson was reading aloud at him. Thus stilled, the gap between 'dies in me' and 'That dies not' represents not only a single breath, one sensation, the tick of a clock, but a pattern of character, something Tennyson lives in every breath he takes.

H. D. Rawnsley remembered how Tennyson read with a drama of pause:

> 'Nor can I forget how, at the intervals or ends of a phrase such as "And sorrow darkens hamlet and hall", the whole voice which had been mourning forth the impassioned lament suddenly seemed to fail for very grief, to collapse, to drop and die away in silence, but so abruptly that the effect upon one was— "He has come to a full stop; he will not read another line." '[50]

'He has come to a full stop'—Rawnsley may not have intended the pun between 'full stop' as a mark of punctuation and as an absolute halt but it seriously conveys how much existential weight Tennyson could put on a stop, the death in 'he will not read another line' and, equally, the courage for living on at a semicolon: 'The life that almost dies in me; / That dies not'.[51]

Tennyson made the pulse sound like a burden in the returning iambic mechanism of *In Memoriam*, VII, and he can also make the breath reverse its significance and tell of the longing to die in the very fibres and motions which keep us going. *In Memoriam*, LXXXVI:

> Sweet after showers, ambrosial air,
>   That rollest from the gorgeous gloom
>   Of evening over brake and bloom
> And meadow, slowly breathing bare

> The round of space, and rapt below
>   Through all the dewy-tasselled wood,
>   And shadowing down the hornèd flood
> In ripples, fan my brows and blow
>
> The fever from my cheek, and sigh
>   The full new life that feeds thy breath
>   Throughout my frame, till Doubt and Death,
> Ill brethren, let the fancy fly
>
> From belt to belt of crimson seas
>   On leagues of odour streaming far,
>   To where in yonder orient star
> A hundred spirits whisper 'Peace'.[52]

'It all goes together', as Tennyson proudly said of the poem to Allingham.[53] One implication of the remark is that the section is hard to read aloud because it has to be taken in one breath and requires good lungs. Hallam Tennyson wrote that the section 'gives preeminently [Tennyson's] sense of the joyous peace in Nature',[54] and we can imagine Tennyson's joy in his own nature, at least in that part of it which permitted him graceful spans of respiration as he read this poem out. But is the 'Peace' the poem concludes with that 'peace in Nature' Hallam speaks of? In so far as the 'spirits' are 'in' a star, however distant, they can be said to be in Nature, and their peace is in there with them. Consider, though, the effect of attempting to speak this poem in a single breath. The exceptionally proficient arch of the verse blends with the climate it describes, the 'ambrosial air' being both a song and an atmosphere, so that the human breath and the world's breeze find a kinship, become 'breath-ren' (the pun is in the poem). Even the best lungs will be weary at the close of the section, will have the air left only to whisper the word which is the destination of this eloquent trajectory, 'Peace'. Said in that way, breathing the reader's last, the word can sound like the peace that death is, the peace of 'Rest in peace'. The spirits may be saying 'hush' to the utterance of the poem ('Peace, peace: / Dost thou not see my Baby at my breast, / That suckes the Nurse asleepe?'[55]) as well as naming a calm which the poem attains. The poem comes to completion by telling itself to speak no more. *In Memoriam*, LXXXVI expresses, in the metaphysical depths of melody nineteenth-century philosophers often heard in music, the longing to be out of Nature, to be dead, and expresses simultaneously a billowing delight in the performing breath as a sign of life.[56] Any vocalization of the poem has the risky privilege of trying to make this balance of absolute impulses audible; on the page, the poise is there to be seen. It creates within the printed voice a feeling for a place 'where beyond these voices there is peace', as the last line of 'Guinevere' has it,[57] by stretching breathing to breaking-point so that utterance of such extremity seems to take one outside of oneself. Gladstone wrote of 'Guinevere': 'No one, we are persuaded, can read this poem without feeling, when it ends, what may be termed the pangs of vacancy—of that void in heart and mind for want of its continuance of which we are conscious when some noble strain of music ceases . . . the withdrawal of it is like the withdrawal of the vital air.'[58] The void in the lungs *In Memoriam*, LXXXVI creates so rapturously does not make us long that we or the poem should be continued, it finishes so perfectly, and the reader who has expended breath to voice this air discovers in the triumph of having done it that he will be content, eventually, himself to have done with life.

Notes

1. First published in Hallam, Lord Tennyson, *Alfred Lord Tennyson: A Memoir by his Son*, 2 vols. (1897), II, 87–88. Probably composed in 1869, 'Reticence' is reprinted in *The Poems of Tennyson*, ed. Christopher Ricks (1969, 2nd edn., 3 vols., 1987). All subsequent references to Tennyson's poems are to the text of this edition, given in the form 'Ricks' and a volume and page number. Thus, for this poem: 'Reticence' (1869), Ricks, III, 628–29.

2. *Memoir*, II, 325.

3. 'Tennyson', in R. H. Hutton, *Literary Essays* (1871, 3rd, enlarged edn., 1888) 372–73.

4. 'Tennyson as Prophet', *Nineteenth Century* (Mar. 1889), in *Tennyson: The Critical Heritage*, ed. J. D. Jump (1967), 412.

5. *King Lear*, V. iii. 263–64; Folio, 11. 3224–25.

6. The phrase is from W. J. Fox's review of *Poems, Chiefly Lyrical*, *Westminster Review* (Jan. 1831), in Jump, *Critical Heritage*, 32.

7. *William Allingham: A Diary*, ed. H. Allingham and D. Radford (1907, rpt., 1967), 62.

8. (1832), Ricks, I, 506.

9. See L. A. Sonnino, *A Handbook to Sixteenth-Century Rhetoric* (1968), 131, quoting Abraham Fraunce, *The Arcadian Rhetorike* (1588).

10. *Hamlet*, I. ii. 73–74; Folio, 11. 252–53.

11. Letter of 7 Apr. 1832, in *The Letters of Arthur Henry Hallam*, ed. J. Kolb (Columbus, Ohio, 1981), 546.

12. Ricks, I, 507.

13. See his *Tennyson* (1972), 98.

14. *In Memoriam*, CXXV (1850), Ricks, II, 445.

15. *The Princess* (1847), Ricks, II, 211.

16. (1859), Ricks, III, 545.

17. 'On Some of the Characteristics of Modern Poetry, and of the Lyrical Poems of Alfred Tennyson' (1831), in *The Writings of A. H. Hallam*, ed. T. H. Vail Motter (New York, 1943), 191.

18. (1842), Ricks, II, 24.

19. 'Mariana in the South' (1832), Ricks, I, 399; 'Claribel' (1830), Ricks, I, 199; 'The Miller's Daughter' (1832), Ricks, I, 410.

20. 'Gareth and Lynette' (1872), Ricks, III, 293; 'Geraint and Enid' (as the second half of 'Enid' 1859), Ricks, III, 351; 'Merlin and Vivien' (as 'Vivien' 1859), Ricks, III, 418.

21. *In Memoriam*, XXVIII, Ricks, II, 346.

22. Kolb, 385; Allingham, 95.

23. *Memoir*, I, 395n.

24. *Memoir*, I, 190.

25. *Memoir*, I, 459.

26. Hutton, *Essays*, 364.

27. Leigh Hunt, *Church of England Quarterly Review* (Apr. 1843), in Jump, 128.

28. 'Personal Recollections of Tennyson' *Nineteenth Century* (Jan. 1925), rpt. in *Tennyson: Interviews and Recollections*, ed. N. Page (1983), 21.

29. *In Memoriam*, XCV, Ricks, II, 413.

30. Letter to J. M. Gaskell, 25 June 1828, Kolb, 212.

31. H. D. Rawnsley, *Memoirs of the Tennysons* (Glasgow, 1900), Page, 68.

32. 'In Memoriam', in *Selected Essays* (1932, 3rd enlarged edn., 1951, rpt. 1976), 337.

33. 'Essay on the Philosophical Writings of Cicero', written 1831, Motter, 175.

34. (1880), Ricks, III, 68.

35. Ricks, II, 612.

36. 'The Two Voices' (1842), Ricks, I, 591.

37. Spinoza, *Ethica in ordine geometrico demonstrata* (1675), trans. as *Ethics* by W. H. White and A. H. Stirling, ed. J. Gutman (New York, 1949), Part III, proposition vi, 135.

38. 'The Two Voices', Ricks, I, 591.

39. Browning, letter to Julia Wedgwood, 27 June 1864, in *Robert Browning and Julia Wedgwood: A Broken Friendship as Revealed in Their Letters*, ed. R. Curle (1937), 31.

40. Quoted in Ricks, III, 137n.

41. Ricks, III, 137.

42. In addition to the examples I discuss below, see 'The First Quarrel' (1880), Ricks, III, 41, especially its cutting lineation of ' "Let bygones be!" / "Bygones! . . ." ' The phrase 'let . . . be' rarely has Tennyson's inquiring richness in other poets of the period. Newman, for example, makes the Soul of Gerontius cry, after the Divine Vision, 'Take me away, and in the lowest deep / There let me be . . .', but the Soul does not wish to be let alone; see *The Dream of Gerontius* in Newman's *Verses on Various Occasions* (1865; Uniform Edition, 1868), 357. On the other hand, Christina Rossetti uses the phrase probably to mean just 'let me alone' in 'Autumn' (1858): 'O love-songs, gurgling from a hundred throats, / O love-pangs, let me be.'—I quote from the variorum edition of Christina Rossetti's poems, ed. R. W. Crump (2 vols., Baton Rouge, 1979), I, 143.

43. *Maud* (1855), I. xiii, Ricks, II, 548.

44. *Maud*, II. iv, Ricks, II, 575.

45. Ricks, II, 234.

46. (1889), Ricks, III, 200–201.

47. 'Tennyson and the Idea of Decadence', in *Studies in Tennyson*, ed. Hallam Tennyson (1981), 204. Compare also Martin Dodsworth's remark that 'the word "unspeakable" receives an almost impossible degree of emphasis', 'Patterns of Morbidity: Repetition in Tennyson's Poetry', in *The Major Victorian Poets: Reconsiderations*, ed. Isobel Armstrong (1969), 26.

48. *In Memoriam*, XVIII, Ricks, II, 337.

49. *The Middle Years* (1917), rpt. in *Autobiography*, ed. F. W. Dupee (1956), 594.

50. Page, 63.

51. Compare also *Maud*, I. xviii, Ricks, II, 555.

52. Ricks, II, 402.

53. Allingham, 328.

54. *Memoir*, I, 313.

55.   *Antony and Cleopatra*, V. ii. 307–9, Folio, 11. 3561–63.

56.   Compare, for example, the climactic 'in des Welt-Atems wehendem All ['in the travailing/lamenting totality of the breath of the world'] in the 'Liebestod' of *Tristan und Isolde* (1865). 'Welt-Atems' is sung on a semibreve high G sharp, the highest and the longest note in the sequence; the control of breathing required and celebrated in this magnificent passage is an extended version of that rapturous extinction asked by Tennyson's poem.

57.   Ricks, III, 547.

58.   *Quarterly Review* (Oct. 1859), in Jump, 259.

Tennyson's Philosophy:
Some Lyric Examples

TIMOTHY PELTASON

Tennyson's bad reputation as the painfully sober and discursive metaphysician of "The Higher Pantheism" has made all talk of his philosophy suspicious. He wrote poetry and not philosophy, of course, but this truism, applied to Tennyson, becomes a form of serious qualification or even dismissal, another echo of W. H. Auden's famous slap: "He had the finest ear, perhaps, of any English poet; he was also undoubtedly the stupidest; there was little about melancholia that he didn't know; there was little else that he did."[1] Tennyson's is indeed a poetry of darkened moods and subtle meters, and in insisting on its philosophical interest I am not denying this or redirecting attention to some neglected and anomalous part of the canon. My examples are among Tennyson's best-known and most widely admired poems, and, in reading them as philosophical exercises, I do not intend to upset received opinion, at least not the opinions of Tennyson's admirers, but to make my own addition to it, trying as well to stand back and talk explicitly about the critical values that underlie an inclination to take Tennyson and his moods seriously. This is to claim for mood its own philosophic dignity and for Tennyson's evocations of mood a strenuous thoughtfulness.

"Tears, Idle Tears" has been blamed and praised for its exclusive attentiveness to a particular mood or state of mind, blamed for the exclusiveness and praised for the attentiveness, but hardly pinned down as to the precise quality and significance of the mood itself. And this is curious because so much of what the poem has to offer it offers so immediately and insistently:

> Tears, idle tears, I know not what they mean,
> Tears from the depth of some divine despair
> Rise in the heart and gather to the eyes,
> In looking on the happy autumn-fields,
> And thinking of the days that are no more.

Reprinted from *Philosophical Approaches to Literature*, ed. William E. Cain (1984), by permission. © 1984 by Bucknell University Press.

Fresh as the first beam glittering on a sail,
That brings our friends up from the underworld,
Sad as the last which reddens over one
That sinks with all we love below the verge;
So sad, so fresh, the days that are no more.

Ah, sad and strange as in dark summer dawns
The earliest pipe of half-awakened birds
To dying ears, when unto dying eyes
The casement slowly grows a glimmering square;
So sad, so strange, the days that are no more.

Dear as remembered kisses after death,
And sweet as those by hopeless fancy feigned
On lips that are for others; deep as love,
Deep as first love, and wild with all regret;
O Death in Life, the days that are no more.

F. R. Leavis, in his largely dismissive commentary, reads the poem as
a skillful piece of nostalgia, a feeling cheap and familiar and uncritically
indulged. Leavis is discussing Tennyson under the heading "Thought and
Emotional Quality" as a writer in whom the latter crowds out the former
entirely. There is no thought in the poem, according to Leavis, because
"there is no attitude towards the experience except one of complaisance; we
are to be wholly in it and of it."[2] And this is true, I think, except for
the seriously misleading assumption that the poem records a single, local
experience of a kind that we might have at one moment or another of our
lives. Rather than offering us "no attitude," I should say that the poem is
all attitude, and that its project is to describe precisely the situation, the
placement, that is, of human consciousness in time. The poem's most articulate admirers—I think particularly of Cleanth Brooks, Graham Hough, and
Harold Bloom—have all pointed toward this fact, or perhaps proceeded from
it, in praising the universality of feeling that the poem achieves. But it is
not a matter of feeling alone.

Certainly, the poem begins in the unabashed emotionalism of those
tears. But their idleness is directly a challenge to thought: In what sense idle
and are tears ever otherwise? And they are the products of thought as well,
of "looking on the happy autumn-fields" that the poem attends to only in
that quick pathetic fallacy, and of "thinking of the days that are no more."
As in "Break, break, break," where the poet's surging feelings are carefully
named as "the thoughts that arise in me," Tennyson here insists on the union
of heart and head in the full human experience of inwardness. At the same
time, taking the shift from looking to thinking as its premise, the poem
quickly steps free of its origins in idiosyncratic perception and attempts to
document another order of experience, something urgent and firsthand, yet

not circumscribed by the conditions of a single person, place, or time. The first-person singular appears in the poem only as the baffled interpreter of the first line. The object of interpretation and meditation is a phenomenon strangely impersonal, the tears of "some divine despair," with the vagueness of "some" and the largeness of "divine" only reemphasized by the oddly categorical mention of "the heart" and "the eyes." The poem was written at Tintern Abbey, Tennyson reports in the *Memoir*, "filled for me with the memory of bygone days,"[3] but neither the place nor any particular memory evoked by it occupies the poet's attention, and he does not present himself in relation to the landscape or even begin to record the significant details of his experience there. Instead, the poem becomes a second-order meditation that does not think about the days that are no more, but thinks about thinking about them. It is not an account of memories, but of memory, the mysterious and equivocal presence of the past. And yet the past and memory are not really the subjects of the poem either, not at least if the past is taken as something that can be separated out from the present and located and observed and not if memory is the faculty or operation of mind that does the locating and observing. The poem describes no act of will or recovery, but rather a condition of being. It reads finally as if written in answer to the question of the philosopher, or, more precisely, of the phenomenologist: "What does consciousness feel like?" Or, to give the question a Heideggerian turn and to take those tears more fully into account, "What is the mood of consciousness?"

For present consciousness really is the exclusive object of the poem's regard. The poem employs no past tenses, depicts no past scenes, never interests itself in the days that are no more as they exist, or existed, independently of consciousness, but only as they appear to consciousness now. The beams that glitter on the sails of otherworldly boats are not fresh or sad in themselves, out there on the horizon, but in our experience here at the center of consciousness. The phrase itself, "the days that are no more," oddly evades naming the past as past, as if such a conception were outside the realm of interest or possibility, just as the idea of falsehood is so alien to Swift's Houyhnhms that they can refer only to "saying the thing which is not." What the straightforward grammar of "the days that are no more" insists on for Tennyson is that paradox of philosophers and poets both, the presence of absence, and this paradox appears ultimately in the poem as "Death in Life," a phrase that wants only a few hyphens to have the true Heideggerian look. But the feel here is thoroughly Tennysonian, and these phrases, along with the adjectives and the gorgeous series of similes that illustrate them, separate out and examine anew the conclusion of "Break, break, break," the rising thought that that poem finally brings itself to utter: "But the tender grace of a day that is dead/Will never come back to me."

Where "Break, break, break," however, is movingly personal and records the struggle of a deeply feeling individual to reconcile himself to loss,

"Tears, Idle Tears" takes place on the far side of reconciliation and risks its composure only in the surprising "Wild with all regret" of the penultimate line. It does not offer the progress of personal consciousness, but the progressively sharpened and deepened portrait of consciousness in its perpetual present tense. Thus, its tears gather but do not fall and, thus, there is no horizontal movement across its imagined sea, but only the rising and sinking at the horizon. Even these movements are not described, but inferred from the still image of the boat on the far horizon, a single image for the boat that comes and the boat that goes. None of the final three stanzas of the poem is even a complete sentence, and each of them seems to start over again, to throw onto the screen of consciousness a new image and a new set of adjectives that attempt to capture the present experience of the days that are no more. In spite of our talk of inwardness, projection does seem the apt metaphor here rather than insight, for it is an exemplary inwardness that the poem presents us with and not a glimpse into the merely private inner visions of the speaker.

But these exclusively visual metaphors are truly adequate only to the image of stanza two. There the poem imagines time as space and present consciousness as an expanse that just contains the past, but only in its moment of appearance or of disappearance. There is no horizontal motion across that sea of consciousness, but there is the gaping horizontal distance between here and the horizon that is the image of an inner emptiness, of the space across which consciousness feels itself stretched thin. The next stanza offers us not a simple picture of the space of consciousness, but a narrative situation. The days that are no more are as sad and strange as first light and first bird-song must be to the eyes and ears of a dying man. The images of this stanza are finely adjusted to the portrayal of liminal states, of first things and last. These dawns are still dark, stabilized only by the intrusion of "summer." The birds are just waking and just singing, the light of nature is just dawning as the light of sense hovers on the verge of extinction, and both these lights are evoked in the image of the glimmering square, an image of brightening and fading at once. Illuminated by the rising sun, the casement window is growing lighter, but is also flattening out into a mere square of light instead of a window to the world outside. The days that are no more in this stanza render consciousness more tenuous still, both more strangely vivid and more fearfully empty, harder than ever to describe and to place. The consciousness of this stanza is not located precisely inside the dying man, who is never named or pictured, not evoked as a full presence, but in the event that connects the dying senses to the strangely distinct call of the bird. To be conscious in time is to be slipping away perpetually from experience into extinction, to be always just sensing and always just losing what is most real and alive. The poem fills out and presses upon us its apprehension of the days that are no more as an urgently present absence by combining ever more vivid imagery with less and less palpable imagined objects. The boat of the first stanza was already less than it seemed, not a boat, but a sail, not even a sail, but a glittering beam. In each of the next two stanzas new intensities of feeling are gleaned from an ever-more-marginal experience of consciousness, as the poem approaches and then passes beyond the boundary of death.

In the final stanza the present is an after life and the past is more vividly and delusively present than ever, the past and the present more deeply and distressingly intimate. Earlier they have been connected, but also separated by the clear distance between here and the horizon or by the less clear, but still estranging, distance between the dying senses and the sounds of earliness that reach them. The past is now like a kiss, but only a remembered kiss, and the objects of memory slip finally away into the virtual existence of the imagined. The poem's desire to see the past only as it lives in the present of consciousness makes it, on the one hand, a fact of consciousness, yet reduces it to the impalpability of all mere facts of consciousness that are not facts of perception as well. And perception has been left behind in the first stanza. Consciousness is never the simple act of looking on the world, but always the linked and complex awareness of "thinking of the days that are no more." And such thinking does not assure the continuing vitality of the past, but fills the present with delusive images. The kisses of actual experience, once that experience is past, cannot be distinguished from the kisses of fancy. The past exists only in the experience of the present, while the present surrenders its fullness, its presence, to the beckoning memories of the past. Experience itself feels tenuous, stretched thin. The poet's self, drawn out at first to the autumn fields, doubles back to the world within, a shared and expansive inwardness, but an inwardness nevertheless. And now the past is "deep" and "wild," adjectives that absorb it entirely into consciousness, as Cleanth Brooks has noted.[4] The erotic longing of the last stanza and the placement of the past at precisely the depth of first love finally identify the inevitable and frustrated reaching out of consciousness to its own past with the most primal and urgent reaching out to others.[5] The "Death in Life" that the poem ends by lamenting is, among other things, the inner vacancy of Romantic desire, and the poem's wild regret is for all the possible forms of connection of which Tintern Abbey would be a potent reminder. But Wordsworth's poem at this spot is so much more mobile and various and ambitious that it can hardly serve as a foil. Tennyson's wild regretfulness can be compared more helpfully and pointedly with the absolute sufficiency of consciousness evoked by Keats's "To Autumn," a poem that Harold Bloom has convincingly identified as the nearest poetic source of "Tears, Idle Tears."[6]

The attitude of consciousness in "Tears, Idle Tears" is introspective and retrospective, and the mood of consciousness is strange, sad, and urgent. Keats's beautifully different meditation on happy autumn fields shares with "Tears, Idle Tears" its conception of the present moment as the repository of the past. For Keats, as John Jones has remarked, "Ripeness is a kind of simultaneity,"[7] and the past endures in the present and fills it up. The fullness of Keats's arrested present and the emptiness of Tennyson's are oddly congruent, but perfectly opposed in mood and attitude. Keats locates his images of fullness scrupulously outside himself in the plants and animals of the observed or imagined scene and in the spirit of Autumn that he insists on presenting in the full externality of personification. And when he thinks of the past and the songs of spring, he assigns even that thought to the objects before him and then quickly brushes it aside. Tennyson, blinded by the tears that have gathered to fullness and that will be his only harvest, hardly sees the world at all, and his poem makes no show of resisting the acknowledgment that its mood is a human imposition and a fact of human consciousness. Keats's is the greater poem, and for reasons to which Leavis's dispraise of Tennyson points the way, but in saying this I intend to give up very little of my claim for Tennyson and not at all to give way to Leavis's contention that their is something emotionally unhygienic or intellectually limited about "Tears, Idle Tears." A mood piece need not be slack or self-indulgent, and a mood piece as beautiful and successful and exemplary as "Tears, Idle Tears" advances the collective human project of consciousness by making available for our examination and for the pleasure of recognition one precisely evoked way of being in the world.

I have referred to the question of mood as Heideggerian. In the first volume of his recently translated lectures on Nietzsche, Heidegger defends the conception of mood as a necessary philosophical category, as a way of describing the situation in which man finds himself in the world:

> Here it is essential to observe that feeling is not something that runs its course in our "inner lives." It is rather that basic mode of our Dasein by force of which and in accordance with which we are always already lifted beyond ourselves into being as a whole, which in this or that way matters to us or does not matter to us. Mood is never merely a way of being determined in our inner being for ourselves. It is above all a way of being attuned, and letting ourselves be attuned, in this way or that way in mood. Mood is precisely the basic way in which we are *outside* ourselves. But that is the way we are essentially and constantly.[8]

A little earlier in the discussion, Heidegger says that "the will cannot directly awaken or create a countermood: for moods are overcome and transformed always only by moods." An exciting and sympathetic account of *In Memoriam* might take that remark as its guide, but I am interested now in reading "Ulysses" and "Tithonus" as mood and countermood, as poems that amplify and enrich one another and that help to fill out a brief account of Tennyson's philosophy. Another way to phrase part of Leavis's objection to "Tears, Idle

Tears" might have been to say that the poem contains no suggestion of its own countermood, a suggestion that I tried to make in the introduction of Keats. Of course, the quickest answer to Leavis would be to point out the immediate context of "Tears, Idle Tears" in *The Princess* and to show the title character herself making just his objections to the lyric, objections that the rest of the poem attempts in turn to answer and surround. But one would refer anti-Tennysonians to *The Princess* only with reluctance, and very few among pro-Tennysonians find its blank verse narrative an adequate complement to the lyrics that interrupt it. "Ulysses" and "Tithonus," however, are evenly and productively matched.

Tennyson wrote "Ulysses" in 1833, a decade or more before "Tears, Idle Tears," and he began "Tithonus" in the same year, although it was not completed and published until 1860. He called "Tithonus" a "pendent" to "Ulysses,"[9] so I follow the poet's own lead, as well as that of many subsequent critics, in examining the two together. And even without Tennyson's comment to point the way, one would hardly miss the purposeful contrast between the two poems. They are matched and opposed as the utterances of Greek and Trojan, victor and vanquished, hero and victim. Surely no reader would miss or mistake the opposition between the upright, active resolve of Ulysses, embodied in the plump assertiveness of a rhetoric that is, like that of Shakespeare's Henry V, a continuing favorite of politicians, and the luxurious passivity of the dying cadences of Tithonus. Yet many readers have perceived as well an odd similarity that makes these contrasts seem misleading or superficial and that makes it hard to distinguish with final clarity and assurance between the moods of the two poems. Robert Langbaum, for instance, hears in both poems, "a certain life-weariness" that is, for him, the true signature of their author,[10] and one must take into account this Tennysonian common denominator without blurring the distinctions between the two poems, distinctions that are too obviously intentional and too important a part of any reader's experience to be merely superficial. One possibility is to consider the subversive stillness of "Ulysses" and the deceptive stillness of "Tithonus" as features of what I have been trying to establish as Tennyson's philosophic attitude.

Tennyson's interest in Ulysses and Tithonus is not an interest in character or dramatic circumstances, and he provides none of the density of social or historical detail that would characterize a monologue by Browning. Rather, these two speakers are cut free from the mythological narratives that suggested them and present in their fixity two ways of being in the world. For Goldwin Smith, a nineteenth-century critic, Ulysses "merely intends to roam, but stands forever a listless and melancholy figure on the shore."[11] And for Christopher Ricks, to whom I am indebted for the Smith quotation, the poem and its speaker reveal an odd and underlying ambivalence toward the future in their curious failure to employ the future tense,[12] a failure that recalls the avoidance of the past tense in "Tears, Idle Tears." Both these poems and "Tithonus," too, are searching out the experience of life from within the present moment and can hardly imagine the past and the future as places actually to find oneself. Nor can they imagine a point of view outside the present moment from which it is just one point in a line. "Tithonus" immobilizes consciousness in a relationship to time and the world quite outside the order of things and by means of the kind of extravagant hypothesis of which some schools of twentieth-century philosophy are fond. And "Ulysses" is not so much a report on an episode in its hero's life as an expansion of the moment in his story that can figure forth an attitude toward all the moments of our own lives. "Yet all experience is an arch wherethrough/ Gleams that untravelled world whose margin fades/For ever and for ever when I move" (19–21). It is like Ulysses and like Tennyson to offer this single image for "all experience," an image that incorporates movement but does not move. Dante's Ulysses approaches the straits of Gibraltar and then leaves them behind in the space of five lines. He tells his story from outside history and the world. Tennyson and his hero share the urgency of a self-consciousness that cannot take for granted its place in the order of things, but must discover, articulate, and so maintain it. Ulysses and Tithonus do not represent for Tennyson significant idiosyncrasies of human character in action, but compelling apprehensions of the situation of human consciousness, and our readings need to discover just what, in their two poems, that situation is.

Tennyson said of "Ulysses" that it expressed, in the dark days after Hallam's death, his sense of the need of going forward, but it would perhaps be more accurate to say of both "Ulysses" and "Tithonus" that they express the desperate necessity of having someplace to go forward to, of being able to imagine a future. At the same time, both poems respond to the pressures of the past, not merely an abstraction here, but the sum of personal, lived experience that challenges or mocks the present. The importance of establishing some vital connection with the past reflects for these speakers an anxiety over the continuity of personal identity that is quite unlike the objectless regret so brilliantly evoked in "Tears, Idle Tears." For Tithonus, too, existence is posthumous, but the transcendental subjectivity of "Tears, Idle Tears" has only a generalized past and nothing like a personal history. Both Ulysses and Tithonus can say with Tiresias, a third classical monologist of this phase of Tennyson's career, "I wish I were as in the days of old." For Ulysses, the admission of personal loss works to confirm a continuing strength of identity: "though/We are not now that strength which in old days/Moved earth and heaven; that which we are, we are" (65–67). Tithonus makes the same admission in a tone of quietly despairing wonder: "Ay me! ay me! with what another heart/In days far off, and with what other eyes/I used to watch— if I be he that watched—" (50–52). Tithonus here expresses a new and radical concern for the contingency of the self. In other of Tennyson's poems, in "Tears, Idle Tears" and also in "Mariana" and "The Lady of Shalott" and others, the experience of time has provoked the sense of continuous and unfulfilled desire, of an emptiness and a need within. But in each of those poems, the world has somehow failed the self. Now Tennyson assumes the mask of age in order to look back over a long life and wonder if it is not the very self that fails.

Ulysses blames his failure to be himself on circumstance:

> It little profits that an idle king,
> By this still hearth, among these barren crags,
> Matched with an aged wife, I mete and dole
> Unequal laws unto a savage race
> That hoard, and sleep, and feed, and know not me.
>
> (1–5)

Whatever the precise tone of this dismissal and whatever praise or blame attaches to it, it does make clear the terms of Ulysses' dissatisfaction with his subjects: they "know not me." Yet surely the citizens of Ithaca do know their king, and the statement can only mean that Ulysses in Ithaca is not "me," not his truest self. In a new verse paragraph, in a rhetoric grand and assertive, Ulysses defines the self to which he would remain true.

> I cannot rest from travel: I will drink
> Life to the lees: all times I have enjoyed
> Greatly, have suffered greatly, both with those
> That loved me, and alone; on shore, and when
> Through scudding drifts the rainy Hyades
> Vext the dim sea. I am become a name;
> For always roaming with a hungry heart
> Much have I seen and known,—cities of men
> And manners, climates, councils, governments,
> Myself not least, but honored of them all,—
> And drunk delight of battle with my peers,
> Far on the ringing plains of windy Troy.
>
> (6–17)

Ulysses defines himself as a man of action and now must struggle to live up to his self-definition, to realize the full significance of being himself. And action, for Ulysses, is taking and giving at once, voracious appetite and profuse self-expenditure. His hungry heart will consume experience, converting all that he meets into his grand sense of himself. Yet he can reverse this flow, too, and say "I am a part of all that I have met." He wants more and more of life, but he will not have the self a mere storehouse of past experience:

Life piled on life
Were all too little, and of one to me
Little remains; but every hour is saved
From that eternal silence, something more,
A bringer of new things; and vile it were
For some three suns to store and hoard myself,
And this gray spirit yearning in desire
To follow knowledge like a sinking star,
Beyond the utmost bound of human thought.

(24–32)

Ulysses has earlier scorned the hoarding of his subjects, and he now finds that to stand watch over them is to hoard himself as well. Both in rejecting such husbandry and in discovering such a coincidence of experience between his subjects and himself, Ulysses distinguishes himself from the consciousness of "Tears, Idle Tears." There the world and the self stood in clear opposition, the realm of looking and the realm of thinking, one happy and one sad. The self was precisely an inner storehouse, painfully empty of all but its images, but still a kind of space to be mapped and described. For Ulysses, however, consciousness does not hold itself from the world, but leans into it, and intensest consciousness is a perpetual process of relationship, extracting from every hour the maximum value by investing in every hour all the energies of the self. Ulysses requires both to know and to be known, and he can be known only in actions that are themselves knowledge-seeking. He is not himself and consciousness is not itself while enthroned on an island, set over against a world of brute facts and mechanical processes.

Whether such a view of the kingship of Ulysses does justice or not to Penelope and Telemachus and the citizens of Ithaca is almost, if not entirely, beside the point. The poem evokes enough of Homer and dwells enough on Telemachus to introduce the possibility of social judgment. But this is the bad conscience and not the true consciousness of the poem. The reduction of Ulysses' kingship to an epistemological paradigm goes beyond the prudent limits of paraphrase in order to reach toward the philosophical understanding that the poem bespeaks. And this is essentially an understanding of what Husserl's phenomenology names as the intentionality of consciousness, its directedness toward the world.[13] The mind and the world are not separately conceivable, but are joined by the temporal activity of consciousness, which is always consciousness of something and never merely the self-awareness of an enclosed container. Marjorie Grene, writing in a tradition distinct from but sympathetic to phenomenology, phrases the matter finely and in language that recalls Tennyson: "But if reason, if self-consciousness, is essentially temporal, then knowledge is never finished, never at rest in 'manifest truth.' We are always beyond ourselves in the venture of knowing, the task of finding and giving as best we can significance to our world, the world which is always beyond us at the horizon, but whose concrescence, whose interpretation, whose meaning we are."[14] So, for Ulysses, the sense of personal history is generated by the interplay of knowing and being known, drawing the world into the self and spending the self in the world.

Yet one can hardly distinguish these two activities in practice, and for a consciousness so purified and purposeful as that of Ulysses, the present danger is solipsism. At the cutting edge of experience, knowing and being known amount to the same ceaseless movement, perhaps because Ulysses so vaguely defines the knowledge that he seeks. If he is a part of all that he has met, no wonder then that when he meets his past again in memory, he meets himself: "Much have I seen and known; cities of men/And manners, climates, councils, governments,/Myself not least, but honoured of them all" (13–15). He has drunk delight and he will drink life, but these are only equivocally external. And when he comes finally to describe a truly external scene— "The lights begin to twinkle from the rocks:/The long day wanes: the slow moon climbs: the deep/Moans round with many voices" (54–56)—he seems to be conjuring up rather than describing the scene, so dreamily appropriate is it to his mood. A sensibility that can convert contingency so readily into significance encourages the suspicion that it never truly engages the world at all, but only its own projections. "I am a part of all that I have met" may be less a boast of influence than a confession of inability to see anything beyond the self.[15] Ulysses does not seek a newer world in order to find it, but to find and be himself in the act of seeking.

But to know the world only in relationship to the self is not to be a solipsist. Ulysses, after all, is only a part of all that he meets, and he does know Telemachus and acknowledge him. Knowledge is relationship and Ulysses knows Telemachus by knowing and articulating the differences between Telemachus and himself. This does not seem to me as humanly unattractive as it has seemed to other readers, and it does, in the poem's allegory of consciousness, suggest accurately the relationship between the two senses of consciousness of which Ulysses and Telemachus are the representatives. Telemachus, the agent of assimilation and order and tradition, represents consciousness as content, the aspect of our inner lives that is generated by true, intentional consciousness but also left behind by it as the father here leaves behind the son.

Yet these are a father and a son, and there is a wife here, too. If Ulysses is not solipsistic, he may at least be selfish. Disgusted with Ulysses for his Romantic irresponsibility, W. H. Auden listened exclusively to what I have called the bad conscience of the poem. As a character and as a psychological case, Ulysses is indeed flawed in many ways and could be accused not merely of stasis, as in the remarks of Langbaum and Goldwin Smith, but of regression. The margin that fades forever and forever might as easily be the past as the future, and the desire to pursue it may not be a desire to progress, but rather to repeat oneself. Only a willingness to accept change, to grow perhaps from an adventurer into a statesman, would indicate true progress of the self. And Tennyson himself has given us further encouragement to suspect the heroism of Ulysses by taking as his source Dante's *Inferno*, where Ulysses has been damned for his presumption and reckless leadership, and then by underscoring this infernal connection with echoes of the rhetoric of Milton's Satan.

Writing soon after Hallam's death, Tennyson would indeed have felt a guilty resistance to the urge to move forward, or even to face forward, into the future. This resistance, in fact, is an important subject of *In Memoriam*. But "Ulysses" is not the vehicle of explicit self-examination, just as it is not a psychological case history. Tennyson may have struggled to reach the mood of "Ulysses," and it may be that kings should not leave their wives and sons and duties behind, but the poem itself is not about Tennyson's struggle or about what some king Ulysses should have done. It abstracts itself from these empirical occasions to present a philosophical, which is not to say a bloodless or impersonal or idealized, attitude: not an attitude toward kingship or mourning, but toward being. Subversive readings of the poem cannot and should not undo its assertive rhetorical power, and it is this power, the evident and persuasive feeling of the poem, with which the philosophical reading attempts to stay in touch. Even though it is possible to expose his heroic, ceaseless activity as motion without locomotion, a kind of busy, aspiring stasis, Ulysses does engage the world in a manner sharply different from that of Tithonus. Whatever the status of his planned, barrier-breaking voyage, Ulysses does move ceaselessly through time toward death, and his triumph is to render this curse of mortality a source of imaginative life. To be perpetually "yearning in desire" defined a mortal dilemma for the many Tennysonian—and Coleridgean and Shelleyan and Byronic—victims of romantic desire. The resolution "To strive, to seek, to find, and not to yield" makes of perpetual frustration a form of heroism. Ulysses will not yield to obstacles and, as the order of these celebrated infinitives makes clear, he will not yield to finding, will not make an end until one is made for him.

It is a matter, once again, of mood, of attunement to the world, of the spirit in which one takes up the given situation of consciousness, and this situation includes the fact of death. Saying flatly that "Death closes all," Ulysses does not use constant movement as a defense against this knowledge, but instead uses this knowledge as the incentive to movement. Facing the future, Ulysses faces always toward his death at the horizon, and it is surprising to notice how unemphatically but also how unequivocally he acknowledges this absolute limitation: "for my purpose holds/To sail beyond the sunset, and the baths/Of all the western stars, until I die" (59–61). This achievement of authentic Being-toward-death, to adopt the existential terminology of Heidegger, makes possible the hopeful intensity of the quest. Ulysses longs for an eternity of aspiration and knows at the same time that aspiration can have meaning only in a finite, death-bound world. Only the fact of death imposes on experience the urgency that renders each hour the source of potential value.

At least, this is clearly the wisdom of "Ulysses" and of "Tithonus," too, but can it really be this easy? We know that Tennyson himself had hardly achieved such composure in the face of death and that he achieved it finally only by assuming a faith in the benign immortality of Christianity. And we notice, too, that Ulysses invokes an agnostic escape clause: "It may be that the gulfs will wash us down;/It may be we shall touch the Happy Isles,/And see the great Achilles whom we knew" (62–64). Death may be death, or it may be another form of living, and neither "Ulysses" nor "Tithonus" advocates the existential heroism that would renounce this uncertainty in favor of a sure and clear negation. Consciousness cannot stand outside itself and it cannot intend the end of intending, its own nonexistence. That this is so in the case of Tithonus will require some later argument. Ulysses, facing his own death, does not face or desire certain extinction, but he does accept and rely on something he calls death, and this is an acceptance of the world as bounded and given. Consciousness discovers the world, but does not choose it. Death and the horizon, whether or not they bring extinction, mark the limits of our intending, "the utmost bound of human thought." It is not a question of choosing death, but of acknowledging the limits of choice. To inhabit a field of choice unlimited by the constraints of death and the horizon is to be in the position of Tithonus.

Tithonus has discovered the curse of fulfillment, of having his carelessly worded wish come true. He lives where no man ought to live, on the other side of the horizon, the other side of the border that Ulysses could only plan to cross. This results in a terrible reversal of the ordinary conditions of human life, but also in some of Tennyson's most extraordinary writing.

> The woods decay, the woods decay and fall,
> The vapours weep their burthen to the ground,
> Man comes and tills the field and lies beneath,
> And after many a summer dies the swan.
> Me only cruel immortality
> Consumes: I wither slowly in thine arms,
> Here at the quiet limit of the world,
> A white-haired shadow roaming like a dream
> The ever silent spaces of the East,
> Far-folded mists and gleaming halls of morn.
>
> Alas! for this gray shadow, once a man—
> So glorious in his beauty and thy choice,
> Who madest him thy chosen, that he seemed
> To his great heart none other than a God!
> I asked thee, "Give me immortality,"
> Then didst thou grant mine asking with a smile,

Like wealthy men who care not how they give.
But thy strong Hours indignant worked their wills,
And beat me down and marred and wasted me,
And though they could not end me, left me maimed
To dwell in presence of immortal youth,
Immortal age beside immortal youth,
And all I was, in ashes.

(1–23)

In the passage from Book 6 of *The Prelude* that Tennyson's opening echoes, Wordsworth describes in nature an "eterne in mutabilitie" beyond the reach of mortal striving: "The immeasurable height/Of woods decaying, never to be decayed,/The stationary blasts of waterfalls" (1805; 6: 624–26). For Tithonus, however, the world of nature represents the mortal estate of which he would be part. From the viewpoint of exile, nature and man are joined in their subjection to time. Tithonus, meanwhile, in his passage beyond the horizon, has fallen out of the natural and temporal orders and now finds himself an anomaly, immortal like Aurora, but subject to decay like the objects of nature. Without the prospect of death, he cannot bend toward the future, cannot feel himself moving toward anything. Neither is the past a source of self-confirmation, for his relationship to it is discontinuous. Aging slowly, inexorably into decrepitude, he ought at least to be able to trace through past time the arc of his decline. But the present stands to the past not as one moment to another in the order of a genetic history, but rather as shadow to substance, or ashes to living fire. It is a wholly different and reduced sphere of being. In becoming immortal, Tithonus has ceased to be himself, has sacrificed his mortal identity.

For Ulysses, who is all that a man might be, the past functions as a usable resource, a potent if also a tyrannical source of energy. With all the momentum of his past activity, he must go forward from the place to which past activity has brought him. The present moment gathers together at once all of the past—this is the gathering accomplished by his meditation—and imagines the future as a straight line breaking forth out of the enclosure of the present. For Tithonus, however, no such connection exists. What he glimpses obscurely through the mist and just beyond the horizon is not the future, but the past, the world of his ordinary mortality: "A soft air fans the cloud apart; there comes/A glimpse of that dark world where I was born" (32–33). Tithonus has been excluded from history. Linear motion lies behind him and not the past, but, appallingly, the future coexists with the present. Looking ahead, he sees no possibility of the motion or change by which the passage of time can be defined. The future is here and now and the same.

Tithonus, having once emerged into this new temporal order, is effectively without a past or a future. His partial transcendence of the human condition has stranded him in a realm where both the perpetual repetitions of God-time and the progression of human time are turned against the self. His desire to achieve a God-like changelessness has been tragically frustrated. Even that original desire, however, arouses suspicion; the poem does not encourage a sense that all would be well if only Tithonus had retained his youth. Perhaps the sexual energy of his relationship with Aurora would have provided the necessary and perpetual renewal of desire, but the sense remains that stasis rather than withering age is the source of misery. The desire for perpetual youth was itself flawed and regressive, and its frustration reveals the inevitable failure of spatial solutions to temporal problems. Tithonus travels to the land of the dawn, but continues to age. The mere absence of death (although its presence, admittedly, could never be called mere) does not resolve the dilemma of temporal existence. It creates instead a time-lessness that is more destructive to the self than the time it seeks to escape. If time threatens to alter the self, then stepping out of ordinary, death-bound time does not stabilize it, but alters it absolutely.

Crossing the horizon and falling out of time, Tithonus confirms by negation the linkage between the temporality and the intentionality of consciousness. Out of time, he is out of the world, a "shadow," a "ghost," a "dream," and he cannot enter into self-confirming relationship either with the world of his birth and his mortality or with the weirdly insubstantial "Far-folded mists and gleaming halls of morn." Aurora herself is real and warm and gorgeously alive, but Tithonus has been reduced to mere spectatorship, and he has no place in the extraordinary erotic drama of the dawn that he describes:

> A soft air fans the cloud apart; there comes
> A glimpse of that dark world where I was born.
> Once more the old mysterious glimmer steals
> From thy pure brows, and from thy shoulders pure,
> And bosom beating with a heart renewed.
> Thy cheek begins to redden through the gloom,
> Thy sweet eyes brighten slowly close to mine,
> Ere yet they blind the stars, and the wild team
> Which love thee, yearning for thy yoke, arise,
> And shake the darkness from their loosened manes,
> And beat the twilight into flakes of fire.
>
> (32–42)

Taunted by these images that he can only describe, Tithonus suffers what the Lady of Shalott would suffer if she could not enter the world and die, but was instead condemned to watch Lancelot reappearing through the ages. "How can my nature longer mix with thine?" Tithonus asks Aurora, and he receives no answer, because it cannot and they are absolutely divided. Tithonus is out of nature, but he is out of this dawn world, too. Aurora speaks to him only through her tears, and these are only the morning dew. Tithonus has none of the privileges of immortality of or mortality, except one. He can speak.

Ulysses, in spite of his rhetoric, knows that he will die, and Tithonus, in spite of his, knows that he will not. What does rhetoric accomplish for these speakers or for their maker, Tennyson? In the case of Ulysses, one has suspected throughout that rhetoric substituted for action. As Arthur Gold has commented to me, the reader often feels that Ulysses' truest quest is to reach the point where he can burst into the majestic eloquence of the poem's last paragraph. Yet how severely ought he to be criticized for this? Is not speech, too, a mode of becoming? "I am become a name." The ambiguity of the verb tense allows this assertion to do double service, primarily to indicate that life has passed already into legend, has already been written, but also to remind us that Ulysses is even now rewriting his own legend, which had mistakenly been brought to conclusion. "I am become a name" joins with "I cannot rest from travel" and "I am a part of all that I have met" in suggesting the constant outward energies of the self. As long as Ulysses is still talking, these energies still flow, and the legend of self remains in vital flux. John Pettigrew has plausibly and perceptively suggested that the poem breaks into an interior and an exterior monologue, that the third and fourth paragraphs "reword for public proclamation" the private meditations of the first two.[16] I find this convincing, but would press further to notice the way in which all of the poem holds open the passage not just between private and public, but between future and past, living potential and dead achievement. The very act of speech combines the taking and giving that characterize Ulysses' progress through the world. As he speaks in the poem, he both reads his past and writes his future, absorbs his own experience through memory and projects it into the imagined future.

Yet speech also defers the future that it struggles to create, and we return to the remark of Goldwin Smith, that Ulysses merely "intends to roam, but stands forever a listless and melancholy figure on the shore." But this penetrating and sensitive criticism goes too far in calling the maker of such heightened speech "listless" and not far enough in seeing only melancholy in Ulysses' posture on the shore. Rhetoric that displaces action may seem to mark a retreat from life. But when action means setting sail at dusk into a glooming, dark, broad sea, the rhetoric that defers it does not retreat from life so much as prolong life in the face of death. The speaker always about to cease speaking and set out offers the same resistance to the death of completion as does the adventurer always preparing to cross the horizon. Like the daughters of Hesperus in "The Hesperides" or the bulbul in "Recollections of the Arabian Nights," Ulysses must sing to sustain the enchantment. But his song is public speech and private consciousness at once, and it does not suspend time, but enters it word by word.

Speech announces presence and life in the face of "that eternal silence" ("Ulysses," 27). For Tithonus, eternity and silence together conspire against being, and his speech in the poem struggles to make a noise and so to emerge from the nightmare of nonbeing that the poem everywhere documents. Tithonus inhabits a "quiet limit," "ever-silent spaces," and has himself faded into insubstantiality: "A white-haired shadow roaming like a dream." Yet he is haunted by memories of a speech magically potent and productive, by gestures of effortless and God-like creativity. He remembers the moment in which his own quick words, "Give me immortality," became sudden and awful reality, and he remembers how Apollo could sing a city into being. Now his own speech cannot bring anything out of the silence. "Lo ever thus thou growest beautiful/In silence, then before thine answer given/Departest, and thy tears are on my cheek" (43–45).

Tithonus is trying to open a closed case. His story has already been written, in his own request, "Give me immortality," and in the dimly remembered saying, "The Gods themselves cannot recall their gifts." Recorded speech here, speech fixed in time, is the mark of doom. Crossing the horizon, Tithonus has left behind not only time and the world, but the ordinary powers and properties of language. Language now is the agent of fate and not of freedom, something that has happened to Tithonus, a sentence and not a power. His future has been spoken, and his own speech is cut adrift, insubstantial as the shadow from which it emanates and the mists in which it dissolves without effect. Tithonus's desire for the earth is not just a desire for the grave, but for connection and substantiality. The problem is not that language and the self are divided, but that they are perfectly coterminous and disembodied, without a home in time and without effect in the world. "Thou seest all things, thou wilt see my grave." Tithonus tries through this play of speech to invest his own word and wish with Aurora's power. But he cannot, and his speech ends in lovely and hopeless bravery, asserting itself against an inalterably fixed destiny:

> Release me and restore me to the ground.
> Thou seëst all things, thou wilt see my grave;
> Thou wilt renew thy beauty morn by morn,
> I earth in earth forget these empty courts,
> And thee returning on thy silver wheels.
>
> (72–76)

But these final lines provoke a few final misgivings and questions. Can we really believe that Tithonus wants to die when his language is so palpably the agent and evidence of a struggle into being and life? And is such language without power altogether, merely because it is without the power to change fate and to move Aurora to action? A. Dwight Culler's summary remark helps us toward some answers: "Both Tithonus and Ulysses want to be released into the human world of Becoming, the world of change, movement, activity, life—and death."[17] Thus Tithonus wants to be dying as evidence that he is alive. And failing that, he can offer in evidence the very fact of his articulated desire. In petitioning Aurora, Tithonus does continue to press himself into the future and against the boundaries of his freedom, and he can do this as long as he holds to any sense of his own being in the world. And he just does hold on, feeling his cold and "wrinkled feet" (67) on the threshold as a late and last evidence of the body and obstinately interpreting the morning dew as the tears of sympathy. So long as the perpetual order of things can be humanized, Tithonus must still be human, able to glimpse his past and to reach into the future. The opportunity to speak offers him a respite, however pathetic, from the contemplation of his changeless fate, and within the space of the poem he can experience temporarily the consolations of teleology. So the paradoxical answer to our questions is that Tithonus must continue to desire death or he will be dead, and he proves his continued desire in his speech.

Speech is all that is left to Tithonus, nearly all that is left of him, and he does not seem in speaking to reach Aurora or to make a noise in his world at all. But this extreme and negative view of his condition finally will not do, because it falsifies our own experience of the poem. We do hear Tithonus, and we hear him because a language out of time and disembodied and dehumanized simply cannot be. Language always has a body and a place in the world and time, or it would not exist for us, and Tennyson's language in this poem imposes on us with all the intensity of Tithonus's imagined need. The mingled pathos and sublimity of "Tithonus," the sense of enervation and intensity at once, testify to the opposed, acknowledged, and fully realized strengths of immovable fate and moving human resistance—a summary that returns us to Ulysses.

Our moods have no power to change the order of things, and "Tithonus" and "Ulysses" describe and emerge from congruent orderings of conscious-ness, time, and the world. But moods do offer us alternative ways to take up the apprehensions of philosophy in our continuing, lived experience, and the two poems thus address different moments or possibilities of our experience. The situation of Ulysses obviously suggests that of any spirit confronting its own mortality and choosing life in the face of it. Although neither Tennyson nor any of his readers lives with the goddess of the dawn, the situation of Tithonus also has its analogue in the sort of youthful vastation that Tennyson and his sister Emily (and, to a lesser degree, his whole family) suffered in the shock of Arthur Hallam's death, which seemed to empty their lives of all secure points of reference, all happy anticipations. M. J. Donohue, in her discussion of the poem's first draft, cites Emily's letter to Tennyson in 1834: "What is life to me! If I die (which the Tennysons never do)."[18] "Ulysses" and "Tithonus" offer the paired challenges of being in time, of consciousness discovering that it must die and discovering that it must live. In "Tithonus," especially, we can hear the shaken, impassioned, and still disbelieving voice of consciousness, just realizing that it must indeed endure the unendurable. And in speaking, the business of enduring and of living begins.

Ulysses and Tithonus do not alter the given conditions of the world with their language, a privilege that is reserved for the gods, but they do enter and, indeed, constitute a human world with their language and thus enact a philosophical truth. In their attentiveness to the ways of speaking and to the life of speech, Ulysses and Tithonus and, finally, Tennyson himself are brilliantly interested parties, and it may be salutary in concluding to distinguish sharply, if somewhat arbitrarily, between philosophy and litera-ture and to lay stress on the distinctly literary character of Tennyson's achieve-ment. The philosophical value of "Ulysses" and "Tithonus" is to identify language and consciousness by presenting their subjection, or, in another mood, their shared access, to time and the world. The literary value of "Ulysses" and "Tithonus" and of "Tears, Idle Tears," too, is also to identify language and consciousness, but this time by the miracle of style that renders these poems distinct from one another and just as distinctly Tennysonian, and that presses their language and Tennyson's consciousness into time and the world. But we must stop just short of the thrilling conclusion that Tennyson lives in his poems and speaks to us from the other side. The poems themselves invite such a mystification in their urgency and personality of voice and also in their readiness to employ death as a metaphor for some of the possibilities of our conscious lives. But they refuse this mystification as well, separating the metaphorical deaths of consciousness from the stillness of a death that is always beyond the horizon, and also separating themselves from the empirical, lived concreteness of life—of Tennyson's life—by their assumption of the exemplary consciousness of the philosophical attitude. Urgency and personality coexist with the philosophical attitude as final evidence that poetry is the form of philosophy that attends most seriously to the body of its language, so that the poem is always its own most compelling philosophical example.

Notes

All quotations from Tennyson's poetry are taken from *The Poems of Tennyson*, ed. Christopher Ricks (New York: Longmans, 1969).

1. W. H. Auden, *A Selection from the Poems of Alfred, Lord Tennyson* (Garden City, NY: Doubleday, 1944), x.

2. F. R. Leavis, *The Living Principle* (Oxford: Oxford Univ. Press, 1975), 78–79.

3. *The Works of Tennyson*, ed. Hallam Tennyson (London: Macmillan, 1908), IV, 225.

4. Cleanth Brooks, *The Well Wrought Urn* (New York: Harcourt, Brace and World, 1947), 172–74.

5. See A. J. Ayer's remarks on the analogy between the problem of making statements about the past and problem of making statements about other minds; in *Philosophical Essays* (London: Macmillan, 1954), 188–89.

6.   Harold Bloom, *Poetry and Repression* (New Haven: Yale Univ. Press, 1976), 163.

7.   John Jones, *John Keats's Dream of Truth* (London: Chatto & Windus, 1969), 217.

8.   Martin Heidegger, *Nietzsche: Volume I: The Will to Power as Art*, trans. David Krell (San Francisco: Harper and Row, 1979), 99.

9.   *Alfred, Lord Tennyson: A Memoir*, ed. Hallam Tennyson (London: Macmillan, 1897), I, 459.

10.   Robert Langbaum, *The Poetry of Experience* (New York: Random House, 1957), 89–90.

11.   Goldwin Smith, in *Saturday Review*, 3 November 1855; rpt. in *Tennyson: The Critical Heritage*, ed. John Jump (London: Routledge and Kegan Paul, 1967).

12.   Christopher Ricks, *Tennyson* (New York: Macmillan, 1972), 125.

13.   The concept of intentionality is explicated many times over by both Husserl and his critics. For the best and clearest account I have found, see Maurice Natanson, *Edmund Husserl: Philosopher of Infinite Tasks* (Evanston, Ill.: Northwestern Univ. Press, 1973), 85 ff.

14.   Marjorie Grene, *The Knower and the Known* (New York: Basic Books, 1966), 91.

15.   So Harold Bloom takes it in *Poetry and Repression* (pp. 158–59), citing Vico and Emerson as analogues.

16.   John Pettigrew, *Tennyson: The Early Poems* (London: Edward Arnold, 1970), 59.

17.   A. Dwight Culler, *The Poetry of Tennyson* (New Haven: Yale Univ. Press, 1977), 98.

18.   *Memoir*, I, 135. Quoted by Donohue in "Tennyson's *Hail Briton!* and *Tithonus* in the Heath Manuscript," *PMLA* 64 (1949), 385–416.

The Skipping Muse: Repetition and Difference in Two Early Poems of Tennyson

MATTHEW ROWLINSON

The Skipping-Rope

Sure never yet was Antelope
    Could skip so lightly by.
Stand off, or else my skipping-rope
    Will hit you in the eye.
How lightly whirls the skipping-rope!
    How fairy-like you fly!
Go, get you gone, you muse and mope—
    I hate that silly sigh.
Nay, dearest, teach me how to hope,
    Or tell me how to die.
There, take it, take my skipping-rope,
    And hang yourself thereby.[1]

"The Skipping-Rope" was among the new poems Tennyson published in 1842, and it continued to appear in editions of his poems until 1850, after which it was not reprinted in his lifetime. A reader of the first edition who for some reason took the trouble could have deduced from the pronouns that the poem represents a dialogue between a skipping woman and her somewhat listless suitor; in the modern standard edition, this deduction is confirmed by a headnote that quotes an unpublished draft beginning "While Annie whirled the skipping-rope, / Said Harry standing by . . ." (Ricks, 657). But the main source of the nervous good humor of the poem cannot thus be found from internal evidence, for Prof. Ricks's headnote also tells us that Tennyson wrote the poem in the end of his copy of John Walker's *Rhyming Dictionary*, and that he took his rhymes in "ope" from its index.

    The index to Walker's *Dictionary* consists simply of lists of rhyme-words, alphabetically arranged, without even the sketchy definitions included in the main body of the work.[2] It thus appears to generate language without discourse by a process of purely mechanical differentiation. In so doing, it

Reprinted from *Victorian Poetry*, Vol. 22 (1984), by permission. © 1984 by West Virginia University Press.

subverts any assumption that sense precedes language in a way that seems to have driven Tennyson to produce "The Skipping-Rope" as a half-joking reaction. As such, the poem claims to naturalize the alphabetic series of the dictionary by supplying for its rhyme-words the context necessary to re-originate them in the dialogue and in the play of desire between its two characters.

Ricks's headnote also aptly cites Tennyson's much later reply to the question of Francis Turner Palgrave: "Did he ever use a rhyming dictionary? He had tried it in earlier days, but found it of little use: 'There was no natural congruity between the rhymes thus alphabetically grouped together.' "[3] The appeal here to a category of naturally congruous rhymes is an odd one. What kind of rhymes would these be? Behind it lies an appeal, not to an empty category of natural rhymes, but to a category of rhymes produced by the poetic imagination, which Tennyson wants to endow with a power of conferring naturalness denied the purely mechanical production of the dictionary.

Such an appeal is implicit in Tennyson's practice in "The Skipping-Rope." Here, in spite of choosing his rhymes arbitrarily from a dictionary, he succeeds in producing something like poetic discourse by displacing his sense of their incongruity onto the characters who speak them. Hence the pairing of a skipping, antelopelike woman with a mopey, would-be hopeful lover. The poem thus naturalizes the mechanical production of difference in its rhymes but only at the cost of a preoccupation with sexual difference. The proliferation of different rhymes in "ope" (and in "oop," "op," and "up," which Walker [338] lists as "allowable rhymes" for "ope") is resolved into what is in this context a much more reassuring scenario of tension between the different sexes.

We shall see later how the process of displacement which is wittily, if defensively, highlighted in "The Skipping-Rope" is in more veiled forms powerfully at work in many of Tennyson's greatest early treatments of sexual tension. But first let us consider at more length what could be meant by the whirling of the skipping-rope itself, the figure which opens and closes in the text the play of sexual difference. It does so, moreover, as itself an image of play; and as such it has two specific characteristics which are particularly worth noting here. One is that it is repeated; the other is that its repetitions enclose a space for a playing woman, in which she can remain, though continually at risk, for as long as her agility will sustain her there.

Different kinds of enclosed space are a recurring motif in Tennyson's early poetry, and, like the space enclosed by the whirling of the skipping-rope, they are characteristically constituted by repetition or doubling and usually more or less at risk. They are frequently inhabited by women, as in "The Hesperides," "The Lady of Shalott," and "Mariana." Even in early poems less obviously akin to "The Skipping-Rope," Tennyson tends to represent interior space as somehow constituted by doubling. This seems to be the case in texts as diverse as, for instance, "The Two Voices," in which the double appears as a threat, and as "O Darling Room," with its mysterious second bed.

In "The Skipping-Rope," moreover, repetition does not simply constitute space, but specifically the space of the subject at the origin of discourse. The play of the skipping woman in the poem should be read as a figure for Tennyson's own play with rhyme there. We know that anxiety about the proliferation of difference in the rhyming dictionary was the occasion of the poem; this anxiety generates the energy it invests in representations of autoeroticism and repetition. The rhymes of the poem thus transform the mechanical production of the dictionary into repetition, as the word "skipping-rope" itself returns to rhyme with itself three times.

The play of the skipping-rope in this text thus represents the play with rhyme that opens out the space of the speaking subject. In so doing, however, it idealizes it, not just as repetition, but as repetition without articulation. There is no mark between any one turn of the rope and the next; its trajectory could only be sounded as a string of vowels: 00000. This idealization shows what is at issue in its appearance here, for the articulation which it denies is one of the elemental forms of linguistic difference. Derrida has written that it is "the becoming-writing of language";[4] he goes on to argue that this "becoming" does not come after the origin of language, but is on the contrary constitutive of it:

> Language could have emerged only out of dispersion. The "natural causes" by which one explains it are not recognized as natural except in so far as they accord with the state of nature, which is determined by dispersion. This dispersion should no doubt be overcome by language but, for that very reason, it determines the *natural condition* of language. . . . In truth, dispersion will never be a past, a prelinguistic situation in which language would certainly have been born only to break with it. The original dispersion leaves its mark within language . . . articulation, which seemingly introduces difference as an institution, has for ground and space the dispersion that is natural: space itself. (232)

We have already seen how the play of the woman's skipping-rope figures a play of rhyme in which difference would not occupy the inceptive and constitutive position it had in the dictionary but would be subordinate to a notion of natural congruity predicated on the continuity of poetic discourse. The passage just quoted from Derrida suggests that the play of rhyme can achieve this naturalization only when difference has been effaced at its origin in space itself; hence the fantasy in this poem of a space without dispersion or difference, enclosed by the whirling of the skipping-rope. Such a space can, however, only be a fantasy, as indeed many of Tennyson's early poems show. Thus in "The Lady of Shalott," the space of the subject at the origin of discourse turns into a space within the subject, while in "The Two Voices," the dream of the subject's hearing its own speech has become a nightmare in which it is constituted as two voices radically at odds. Even in the present relatively sketchy text, the skipping-rope, initially a figure for an idealized repetition enclosing a space without difference, eventually, when repetition has been breached, introduces a threat of hanging—a return of articulation that would be final.

In this reading, the poem represents the discourse of two kinds of desire, the relations between which are ambivalent. The man's desire is for the woman constituted as other; like the poem as a whole, his discourse exists in the space opened up by sexual difference. The woman's desire, on the contrary, is for a self which is constituted by repetition, figured in the whirling of the skipping-rope. If the uneasy intensity of this representation of sexual difference is determined by the casting-out of difference from language, its representation of auto-affectionate play is a figure for the language thus produced. What "The Skipping-Rope" can show us is that these two kinds of discourse are related as respectively the anxious and the wishful versions of the same fantasy. But the displacements and suppressions which produce them here can also be found under various elaborations and revisions as the necessary preconditions of discourse in some of Tennyson's most powerful early poetry, where indeed the play of autoeroticism and sexual difference is a recurrent theme.

If the appeal of "The Skipping-Rope" for the critic is founded on the evidence we have for its origin, the perhaps more respectable appeal of "The Hesperides" has a lot to do with its impenetrability. In the song of Hesperus' daughters, Tennyson produces discourse whose function is not to open out meaning but to protect a mystery. In a very literal sense, this is a poem against dispersion; Hanno, hearing the Hesperides' song, sails on by without paying any attention. Language, as Tennyson represents it here, is not a commodity for export; and, indeed, the question of trade is relevant to this text, for the historical Hanno was a Phoenician, a member of the most active trading nation of the ancient world.

The possibility "The Hesperides" refuses, that the golden apples could be taken away from the garden and made into objects of exchange, or signifiers, Tennyson indeed describes in "Oenone," a poem contemporary with "The Hesperides" in which he tells the story of the judgment of Paris. Here, the golden apple has become an index of desire, inscribed with the words "For the most fair," which Paris is to award to one of the three goddesses, Hera, Athene, or Aphrodite. During the competition, each of the goddesses offers Paris a favor in exchange for the prize: Hera offers power, Athene, wisdom, and Aphrodite, "The fairest and most loving wife in Greece" ("Oenone," 183). The catastrophe of the story is Paris' choice of Aphrodite, for which she rewards him with assistance in the abduction of Helen, and which leads to the Trojan War.

The poem is narrated by Paris' first love, the nymph Oenone. She speaks on the slopes of Mt. Ida, where the judgment took place, and addresses the mountain as her mother. Her narrative is framed as an extended lamentation over Paris' desertion; such is the closeness of her relation to the landscape in which she speaks that in her account of his transgression it becomes virtually a transgression against the landscape and against nature itself. Thus at the end of the poem Oenone describes the ruin of the glen where she stands to fix the blame for it on the golden apple and on the goddess of strife who had maliciously first produced it as a prize:

> I wish that somewhere in the ruined folds,
> Among the fragments tumbled from the glens,
> Or the dry thickets, I could meet with her
> The Abominable, that uninvited came
> Into the fair Peleian banquet-hall,
> And cast the golden fruit upon the board,
> And bred this change.
>
> (217–223)

The golden apple introduces transgression against the natural here because it represents the differential, denatured structure of desire, and, more generally, the fact of writing. In the scene of Paris' judgment, desire is not naturally attached to its object but constituted as a written sign, referring only to other signs, and available for arbitrary exchange. The goddesses thus compete, not to induce the affect of desire in Paris, but to possess the apple which signifies that affect. The question of which goddess is actually— naturally—the fairest is not possible here; fairness becomes a quality constituted as possession of the apple bearing the inscription "For the most fair." In each case, the apple as signifier usurps upon, replaces, the affect of desire or the quality of desirability which it claims only to represent. Similarly, if from the perspective of Paris, Helen is the ultimate object of desire in this scene, she too is represented by a formula constituted as pure difference: "The fairest and most loving wife in Greece" (183). Like the desire of the goddesses, Paris' desire can define its object only as the sign of value, or only in terms of exchange with other objects.

This proliferation of difference in "Oenone" is introduced by writing in the form of an inscription on the golden apple; it ends in the Trojan War, which Cassandra foresees at the conclusion of the poem: "A fire dances before her, and a sound / Rings ever in her ears of armed men" (260–261). But in "The Hesperides" the apple is uninscribed; and the catastrophe which is to result from its inscription is part of the world which the sisters shut out of their garden, as they sing: "The world is wasted with fire and sword,/ But the apple of gold hangs over the sea" (104–105). The poem represents a fantasy of the sign before writing, which is to say of meaning and value without difference, as categories in a nature which they would constitute, rather than as arbitrary and exchangeable marks upon a nature which always, as in "Oenone," vanishes beneath them.

Like "The Skipping-Rope," then, "The Hesperides" defends the possibility of naturalized language against the proliferation of difference. In a seminal essay, G. Robert Stange has seen that the principal theme of the poem is the relation of the production of the Hesperides' song to the growth of the fruit on their tree.[5] He quotes at length from the first section of the song, ending with the lines:

> For the blossom unto threefold music bloweth;
> Evermore it is born anew;
> And the sap to threefold music floweth,
> From the root
> Drawn in the dark,
> Up to the fruit,
> Creeping under the fragrant bark,
> Liquid gold, honeysweet, through and through.
>
> (30–37)

Stange comments on this passage that "The conception by which the burgeoning of the fruit depends on the charmed music of the Hesperides and they, in turn, draw their vitality and find the source of their song in the root and the tree, is a figure of the connection among the artist, his art, and his inspiration" (103). Later, this connection becomes a unity:"The root, the bole, and the fruit are the elements of a living unity . . . [which] not only symbolizes the process of growth and the nature of artistic creation, but also suggests the ancient distinctions among body, soul, and spirit, as well as the organic principle of multiplicity in unity" (108–109). And in fact, living unity is the implicit subject of the first of Stange's claims as well as of the second. In his initial account, the unity of the tree and the fruit is actually constituted in the Hesperides' song, which he paradoxically identifies with both. In Stange's analysis, the song both grows out of the tree like the fruit and fosters the growth of the fruit like the natural vitality of the tree.

What is at issue in the poem as Stange reads it is thus not so much the notion of a language whose living unity is derived by analogy with nature as that of a language whose undifferentiated unity constitutes it as the natural. As Stange sees, what grows naturally in the garden of the Hesperides is language; it is, in his terms, a "garden of art." His analysis goes on, however, to transform this insight into a discussion of Tennyson's views on the morality of art. For him, the poem is finally an "assertion of a desire to retreat from purposive moral activity" (111); it is this moralized reading that has established the terms in which much of the subsequent discussion of the poem has taken place.[6]

It should by now be possible to evolve a more sophisticated account than Stange's of the determinants of what is after all a rather stranger text than his reading allows. If "The Hesperides" is like "The Skipping-Rope" in defending a fantasy of naturalized language, it does so, also like "The Skipping-Rope," by producing language as autoerotic repetition. Indeed, the erotic charge that the Hesperides' song attaches to the regularity of its own rhythm and its insistence on the sleeplessness of its singers give it the quality of a masturbatory fantasy: "If ye sing not, if ye make false measure,/ We shall lose eternal pleasure,/Worth eternal want of rest" (23–25). The same quality extends, moreover, to the representation of the production of language in the growth of the golden fruit, which also fairly clearly figures masturbatory activity; let us recall the passage that Stange quotes:

> the sap to threefold music floweth,
> From the root
> Drawn in the dark,
> Up to the fruit,
> Creeping under the fragrant bark,
> Liquid gold, honeysweet, through and through.
> (32–37)

In connection with this poem it is worth recalling Stephen Marcus' analysis of the economic basis of Victorian fantasies about masturbation, in which he takes as an exemplary text William Acton's *The Functions and Disorders of the Reproductive Organs* (1857). He concludes his discussion of Acton on adolescent masturbation as follows:

[According to Acton,] in the masturbating boy, "the large expenditure of semen, has exhausted the vital force." The continent boy, however, has "not expended that vital fluid, semen, or exhausted his nervous energy, and his youthful vigor has been employed for its legitimate purpose, namely, in building up his growing frame." . . . The fantasies that are at work here have to do with economics; the body is regarded as a productive system with only a limited amount of material at its disposal. And the model on which the notion of semen is formed is clearly that of money. Science, in the shape of Acton, is thus still expressing what had for long been a popular fantasy: up until the end of the nineteenth century the chief English colloquial expression for the orgasm was "to spend." . . . Furthermore, the economy envisaged in this idea is based on scarcity and has as its aim the accumulation of its own product.[7]

Against this background we can see in the perpetual generation of "liquid gold" and in the delight that "Hoarded wisdom" (37, 48) brings in Tennyson's garden the record of what Marcus would describe as a fantasy of unlimited production which bears nonetheless the traces of a strong prohibition against masturbation.

The possibility that the song includes material originating in autoerotic fantasies is a useful one because it opens up an explanation, not only of its hothouse eroticism, but also of the sense that this eroticism depends upon the fantasized evasion of a taboo. It is explicit throughout that the song and the pleasure it produces require secrecy—that "Out of watchings, out of wiles, / Comes the bliss of secret smiles" (77–78). Oddly enough, one of the powerful defenders of this secrecy seems to be the father, who is repeatedly exhorted to "watch, watch, night and day" (68). In fact, in this respect, as in others, Father Hesper is the wishful inverse of the father we all suppose ourselves to have in childhood. Instead of being a continuously watching figure who prevents his children from gratifying their desires, he is here a watcher entirely subject to their will, whose attention and whose wrath they can continuously direct away from them. The result of this inversion is that the father becomes, within the garden, an aged and curiously insubstantial figure, characterized chiefly by his "silver hair" and "silver eye" (44), who is apparently incapable of any action or speech that might even momentarily interrupt his daughters' continuous outpouring of song.

The anxiety induced by the autoerotic activity embodied in the Hesperides' song is not, however, entirely suppressed. It is rather cast out of the garden to reappear in displaced form in the disturbingly threatening imagery the singers use to describe the world outside. This world, they sing, is "wasted with fire and sword" (104); and their father is exhorted to watch specifically "Lest the old wound of the world be healed" (69). It is hard not to see in this bizarre line an externalization of castration anxiety, which the autoeroticism invested in the song would at once defend against and intensify. In the most schematic reading, the repetitions and numerations of the song would amount to the multiplication of phallic symbols and repeated assertions of the presence of the phallus which accompany the return of castration anxiety, while the "old wound," which the song itself sustains, would at once reassuringly externalize the threat of castration while paradoxically implicating the song itself as the transgression with which it originates.

At this level, it should by now be clear, the fantasy material in this text derives from a specifically male autoeroticism. Here, as in "The Skipping-Rope," Tennyson distances himself from his own wish to find autoerotic gratification in the production of language by displacing a representation of its fulfillment onto female characters. The greater elaboration of "The Hesperides" makes the nature of this displacement clearer than it was in "The Skipping-Rope," where less psychic material is engaged. In the masturbatory content of "The Hesperides" we can see some of the taboo material which makes such a displacement necessary.

We now need to ask how a text whose essential subject is language comes to be so powerfully overdetermined by masturbatory fantasies. It is certainly true that the fantasized economy of bodily fluids which Stephen Marcus has shown organized Victorian notions of masturbation bears a marked affinity to the economy of the signifier as Tennyson represents it in "The Hesperides" and "Oenone." Both structures are constituted around fantasies of the natural origin of the sign; thus, in the passage Marcus quotes from William Acton, semen is not figured simply as money, but also as deriving its value from its specifically natural function of "building up [the] growing frame" rather than as the subject of dissemination and exchange. At work here are fantasies, not only about the function of semen, but about that of money as well.

But the availability of an analogy between contemporary wishes about the economy of the body and Tennyson's fantasy of the natural production of poetic discourse does not of itself explain why that analogy should have been so important in determining the text of "The Hesperides." To put it another way, it does not seem necessary that the wish to identify language as an autoerotic object, which we have already seen in "The Skipping-Rope," must necessarily be associated, as it is here, with a purely genital autoeroticism, and with the taboo that that eroticism calls up.

We have seen that a central mechanism in dealing with taboo material in the text is its displacement of the consequent anxiety away from the place where this material is represented, in the song and garden of the Hesperides, and onto a world at large against which the song is specifically a defense. To pursue the question of why the notion of a taboo that has to be defended against appears in the poem at all, let us consider in more detail its principal representation of this world outside the garden, in the character of Zidonian Hanno. Hanno has very little place in the canonical reading of the poem that has been initiated by Stange's essay, and yet its account of his journey and of his swerve away from the voices that he hears is surely one of the strangest things about it.

In the *Periplus*, Tennyson's source for the explorer's name and itinerary—though not for an encounter with the Hesperides—Hanno sailed south along the west coast of Africa until he ran short of provisions, whereupon he turned around and returned to his starting-point in Carthage. It is hard to imagine Tennyson's Hanno doing likewise. His journey to "the outer sea" ("The Hesperides," 13) sounds much more like that of Ulysses, who announces his purpose "To sail beyond the sunset, and the baths / Of all the western stars, until I die" (60–61). Moreover, the Dantean Ulysses who took the journey Tennyson's character anticipates in these lines followed a route very similar to Hanno's, sailing out beyond the Pillars of Hercules and then turning south. But that story ends, of course, with Ulysses' death when a vast wave overwhelms him and his ship.

The idea of death as a sea voyage into the west, which Tennyson found in Celtic mythology as well as in Dante and classical sources, seems to have held an enduring fascination for him. It figures not only in "Ulysses," but also in "Morte d'Arthur," and in *In Memoriam* CIII, as well as in the late poem "Merlin and the Gleam" (1889). In "The Voyage of Maeldune" (1880), a similar voyage ends, not with the protagonist's own death, but with his reconciliation to his father's—a theme which is also implicit in "Ulysses," "Morte d'Arthur," and *In Memoriam*, each of which has at least partly at issue the son's response to the death of a father-figure.[8] The account of Hanno's voyage in "The Hesperides" anticipates this group of texts, also in the context of the father's death. We have already seen that the song of the Hesperides is produced at the expense of the father within the garden; outside it, the attenuated figure of Hesper seems to have his double in Hanno, in whose ambiguous fate the defensive measures necessary to produce the song find their fullest representation.

In the opening lines of the poem, Tennyson lists not only the places Hanno passed by on his journey, but also, more oddly, the sounds which he did not hear:

> The Northwind fallen, in the newstarrèd night
> Zidonian Hanno, voyaging beyond
> The hoary promontory of Soloë
> Past Thymiaterion, in calmèd bays,
> Between the southern and the western Horn,
> Heard neither warbling of the nightingale,
> Nor melody o' the Lybian lotusflute
> Blown seaward from the shore.
>
> (1–8)

The catalogue of place names comes from the *Periplus*; but the sounds have a source closer to home. They refer in a concise shorthand to two of Keats's odes, "To a Nightingale," and "On a Grecian Urn," both written in the spring of 1819. In each of these odes, a wishful version of poetic inspiration is figured by one of the sounds to which Tennyson alludes—in the former, by the song of the nightingale, and in the latter, by the music of the piper represented on the urn as a "happy melodist, unwearied, / For ever piping songs for ever new" (23–24). In a loose paradox, the melodies which Hanno does not hear recall the unheard melodies of the "Ode on a Grecian Urn."

If Tennyson records in this passage a swerve away from the figurations of Keats's spring odes, he attempts in the song of the Hesperides itself, which Hanno does hear, to achieve what Harold Bloom would call transumption of the later "To Autumn."[9] For "To Autumn" is itself a swerve away from the achievements of the spring of 1819. Keats wrote it that September, in a period when it seemed that he had not the means to continue writing poetry, and at about the time when he decided that, for a second time, he would have to give up his plan for an epic on the Hyperion story. The poem is a crisis-lyric, whose closest contemporary analogue is Shelley's "Ode to the

West Wind," in which the poet works through a period of blockage to a renewal of the poetic gift. The question "Where are the songs of Spring?" in "To Autumn" should, as Helen Vendler has implied, be read as Keats's nostalgia for the inspiration of the preceding April and May—a nostalgia which of course finds its rebuke in the lines which follow.[10]

Hanno is Tennyson's version of the Keats of "To Autumn." Having passed the song of the nightingale and the music of the pipes, he hears, not the music of autumn, but the song of the Hesperides. For Hanno, the song is a phenomenon of the limit; it is the last thing he hears before he vanishes, for the purposes of the poem, into the "outer sea" (13). And from Tennyson's point of view, the music of autumn which the Hesperides' song replaces was for Keats a phenomenon of the limit in a precisely analogous sense. In 1830, Tennyson could have known nothing of *The Fall of Hyperion*, and so for him, even more obviously than for us, "To Autumn" was the last great achievement of Keats's life. When in "The Hesperides" he came to write his own revisionary version of Keats's text, the liminal song of its final stanza consequently returned as a song marking the limit of Keats's own life.

Song actually is constituted in a liminal moment in "To Autumn"; it marks the limit, however, not of the poet's life, but of the figural proliferation of the opening stanzas, and, if it comes to that, of Keats's own earlier poetry. The voice which returns to autumn after the invocation of line 24 seems to be the voice of time itself. As such, it speaks the very thing that figuration denies and dissolves the representational stability of the first two stanzas of the poem into a moment constituted as difference.

It is from this first part of "To Autumn" that Tennyson takes his central image of the golden apple. The fruit in "The Hesperides" which "clustereth mellowly, / Goldenkernelled, goldencored, / Sunset-ripened above on the tree" (101–103) recognizably derives from the fruit filled "with ripeness to the core" of "To Autumn" (6). But where in Keats the apple is a figure which, claiming too much for itself, seems to block poetic utterance, in Tennyson, as we have seen, the apple stands for an utterance which precedes the figurative. This naturalizing misreading of an ironically excessive figuration opens Tennyson's defense in "The Hesperides" against the voice at the end of "To Autumn" which constitutes itself as the limit of figuration.

This defensive revision is central to "The Hesperides," for the notion of the liminal which Tennyson casts out of his representation of poetic discourse reappears as the dominant obsession of this peculiarly obsessive poem. The refusal of the text to articulate a limit within its own language manifests itself in its characteristic figuration of the garden, the place where language is produced, as the limit of something else. This figuration is introduced by the ambiguous ending of the voyage of Hanno, which marks the garden as standing at the limit of the world. Its fruit thus grows, without itself being limited, in what appears as a liminal moment in time:

the western sun and the western star,
And the low west wind, breathing afar,·
The end of the day and beginning of night
Make the apple holy and bright.

(89–92)

The notion of the liminal moment also determines the forebodings of apocalypse that pervade the characterization of the world outside the garden—
forebodings which are moreover themselves linked to its weird representation
of its own discourse, the Hesperides' fruit, as preceding and constituting the
limits of consciousness as that which can be known: "If the golden apple be
taken / The world will be overwise" (63–64).

"The Hesperides," in short, anxiously revises Keats's representation in
"To Autumn" of poetic language as belated figuration, limited in a moment
constituted purely as difference. The power of this representation is that it
closes off the possibility of subsequent figural language; in consequence,
"The Hesperides" begins by claiming its own priority to Keats's text, representing, in the figure of Zidonian Hanno, Keats himself as a belated quester,
to whose quest the Hesperides' song marks a limit. This subversion of its
precursor text is the specific transgression against the father which Tennyson's
fantasy of naturalized language must suppress. In this reading, the silence
of Father Hesper, as well as representing the wishful suppression of anxiety
called up by masturbatory fantasies, also marks Tennyson's suppression in
his text of the voice of Keats. In fact, it seems that the suggestions of
masturbatory guilt in the poem should be read as its playing out of a
transgression whose real origin is the origin of Tennyson's poetic self.

In certain of its configurations, then, "The Hesperides" bears a marked
resemblance to "The Skipping-Rope." Here, as in "The Skipping-Rope,"
Tennyson's investment in a representation of poetic discourse as autoerotic
repetition derives from a fantasy of a naturalized language, in which significance would be inherent in signs rather than constituted in the relations of
exchange between them. In both poems, this fantasy is preserved by a
displacement which excludes difference from the origin of language and
represents it elsewhere obsessively intensified. In "The Skipping-Rope," as
we saw, the difference suppressed in language reappeared as exaggerated
sexual difference, while in "The Hesperides" it reappears most markedly as
difference between the inside and the outside of the garden in which the
sisters sing.

All the same, the text of "The Hesperides" is clearly far more richly
overdetermined than that of "The Skipping-Rope." The ambivalence in "The
Skipping-Rope" toward autoerotic repetition as at once suppressing and
proliferating difference represents itself in "The Hesperides" as a transgression of the taboo against masturbation, and plays itself out in terms of

ambivalence to the father who institutes this prohibition. This representation is however also determined by the origin of the poem in difference from a prior text, as a troping on Keats's "To Autumn." The investment of the poem in autoerotic repetition is specifically an investment in suppressing this origin and in effacing in itself the traces of its precursor; in consequence, the Hesperides sing before a wishfully weak and silent father.

Taken together, however, these two texts open up a way of reading that group of Tennyson's poems—most obviously "The Lady of Shalott" and "The Palace of Art"—in which writing is figured by narcissistic or autoerotic activity in women. Especially if we enlarge this group to include related texts in which the poet's function is not explicitly thematized, like "Mariana" and "Tithonus," we can see that all of them represent scenes of exaggerated sexual difference or tension, in which the woman is characterized by self-involvement and repetitive activity. Under different displacements, then, each of these poems describes the scene which in "The Skipping-Rope" and "The Hesperides" appeared as Tennyson's anxious representation of the scene of writing itself. In each case, the woman's repetitions figure a fantasized poetic discourse whose meaning would be constituted in itself and in its doublings of itself, and not in a difference from something else which it could only speak as belatedness or lack. And in each case, the lack, or space, which is not spoken within language returns as a space outside it—as sexual difference, or, more abstractly, as the articulation between artistic and historical phenomena which we invoke when we interpret these texts as being about "art for art's sake."

In "The Hesperides," this fantasy of the scene of writing was produced to suppress the true scene of a rewriting of Keats's "To Autumn." Here the difference which Tennyson's text is engaged in casting out is specifically its own difference with a precursor. This point is of some literary-historical importance. For the group of texts cited above, including "Mariana," "The Lady of Shalott," "The Palace of Art," and "Tithonus," as well as "The Hesperides," became powerful sources of influence on the work of later writers—and painters—such as William Morris, D. G. Rossetti, and Yeats. Indeed, they introduce what became a characteristically Victorian figuration of narcissistic women. And they do so in the course of a revision of specific figures in certain texts of the High Romantic period—not just in "To Autumn," but also, in the cases of the poems listed above, in "Isabella," "Hyperion," in Wordsworth's "The Solitary Reaper," and in Book I of *The Excursion*.

It is perhaps no news that the line in English poetry that begins with the early Tennyson and extends through the Pre-Raphaelites originates in a reaction to the Romantics. But most academic Victorianists, like Stange, locate this reaction in the wrong place, on the high ground of ethical or ontological claims about the status of the artist, in the assumption that such claims constitute stable referents for the shifty figuration of the texts. In fact, however, such an assumption only weakly repeats the wishful escape of the texts from figuration and obscures the revisionary struggle in which they have their origin.

Notes

1. "The Skipping-Rope," in *The Poems of Tennyson*, ed. Christopher Ricks (London, 1969), 657. Quotations from Tennyson's poems are from this edition and will be cited parenthetically in the body of the text.

2. John Walker, *A Rhyming Dictionary: Answering at the same time, the purposes of spelling and pronouncing the English Language* (London, 1806). I have unfortunately been unable to find a copy of the 1800 edition which, according to Prof. Ricks, Tennyson actually owned.

3. The remark is quoted from Hallam Tennyson's *Alfred Lord Tennyson: A Memoir by his Son* (London, 1898), II, 496.

4. Jacques Derrida, *Of Grammatology*, trans. Gayatri C. Spivak (Johns Hopkins Univ. Press, 1976), 229.

5. "Tennyson's Garden of Art: A Study of 'The Hesperides,' " *PMLA*, 67 (1952); rptd. in John Killham, ed., *Critical Essays on the Poetry of Tennyson* (London, 1960), 99–112.

6. Commentators on the poem who follow or elaborate Stange's views include J. H. Buckley in *Tennyson, The Growth of a Poet* (Harvard Univ. Press, 1960), 47, and, with some reservations, Valerie Pitt in *Tennyson Laureate* (London, 1962), 59–60. In "The Poet as Heroic Thief: Tennyson's 'The Hesperides' Reexamined," *Victorian Newletter*, 35 (1969), 1–5, James D. Merriman retains the moral categories that Stange finds in the poem but reverses his reading, arguing that the poem is a "hard-headed examination of the moral evil, the psychological failure and the pragmatic inadequacy of retreat," and that Tennyson's identification is really with Hercules, the heroic thief who eventually steals the apple.

Since, then, A. Dwight Culler, reading the Hesperides' apples as representing a privileged poetic knowledge, has acutely argued that the enigmatic response of Hanno to their singing figures the problematic relation of poetic or visionary language to the phenomenal world. See *The Poetry of Tennyson* (Yale Univ. Press, 1977), 49–51. Even more recently, Kerry McSweeney's *Tennyson and Swinburne as Romantic Naturalists* (Univ. of Toronto Press, 1981), 45–47, begins a discussion of "The Hesperides" by citing Stange, though McSweeney goes on to suggest that the poem does not describe the actual conditions of Tennyson's art, but a wishful version of them.

In spite of the sensitivity of many of these readings of the poem, none of them has improved on Stange's outline of its problems, which accounts for the continuing influence of his article; moreover, no one has made any advance on his critical practice, which is essentially to produce stable meaning in the text by thematically privileging certain elements in it. Some critics (e.g., Merriman) betray a certain uneasiness with the results of this method; none to my knowledge points out its theoretical inadequacy to a text so clearly not thematically determined as "The Hesperides." To all of this, as to any generalization about recent writing on Tennyson, Harold Bloom's chapter in *Poetry and Repression* (Yale Univ. Press, 1976), 143–74, stands as a notable exception. I wish to acknowledge my large debt to Bloom's theorizing throughout this book, as well as to his teasingly brief discussion of "The Hesperides" on pp. 155–57.

7. *The Other Victorians* (New York, 1964), pp. 21–22.

8. All three of these poems were of course written primarily in response to the death of Arthur Hallam in 1833. They also seem colored by the death of Tennyson's father, which had occurred two years earlier. In the case of "Morte d' Arthur," this was first suggested by W. D. Paden in his *Tennyson in Egypt: A Study of the Imagery in His Earlier Work* (Univ. of

Kansas Pub. No. 27, 1942), 86–87; the same suggestion applies at least to *In Memoriam* CIII, which is a self-conscious reworking of the earlier poem. None of this biographical material is directly relevant to "The Hesperides," which was completed by 1830, when both Hallam and Tennyson's father were still alive. However, its affinity with the later texts, if it can be taken as evidence of its similar concerns, thus suggests all the more strongly that representations of the father's death have in Tennyson's poetry more than a narrowly biographical importance.

9. Transumption has been much in the air lately. For recent accounts, see John Hollander's "Appendix: The Trope of Transumption" in *The Figure of Echo* (Univ. of California Press, 1981), 133–49, and Chapter 3 of Harold Bloom's *The Breaking of the Vessels* (Univ. of Chicago Press, 1982). Bloom's most stripped-down formulation may be useful here: "Transumptive or metaleptic literary criticism relies upon a diachronic conception of rhetoric, in which the irony of one age can become the noble synecdoche of another" (p. 74). In what follows, I argue that the golden apples of the Hesperides, which are certainly something like a noble synecdoche carrying the burden of Tennyson's aspirations regarding his own discourse, derive from the ironically belated and figurally overloaded apples of Keats's "To Autumn."

10. "The Experiential Beginnings of Keats's Odes," *Studies in Romanticsm*, 12 (1972), 604–5.

A Blessing and a Curse: The Poetics of Privacy in Tennyson's "The Lady of Shalott"

When, in his famous review of *Poems, Chiefly Lyrical* (1830), Arthur Henry Hallam claims that Tennyson "belongs decidedly to the class we have . . . described as Poets of Sensation,"[1] he places his friend squarely within certain main currents of English Romantic aesthetics. Opposing Tennyson's work to Wordsworth's discursive, "reflective" poetry, he argues that Tennyson's poetics are patterned on the examples of the most perfect previous "Poets of Sensation": Shelley and Keats. And he fleshes out his argument by defining the poet of sensation's characteristic notions of beauty, imagination, and audience. Such a poet's "predominant motive," he writes, is not "the pleasure [one] has in knowing a thing to be true," but rather "the desire of beauty" (184–185, 184). Discussing Shelley and Keats, he describes the kind of imagination needed to sustain the predominance of that desire, claiming that "they lived in a world of images; for the most important and extensive portion of their life consisted in those emotions which are immediately conversant with sensation" (186). Finally, he notes that the poet of sensation is likely to be unpopular, because "to understand his expressions and sympathize with his state . . . requires exertion," and "this requisite exertion is not willingly made by the large majority of readers" (188).

    This aesthetic position, which Hallam sees as fundamental to Tennyson's early work, is rooted in what later critics have defined as the Romantic ideal of the autonomy of the work of art. Hallam's rejection of Wordsworthian "poetry of reflection" and his preference for pleasure in beauty over pleasure in the truth of referential discourse, for example, are closely allied to the notion, defined by M. H. Abrams, "that a poem is an object-in-itself, a self-contained universe of discourse, of which we cannot demand that it be true to nature, but only, that it be true to itself."[2] His claim for an immediate union of emotion and sensation in the image, with its implication that the poet's emotions are immediately evoked by objects of sensation, leads directly to Paul de Man's claim that the language of Romantic poetry seeks to recapture such immediacy by reconstituting the object: "[Romantic] poetic

Reprinted from *Victorian Poetry*, Vol. 24 (1986), by permission. © 1986 by West Virginia University Press.

language seems to originate in the desire to draw closer and closer to the ontological status of the object, and its growth and development are determined by this inclination."[3] And his observation that the "exertion" required to understand the poet of sensation's "expressions" is "not willingly made by the large majority of readers" assumes the same alienation of art from common life that Frank Kermode defines when he describes the Romantic artwork as "out of the flux of life, and therefore, under one aspect dead; yet uniquely alive because of its participation in a higher order of existence. . . ; resistant to explication; largely independent of intention, and of any form of ethical utility."[4] Each of the characteristics Hallam accords the poet of sensation—the privileging of beauty, the immediate union of emotion and sensation, the alienation from any wide audience—thus also appears in twentieth-century discussions of the autonomy of Romantic artwork, its status as a self-contained object divorced from everyday life and language. To be a poet of sensation, then, to be the Alfred Tennyson of *Poems, Chiefly Lyrical*, is also to be a poet of autonomy.

Hallam's aesthetic harmonizes not only with the Romantic ideal of the autonomy of the artwork, but also with another important Romantic aesthetic ideal: the identification of the artwork with femininity. Hallam himself hints at this harmony when he points out that "a considerable portion of this book [*Poems, Chiefly Lyrical*] is taken up with a very singular and very beautiful class of poems on which the author has evidently bestowed much thought and elaboration. We allude to the female characters, every trait of which presumes an uncommon degree of observation and reflection" (197). Carol T. Christ reaffirms this point when she notes that "many of [Tennyson's] poems which most clearly typify Hallam's definition of the poetry of sensation bear as titles women's names."[5] These observations suggest that one can say of the early Tennyson's "poetry of sensation" something very close to what Kermode says of Romantic poetry in general: "the beauty of a woman, and particularly of a woman in movement, is the emblem of the work of art or Image" (71). The poem, that is, not only claims autonomy, but also identifies itself as feminine: Keats's Grecian urn is a "still unravished bride of quietness"; Coleridge's Eolian harp is "Like some coy maid half yielding to her lover"; and Shelley's skylark sings not only "Like a Poet hidden / In the light of thought," but also "Like a high-born maiden/ In a palace tower." Even inanimate or animal emblems for the work of art—urn, harp, skylark— must themselves be emblematized by figures of autonomous (unravished, coy, maidenly) femininity. The autonomy and femininity of the Romantic artwork or poem of sensation, indeed, seem to be inextricably interlinked. The woman who is the emblem or the topic of such an artwork can be ascribed the same qualities—self-containment, objectified otherness, removal from the flux of life, participation in a higher order of existence—through which that artwork claims autonomy. The "female character," then, would seem to be a fitting genre for a poet of sensation like Tennyson because, identifying a poem as feminine, that genre also endows the poem with autonomy.

However, the ideals of femininity and autonomy fundamental to Hallam's notion of the poetry of sensation are radically challenged by one of Tennyson's most important "female characters": "The Lady of Shalott." This poem, the first version of which appeared only two years after Hallam's review, has often been read as yet another allegory of artistic autonomy, albeit one which, tinged with Victorian pessimism, emphasizes the costs of such autonomy for the artist. According to Jerome Buckley, the poem "explores the maladjustment of the aesthetic spirit to ordinary living"; A. Dwight Culler asserts that the curse which separates the Lady from her world "is simply the inescapable condition of the poet's art"; and W. David Shaw argues that the poem portrays a "death of the imagination such as Wordsworth suffered" as "the price the artist may have to pay for trying . . . to make his world human."[6] All of these critics see the Lady's death as a sign of some conflict between art and "ordinary living," or between the artist and "*his* world" (my emphasis). None sees the Lady's femininity as having anything to do with that death.[7] But her particular form of femininity is precisely what gives that death its meaning. Through her femininity, the poem calls into question the relations between the "aesthetic spirit" and "ordinary living," that is, between art and the social world.

The poem poses its questions by deploying a tactic Kermode defines in his discussion of the self-emblematizing of Romantic artwork. Although he points out that the Romantic artwork often identifies itself with an emblematic image of autonomy and femininity (an unravished bride, a coy maid, a maiden in a tower), Kermode does not follow the implication of this idea: to claim autonomy and femininity by representing them in an emblematic image is to acknowledge that those qualities are, like Keats's Lamia and her palace, illusory. "The Lady of Shalott" takes up this tactic of self-emblematizing not only to define itself as autonomous and feminine, but also to examine the illusions and contradictions which these definitions engender. In the Lady, the poem offers an emblem of both the poet and the poem of sensation; but this emblem, isolated in a zone of shadows and illusions, questions the definitions—the ideals of femininity and autonomy—which constitute its very being.

When Christ notes that the Tennyson poems which best exemplify Hallam's notion of the poetry of sensation often "bear as titles women's names," she also points out that it is difficult to tell whether the women named in those poems are perceiving subjects or perceived objects.[8] Her observation suggests that Tennyson presents the woman not simply as an emblem for the art object which endows that object with an (illusory) autonomous otherness, but also as a figure for the artist's subjectivity, a subjectivity confined to imaginative privacy as the woman is confined to domestic privacy. The woman who gives her name (insofar as it is a name at all) to "The Lady of Shalott" plays this double role very explicitly. As the topic or object of the poem which bears her name, she confirms the harmony between Hallam's aesthetic and the Romantic identification of the artwork with femininity. As the artist or subject of that poem, however, she also makes audible the dissonant voices that whisper within that harmony, the voices of the social and sexual contradictions which lurk behind the Romantic ideal of autonomy. These contradictions are produced by the problem that Robert Bernard Martin sees at the core of "The Lady of Shalott": "the conflict between privacy and social involvement."[9] Privacy, in other words, is the social equivalent of the aesthetic condition of autonomy, as the association between femininity and art in "The Lady of Shalott" demonstrates. And despite the feudal setting of the poem, the problems of privacy and autonomy it confronts are not specifically medieval ones; for it is Tennyson's own social order, not the one from which he drew the Lady and Lancelot, that makes autonomy and privacy fundamental conditions of femininity and of art. Just as the Lady's isolation and gender define Shalott as a private, domestic domain (the domain which was becoming increasingly important to the social structure of nineteenth-century England), so her isolation and occupation—"she weaves by night and day / A magic web with colours gay"—define it as also an artistic realm, as the apparently autonomous social place art (especially Romantic art) inhabits.[10] The privacy that structures the Lady's femininity also determines her fate as an artist and the fate of her artwork.

Or, to state this claim in a different way: Tennyson is not the only poet of sensation whose name appears in *Poems* (1832); the Lady of Shalott is another. And in order to see how her gender makes her a particularly apt figure for the poet of sensation, we need to examine the links between her particular form of femininity and the qualities Hallam ascribes to such a poet. The Lady's femininity is first defined by her situation: her confinement within the walls and towers of her "silent isle." The cultivated barley fields and the busy road and river surrounding the island, as well as the reapers who hear the Lady's song and the various social types that go by in her mirror, define Shalott and the femininity it "imbowers" as unmoving, unchanging, cut off from all useful social activity. The Lady, unlike the "market girls," the "troop of damsels glad," or the "two young lovers lately wed" in her mirror, remains outside the cycles of economic and sexual exchange: "She hath no loyal knight and true" (62). And this separation is fundamentally a denial of the Lady's substantiality, of her participation in material exchange, even of her corporeality:

> who hath seen her wave her hand?
> Or at the casement seen her stand?
> Or is she known in all the land,
>   The Lady of Shalott?
>
> (24–27)

The only evidence the outside world has of her existence is the song—disembodied sound—that reapers hear in the wee hours of night and morning. To the active social world she is mysterious, insubstantial, shadowy.

This same denial of the Lady's substantiality is implicit in her relation to the magic mirror, the central symbol of her separation. That mirror, showing her "Shadows of the *world*" (my emphasis) rather than her own reflection, indicates that she is utterly dependent upon the world from which she is separated. The absence of her own reflection in the mirror (which suggests that she, like a shadow, cannot cast her image there) is a sign that she has no independent existence, even if she has a separate one. Traditional portrayals of a woman gazing into a looking-glass or pool (Milton's Eve in Book IV of *Paradise Lost*, for example) invoke a feminine autonomy achieved through narcissism. The glass or pool represents the woman as one who is her own object of desire and thus achieves a kind of sexual self-sufficiency (though it also implies that the woman's role as an object of masculine desire structures even her own sexual constitution, that she cannot escape the condition of otherness and objectification even in her own patterns of desire). The Lady's magic mirror, however, reveals the illusoriness of such narcissistic autonomy even as it imposes it. Insistently referring to that mirror as a "there," the poem suggests that instead of representing the "here" of the Lady's subjectivity as also the "there" of a desired other, the mirror's "there" in fact constitutes the Lady's "here":

> There she sees the highway near
>   Winding down to Camelot:
> There the river eddy whirls,
> And there the surly village-churls,
> And the red cloaks of market girls,
>   Pass onward from Shalott.
>   (49–54)

Showing the Lady no image of herself, the mirror reveals that the Lady's apparently autonomous subjectivity and desires—her "here"—are shadows or effects of the sights that appear in it, that no matter who she is or what she loves, her identity and desires are always already another's. This other is no single individual (such as a father- or mother-figure), but rather the public world that surrounds her. Her identity and desires are effects of identification with a whole ensemble of social types and relations: village-churls, market girls, damsels, the abbot, the shepherd, the page, the knights, the funeral party, the newlywed lovers, and the interactions between these. The autonomy and independence her isolation grants her, then, turn out to be fundamentally illusory, since she is granted them only at the cost of becoming just as shadowy as the images the mirror shows her.

The Lady's insubstantiality, her absence in the eyes of the world and in the scene in the mirror, is complemented by the insubstantiality of the world, in her own eyes. Her mirror shows her only *"Shadows* of the world" (my emphasis). The pattern of double insubstantiality thus constructed is fundamental to the Lady's femininity, as we can see by comparing this version of that pattern to one Tennyson sets up when he is explicitly concerned with defining an ideal femininity: a famous passage from *The Princess* in which the Prince describes his mother as

> one
> Not learnèd save in gracious household ways,
> Not perfect, nay, but full of tender wants,
> No Angel, but a dearer being, all dipt
> In Angel instincts, breathing Paradise,
> Interpreter between the Gods and men,
> Who looked all native to her place, and yet
> On tiptoe seemed to touch upon a sphere
> Too gross to tread, and all male minds perforce
> Swayed to her from their orbits as they moved,
> And girdled her with music.
>
> (VII. 298–308)

Like the Lady of Shalott, this feminine-ideal is both corporeal and insubstantial. She can experience "tender wants" just as the Lady can experience delight and disgust. But those wants are also "Angel instincts," which ensure that this feminine-ideal will touch a "sphere / Too gross to tread" only "On tiptoe," just as the isolation of the Lady ensures that her entire experience of the outside world remains utterly shadowy. This feminine-ideal's place is identified when the Prince calls her "Not learnèd, save in gracious household ways." She clearly inhabits the realm of the private domestic household, a zone surrounded by the public—by the "male minds" that grapple with public conflict and "[girdle] her with music"—but which somehow escapes the grossness and materiality of the public realm. The social place of the Lady of Shalott, though it is clearly an artistic as well as a domestic realm, also shares the privacy of the domestic household. It too is a zone of insubstantiality, a zone apart from though surrounded by that "sphere / Too gross to tread" which one could also call Camelot.

The double insubstantiality of self and world that structures the Lady's femininity also structures her artistry. It forms a model of the artist's experience of the world, a model just similar enough to that which Hallam prescribes for the poet of sensation to identify the Lady as such a poet—just similar enough, indeed, to raise important questions about Hallam's model as well. That the Lady's mirror shows her only "shadows" suggests that she, like the poet of sensation, lives "in a world of images." Poets of sensation like Shelley and Keats, according to Hallam, lived in such a world because "the most important and extensive portion of their life consisted in those emotions which are immediately conversant with sensation." As the following passage shows, the relation between the Lady's emotions and her sense experience fits this definition closely enough to bring to light the social implications of its terms:

> But in her web she still delights
> To weave the mirror's magic sights,
> For often through the silent nights
> A funeral, with plumes and lights
>   And music, went to Camelot:
> Or when the moon was overhead,
> Came two young lovers lately wed;
> 'I am half sick of shadows,' said
>   The Lady of Shalott.
>
> (64–72)

As the conjunction "For" in the third line of this stanza suggests, the funeral evokes the Lady's delight in weaving "the mirror's magic sights"; by the same token, the semicolon in the seventh line of the stanza suggests that the Lady's declaration, "I am half sick of shadows," follows immediately upon, and thus is caused by, the sight of the "two young lovers lately wed." The Lady's emotions—as well as her work of weaving—seem wholly bound up with virtually the only sense experience she is permitted on her "silent isle": the images of the mirror. Those images or "shadows," however, are by no means simple sensations, as the Lady's unconventional emotional responses to them hint. Rather, those images undergo several stages of mediation before they reach the Lady's eyes. First, they are socially constructed; the funeral and the newlywed lovers are both intimately connected to important social rituals. Second, they do not appear directly to the Lady's eyes, but move "through a mirror clear / That hangs before her all the year." Finally, they do not appear directly to the mirror either; instead, they are "magic sights" which appear in the mirror only via the "magic" agency of representation. Even when they reach the Lady's vision, those images undergo a further stage of mediation when she weaves them into her equally "magic" web. The images, the mirror, and the mirror's "magic" (all of which work to produce the Lady's sensations), as well as the Lady herself and her magic web, thus form links in a long chain of mediations and representations. And just as the Lady's sensations are subject to mediation and representation, so are her emotions. Her delight and half-sickness would be the socially proper (and thus ostensibly "immediate") responses to the newlyweds and the funeral, except that they too apparently undergo the mirror's mediation: following the pattern of reversals mirrors impose, the funeral evokes the Lady's delight, the newlyweds her half-sickness.

That the Lady's experience is so closely bound up with various sorts of "reflection," representation, and mediation does not undermine her status as a poet of sensation so much as call into question the model of imagination which that term names. Even an artist so completely removed from the temptations of discursive reflection as the Lady, the poem suggests, can never achieve an immediate relation between emotion and sensation; other forms of "reflection" or representation inevitably intervene. And this questioning of the model of imagination Hallam claims for the poet of sensation is based not only on epistemological grounds, but also on social grounds. The magic mirror is a figure not simply for universal human processes of perception and imagination which mediate emotion, but also for a particular form of perception and imagination: the form which isolates the artist from any active participation in public social life, which renders the world shadowy in the eyes of the artist and the artist shadowy in the eyes of the world. The mirror, then, may be a figure for imaginative mediation in general, but it is also a figure for the specific form of imaginative mediation privacy creates. For what the Lady sees in that "mirror clear / That hangs before her all the year"—highway, river, girls, churls, damsels, abbot, shepherd-lad, page, knights, funeral, and lovers—is the social realm of activity and exchange which privacy shuts out. The mirror unceasingly shows her that realm; but, equally unceasingly, it attests to her separation from and her dependence upon that realm. The magic of the "magic sights," then, consists in making such separation and dependence—and all of their psychic and perceptual consequences—the fundamental conditions of both her femininity and her artistry.

If privacy is what divorces the Lady—as a woman and as a poet of sensation—from the social realm that surrounds her, what power enforces this divorce, this splitting of the world into private and public zones? The answer clearly lies in the identity of the voice that whispers the curse under which the Lady lives: "She has heard a whisper say,/A curse is on her if she stay/To look down to Camelot" (39–41). Two voices in the poem speak this curse. The first is the voice of the "reaper weary" who, hearing the Lady's song, "whispers ' 'Tis the fairy / Lady of Shalott'." This whisper precedes the curse-whisper so closely (only two lines and a section-break separate them) as to suggest that the Lady hears the reaper's whisper as the curse. Indeed, this whisper can be seen as part of an indirect conversation between the reaper and the Lady—a conversation broken by the river and, at the typographical level, by the break between sections I and II: the Lady sings; the reaper hears her song and replies with a whisper; the Lady hears his whisper and interprets it as the curse. The reaper's whisper, defining the Lady as "fairy" (that is, insubstantial) and as an inmate of Shalott (a realm whose essence is its separateness), is identical in content to the curse-whisper, which confines her to those conditions of insubstantiality and separateness. The former identifies the Lady; the latter imposes the condition which constitutes her identity. The reaper's whisper, crossing the river, becomes the curse, thus taking on the force of a speech act which makes the Lady what it names. Even if this notion may violate the sequence of events in the poem (since the Lady is already confined to Shalott when the reaper whispers), it accords perfectly with the combined power of the voices that speak the curse.

The second voice that speaks the curse is the only other voice outside Shalott that speaks in the poem: Lancelot's. His speech is both a blessing and the curse: " 'She has a lovely face;/God in his mercy lend her grace,/The Lady of Shalott' " (169–171). If one follows the logic of juxtaposition which shows the reaper's whisper and the curse-whisper to be the same, one can see that these three lines add up to a statement almost identical to those two whispers. What prompts Lancelot to wish the Lady God's grace, as both the juxtaposition of the first two lines of the passage and the rhyme between them suggest, is her "lovely face." This blessing, apparently the opposite of the curse which confines the Lady to insubstantiality and separateness, recognizes her physical appearance (both her beauty and her presence) and welcomes her into the public social order (under the sign of religion). But by making the Lady's physical appearance something like a precondition for her welcome into the public realm, Lancelot calls attention to the Lady's loss of the physical life which might have made such a welcome worth having. His blessing, then, rather than countering the curse, instead restates it in other terms. That blessing is simply the reversed mirror-image of the curse, as though what appears as a curse on the Shalott side of the magic mirror appears as a blessing on the Camelot side. And the fact that it is Lancelot, the catalyst for the curse coming upon the Lady, who offers this blessing confirms the fundamental similarity of the two statements, as does yet another juxtaposition: the line in which Lancelot says, " 'God in his mercy lend her grace,' " appears at exactly the same point in Part IV where the line in which the Lady cries, " 'The curse is come upon me,' " appears in Part III.

The fundamental similarities between the blessing and the curse— between the reaper's whisper, the curse-whisper, and Lancelot's speech— identify the power that enforces the Lady's isolation in Shalott as the masculine voice in the poem. This voice is not, however, a single voice; it belongs to reaper, to knight, and to no one at all. It speaks from every level of the social world of the poem, imposing and enforcing the private/public split fundamental to the Lady's position as both a woman and an artist. The curse-whisper imposes the condition of privacy; the reaper's speech names it. These two voices, indeed, constitute Shalott as a private realm not only through the content of their speeches, but also through the way in which they speak of it, which is to use the softest possible tones and to address the smallest possible audience: the reaper whispers about that realm only in the wee hours of morning "In among the bearded barley"; and the curse-whisper, whatever its source, speaks only in the hearing of the one who must inhabit the realm its speech defines. These voices, that is, enforce Shalott's privacy by speaking of it only in strictest privacy. Lancelot's voice, on the other hand, speaking out loud, makes the Lady public: immediately after his " 'Tirra lirra' ," "she look[s] down to Camelot," thus dissolving Shalott's privacy; and immediately after her song ceases, his blessing defines her public identity and value. Assigning the Lady a public identity, Lancelot's voice reinstates and reinforces the private/public split momentarily collapsed by her emergence into the public world, thus neutralizing the threat she poses to "All the knights at Camelot," who "[cross] themselves for fear" as she floats by.

The process by which the Lady is made public, initiated by Lancelot's song and consummated by his blessing, defines the fates of both her sexuality and her artistry. As argued above, the Lady's sexual identity is a privatized, domestic femininity—a femininity sheltered from the "sphere / Too gross to tread" of public conflict and exchange. When the Lady looks at Lancelot and sets the curse in motion, her privacy is publicized, her domesticity dissolved, her femininity objectified. And the operation of this curse follows precisely the pattern of its imposition. Just as the reaper's whisper, unbeknownst to the whisperer, seems to become what the Lady hears as the curse, so Lancelot's flashing "into the crystal mirror" and singing " 'Tirra lirra' " are experienced by the Lady as a kind of rape, a rape all the more devastating because it is, on Lancelot's part, unwitting. The description of Lancelot is studded with sunlit, phallic imagery: he rides "A bow-shot from [the Lady's] bower-eaves"; his "helmet and the helmet-feather / [Burn] like one burning flame together" and are likened to "Some bearded meteor, trailing light"; "coal-black curls" flow "From underneath his helmet." Combined with all of his noisy, metallic accoutrements—"brazen greaves," "shield," "gemmy bridle," "bridle bells," "mighty silver bugle," and ringing armor—this imagery marks Lancelot as a masculine machine of desire. A metallic phallus, he cracks "from side to side" the "crystal mirror" which has formed the barrier between the Lady's privacy and public Camelot. And as befits his metallic body, he performs this rape without even knowing it.

The discrepancy between Lancelot's experience of this rape and the Lady's is summed up in the lines that immediately follow his flashing into her mirror:

> She left the web, she left the loom,
> She made three paces through the room,
> She saw the water-lily bloom,
> She saw the helmet and the plume,
> She looked down to Camelot.
> (109–113)

The contrast between the delicate, vaginal water-lily and the metallic, phallic helmet, the first objects the Lady sees without the mediation of the mirror, defines a discrepancy of power and value. The Lady's static realm of shadows and silence is utterly vulnerable to Lancelot's mobility, solidity, light, and noise. Her privacy, constituted by and dependent upon the discourse of masculine, public voices, is instantly dissolved by the intervention of that discourse, by Lancelot's " 'Tirra lirra'." Once this dissolution occurs, the Lady finds herself in a position peculiarly similar to that of the freed prisoner in Plato's allegory of the cave: having made his way out of the shadowy cave, the prisoner discovers "that it is the Sun that produces the seasons and the course of the year and controls everything in the visible world, and moreover is in a way the cause of all that he and his companions used to see."[11] Yet unlike Plato's, Tennyson's allegory is not primarily an epistemological one, built on an opposition between illusion and truth, but fundamentally a social one, built on oppositions between feminine and masculine, private and public. The Sun in "The Lady of Shalott" is Lancelot, whose "broad clear brow in sunlight glowed," and who, as part of a patriarchal social ensemble, "controls everything in the visible world" of Camelot. Thus the Lady's emergence from shadowy Shalott is a Platonic, epistemological "upward journey of the soul into the region of the intelligible" only insofar as masculine voices determine what is and is not intelligible in the world of the poem (Plato, 231). That emergence is also, and more importantly, a process which radically alters the Lady's femininity. Her journey toward masculine Lancelot and public Shalott is also a journey toward death, a journey she makes dressed as a bride—"robed in snowy white / That loosely flew to left and right" (136–137). This journey is the death of the Lady's particular form of femininity, a femininity which, though private and confined, maintains at least the illusion of an autonomous subjectivity. It is also, perhaps, her initiation into the objectified form of femininity defined (if only by negation) by Lancelot's oblivious, omnipotent desire; this desire, finding its consummation in the utter objectification of the other—the Lady—would be equally satisfied through her marriage (her transformation into an object) or her death (her annihilation as a subject).

The dissolution of the privacy that confines and shelters the Lady's femininity is also a dissolution of the autonomy of her artwork and of her position as an artist, a poet of sensation. The consequences of this second dissolution are summed up by the contrast between the Lady's look at Lancelot and Lancelot's look at the Lady, a contrast which defines a discrepancy of value. While the Lady dies for her look at Lancelot, Lancelot's reaction to the sight of her dead form is to "[muse] a little space" and to offer a blessing that is merely appreciative, suspiciously close in tone to a museum-goer's casual comment on a painting after a momentary glance. Just as the Lady, looking at Lancelot and dying, is consumed by what she sees, so he, glancing at her and appreciating her beauty, takes the role of consumer. Like Plato's freed prisoner, the Lady finds that the sun of her world—Lancelot— controls everything, including the value she is assigned in the public realm. Lancelot's blessing, assigning the Lady a value and making her intelligible to "Knight and burgher, lord and dame," defines the fate of the poet of sensation in the public realm. Such a poet, whose unpopularity Hallam ascribes to his unintelligibility, to the "exertion" required "to understand his expressions and sympathize with his state," will (as Hallam recognizes) face the kind of reading Lancelot offers in his blessing, a reading which betrays no understanding and precious little sympathy.

This discrepancy of value structures the whole process of artistic production in the poem. Although "the mirror's magic sights," for example, are the thematic content of the Lady's "magic web," the figures that populate the mirror have little or no notion of the existence of the web. Even when, the curse invoked, her art enters the public world, it seems to travel beyond the bounds of the Camelot it represents and get lost: "Out flew the web and floated wide." Both the mirror and the web, then, set up discrepancies of value identical to that which Lancelot's blessing defines, the former with reference to the process of artistic work, the latter with reference to that work as product. Both the Lady as artist and the web as artwork are wholly dependent upon a public world which accords them no stable or certain value at all. An antidiscursive poet of sensation, the singer of a song whose words we never hear, the Lady is not even recognized as an artist when she emerges into the public world that has been the sole theme of her art.

Although the Lady gains no recognition as an artist, she does seem to gain recognition as an artwork. For, as Sandra Gilbert and Susan Gubar point out, the Lady's "last work of art is her own dead body" (43). At the moment of her glance, when the mirror cracks and the web floats wide, she begins to reenact with her body the same process of artistic production that issued in the web. Lying down in the boat, floating down the river, she sends her body into the world as an artwork which she signs—"round about the prow she wrote / *The Lady of Shalott*"—and whose appearance and origin she announces by "singing her last song." The process of dying which the curse sets in motion is also the process by which the Lady—the artist, the apparently autonomous subject—makes herself into an object of art, an object finished and perfected when, entering Camelot, she dies: "A gleaming shape she floated by, / Dead-pale between the houses high, / Silent into Camelot" (156–158). This process, then, objectifies not only the Lady's femininity, but also her artistry—and this in the most literal way possible: the artist becomes the art-object, the work of producing art is subsumed by the artwork as product. And this process of artistic objectification is wholly bound up with the process of becoming public, as the direction of the Lady's dying gaze shows: the Lady's carol is heard "Till her blood was frozen slowly, / And her eyes were darkened wholly, / Turned to towered Camelot" (147–149). Dying into objectivity, the Lady's whole attention is fixed on the public realm of "towered Camelot." The inward space of her autonomy dissolves, and, bereft of that interiority, she can only gaze outward. Just as the magic mirror calls into question the autonomy of the model of imagination and artistic creation implicit in Hallam's poet of sensation, so the Lady's death thus calls into question the autonomy of what we might call the poem of sensation—the Romantic artwork. For as the Lady's gaze indicates, that artwork turns out to exist wholly for others, to lose in the process of public consumption the heterocosmic autonomy it claims for itself. It becomes a beautiful, lifeless body, "A gleaming shape," "a lovely face."

By making the Lady an emblem for the artist and the Lady's body an emblem for the artwork, then, this poem raises fundamental questions about both her femininity and her artistry. It questions the viability of both a femininity constituted through domestic, privatized subjectivity (the very femininity Tennyson later endorses in *The Princess*) and an aesthetic which insists on the privileged, autonomous nature of the artistic imagination (the aesthetic Hallam sees as basic to Tennyson's early work). As a feminine emblem of the artist and the artwork, the Lady undermines artistic autonomy by revealing it to be another form of the same kind of confining privacy which removes certain women from the public social world. As an artist and eventually an artwork representing the situation of a certain form of femininity, the Lady undermines the privatized subjectivity of that femininity by revealing it to be vulnerable to the same annihilating objectification Hallam sees the public meting out to the poet of sensation and his works.

This reciprocal identification of the woman with the artist and artwork not only calls into question Romantic ideals of femininity and artistry, but also leads to a subversion of the very private/public split that shapes those ideals. One example of such subversion is the Lady's voyage out of private Shalott toward public Camelot and the fear her appearance provokes among Camelot's knights. This fear seems to be provoked by the collapse of the split between Shalott and Camelot which the Lady's appearance signals, though it is finally allayed by Lancelot's blessing. Two features of the poem, however, suggest that his blessing does not fully restore the private/public split—that this split, indeed, was always at some level an illusory one.

The first of these features is the shift of seasons which occurs when the curse is invoked. The summery sun "dazzling through the leaves" and "blue unclouded weather" of Lancelot's ride give way to the autumn of the Lady's voyage:

> In the stormy east-wind straining,
> The pale yellow woods were waning,
> The broad stream in his banks complaining.
> Heavily the low sky raining
>   Over towered Camelot.

(118–122)

Lancelot and Camelot seem to appear sunlit only from within the confining shelter of the privacy of Shalott, its "Four gray walls, and four gray towers."

Once outside those walls, the Lady, unlike Plato's freed prisoner (and this is the key to the differences between them), finds a world just as gray as the one she has left. The radiance and intelligibility of Camelot turn out to have been just as illusory as the mysterious privacy and autonomy of Shalott. A single climate, a single social atmosphere, governs both realms, even though each appears to the other as its opposite.

The second feature which subverts the private/public split is the *combinatoire* of rhymes formed by the only proper names in the poem: Shalott, Lady of Shalott, Camelot, Lancelot. These rhymes (or repetitions, in the case of Shalott/Lady of Shalott) set up a pattern of identifications between the individuals named and the places they inhabit. The Lady and Lancelot are identified by rhyme or repetition both with the places they inhabit—Shalott and Camelot, respectively—and with the places where they appear as outsiders—Camelot and Shalott, respectively. They are also identified by rhyme with each other (Lady of Shalott/Lancelot), as are the places they inhabit (Shalott/Camelot). And each of these identifications is reinforced by a narrative element: habitation, Lancelot's ride by Shalott, the Lady's voyage to Camelot, the curse/blessing, the shift in climate. Thus, the differences (feminine/masculine, aesthetic/social, private/public) which the narrative establishes between the Lady and Lancelot and between Shalott and Camelot are deeply undermined by a set of identifications forged both by rhyming proper names and by certain elements in the narrative itself. These identifications suggest that there is something illusory about those differences, that the Lady's confinement is inseparable from Lancelot's dominating mobility, that Shalott is shadowy and mysterious precisely because Camelot constitutes itself as the realm of light and intelligibility. The difference the poem defines between these two individuals, then, is not reducible to an absolute biological dichotomy between women and men, nor is the difference between the places they inhabit reducible to some fundamental ontological or epistemological opposition between art and society. These differences, rather, are defined by the purely social split between private and public, and thus share in the ultimately artificial, ideological, illusory nature of that split. These differences are produced by the same social and economic forces that produce the private/public split, a set of forces that operate with particular strength in nineteenth-century England.

The two features which enable one to see through these differences—the narrative detail of the shift of seasons and the technical device of rhyming proper names—are, of course, background elements, neither being absolutely central to the drama the poem presents. These features contrast obliquely with the foreground situation, in which the Lady succumbs to the same "curse"—the private/public split which structures her self and her world—that they define as purely social, and thus ultimately ideological and illusory. They contrast more directly, however, with a third background element of the poem: its medieval setting. And this background contrast sets up a struggle between opposing readings of the foreground situation—between, that is, this reading and those less historically specific. One could argue, if one were to read the poem as a modernized medieval tale, that the setting renders irrelevant the nineteenth-century aesthetic and social categories fundamental to the reading of the poem proposed in this paper. Or one could argue that this setting, removing the narrative situation of the poem from the historical era in which the poem was written, is meant also to remove the artistic or even the sexual problems the poem poses from the flux of history, to suggest that those problems are simply inherent in art or sexual difference in general. Both of these arguments rely on an assumption implicit in the historical distance that the setting imposes between the narrative situation of the poem and that of its audience: the dilemma the poem describes is universal and supra-historical; it confronts all women and/or all artists in all eras. One can also argue, however, that the setting simply reinscribes at the level of the relation of the poem to its audience the fundamentally ideological and illusory differences between the Lady and Lancelot and between Shalott and Camelot, differences predicated upon the private/public split characteristic of nineteenth-century England. Like the magic mirror, the setting divides a shadowy world of images (the poem) from the surrounding contemporary social world of the audience, thus contradicting the implications of the shift of seasons and the rhyming proper names, which show those worlds to be fundamentally a single world, a world governed by a single climate and identified by insistently echoing names. As that climate and those names suggest, the setting does not utterly remove the poem from history, but simply veils the historical specificity of the poem within the same shadow—and by means of the same divisive strategy or "curse"—that isolates the Lady. (Indeed, considered as yet another avatar of the nineteenth-century private/public split, that setting, which appears to deny the historical specificity of the poem, turns out to be one of its most historically specific features.)

To read the poem as an updated medieval tale or as an allegory of a universal, unchanging artistic or sexual dilemma, to deny the historical specificity that the shift of seasons and the rhyming proper names oppose to the historical distance of the setting, is, then, to interpret the poem in somewhat the same way that Lancelot interprets the Lady's body—as "A gleaming shape" or "a lovely face." Although such a reading may be extremely attentive and sensitive, it will tend to ignore the privatized conditions of the production of the poem (including the audience's own complicity in creating those conditions) and to neutralize any threat the poem poses to those conditions by bestowing the blessing of an evaluation of the poem as a thing of beauty. It will restore to the poem the very autonomy which the Lady's death so radically questions.

In order to refuse such a reading, we must put ourselves in the Lady's place. We must risk a glance that focuses not on the illusory historical distance of the setting, but on the particular nineteenth-century aesthetic and sexual problems the poem confronts—the social contradictions that structure the Lady's subjectivity. To risk this glance means refusing the poem the autonomy which the setting claims and which the shift of seasons and the rhyming proper names question. It means refusing the naturalness or necessity of the Romantic connection between the feminine body and the artwork. And it means recognizing that the specific ideals of femininity and autonomy which Romantic artworks invoke are inseparable from the conditions of private isolation and public objectification which the Lady confronts. The "blue unclouded weather" that shines in the magic mirror where the Romantic artwork displays its feminine, autonomous emblems of itself is inevitably shadowed by the same "stormy east-wind straining" of isolation and objectification that shadows "The Lady of Shalott."

Notes

1. "On Some of the Characteristics of Modern Poetry, and on the Lyrical Poems of Alfred Tennyson," in *The Writings of Arthur Hallam*, ed. T. H. Vail Motter (New York, 143), 191.
2. *The Mirror and the Lamp* (Oxford Univ. Press, 1953), 272.
3. "The Intentional Structure of the Romantic Image," in *The Rhetoric of Romanticism* (Columbia Univ. Press, 1984), 7.
4. *Romantic Image* (London, 1971), 56–57.
5. *Victorian and Modern Poetics* (Univ. of Chicago Press, 1984), 60.
6. Buckley, *Tennyson: The Growth of a Poet* (Harvard Univ. Press, 1960), 49; Culler, *The Poetry of Tennyson* (Yale Univ. Press, 1977), 46; Shaw, *Tennyson's Style* (Cornell Univ. Press, 1976), 65.
7. Among critics who grapple with the question of the Lady's femininity, Lionel Stevenson (who does not see this question as the central issue of the poem) identifies her and other "high-born maidens" in Tennyson with the Jungian concept of the *anima*, an image always feminine in the male psyche ("The 'High-Born Maiden' Symbol in Tennyson," in *Critical Essays on the Poetry of Tennyson*, ed. John Killham [London, 1960], 135). Lona Mosk Packer extends Stevenson's interpretation of the poem by arguing that the Lady's contact with Lancelot represents an emotional and sexual fruition ("Sun and Shadow: The Nature of Experience in Tennyson's 'The Lady of Shalott,' " *Victorian Newsletter*, 25 [Spring, 1964], 4–8). Sandra Gilbert and Susan Gubar, in a brief analysis that in some ways anticipates my own, argue that the Lady is a *poète maudite*, a "*memento mori* of female helplessness, aesthetic isolation, and virginal vulnerability carried to deadly extremes" (*The Madwoman in the Attic: The Woman Writer and the Nineteenth-Century Imagination* [Yale Univ. Press, 1979], 618).
8. Discussing "Mariana," Christ writes: "Tennyson builds into the poem a blurring of subject and object that leaves ambiguous its organizing principle," *Victorian and Modern Poetics*, 59.
9. *Tennyson: The Unquiet Heart* (Oxford Univ. Press, 1980), 162.
10. *The Poems of Tennyson*, ed. Christopher Ricks (London, 1969), 11. 37–38. All subsequent quotations from Tennyson's poems will be taken from this text.
11. *The Republic*, trans. Francis McDonald Cornford (Oxford Univ. Press, 1941), 230. Culler also notes the analogy between Plato's allegory of the cave and the artist's situation in

his discussion of "The Lady of Shalott," but, proceeding from a notion of art much more generalized than my own, argues that the analogy is a false one, that the Lady is wrong to see her world of art as simply a confining realm of shadows (*Poetry of Tennyson*, 46). I would agree with Culler that the cave is not an apt analogy for *all* worlds of art, but it does fit, I believe, the specific world of art that I see Shalott representing: the privatized world of art of nineteenth-century English Romanticism.

Personification in "Tithonus"

Daniel A. Harris

"Tithonus" (1833–60) opens in deadmarch cadences that echo the lament of conventional elegy for the transience of earthly phenomena:

> The woods decay, the woods decay and fall,
> The vapours weep their burthen to the ground;
> Man comes and tills the field and lies beneath,
> And after many a summer dies the swan.

But far from being an expression of sorrow, these lines embody Tithonus' passionate envy of the very mortality he had once, in youth, sought to elude. The passage explodes in a helpless outcry against a wastage he cannot escape. "Me only cruel immortality/Consumes." This rage against fate—marked by the attenuation of the long "ee" vowel, the brutal insistence of the inverted syntax, and the bitter oxymoron "cruel immortality"—points to a bleak pain so intense that Tithonus would give up the eternal life for which most Victorians yearned. The nature of that pain is too complex to be codified as Tennyson's response to the death of his friend Arthur Henry Hallam; and the poem, even in its early version as "Tithon" (1833), is more than the "pendent to 'Ulysses' " (1833) that Tennyson deceptively named it; one notes, of course, that Tennyson's interest in the "Tithonus" theme begins with "The Grasshopper" (1830), a poem that patently predates Hallam's death.[1] To take Tithonus' rebellion against "cruel immortality" as a hyperbole for Tennyson's guilty hatred of his ongoing life—a life that continues despite Hallam's death—is to adopt an interpretation that has little to do with the poem's language or Tithonus' character. Tithonus' pain results not only from his lost virility and sexual victimization by Eos, the Dawn. It reflects as well his very mode of conceiving his experience: his pain is the consequence of his linguistic behavior. His oxymoron, "cruel immortality," hints at the problem: he personifies an abstraction, endows it with threatening power and hostile motive; simultaneously, the phrase is an epithet for the Dawn that, as such, partly reduces her to an abstraction even while it renders her—and her malevolence—infinite. To remember that the Dawn is already a

Excerpts from *Tennyson and Personification: The Rhetoric of "Tithonus,"* © 1986 by Daniel A. Harris, are reprinted by permission of UMI Research Press, Ann Arbor, MI.

phenomenon personified by Tithonus is to realize that Tennyson's monologist personifies throughout the poem, that he shifts uncertainly between abstraction, personification, and phenomenon, and that he sometimes cannot tell the difference between them. With such a complexity of contradictory linguistic procedures embedded in the term "immortality," it is no wonder that Tithonus cannot escape his condition, for he cannot recognize his jailor: his mind. The pain he experiences is that induced by a perceptual *cul de sac*, the paralysis of a mind that repeats its entrapment—and thus its self-grating frustrations—because it cannot find access to self-criticism.

What thus differentiates Tithonus' paralysis from that of other Tennysonian characters is neither the subject nor the emotional quality of his fixation. Rather, it is Tennyson's deliberate attention to the problem of personification itself, as, simultaneously, an issue in literary and psychological form. "Tithonus," his most concentrated and thorough study of personification, illustrates with supreme finesse the tension between individual and type that Hallam observes in Tennyson's method: "He collects the most striking phenomena of individual minds until he arrives at some leading fact, which allows him to lay down an axiom or law; and then working on the law thus attained, he clearly discerns the tendency of what new particulars his invention suggests, and is enabled to impress an individual freshness and unity on ideal combinations."[2] The "axiom or law" that recurs within "the most striking phenomena of individual minds," the constant element by which they are generalized, is like the contours of Tithonus' fixation; the accidents of emotional color give "individual freshness" to the type. This persistent concern with laws of behavior leads Tennyson to seek not simply a generalized psychology but, insofar as law suggests constraint, a focussed analysis of personification that simply extends his proclivity for representing individual states of mind. The great recognition embedded in "Tithonus," and preceded by his earlier studies of character, is that personification is a literary and psychological procedure that can "happen" to persons as well as to abstractions or inanimate things. While the trope is usually construed as the animate personating of concepts or non-human phenomena, "Tithonus" shows that personification, when applied to human beings, generates a reduction of self, a dehumanization whereby a figure becomes, as in Spenser, a "type" of Despair. The inanimating of the human that occurs in this depersonating complements the opposed dynamics of "conventional" personifying, which animates the non-human. In "St. Simeon Stylites" (1833), comparably, the monologist's obsession with gaining a sanctified fame leads him to depersonate himself into the very stone pillar on which he sits, the epithet by which he has his identity: he names himself, "I, Simeon of the pillar, by surname / Stylites, among men; I, Simeon, / The watcher on the column till the end" (lines 158–60).[3] The symbiosis of personification and depersonation is everywhere evident in "Tithonus." But when it is asked, "Of what is Tithonus the personification?" (for his name signifies no quality or emotion that he typifies), we must say that he personifies the personifying process itself, the habit, "axiom or law" by which the mind thinks in terms of personifications and transforms the objects of its perception, including the thinker's own thoughts and behaviors, into manifestations of a literary and psychological trope. It is crucial to observe that Tithonus actually personifies an otherwise inanimate dawn, endows it with animate spirit and bodily form, recreates it as a goddess and temptress:

> . . . with what another heart
> In days far-off, and with what other eyes
> I used to watch—if I be he that watch'd—
> The lucid outline forming round thee . . .
> (50–53)

It is Tithonus who envisages a "lucid outline" that supplies the phenomenon of dawn with figural form, that is, anthropomorphic identity; and although Tithonus takes the Dawn's bodily reality as a given, it is plain that Tennyson means the reader to understand the process of personifying by which Tithonus himself initiates the disaster of his own subsequent history and to criticize the imaginative distortions in which he engages.[4] Tithonus' act of inventing the Dawn by personification is but the chief of many occasions in the poem in which Tithonus personifies his experience. When he speaks of "Immortal age beside immortal youth" (22)—to give another instance—he links himself with the Dawn as paired personifications and implies (beyond his knowing) the trade-off in animation that the personifying process entails: he loses animation as the Dawn gains it. Part of the strength of "Tithonus," indeed, lies in Tennyson's attention to the linguistic character of the personifying act; it is a version of naming, Tennyson shows, and as such flourishes most readily in a social context (real or imagined) in which the personifier has opportunity to renew or alter his/her formulation of a phenomenon or abstraction into a personification that controls otherness, that element in experience that constantly challenges the "I" and its shaping powers. Where the isolated Mariana suffers a linguistic impoverishment that renders her fixation opaque even as it reveals the horrific starkness of her paralysis, Tennyson has adroitly situated his examination of personification within the genre of dramatic monologue, a form predicated on loquacity and thus on the identifiable recurrence of particularizing habits (such as personification) within the speech acts. The form invites (if it does not necessitate) linguistic interaction between monologist and auditor; Tithonus can thus be shown not once, but repeatedly, to be metamorphosing the dawn into his divine mistress, and to be doing so as a natural act of conversation rather than as the "poetic" act of invocation found in lyric. In this poem, as contradistinguished from all others in the genre, Tithonus' act of personifying virtually creates the auditor (the Dawn), an enabling act that permits his utterance to achieve its identity as a dramatic monologue: remove his perceiving of the dawn's "lucid outline" and his utterance has no auditor, his psyche no personal engagement with his lover.

The particular kind of personification in which Tithonus is embarked amplifies his fixation yet more. The Dawn is a divinity, a figure who, as by her sexual power, doubles, by virtue of the gods' authority, the magnetic attachment already intrinsic in the personifying process. From a psychological point of view, the divine status of the personification confirms the magical, or neurotic, aspect of the personifying process by enacting that personifying at the highest level. But from a theological perspective, something very different is afoot. "Tithonus" is a poem about theogony, god-formation: the Dawn's reality is posited solely as the consequence of a linguistic event in Tithonus' discourse, the envisaging and naming of her "lucid outline"; Tennyson's recourse to the rhetorical trope of personification as the foundation of theogony allows him to dramatize god-formation without reference to any transcendental ontology; and even though the Dawn, as Eos, has her sanction from both Hesiod and the Homeric *Hymn to Aphrodite*,[5] Tennyson explicitly treats her emergence as the function of Tithonus' private imagination. What cannot be missed here is Tennyson's daring: he has chosen to examine personification in the most abrasive context he could have risked, one which adopts a thoroughly skeptical and rationalist view of the gods by illustrating the typical human psychology—manifested in a common literary trope—by which the gods are brought into being. The poem exhibits a post-Enlightenment understanding of natural theology—not simply Tennyson's doubt that the natural universe itself, without benefit of divine revelation, implies the existence of supernatural deities, but also his view that the gods as envisaged are the product of human mentation, earthbound psychological needs. Tennyson at Cambridge, it will be recalled, was tutored by Connop Thirlwall and Julius Hare, both of them, then, in the rationalist phases of their careers; at a meeting of the Apostles at which the question was debated, "Is an intelligible First Cause deducible from the phenomena of the Universe?" he voted "no"; and his faith was both less coherent and less Christian than Hallam's.[6] Even at the end of his life, Tennyson felt, as his son indicates, that "our highest view of God must be more or less anthropomorphic."[7]

Tennyson's exposure of Tithonus' personification of the Dawn results from the tension between Tithonus' attitude towards the Dawn (she is a divinity) and Tennyson's (the dawn is a phenomenon that the protagonist has personified). That ironic discrepancy, in turn, derives from Tennyson's handling of dramatic monologue. "Tithonus" demonstrates more exactly than other dramatic monologues the manner in which the genre intermixes the two overlapping but divergent meanings of *prosopopoeia* designated by traditional rhetoric: personification vs. impersonation. Although Tithonus' acts of personifying are independently evident as rhetorical engagements in stereotypical thinking, it is not until they are understood in contradistinction to the poet's own activity as he impersonates Tithonus that they acquire negative connotations as participations in delusion; the credence Tithonus mistakenly grants his own personification is judged against Tennyson's conscious impersonation of his monologist. "Tithonus" exhibits both versions of *prosopopoeia*—personification and impersonation—in fruitful tension. Tennyson uses the author's impersonating of his monologist to expose his monologist's personification of the dawn as such: the Dawn appears as a fiction, not a goddess or a "real" character. The exposure happens because the poet's evident creation of a fictive character is structurally duplicated in the monologist's relations with his auditor. The fictive nature of Tithonus (hypothecated or projected by Tennyson) is carried over to insinuate the fictive nature of the Dawn (personified—rather than perceived—by Tithonus). In "Tithonus" the form of the dramatic monologue emphasizes what is already problematic, the Dawn's identity; alone in the tradition of the genre, the auditor is not a human being. Because Tithonus converses with a pagan "divinity" already construed by Tennyson's readership as a fiction, the tendency to view the Dawn as an invention is felt as a matter of course; when the Dawn's fictiveness is confirmed by Tithonus' language of personification, the parallel between Tithonus' creation of the Dawn and Tennyson's self-masking as Tithonus falls into place. Tennyson's self-disguise, in turn, an enactment of the basic strategy of dramatic monologue, is seen to be echoed in Tithonus' personification, and in such a manner that, by parallel, the act of personifying emerges as an act of projection. The similitude between impersonation and personification becomes a revealing difference. As Dallas rightly observes, impersonation is an act of the sympathetic imagination, while personification reflects egocentric, imperialist tendencies to absorb or co-opt.[8] Tennyson enters Tithonus, much as Browning disguises himself as Fra Lippo Lippi; but Tithonus crafts the Dawn in his own image. "Tithonus" thus shows through unusually sharp contrasts (Tennyson creates a human being; Tithonus invents a goddess) the self-mirroring structure that is intrinsic to dramatic monologue; the self-reflexiveness of the form itself constitutes the skeptical perspective in which the poem situates Tithonus' mental activity. It is the doubt-engendering analogical structure of dramatic monologue that casts Tithonus' credulous belief in the Dawn into disrepute.

The duplicated impersonations of "Tithonus" change the poem's method into its chief preoccupation. Because the self-mirroring relations are discordantly similar, not exactly correspondent, the poem illustrates the manner in which dramatic monologue questions the notion of "person." The existential status of the impersonated monologist (Tennyson's Tithonus) becomes no less subject to redefinition than the personification or "imaginary Person" (Tithonus' Dawn), and the poet's self-projection (such that his monologist becomes his personification) becomes an element that is structurally characteristic of all dramatic monologues, with the consequence that the speech of these poems is spoken doubly, from two sources simultaneously, but not with consonant meanings. The opening of "Tithonus" offers an outstanding instance of this mystery of speech in dramatic monologue: what is, to Tithonus, a language by which he envies "the power to die" is for Tennyson a language that mimics the lament of classical elegy to show his classical monologist Tithonus to be out of phase with classical literary forms.[9] The doubling structure evident in "Tithonus" shows the status of the auditor to be no less vexed: if the Dawn is invented, personified by Tithonus the speaker, are all auditors, even when fully human, merely the inventions of the speakers who address them? Are they but reflections of particular psychological features that the speakers attach to convenient outward forms?[10] In such a case, a common dramatic monologue would be typically composed of at least four characters: the actual speaker and the auditor whose image the speaker invents or surmises; the actual auditor and the speaker whose imagined image shapes the manner in which the auditor hears; add to these four figures various versions of the poet and the reader, and you have a case in which, as Yeats observed, "Mirror upon mirror mirrored is all the show" ("The Statues").

As Tithonus describes the Dawn's perpetual silence (lines 43–45), he understands that silence as being intrinsic to her beauty and her growth alike. Tennyson grounds his examination of silence in the specific dramatic context of Tithonus' crisis, and thus reflects the larger discovery of nineteenth-century culture that silence is a reality, not merely an absence or space. Tennyson takes advantage of his form to pass beyond the limits of lyric to the social context of speech: dramatic monologue perpetually promises a conversation between participants yet scotches the reality of such a dialogue; the form tempts the auditor into speech while denying its possibility. The Dawn's unresponsiveness thus surrounds Tithonus' utterance, and his speech seems fringed by hollowness and echo as it fails to provoke answer; Tennyson dramatizes the tension between speech and silence that is found in all discourse by situating it in the most charged context available, a dialogic relation between deity and mortal in which the deity refuses (?) to participate. Here "Tithonus" mordantly demarcates mortals from divinities in a fashion not typical of Western traditions: a man may achieve immortality (even without dying), may even have sexual intercourse with a goddess—but he cannot converse with her, cannot receive verbal reply, is constrained to know only her body.

Such a silence Tithonus cannot tolerate. Thus, he constantly seeks to make the Dawn talk: questions, requests and imperatives—forms meant to elicit responses—mark the syntax of both "Tithon" and "Tithonus." He strives, as it were, to break the very genre of dramatic monologue, to end the linguistic isolation of the monologist by compelling the auditor to answer. He strives, moreover, against the very subject matter Tennyson has chosen, for the dawning, in all its sublime loveliness, is a silent phenomenon; Tithonus, as he tries to force the dawn's personification to utter sound, unwittingly rebels against natural law. The contrast between the phenomenon and what Tithonus wants from the personification is so sharp that it is impossible to think Tennyson unconscious of forcing an exposure of the personifying process. Tithonus' effort to compel the Dawn's speech renders his utterance a power struggle; like many other dramatic monologues— Browning's "Andrea del Sarto," Tennyson's "Columbus"—this one is fought over language use: the monologist requests the audience to speak; the audience refuses to answer—or, indeed, to heed spoken language. Unlike Tennyson, who has a formal knowledge that the Dawn as an imagined figment *cannot* speak, Tithonus has only a psychological understanding by which he thinks she might speak but *will* not: he feels a problem of motive or personal compatibility where Tennyson simply works within generic constraints. Tithonus daily repeats his effort to make the Dawn give verbal response (lines 43–44), obsessively refusing to acknowledge that human discourse can fail to provoke response; as Tennyson contrasts Tithonus' obsessive linguistic repetition with the natural repetitions of the Dawn's behavior, he correlates the recurrence of Tithonus' linguistic needs with the poem's other major cycles. What troubles Tithonus in the Dawn's disappearance, as she vanishes into the dawn she personifies, is his lost opportunities to compel her response.

At the end, then, Tithonus talks to no one, air; his dramatic monologue has become a soliloquy.[11] This internal change in the poem's form is the outward sign that he has again failed to impose his will on the goddess; Tennyson's careful inversion of the pattern of Wordsworth's "Lines Composed A Few Miles Above Tintern Abbey"—a poem that moves from soliloquy to dramatic monologue—shows the loss of community that accompanies his linguistic inadequacy. Tithonus must use the Dawn's visual appearance alone—and not any supposition of speech—as the basis from which to deduce her emotional responses. Three times he refers to her tears (lines 26, 45, 46), as if wishing to believe their conventional meaning. Yet he must fail to credit her sorrow, and not only because those tears—when understood literally as the personified metaphors of the morning dew—are affectively neutral. He fails, further, because our knowledge of another's emotion—or our justification in imputing it—depends on our assumption of a shared language use. Signs, in the absence of a linguistic context, become ambiguous. While the Dawn's tears may seemingly signify her affectionate compassion and sorrow, she cannot—or will not—confirm such an interpretation verbally, and the absence of a definite reading heightens Tithonus' anxiety. Thus Tennyson deftly brings Tithonus to acknowledge psychologically that the Dawn *does* not do, by nature, what dramatic monologue, by genre, formally insists she *cannot* do: speak. (It is part of Tithonus' failure that he never recognizes that the Dawn does not do what the phenomenon of dawn cannot.) This is the critical juncture at which Tennyson, theologically alert to the spawning of false deities, shows Dawn the goddess to be merely Tithonus' personification of dawning. The auditor's silence, construed by Tithonus as the silence of the goddess, is also, for Tennyson, the silence of the trope. For Tennyson, speech is the final test of *prosopopoeia*, the test by which the visual metamorphoses of an object or idea into the trope succeed or fail; speech reveals whether the trope is an imaginative truth or a transparent fiction. Tithonus' inability to endow his personification with voice is Tennyson's sign that his character cannot create another "I," that Tithonus can only envisage an externalized projection of himself—and that, a corporeal image only. Tithonus, Tennyson suggests, cannot tell a goddess from a personification.

In two gorgeous passages (lines 34–38, 50–61), Tennyson twice shows Tithonus personifying the dawn; the poet's repetition is as deliberate as the monologist's is not. The first passage occurs as Tithonus addresses the auditor of his utterance; the second recalls the occasion of his original personifying: together, they render Tithonus' personifying as an historically continuous activity, a persistent habit of mind. Tennyson here makes two major deviations from the typical dramatic monologue. First, whereas monologists rarely allude to earlier encounters with their auditors (as if to do so would threaten the reality of the present conversation), Tithonus vividly recollects the first time he saw the dawn as an anthropomorphic goddess (lines 50–61). While the intensity of his memory partly measures his flamboyant mourning for lost sexual joy, it also reflects his ongoing need for a conventional speech situation through which he can not only reiterate his request for deliverance but experience a semblance of human intercourse: *then*, in that magical past time, the Dawn seemed most capable of speech (if only "Whispering"). Tennyson's second, and more significant, deviation emerges from this first one. Whereas other monologists can assume their auditors' prior existence as human beings, bodily, sentient, and intelligent, Tithonus invents his auditor out of insubstantial light and air. This fictive quality in the Dawn, twice created from scratch for the reader, cannot be mistaken; whereas most monologists, taking their auditors' bodily presence as a given and thus progressing to other topics of conversation, Tithonus dwells on the very existence of the auditor as the primary material of his discourse. And so, from a different perspective, does Tennyson: in the second passage, he demarcates the historical moment when Tithonus first personifies the dawn as his auditor. While all monologists engage in the dynamics of transference, endow their auditors with particular psychological images and thus "make" them as imaginative constructs, Tithonus' attempt to alter the dawn from natural phenomenon into anthropomorphic auditor is a more radical imaginative gesture, one which suggests the tyranny of his desire, his will to reshape the natural world.

Tennyson's stress on Tithonus' invention of Dawn constitutes his central conceptual revision of the poem. The crucial motif of Tithonus watching "The lucid outline forming round thee" (line 53) does not appear until the final version of 1860.[12] The Dawn—a "real" person or goddess in "Tithon" and its drafts (see "Tithon," lines 41–46)—has been revised into a personification. The final poem shows Tithonus' primary act of personifying as he simultaneously bestows upon the dawn a bodily shape, sex-casts the shape female, and, altering "it" to "you," animates it.[13] That the legendary Dawn may pre-exist this individual occasion of theogony disguised as a divine *parousia* is irrelevant: at the least, Tithonus envisages his personal embodiment of a general notion, imagines the Dawn's private visitation. In Tennyson's emphasis on that "lucid outline," Tithonus' personifying appears as a process of hallucinating: the dawning light, construed as a fire immanent in the Dawn, emanates from her invisible body to envelop her in a shimmering corolla which forms as it illumines her shape. This central hallucination is the most complex and dramatic instance of a phenomenon frequent in Tennyson's poetry; compare "Tiresias" (lines 42–43) and "St. Simeon Stylites" (lines 199–206), as well as "Rizpah" and "Romney's Remorse." But what differentiates the handling of hallucination in "Tithonus" from that in the other poems is that, instead of simply dramatizing the hallucination, Tennyson makes it both the monologist's primary psychological focus and the center of the poem's problematic quality as a dramatic monologue spoken by a mortal to a goddess/personification.

Tithonus' initial hallucination is of the schematized abstraction of the human form; not until later does her two-dimensional outline gain contour, mass, detail. If he conceives the idea of the Dawn's person ("thee") prior to her personified embodiment, he does so just barely: his notion of a goddess in the dawn is virtually dependent upon her anthropomorphic manifestation.[14] Tennyson uses the word "lucid" to accentuate the wavering fluidity that characterizes Tithonus' hallucination.[15] Yet Tithonus recounts this emergence of figural shape from a "fluid haze of light" with a disconcerting credulity; he knows less of his own mind's capacity for invention than the speaker of the "Ode to Memory," who consciously seeks to shape the *kind* of personification of Memory that visits him (lines 8–14). Once Tithonus has personified the Dawn—and not until then—he can marvel at the "mystic change" of her diurnal dissolution into the morning lights. In the passages above, Tennyson's careful counterbalancing of past and present acts of personifying correspond with the embodying and the vanishing of the Dawn's figure as Tithonus endows "her" with human shape. What Tennyson here illustrates is that Tithonus, fascinated by the magical vanishing of the Dawn's body, takes for granted, as a reality, what he has initially invented: a person(ifica-tion). The personifier, having made his trope, discards the psychological truth of his mind's fictionalizing and thus becomes enthralled by the externalized form of his projection.

All subsequent animations—Tithonus' imputation of bodily action, will, personality, speech capacity—depend upon this initial positing of the Dawn's "lucid outline." Tithonus' personifying thus turns not on his presuming a spirit in the dawn (the usual premise of "animism") but upon an antithetical mental process, the transference of his own human shape to a foreign phenomenon: belief in the Dawn's animated spirit *follows* his creation of "her" body. The emphatic corporeality of Tithonus' attempt to bring the dawn "nearer to a resemblance" with himself[16] more specifically indicates Tennyson's kinship with Locke. As Locke remarks, it is our perception of the "outward figure" that we make "essential to [our notion of] the human species"; "it is the shape, as the leading quality, that seems more to determine that species [of humankind], than a faculty of reasoning, which appears not at first."[17]

While the forging of the Dawn's body might seem difficult, Tennyson shows it to be astonishingly simple. Tithonus merely overrides exterior reality, reorganizes his perceptual experience into a completely different imaginative entity modelled on his own material body; we may compare the brashness of his procedure with the shy cautiousness of Tennyson's speaker in predicating Hallam's body in *In Memoriam*. As Tithonus designates the dawn an anthropomorphic form, he virtually renames it. In the language of Locke's philosophic nominalism, he provides the dawn with a new "nominal essence"; he takes the liberty to do so because, in Locke's view, "the species of things to us are nothing but the ranking them under distinct names, according to the complex ideas in *us*, and not according to precise, distinct, real essences in *them*."[18] In this metonymic action, he detaches his own image so that he can transfer it elsewhere, dissolves the exterior phenomenon so that it seems a blank vacancy needing new definition, and inscribes that void with his own ready image. By the time the Dawn's "dim curls kindle into sunny rings," the metamorphosis of the dawn into the personified Dawn is both complete and invisible, for the process of decomposing the phenomenon and recreating it in hallucinated human form seems perceptual rather than mythical.

Tithonus' metamorphosis, although it has received scant attention, is no less significant than the Dawn's "mystic change" into the dawn. In Tithonus the common interdependence of body and mind dissolves. In consequence, he periodically cannot say "I," state his selfhood. He speaks of himself in the third person (lines 8, 11–14, 52)—far more often than Ulysses, who does so only once (line 1). Thus separated from his utterance, he duplicates as a *person* his earlier failure to attribute speech capacity to a *personification*, the Dawn: without the sense of language as an integral part of his system, he cannot be sure that he manifests the primary sign of anthropomorphic life, and in his life *like*ness he resembles nothing so much as a personification, a fiction that is neither an idea nor a person.[19] In this linguistic self-division that repeats the poem's chief rhetorical and formal problem, Tithonus thinks himself both a personification and a person: at one moment personifying himself as "Immortal age," he next differentiates his "I" ("And all I was in ashes," line 23). He doubts his historical continuity— "if I be he"—and thus, in his ahistorical character, imitates the atemporal nature of personifications.[20] Ultimately, in the extremity of depersonation, he loses cognizance of his bodily coherence: in line 58 ("Mouth, forehead, eyelids, growing dewy-warm"), no possessive pronoun controls the ablative construction; like Yeats' Leda "laid in that white rush" of the swan's power, he can no longer distinguish his body from the Dawn's. The exchange of bodies—hardly the stereotypical fusion of subject and object in sexual bliss—illustrates in starkly literal terms how personifying expends the personifier.

Tithonus' efforts in depersonation fail, however: language ultimately cannot cloak his bodily decrepitude any more than he can provide the Dawn's personified body with linguistic animation. As the Dawn's "rosy shadow" brightens to illumine his "gray shadow" (lines 66, 11), Tithonus is compelled to see his "wrinkled feet" (line 67)—not the attributes of a personified abstraction exempt from age but the grim corporeal metonyms of the constant physical decline which he, unlike the Dawn in her self-recreating cycle, can never escape. Tithonus is thus pushed to hate what he most adores—the Dawn's gorgeous lights, her beautiful "mystic change" that shows him his person's ugliness; and in this mean twisting of his affections he again suffers punishment for misconstruing his erotic devotion. His last attempt to avoid knowledge of his depersonation ambiguously admits that only the death of his bodily person can halt his consciousness:

> Release me, and restore me to the ground.
> Thou seëst all things, thou wilt see my grave;
> Thou wilt renew thy beauty morn by morn,
> I earth in earth forget these empty courts,
> And thee returning on thy silver wheels.
>
> (72–76)

Tithonus' temporary acceptance of mortality is less significant here than the way in which he dissolves his body: echoing the burial service, he renames his body "earth" and then buries his depersoned epithet in the earth itself. "I earth in earth," a triumph of undifferentiated matter, exposes the illusion of animation on which personification rests, for Tithonus—no longer animating nature as he had the dawn—seeks from earth its refuge of inanimacy, insentience.[21] More ironic still is the verb "forget." Tithonus will stop thinking about the personified Dawn only because he "forgets" the daylight, not because he has died and has no sensory or cognitive powers. Thus, he implicitly ascribes a continued consciousness to himself after death (even though he imagines a mental oblivion *like* death), and in so doing he hypothesizes a continued life during which, having forgotten the Dawn, he can later remember her and thus resume the cycle of fixation. Like Maud's lover, who thinks that, dead, his "heart would hear her and beat, / Were it earth in an earthy bed" (*Maud*, I.919–20),[22] Tithonus is too proudly and neurotically committed to his image-making power to surrender his mental activity to death. The last line renders wonderfully his continued obsession with his personification. Although it partly embodies Tithonus' present desire for the Dawn's return ("this evening," half a day away), it also shows the Dawn, paradoxically, as the future object of Tithonus' forgetfulness: Tennyson, *showing* what is to be forgotten (= remembered) and making the absented thought present, again implies Tithonus' inability to forget. Tacitly, he suggests that Tithonus' avowed desire for release is, ambivalently, balanced by his helpless wish to remain the Dawn's thrall.[23] Because Tithonus can neither die nor forget his personified Dawn, he becomes a rhetorical icon, a personification of the personifying process. Like Spenser's Despair—who cannot kill himself, lest, according to the canons of personification, he cease to be his name, the embodiment of living despair (*The Faerie Queene*, I.ix.54)[24]—Tithonus must perpetually re-enact his habit of personifying.

The Dawn's "mystic change"—so dangerously alluring to Tithonus— is what most engages Tennyson's intellectual attention. Tithonus' phrase, which Tennyson did not introduce until the 1860 text, ironically indicates, beneath Tithonus' baffled awe, his own experiment in personification, an experiment which—elasticizing the supposed fixity of personifications into an "airy thinnesse"—poses sharp questions about the trope's nature and function. In dealing with the "mystic change" in the Dawn's body, Tennyson consciously makes the Dawn a hybrid "figure" that perpetually changes from dawn the phenomenon into Dawn the personification—and back again into nature. This diurnal cycle, reflecting the rhythms of Tithonus' obsession, renders the Dawn a conception "eterne in mutabilitie." Unlike Spenser's metamorphic Nature, however, who remains a figure literally veiled from our inspection, subject only to third-person narrative (*The Faerie Queene*, VII.5) the fluid Dawn appears dramatically, through Tithonus' immediate experience, as an elusive principle of shape-changing that must be confronted as such; indeed, she is magical to him precisely because her change *is* "mystic." To what extent, Tennyson asks, can a personification become diaphanous and still regain figural form without compromising the underlying presence of the trope? How far can the trope be dissolved without destroying the poem's generic character as a dramatic monologue that, depending on dialogic relations for its form, nevertheless has an auditor who is a personification rather than a human being? The alteration in physical form between Dawn and dawn parallels a crucial fluctuation in the manner of conceiving the Dawn herself: to Tithonus, she appears as a goddess; to Tennyson, as a personification. The paradox in the ironic intersection of these categories of interpretation is saliently augmented by the Dawn's changing relation to the phenomenal referent (the dawn) from which she derives. Tennyson begins with the Dawn as standard personification: as her horses thrillingly "beat the twilight into flakes of fire" (line 42), making the dawn flash from the sparks of their hoofs, she is a principle of causation, she "makes the dawn happen." Yet, aloof from her effect, returning each evening on her "silver wheels," the Dawn is plainly the goddess *of* the dawn, a personified deity whose identity is paradoxically not bound by the phenomenon from which she takes her name; already Tennyson strays from conventional usage. Contradicting this second view, however, in which the Dawn transcends her referent, Tennyson poses a still more radical vision: the dawn is immanent within the Dawn's body, emanates from it with a fiery intensity. Here, as the figural form and the material phenomenon conjoin, the Dawn *is* the dawn, as in metaphor; the goddess no longer transcends her occasion for being. Next, in a continuation of this equation that significantly redistributes its emphases, the Dawn also becomes the spirit *in* the dawn as the phenomenon itself envelopes her person in the brightening halo that becomes morning, "the glow that slowly crimsoned all / Thy presence." With wry skepticism Tennyson juxtaposes each of these relations between spirit and matter. Showing their incompatibility, he both induces and replicates some typical Victorian anxieties about the unstable definitions of matter, the order and regulation of Nature and natural phenomena, the unknown limitations of consciousness, and the problematic "location" of spirit (or mind) in any ontology that seeks to integrate spirit with matter.

To destabilize his trope, Tennyson must first detach the Dawn from the periphrastic tradition he inherits. Following the post-Homeric *Hymn to Aphrodite*, which renders the Dawn as a full dramatic character, Tennyson undermines her status as a trope by giving her a naturalized, humanized body whose details he treats realistically. Tennyson can envisage such a paradoxical fusion because he denies the convention that personifications are defined by their attributes. Stressing a reciprocity between personification and referent, Tennyson sees the danger that "attributes" fail to remain indices of the phenomenon personified; they become the possessions of the anthropomorphic personification. As such, detached and abstracted from the referent, they cancel the value of the referent as well as its presence; limiting consciousness of the referent's existence, they alter the use of the aspect usurped—as Aurora's "golden lockes" (*FQ.*, I.xi.51) signify her Caucasian beauty rather than the dawning sky. Tennyson eliminates "attributes" altogether from the personified Dawn, and the daring procedure engages him in a difficult choice. Either he must represent the Dawn, anarchically, as a personification having no pictorial or iconographic relation to the phenomenon she arbitrarily symbolizes; or he must have the Dawn signify that relation through the only other material available: her own body. Tennyson's stress on the "mystic change" in the Dawn's material form thus results logically from his quest for new modes of personifying.

The mimetic requirements for personifying a time unit are especially stringent: the concept of duration dictates that the Dawn embody a particular (but shifting) period of early morning; it must be mutable—growing in brightness and intensity from night to day—without compromising its basic identity. Tennyson, however, deliberately exploits this difficulty in representational accuracy: the poem ends with Tithonus' vision of the Dawn's diurnal return each *evening*, the wheels of her chariot silvered in twilight. With this exposure of the Dawn's split identity, Tennyson points towards an animating spirit which paradoxically disappears yet survives: where, and in what form, is such a spirit located? It will be useful, in exploring such questions, to consider Tennyson's debts to Keats' "To Autumn." Tennyson—personifying a time period, rendering the Dawn mutable, juxtaposing a phenomenon against its personification—develops the very methods of "To Autumn." Keats' speaker stresses bodily metamorphosis throughout: he conceives a time period which changes imaginatively from a natural phenomenon ("Season of mists," line 1) to a perceived personification ("Who hath not seen thee oft amid thy store?," line 12); the personified body of Autumn—lovingly coaxed into shape by meticulous naturalistic detail in the first stanza—then vanishes in the last, much as Tithonus' Dawn dissolves. So tactful is this progression that the initial personifying—"Close bosom-friend" (line 2)—is hardly noticed. Keats' interest in transformation of course recalls Wordsworth's indeterminate fusion of "huge stone" and "sea-beast" to resemble the aged leech-gatherer in "Resolution and Independence" (IX), whose marvellous simile is far more wily in its understanding of personification than Wordsworth's theoretical rejection of the trope. But where Wordsworth generates a static configuration of merged objects in which, he rightly says, the "aged Man . . . is divested of so much of the indication of life and motion as to bring him to the point where the two objects unite and coalesce in just comparison," Keats' image radiates a slow-motion but incessant kinesis in which the figural instability coincides with a richly original treatment of time as observable metamorphosis; his conception passes beyond that of Wordsworth as well as of Thomson and Collins.[25] For the time period of Autumn is itself represented as both a daily transformation (as morning mists burn off by noon, as afternoon darkens to dusk) and the annual transition from late summer to early winter. Always distrustful of fixity, lured by oxymoron, Keats here uses the fluid, overlapping simultaneity of time-categories to approximate the rhythms of eternity.

"Tithonus" diverges from its immediate poetic model because Tennyson pursues abrasions which "To Autumn" skirts. This is particularly true of the "double conformity" which both Keats and Tennyson acknowledge in personifying temporal phenomena. Where Keats observes the necessary mimetic constraints, Tennyson intentionally violates them, and he learns his violations from Keats' caution. Tennyson, admiring Keats' suppleness in managing Autumn's vanishing so that the personification remains consistent with natural law, also sees the advantages of breaching such a conformity. The end of "Tithonus"—"And thee returning on thy silver wheels"—exposes precisely the collision between trope and referent (here, the Dawn's inappropriate return in evening) that Keats so deftly conceals. How the Dawn passes "the sunny *interval* of day" ("Tithon," line 26; my italics) and then returns at dusk is the kind of question Keats eludes when he retracts Autumn's

temptation to "think"—inconsistently—of Spring's music. Tennyson focuses the inconsistency of the Dawn's return yet more sharply by stressing,
as throughout, her corporeal presence: Tithonus' picture of her chariot's suave
return has a sumptuous tactility. Here, too, Tennyson departs from Keats,
who accepts the periphrastic convention that personifications have bodies
more in theory than in actual representation. Yet Keats' own aim in minimiz-
ing bodily form, the "lucid outline" stressed by Locke and Tennyson—note
that Autumn has typical poses but virtually no physical characteristics, no
insignia—springs from the desire to avoid all kinds of material fixity. Rejecting the eighteenth-century demand that a personification be a single clear
image, Keats represents Autumn in stanza two as *several* bodies, multiple
personifications, "alternative images, one after the other."[26] Even this innovation, however, displaying a critical shift of interest to the processes of the
personifying mind, skirts the problems of mental behavior and corporeal
animation Tennyson seeks to broach: for, with several versions of Autumn
instead of one, the individuated psychological habits of a distinct "personality" cannot emerge to suffer a self-contradictory dissolution. Tithonus by
contrast needs the Dawn's bodily coherence as an individuated causal agent
and as the fetishistic object of his "erotic devotion." His demand that the
Dawn *be* the phenomenon she functions to express is precisely what makes
so startling her transcendence of her fixed time designation. Where Keats'
relaxed, self-possessed speaker has the "negative capability" to be "in uncertainties, Mysteries, doubts, without any irritable reaching" for a stable image
of Autumn,[27] Tithonus *must* see the "lucid outline forming" around the
Dawn; tyrannically, he can tolerate no "mystic change" but hers. Where
Keats' speaker democratically shares his commonplace perception with others
(line 12), Tithonus claims that his vision of the Dawn is private, privileged,
marked by that specialness which the possessive imagination typically demands. Both poems concern the diaphanous disappearance of kinetic personifications: but where Keats' speaker serenely accepts the diffusion of Autumn's
various figures into a disembodied "music" (line 24), Tithonus experiences
the dissolution of the Dawn's anthropomorphic body with the deep anxiety
of personal loss.

Although "Tithonus" has a distinct theological cast, engendered both
by Tithonus' address to a "goddess" and by Tennyson's own manipulations
of personification, Tennyson's interest in theology may seem unlikely to some
readers; so also, the link between personification and incarnation. The curious
alignment of "Tithonus" with High Church and rationalist developments in
religious speculation results from the poem's manner and style; it confirms
a theological—not merely "religious"—sensibility in Tennyson that commentators have normally denied him. One need not contend that Tennyson
pursued contemporary theological debate as avidly as Browning—or that,
like Hallam, he kept abreast of Biblical criticism—to see that the theological
ramifications of "Tithonus" emerge from Tennyson's handling of dramatic

monologue. For Tennyson was theologically inquisitive. At Cambridge he trained with Connop Thirlwall and Julius Hare during the years they were translating Niebuhr's radical *History of Rome* (1828–32), a work certainly familiar to Hallam, and promulgating central works of Germanic criticism that would have a major role in the controversy over *Essays and Reviews* years later; he had read Locke and Hume.[28] Long before Browning's "An Epistle Concerning the Strange Medical Experience of Karshish," Tennyson's treatment of Lazarus in *In Memoriam* (section XXXI [1833]) manifests his familiarity with the fundamental problems of literary analysis on which the Higher Criticism rests: the possibility of problematic *lacunae* in canonical texts, the unreliability of authorship, the uncertainty of narration. Similarly, Tennyson in "The Vision of Sin" (1842) exploits an indeterminate syntax—"God made himself an awful rose of dawn," (lines 50, 224)—to create rich doctrinal ambiguities on the same incarnationist theme as "Tithonus." To rationalize the syntax is to see in the omission of the preposition some fine theological ramifications. In "God made [for] himself an awful rose of dawn," a transcendent deity severs himself (like Spenser's Aurora) from the natural phenomenon he makes solely to pleasure himself; in "God made himself [into] an awful rose of dawn," He metamorphoses himself pantheistically into material nature, depersonates himself much as Tithonus' Dawn becomes the dawn or as Hallam becomes the child of his Elder Brother. The entire line, offering contradictory notions about the location and characteristic activity of God's divine spirit that Tennyson leaves unreconciled, encompasses all the shiftiness of personification found in "Tithonus" and shows Tennyson's attentiveness to matters of doctrine.

Classical rhetoric terms personification, and regards as the consequence of normative mental processes, what the Christian tradition names the central and unique event in world history, Christ's Incarnation. Personification incarnates and thus makes realizable an idea or phenomenon, humanizes it with body and mind. "The Idea must be cloathed in a bodily Form, to make it visible and palpable to the gross Understanding," writes the eighteenth-century philosopher Fordyce, typifying a standard viewpoint. Wordsworth, while denying that abstract personifications have the "flesh and blood" he demands of poetic language, nevertheless claims that poetry itself, as the very epitome of personification, is "incapable to sustain her existence without sensuous incarnation."[29] The trope mediates between realms presumed opposite or disjunct—mind and world, God and humankind: as Hallam remarks, "the great effect of the Incarnation . . . was to render love for the Most High a possible thing."[30] Christ, incarnating God, makes Him comprehensible; in parallel fashion, the personified Dawn permits Tithonus to love the phenomenon by means of her "person." Consider this mediation, first, as it operates in common personification.

The trope postulates no necessary connection between the referent (dawn), the linguistic signifier (Dawn), and the signified (Dawn the personification): the putative relation between phenomenon and anthropomorphic personification must be presumed on faith; similarly, the composite figure of the god-man is presumed to incarnate the divine spirit. The repetition of the *same* word in different contexts (dawn, Dawn) seemingly renders identical the discontinuous worlds of phenomenon, signifier, and signified. Repetition generates, while pretending to simulate, this critical coalescence between experience, language, and truth by which personification comes to seem an Adamic language; as Fordyce says, "Things are delineated to us not in Show or Fiction merely, but according to their Realities and specific Natures. . . . For, whereas there is only an *Arbitrary* Connection between [normal language] and the Ideas it is brought to express, there is an obvious, a *Natural* Connection and Relation, between this kind of Language [personification] and the Ideas conveyed by it; nay; the Language is evidently built upon that Connection or Similitude."[31] Personification thus appears to encapsulate that elusive "double conformity" whereby mind and "reality" achieve a true coincidence in language; "nominal essences," so insidious in their underlying fictiveness, are finally ratified as "real essences," since word and thing (Dawn and dawn, Christ as divine spirit and as flesh) become the same.

Fordyce gains his faith in that "*Natural* Connection" between word and referent, however, by conveniently ignoring the unnatural introjection of a completely extraneous third term which invisibly joins the disparate parts of the trope in apparent seamlessness. This is the *hidden* referent from which, as a Lockean analysis of the trope makes evident, all personifications derive: the human body. Whatever the exterior referent (tree, dawn, pity), it is the human image which links the exterior referent to both the word and the personification. Two metaphoric transferences occur in personification to make this coalescence plausible. The word "dawn," subjected to the person-imagining impulse, becomes the name of a personification (Dawn); the hidden referent, the anthropomorphic image, next permeates the signifier (Dawn), which, because it is the same word as both the personification and the designated phenomenon, intrudes the anthropomorphizing element into the phenomenon so that the phenomenon ultimately seems incarnate in the person(ification). The first and indispensable change is a nearly untraceable occurrence within language, the "mystic change" in the *speaker's* field of reference upon which all personification rests: Tithonus transforms the general noun (dawn) into an anthropomorphic signifier by transferring his human image to it.

When personification is renamed Incarnation, the translation of terms seems initially improbable. What makes the Incarnation unrecognizable as personification is that Christ the anthropomorphic signifier of God's spirit already pre-exists his Incarnation as Jesus, in the sense that, because God has already been anthropomorphized by His self-projection into humankind (Genesis 1:26), there appears to be no difference between Christ's anthropomorphic form and God's. In the same way, the God of "The Vision of Sin"

cannot be thought to depersonate himself into the dawn unless his prior
change from human idea into anthropomorphic deity is already assumed. In
this transcendental anthropomorphism, the Incarnation thus confirms the
original act of anthropomorphizing the divine spirit: this second anthropomorphizing conceals the first by purporting to be unique, and it paradoxically
conceals it by repeating it. Even in the Broad Church theology of Thomas
Arnold, the Incarnation creates a similitude with humankind that reiterates,
specifically in its anthropomorphism, the similitude with God: "They do not
violate it [God's commandment against the making of graven images], who
represent him . . . under an image which he himself has sanctioned—the
human form of the man Christ Jesus. For *this* similitude of God, we have
God's warrant."[32] Because Christ gives anthropomorphic form to a spirit
which is itself construed anthropomorphically, even before the Incarnation,
the pretext of a continuous relation between referent and signifier already
obtains: this is the business that secular personification always needs to
accomplish and that "Tithonus" exhibits so acutely. The Incarnation proposes
to personify the divine spirit, whereas it actually duplicates the original act
of anthropomorphizing; in substituting the hidden referent (the human body)
for the supposed referent (the spirit), it can claim to be the only case of
personification in which "referent" (really, the hidden referent) and signifier
(Christ's anthropomorphic form) are the same. Further, Christ's divinity
newly designates the hidden referent of the human body as being mortal or
immortal; in secular personification, the distinction is less apparent, but
nonetheless operative. When the hidden referent is mortal, the use of the
human form to make a personification (as for Tithonus) becomes a kind of
self-deification, the gaining of a surrogate immortality. When the hidden
referent is sacralized as the mystical body of Christ, the use of the human
image merely *seems* to privilege the mortal body because Christ condescends—
I use Hopkins' hieratic and precise verb—to enter it; the real message is that
Christ's consecrated body annuls the value of the "lucid outline" he assumes.

   "Tithonus" is a Janus-poem of signal importance. Capitalizing on Keats'
techniques of fluid personification, implying the main points of argument in
Tractarian debates about the Eucharistic presence, it symbolizes the long
historical transition from the "*animating* Metaphor" (Spence's term for personification) to Tylor's animism. The shift from one conception of spiritual
embodiment to the other is marked by the change from the participial
"animating" to its abbreviated noun: eighteenth-century theory concerns
the process, normally conscious, of bestowing life; the attitudes towards
incarnation discussed by Tylor, like the instances of "serious personification"
adduced by Priestley, presume a spiritual life already present in rock or tree,
seemingly independent of human imputation. If animism, as the theory
develops before Durkheim, too little heeds the rhetorical activity of the
human imagination upon which religious structures partly rest, and if
Spence's formulation, typical of his age, too much withholds credence from

the world of spirits as such, "Tithonus"—remarkably—presents both views simultaneously.

What Tennyson constructs as Tithonus' unconscious deployment of an *"animating* Metaphor" is also Tithonus' active belief in animism, construed as a natural or unconscious, not artificial, habit of thought which aptly reflects (instead of inventing) the natural world. In this ironic conflict between skepticism and naiveté one discerns not only Tennyson's roots in the Enlightenment but his understanding that dramatic monologue is the very form of skeptical inquiry. It is the form that most offers its author—as Browning's "A Death in the Desert" also shows—the opportunity to present the improvisatory fullness of a major cultural habit as individually experienced while maintaining the privilege and capacity to judge and criticize the event by rationally exposing the behavior, the modes of thought of a monologist whose responses are ultimately construed as exemplary, not unique.[33] Tennyson's manipulation of dramatic monologue is comparable, decades later, to the anthropological efforts to chart disinterestedly (?) the lineaments of foreign thought processes that are inaccessible even to their thinkers—while still attempting to render those imaginative habits in their experienced truth; indeed, from the time of Cowper's "The Negro's Complaint" and Wordsworth's "The Complaint of a Forsaken Indian Woman," dramatic monologue has quite properly exhibited a particular predilection for anthropological "subjects." The speakers, distanced in space or historical time, are nevertheless—like "St. Simeon Stylites" or Browning's "Pictor Ignotus"—cultural models of normative behavior. Tennyson's ability to perceive personification as a major trope of collective religious experience—a perception certainly abetted by Hallam's comments on the process of transference that links the trope with anthropomorphism—is, in "Tithonus," the aspect which, in its critical insight, its synthetic power, and its subtle anticipations of future theory, most gives evidence of Tennyson's mental rigor. It is but a fortuitous confirmation of Tennyson's vision that, in an historical spectrum, "Tithon" (1833) of its subsequent revisions emerge roughly midway in Freud's quotation (1913) of Tylor's citation (1871) from Hume's remarks (1757) on the anthropomorphizing imagination.[34]

The depth of the poem's contemporaneity marks its magnitude: the drafts of "Tithonus," increasingly capacious in their handling, encompass both the Tractarian controversies and the emergence (to which Tylor's *Primitive Culture* greatly contributes) of mythography as a modern discipline. "Tithonus" focuses both movements and suggests their interrelationship, not only by pointing to their common origin in the historical revaluation of metaphoric procedure that "Tithonus" also exemplifies, but by showing the curious compatibility of High Church dogmatics and a rationalist exposition of non-Western mythologies. Some of Tylor's categories for a secular analysis of spiritual incarnations plainly derive from the Tractarian context; Tractarianism itself is partly the anxious, high-strung attempt to maintain intact the doctrine and historical uniqueness of the Incarnation in the face of a burgeoning Romantic interest in mythology that everywhere observes in tribal rites and primitive customs parallels and analogues to the Incarnation which render its specialness suspect. In "Tithonus" both positions meet. The poem represents the new and open attitude towards mythology in that it refuses to treat Greek myth as an inadequate heathen anticipation of the Christian dispensation or as an irrelevant realm of fable from which subsequent generations can learn nothing; nevertheless, it rejects the Romantic enthusiasm for autotelic mythmaking, balances a guarded sympathy with a critical interest in the general process of personifying. Once again, the double vision of dramatic monologue is indispensable to Tennyson's purpose. Furthermore, precisely because Tennyson will not shape an explicit comparison between Christian and Greek myths, the poem permits conservative Christian readers to imagine that, even if the process of theogony by personification is common to all cultures, the results in Greek thought do not much resemble the Christian faith in the mystery of the Incarnation: the poem, after all, conformable as it is with Locke's notions of perception and the human body, demonstrates the underlying materialism of Tithonus' vision and declines to portray the Dawn as a Real, spiritual Presence. More important than this implied accommodation, however (surely the least interesting way to approach the poem) is that the poem links anthropological and theological perspectives by examining, with great psychological acuity, the system of signification which results from Tithonus' need to spiritualize matter. As his Dawn hovers between phenomenon and personification, personification and goddess, as Tennyson shows Tithonus's psychic pain as he is buffeted by the extremes of her "mystic change," he shows how very much Tithonus is prepared to sacrifice in order not to endure a spiritless world.

Notes

1.   I have used the texts established by Christopher Ricks in his edition of *The Poems of Tennyson* (London: Longman Group, 1969); the date is that of composition, as given by Ricks. Tennyson himself is responsible for the notion that "Tithonus" was meant as a "pendent" to "Ulysses" (Hallam Lord Tennyson, *Alfred Lord Tennyson: A Memoir by His Son*, 2 vols. [London: Macmillan, 1897], I, 459), and it has been received into critical opinion with very little scrutiny. Among those propounding it: Jerome Hamilton Buckley, *Tennyson: The Growth of a Poet* (Cambridge, Mass.: Harvard University Press, 1960), 61; Henry Kozicki, *Tennyson and Clio: History in the Major Poems* (Baltimore: Johns Hopkins University Press, 1979), 40; Clyde de L. Ryals, *Theme and Symbol in Tennyson's Poems to 1850* (Philadelphia: University of Pennsylvania Press, 1964), 133. When Tennyson articulated the connection, however, he was plainly referring to the "Tithon" of 1833, not to the very different "Tithonus" of 1860; see Linda K. Hughes, "From 'Tithon' to 'Tithonus': Tennyson as Mourner and Monologist," *Philological Quarterly*, 58 (1979), 87. Tennyson's revisions have been extensively analyzed by Mary Joan Donohue, "Tennyson's 'Hail, Briton!' and 'Tithon,' " *PMLA*, 64 (1949), 400–416. Tennyson's commentators have nevertheless ignored the distinction and

have written as if the later poem dated from 1833. This procedure is particularly suspect when the "pendent" theory is construed autobiographically, as it usually is, in the light of Tennyson's grief at the death of Arthur Henry Hallam: deceptively, the emotion and design of "Tithonus" thus seem unchanged from 1833. "Tithonus" has been autobiographically interpreted by the following: A. Dwight Culler, *The Poetry of Tennyson* (New Haven: Yale University Press, 1977), 87; E[dward] D. H. Johnson, *The Alien Vision of Victorian Poetry* (Princeton: Princeton University Press, 1952), p. 14; Donohue, 415–16; Frederick L. Gwynn, "Tennyson's 'Tithon,' 'Tears, Idle Tears,' and 'Tithonus,' " *PMLA*, 67 (1952), 572; James Kissane, "Tennyson: The Passion of the Past and The Curse of Time," *ELH*, 32 (1965), 198; W. David Shaw, "Tennyson's 'Tithonus' and the Problem of Mortality," *Philological Quarterly*, 52 (1973), 274–75, 282; Christopher Wiseman, " 'Tithonus' and Tennyson's Elegiac Vision," *English Studies in Canada*, 4 (1978), 213–14, 217, 221. Among the few to oppose the "pendent" theory: Hughes; Arthur D. Ward, " 'Ulysses' and 'Tithonus': Tunnel Vision and Idle Tears," *Victorian Poetry*, 12 (1974), 311–19; Theodore Redpath, "Tennyson and the Literature of Greece and Rome," in Hallam Tennyson, ed., *Studies in Tennyson* (London: Macmillan, 1981), 121, 126; Arthur L. Simpson, Jr., "Aurora as Artist: A Reinterpretation of Tennyson's *Tithonus*," *Philological Quarterly*, 51 (1972), 905–21, who considers the poem an allegory of the "socially alienated, self-indulgent, detached artist" (905); James O. Hoge, "Keatsian Lovemaking in Tennyson's 'Tithonus,' " *Victorians Institute Journal*, 4 (1975), 13–15, who agrees largely with Simpson: "Eos represents an enchanting fantasy which is served by the poetic dreamer but which must be rejected by the artist whose ultimate concern is the human condition" (14). Culler, 87, and Harold Bloom, "Tennyson: In the Shadow of Keats," in *Poetry and Repression: Revisionism from Blake to Stevens* (New Haven: Yale University Press, 1976), 161, 166, also consider the poem as an allegory of the poet; like Simpson, neither argues from the language of the text in so doing; see also Matthew Rowlinson, "The Skipping Muse: Repetition and Difference in Two Early Poems of Tennyson," *Victorian Poetry*, 22 (1984), 362. F. E. L. Priestley, *Language and Structure in Tennyson's Poetry* (London: Andre Deutsch, 1973), 38–39, summarizes the "aesthetic" allegory.

2. Arthur Henry Hallam, "On Some of the Characteristics of Modern Poetry, and on the Lyrical Poems of Alfred Tennyson," in *The Writings of Arthur Henry Hallam*, ed. T. H. Vail Motter (New York: Modern Language Association, 1943), 197.

3. Herbert F. Tucker, Jr., "From Monomania to Monologue: 'St. Simeon Stylites' and the Rise of the Victorian Dramatic Monologue," *Victorian Poetry*, 22 (1984), 128, has remarked Simeon's tendency to reify himself; but he sees these reiterated self-namings as oppositional self-expressions and thus instances of self-division—or, of "a subjectivity subject to negotiation."

4. Compare Tucker, 137, who glorifies Tithonus' personifying by claiming that he seeks "a hidden yet imaginable god abiding apart from nature and history"; Tucker further argues that the poem, unlike other dramatic monologues, eschews the critical perspectives typical of Browning and, without irony, eyes the possibilities of a transcendental selfhood with an intensity "unmatched anywhere but in the most daemonic poems written in English during the last two hundred years." The claims are excessive; they mistake both the poem's tone and Tennyson's attitude towards his monologist; and they scant—like so much Tennysonian criticism—the crafty intelligence of the skeptical Tennyson.

5. Hesiod, *Theogony*, in *The Homeric Hymns and Homerica*, trans. Hugh G. Evelyn-White (London: Heinemann, 1914), 107; *Hymn to Aphrodite*, ibid., 421–23.

6. For general background on Thirlwall and Hare, see Martha McMackin Garland, *Cambridge before Darwin: The Ideal of a Liberal Education, 1800–1869* (Cambridge: Cambridge University Press, 1980). Robert Bernard Martin, *Tennyson: The Unquiet Heart* (Oxford: Clarendon Press, 1980), makes no mention of Thirlwall and Hare as Tennyson's tutors; compare Thomas R. Lounsbury, *The Life and Times of Tennyson* (New Haven: Yale University Press, 1915), 67–68; Charles Tennyson, *Alfred Tennyson* (1949, rpt. London: Macmillan,

1950), 68. It is a hindrance to our understanding of Tennyson's intellectual development to assume his lack of familiarity with skeptical tendencies in contemporary debate. For Tennyson's vote at the Apostle's meeting, see Hallam Lord Tennyson, *Memoir*, I, 44 nl; for a brief but trenchant comparison of Tennyson's skepticism and Hallam's religious belief, see Philip Flynn, "Hallam and Tennyson: The 'Theodicaea Novissima' and *In Memoriam*," *Studies in English Literature*, 19 (1979), passim, esp. 707, 714–15.

7.   Hallam Lord Tennyson, *Memoir*, I, 311.

8.   E. S. Dallas, *The Gay Science*, 2 vols. (1866; rpt. New York: Johnson Reprint Corporation, 1969), I, 274, 281.

9.   Compare Shaw, "Tennyson's 'Tithonus,' " p. 276; James R. Kincaid, *Tennyson's Major Poems: The Comic and Ironic Patterns* (New Haven: Yale University Press, 1975) 46; Wiseman, 218; Michael E. Greene, "Tennyson's 'Gray Shadow, Once a Man': Erotic Imagery and Dramatic Structure in 'Tithonus,' " *Victorian Poetry*, 18 (1980), 294, all of whom regard the passage without irony. Ralph W. Rader, "Notes on Some Structural Varieties and Variations in Dramatic 'I' Poems and Their Theoretical Implications," *Victorian Poetry*, 22 (1984), 104, has observed this doubleness or ambiguity in the source of language, but he has not identified either writing or speech as such in any given case; yet dramatic monologue in the nineteenth century flourishes in the middle ground between oral and written cultures.

10.   Dorothy Mermin, *The Audience in the Poem: Five Victorian Poets* (New Brunswick: Rutgers University Press, 1982), 31, excludes "Tithonus" from the general category of dramatic monologue precisely because Tithonus' "auditor is not a human being"; but the exclusion unfortunately serves to mask the poem's profound—because extreme—exemplification of the problems of doubled and projected images found in conventional dramatic monologues and common conversation alike.

11.   Compare William E. Fredeman, "One Word More—on Tennyson's Dramatic Monologues," in Hallam Tennyson, ed., *Studies in Tennyson*, 171, who has generalized that Tennyson's monologues, because of their "persistent effect" of "stasis" rather than movement, "might, with more accuracy, be called dramatic soliloquies than dramatic monologues." This view belittles the psychological investment that Tennyson's monologists have in their auditors; further, it obscures Tennyson's interest in significant formal metamorphoses *within* a particular work. In "Tithonus," the emergence of soliloquy is the consequence not of the poem's predetermined cast but of the intrusion of an action (the Dawn's departure), the result, that is, of precisely that factor that Fredeman thinks absent in Tennyson's monologues.

12.   Compare Donohue, 403, who considers Tennyson in his revisions to have aimed chiefly at producing "this sense of the persistent and slow which permeates ["Tithonus"] . . . One of the main sources of this effect is a rhetorical one, a kind of balanced repetition." Donohue's analysis focuses primarily on patterns of repetition in the 1860 version. Compare also Hughes, 86: "The central difference between 'Tithon' and 'Tithonus,' then, is the latter's introduction of an informing motive behind Tithonus' attainment of immortality." See also Culler, *The Poetry of Tennyson*, 88: "The main change that Tennyson made in the latter revision of the poem was to omit Tithonus' threat to introduce Death into the halls of Aurora." For the excision to which Culler alludes, see Ricks, *Poems of Tennyson*, 1116.

13.   Most commentators on personification point out that the trope depends on the sexualizing pronoun (he, she)—among other indices—for the making of the anthropomorphic image. See, e.g., Joseph Priestley, *A Course of Lectures on Oratory and Criticism* (1777; rpt. Carbondale: Southern Illinois University Press, 1965), 260; Hugh Blair, *Lectures on Rhetoric and Belles Lettres*, ed. Harold F. Harding, 2 vols. (1783; rpt. Carbondale: Southern Illinois University Press, 1965), 328; Bertrand Harris Bronson, "Personification Reconsidered," in *Facets of the Enlightenment: Studies in English Literature and its Contexts* (Berkeley: University of California Press, 1968), 126. See also Edward Burnett Tylor, *Primitive Culture: Researches into the Development of Mythology, Philosophy, Religion, Language, Art, and Custom*, 2 vols. (1871; 5th ed. London: Murray, 1913), I, 301–2, on "grammatical gender" in inflected languages.

Virtually all of Tennyson's critics assume that the Dawn is presented solely as a goddess, a being having her own ontological reality apart from Tithonus' creation of her. See, e.g., Donohue, 403; Simpson, 916; Wiseman, 216; Shaw, "Tennyson's 'Tithonus,' " passim; Christine Gallant, "Tennyson's Use of the Nature Goddess in 'The Hesperides,' 'Tithonus,' and 'Demeter and Persephone,' " *Victorian Poetry*, 14 (1976), 158; Kincaid, 47. Shaw, *Tennyson's Style* (Ithaca: Cornell University Press, 1976), 234–35, gives an interesting account of the language Tennyson uses to create the Dawn's reality, although he nevertheless ignores the Dawn's fictiveness.

14.   Tennyson further indicates Tithonus' subjective conception of the Dawn by having "her" light emanate first from her "pure Brows" (line 35); in thus likening the Dawn to Athena, he suggests that she is a mental construct whose source in Tithonus' mind (as in that of Zeus) has been transferred to the mind predicated of the personification.

15.   The word "lucid" refers technically to the gaseous formation of starry nebulae as described by LaPlace: see *The Princess* II. 101. For Tennyson's use of LaPlace, see John Killham, *Tennyson and The Princess: Reflections of an Age* (London: Athlone Press, 1958), 232–33; see also the drafts to "The Palace of Art" (1832)—"Regions of lucid matter taking forms"—and Ricks' commentary, *Poems of Tennyson*, 412–13. But the word "lucid" also connotes a fiery female sexuality that the beholder finds irresistible: the Dawn's "lucid outline" recalls the "lucid well" from which Pallas Athena emerges in "Tiresias" (line 41); Athena's light emerges "from her virgin breast" as well as from her hair, and she thus resembles the temptress Helen in "Lucretius," from whose breasts flames "The fire that left a roofless Ilion" (line 65). The figures of Athena and Helen are glosses, as it were, on the awesome sexual energy with which Tithonus fills the Dawn's "lucid outline."

16.   David Hume, *The Natural History of Religion*, ed. H. E. Root (1757; rpt. Stanford: Stanford University Press, 1957), 30.

17.   John Locke, *An Essay Concerning Human Understanding*, ed. Alexander Campbell Fraser, 2 vols. (1894; rpt. New York: Dover, 1959), II, 76, 159.

18.   Locke, II, 63; Locke's italics. See also II, 66: "The mind getting, only by reflecting on its own operations, those simple ideas which it attributes to spirits, it hath or can have no other notion of spirit but by attributing all those generations it finds in itself to a sort of beings; without consideration of matter."

19.   Tennyson's drafts, fluctuating between "shade" and "Shade," reveal a similar process of ghostly self-personification. For Tennyson's use of Dream as an anthropomorphic shadow, see "Demeter and Persephone," lines 87–92, 99.

20.   Christopher Ricks, *Tennyson* (London: Macmillan, 1972), 132, has made some useful remarks on Tennyson's deployment of the pronoun throughout the poem. See also Emile Benveniste, "The Nature of Pronouns," in *Problems in General Linguistics*, trans. Mary Elizabeth Meek (1966; Coral Gables, Fla.: University of of Miami Press, 1971), 217–22.

21.   The procedure of comparison in this image is consistent with what Josephine Miles, in *Pathetic Fallacy in the Nineteenth Century: A Study of a Changing Relation Between Object and Emotion* (1942; rpt. New York: Octagon Books, 1976), 21, describes as "inverted simile" in nineteenth-century anthropomorphism: "Instead of having natural objects borrow feeling from men, men by simile feel in the manner of natural objects." Note of course the irony that earth is insentient. Compare Bloom, *Poetry and Repression*, p. 168, who finds the closing lines both superfluous and unconsciously sadistic; Shaw, "Tennyson's 'Tithonus,' " 281, who thinks, that at the end, "Tennyson and Tithonus are now speaking in unison" and that "to the majestic auroral cycle Tennyson adds the poignant human cycle of 'earth in earth,' a cycle which the reader like Tithonus can now value and accept" (282); and Kincaid, p. 46, who sees Tithonus' last request as a "grotesque bribe," a reading which at least preserves the strain of irony intrinsic to dramatic monologue.

22.   See also "The Two Voices" (lines 109–11), where the dead remain, in their pride, *conscious* of their earthly fame; and compare the similar passage in Browning, "The Bishop

Orders His Tomb at St. Praxed's," lines 80–84, where the bishop cannot imagine that his death will conclude his conscious rivalry with Gandolf.

23.   The fallacious notion that Tithonus desires absolutely and unambiguously to escape from the Dawn has been propounded by many commentators. See, e.g., Donohue, 403, who writes of Tithonus' "rejection of Eos' terms"; Simpson, 913, who speaks of the "impossible situation" Tithonus "seeks to escape" and the despair that results from "the distinct possibility that Tithonus may not be able to leave Aurora's world." See also Buckley, 62; Hughes, 88; Redpath, 125; Ryals, 132. Wiseman, 220–21, sees Tithonus' ambivalence; so also Shaw, *Tennyson's Style*, 95 (but compare Shaw, "Tennyson's 'Tithonus,' " 281).

24.   Compare H. Walwyn, "A Countrey Seat" (1699): "And acting his Despair, himself in *Wye* he throws" (cited in Robert Arnold Aubin, *Topographical Poetry in Eighteenth-Century England* [New York: Modern Language Association, 1936], p. 119). Angus Fletcher, in *Allegory: The Theory of a Symbolic Mode* (Ithaca: Cornell University Press, 1964), 38–50, 66–67, discusses the constricted mental functions of personifications and likens the psychic behavior of personifications to that of obsessional neurosis and compulsive ritual (286–89, 291–93).

25.   William Wordsworth, "Preface to the Edition of 1815," in *Poetical Works*, rev. ed., ed. Ernest de Selincourt (1904: London: Oxford University Press, 1936), 752. For Collins, see Chester F. Chapin, *Personification in Eighteenth-Century Poetry* (New York: Columbia University Press, 1955), 76–77, who rightly argues that Collins in the "Ode to Evening" seeks the "intermixture of personification with scenes of natural beauty" that is the Keatsian vision. Twice, however, Collins fails to achieve the fusion: "thy religious Gleams" (line 32) cannot be both the eye's glances and the evening light (compare "Tithonus," lines 34–35); "Thy Dewy Fingers" (line 39) cannot be both the personification's fingers and the skyey source of evening rain.

26.   Ian Jack, *Keats and the Mirror of Art* (Oxford: Clarendon Press, 1967), 235.

27.   John Keats, *The Letters of John Keats*, ed. Hyder Edward Rollins, 2 vols. (Cambridge, Mass.: Harvard University Press, 1958), I, 193.

28.   For Hallam's readings, see Arthur Henry Hallam, *Writings*, 147 n4. Niebuhr's work, founded on Wolf's analysis of the Homeric poems and Eichhorn's signal distinction between history and legend in the consideration of biblical narrative, was a major influence on Macaulay's preface to the *Lays of Ancient Rome*. Tennyson's friend and (later) brother-in-law Edmund Lushington read Strauss' *Das Leben Jesu* in 1837 (Peter Allen, *The Cambridge Apostles* [Cambridge: Cambridge University Press, 1978], 174), the year after Marian Evans translated it, and it is likely that Tennyson was conversant with this major document as well. For Tennyson's readings, see Hallam Lord Tennyson, *Memoir*, I, 43–44.

29.   David Fordyce, *Dialogue Concerning Education* (1745), 366, cited in Earl R. Wasserman, "The Inherent Values of Eighteenth-Century Poetry," *PMLA*, 65 (1950), 452; William Wordsworth, "Preface to the Second Edition of *Lyrical Ballads*," in *Poetical Works*, 736; ibid., "Essay, Supplementary to the Preface," 744.

30.   Hallam, "Theodicaea Novissima," in *Writings*, 210.

31.   Fordyce, cited in Wasserman, 453; Fordyce's italics. Robert Lowth, *Lectures on the Sacred Poetry of the Hebrews*, 2 vols. (1753; rpt. of 1787 ed., New York: Garland, 1971), 288, separates the personification of abstract ideas from the personification of inanimate objects and thus can easily evade explaining how the similitude is made. Wasserman, 453–54, ignores the bodily referent in his analysis of the linguistic perfection personification purported to represent. Chapin, *Personification*, 29–30, is more conscious of the difficulties over which theories like Fordyce's gloss: "The personified abstraction had its prototype in nature so far as it required the attribution of specific human traits, but the abstract quality itself had no such prototype in the world of material reality." Yet even here, as Chapin approaches the discontinuities within personification, he suppresses the anthropomorphic referent, only to stress it again in its metaphoric, not real, form.

32. Thomas Arnold, "On the Right Interpretation of Scripture," in *Sermons*, 4th ed., 2 vols. (London: Fellowes, 1845), II, 392–93.

33. Compare Robert Langbaum, *The Poetry of Experience: The Dramatic Monologue in Modern Literary Tradition* (New York: Norton, 1957), passim (e.g., 93), who stresses the "extraordinary" aspects of dramatic monologue.

34. Sigmund Freud, *Totem and Taboo*, trans. James Strachey (1913; rpt. New York: Norton, 1962), 77; Tylor, *Primitive Culture*, I, 477; Hume, *Religion*, 29. Morse Peckham, *Victorian Revolutionaries: Speculations on Some Heroes of a Culture Crisis* (New York: Braziller, 1970), 194–95, remarks Hume's influence on Tylor.

Tennyson's *Princess*:
One Bride for Seven Brothers

EVE KOSOFSKY SEDGWICK

It has seemed easiest for critical consensus to interest itself in the Gothic on "private" terms and in mainstream Victorian fictions on "public" terms; but just as the psychological harrowings of the Gothic are meaningful only as moves in a public discourse of power allocation, so the overtly public, ideological work of writers like Tennyson, Thackeray, and Eliot needs to be explicated in the supposedly intrapsychic terms of desire and phobia to make even its political outlines clear. *The Princess* in particular claims to be a major public statement, in a new form, about the history and meaning of femininity; but male homosocial desire, homophobia, and even the Gothic psychology of the "uncanny" are ultimately the structuring terms of its politics—and of its generic standing as well.

To generalize: it was the peculiar genius of Tennyson to light on the tired, moderate, unconscious ideologies of his time and class, and by the force of his investment in them, and his gorgeous lyric gift, to make them sound frothing-at-the-mouth mad.

Tennyson applied this genius with a regal impartiality that makes him seem like a Christmas present to the twentieth-century student of ideology, but made him something less reassuring to many of his contemporaries. We have suggested that the whole point of ideology is to negotiate invisibly between contradictory elements in the status quo, concealing the very existence of contradictions in the present by, for instance, recasting them in diachronic terms as a historical narrative of origins. For a writer as fervent, as credulous, and as conflicted as Tennyson to get interested in one of these functional myths was potentially subversive to a degree that, and in a way that, Tennyson himself was the last to perceive. Where he did perceive it, it was most often as a formal struggle with structural or stylistic incoherence in his work. These formal struggles, however, also answered to the enabling incoherences in his society's account of itself.

If *Henry Esmond* is an ahistorical diagram of bourgeois femininity disguised as an account of historical change, *The Princess* is in some respects the

Reprinted from *Between Men: English Literature and Male Homosocial Desire* by Eve Kosofsky Sedgwick (1985), by permission. © Columbia University Press, 1985.

opposite. Its myth of the origin of modern female subordination is presented firmly *as* myth, in a deliberately a-chronic space of "Persian" fairy tale. On the other hand, the relation of the myth to its almost aggressively topical framing narrative is so strongly and variously emphasized that the poem seems to compel the reader to search for ways of reinserting the myth into the history. The mythic narrative is sparked by a young woman's speculation about the male homosocial discourse from which she is excluded: "—what kind of tales did men tell men,/She wonder'd, by themselves?"[1] Its substance, as well, is about the enforcement of women's relegation within the framework of male homosocial exchange. Some effects of uncanniness result from this magnetic superposition of related tales—along with more explicable historic and generic torsions.

The "mythic" central narrative begins with the astonishing vision of a feminist separatist community, and ends with one of the age's definitive articulations of the cult of the angel in the house. The loving construction of a female world, centered on a female university, looking back on a new female history and forward to a newly empowered future; and then the zestful destruction of that world root and branch, the erasure of its learning and ideals and the evisceration of its institutions—both are the achievements of Tennyson's genius for ideological investment.

One important feature of the myth propounded in *The Princess*'s inner narrative is that it traces the origin of nineteenth-century bourgeois gender arrangements directly back to the feudal aristocracy. Even there, however, the angel in the house does not seem to be new; for the Prince describes his ideal of womanhood as coming directly from his own mother, and describes it in terms that any middlebrow Victorian would have recognized:

> one
> Not learned, save in gracious household ways,
> Not perfect, nay, but full of tender wants,
> No Angel, but a dearer being, all dipt
> In Angel instincts, breathing Paradise,
> Interpreter between the Gods and men,
> Who look'd all native to her place, and yet
> On tiptoe seem'd to touch upon a sphere
> Too gross to tread, and all male minds perforce
> Sway'd to her from their orbits as they moved,
> And girdled her with music. Happy he
> With such a mother!
>
> (VII.298–309)

Toward this destiny (presented as both idealized past and paradisal future) Ida, too, is being propelled. At the same time, it is significant that this nostalgic portrait of the Prince's mother is not arrived at until the last pages

of the poem; for the poem until then at least gestures at a critique of the
aristocratic feudal family that, if not thorough or consistent, is nevertheless
part of its purpose. Although the mother who is its product is a good old
angelic mother, the family that has created her is the bad old baronial family:

> My mother was as mild as any saint,
>
>   . . .
>
> But my good father thought a king a king;
> He cared not for the affection of the house;
> He held his sceptre like a pedant's wand
> To lash offence, and with long arms and hands
> Reach'd out, and pick'd offenders from the mass
> For judgment.
>
> (I.22–29)

The old king thinks his son is lily-livered as a wooer:

> "Tut, you know them not, the girls.
>
>   . . .
>
> Man is the hunter; woman is his game:
> The sleek and shining creatures of the chase,
> We hunt them for the beauty of their skins;
> They love us for it, and we ride them down.
> Wheedling and siding with them! Out! for shame!
> Boy, there's no rose that's half so dear to them
> As he that does the thing they dare not do,
> Breathing and sounding beauteous battle, comes
> With the air of the trumpet round him, and leaps in
> Among the women, snares them by the score
> Flatter'd and fluster'd, wins, tho' dashed with death
> He reddens what he kisses: thus I won
> Your mother, a good mother, a good wife,
> Worth winning"
>
> (V.144–60)

The Prince is an authentic liberal. His tactic in response to his father
here is to present Princess Ida's feminism as a mirror-image extreme of his
father's crudely patriarchal style, and himself as forging a new dialectic
between them, arriving at the moderating terms of a compromise. To Ida,
" 'Blame not thyself too much,' I said, 'nor blame/Too much the sons of
men and barbarous laws' " (VII.239–40). As we see when Ida is forced to
turn into a version of the Prince's mother, however, far from forging a new
order or a new dialectic he is merely finding for himself a more advantageous
place within the old one. Finding one, or preserving it: since one way of
describing the Prince's erotic strategy is that, while maintaining the strict

division of power and privilege between male and female, he favors (and permits to himself) a less exclusive assignment of "masculine" and "feminine" personal traits between men and women, in order that, as an "effeminized" man, he may be permitted to retain the privileged status of baby (*within* a rigidly divided family) along with the implicit empowerment of maleness. (The privileged avenue from a baby's need to a woman's sacrifice is one of the most repetitively enforced convictions in this inner narrative, and most especially in the lyrics.) In short, the Prince's strategy for achieving his sexual ends in battle differs from his father's only in a minor, stylistic detail: he gets what he wants by losing the battle, not by winning it.

The meaningfulness of the concept of fighting *against* a man *for* the hand of a woman can barely be made to seem problematical to him, however. And in general, the Prince's erotic perceptions are entirely shaped by the structure of the male traffic in women—the use of women by men as exchangeable objects, as counters of value, for the primary purpose of cementing relationships with other men. For instance, it never for one instant occurs to him to take seriously Ida's argument that an engagement contracted for reasons of state, by her father, without her consent, when she was eight years old, is not a reason why the entire course of her life should be oriented around the desires of a particular man. Similarly, as in Tennyson's own life, the giving of a sister in marriage to cement the love of the brother for another man is central in this narrative. Although romantic love is exalted in the Prince's view, as it is not in his father's, nevertheless its tendency in the mythic narrative must always be to ratify and enforce the male traffic in women, not to subvert it.

This emphasis on a chivalric code in which women are "privileged" as the passive, exalted objects of men's intercourse with men, is part of the point of drawing a genealogy straight from the Victorian bourgeois family to the medievalistic courtly tradition. To cast the narrative in terms of a "Prince" and a "Princess" is both a conventional, transparent fairytale device, and a tendentious reading of history that accomplishes several simplifying purposes. First, it permits a view of the Victorian middle-class family that denies any relation between its structure and its economic functions. By making the persistence and decadence of a stylized aristocratic family look like a sufficient explanation for contemporary middle-class arrangements, it renders economic need invisible and hides from the middle-class audience both its historical ties to the working class and also the degree to which, while nominally the new empowered class or new aristocracy, most of the middle class itself functions on a wage system for males and a system of domestic servitude for females. Even though the fit between the structure of the ideologically normative family and the needs of capital for certain forms of labor-power is anything but seamless, nevertheless the new middle-class family reflects these imperatives in its structure at least as strongly as it reflects internal contradictions left over from the aristocratic family of feudal times. Thus, the appeal to high chivalry obscures the contemporary situation by glamorizing and in fact dehistoricizing it.

As we will see, though, the mock-heraldry of tracing the bourgeois family back to aristocratic origins in feudal society is not the only ideologically useful way of legitimating it. The *Adam Bede* model, the genealogy through the yeoman and artisan classes, has its uses as well: for instance, instead of excluding work and the facts of economic necessity, it incorporates them centrally, but in a form (individual artisanship evolving into a guildlike system of workshop production) that both affirms some of the features of modern industrial discipline (such as the exclusion of women) and conceals its discontinuity from more individualistic modes of work.

Why then is Tennyson's defense of contemporary social arrangements in *The Princess* cast in the archaizing, aristocratic mold? It is through this question, I think, that we can move to a consideration of the fascinating frame narrative of the poem. For the poem takes place in a very particular England of the present (i.e., 1847), an England that, with Tennysonian daring, seems almost to represent a simple projection into the present of the inner narrative's fantasy of a feudal past. Like *Wives and Daughters*, *The Princess* begins on a great estate, on the day of the year on which it is opened up to the tenantry and neighborhood:

> Thither flock'd at noon
> His tenants, wife and child, and thither half
> The neighbouring borough with their Institute
> Of which he was the patron. I was there
> From college, visiting the son, . . .
>   . . . with others of our set,
> Five others: we were seven at Vivian-place.
> (Prologue 3–9)

As these lines suggest, *The Princess* is unlike *Wives and Daughters* in locating its point of view among those who might be at Vivian-place even on a normal, non-open-house day; it is also different from any Gaskell novel in viewing all the activities of the neighborhood, *including* the industry-oriented sciences of the Institute, as firmly and intelligibly set within a context of aristocratic patronage. In fact, with a characteristic earnest bravado, Tennyson goes out of his way to underline the apparent incongruity of the juxtaposition of on the one hand ancient privilege and connoisseurship, and on the other hand modern science; like a small-scale exposition of arts and industry, the open grounds of Vivian-place are dotted for the day with "a little clockwork steamer," "a dozen angry model [engines] jett[ing] steam," "a petty railway," a miniature telegraph system where "flash'd a saucy message to and fro/Between the mimic stations," and so forth, displayed along with the permanent family museum of geological specimens, Greek marbles, family armor from Agincourt and Ascalon, and trophies of empire from China, Malaya, and Ireland (Prologue 73–80, 13–24). The assertion that science, or technology, is the legitimate offspring of patronage and connoisseurship, that all these pursuits are harmonious, disinterested, and nationally unifying, that the raison d'etre of the great landowners is to execute most impartially a national consensus in favor of these obvious desiderata—the frame narrative assumes these propositions with a confidence that is almost assaultive.

Along with the breathtaking ellipsis with which *class* conflict is omitted from Tennyson's England, the aristocratic-oriented view of progress-as-patronage affects the *gender* politics of the poem, as well. The feminism presented in Princess Ida's part of the poem is a recognizable, searching, and, in its own terms, radical feminism. Some of the elements of it that are taught or practiced at the University include separatism, Lesbian love, a re-vision in female-centered terms of Western history, mythology, and art, a critique of Romantic love and the male traffic in women, and a critique of the specular rationalism of Western medical science. How is it possible for this elaborately imagined and riveting edifice to crumble at a mere male touch? What conceptual flaw has been built into it that allows it to hold the imagination so fully on its own terms, and yet to melt so readily into the poem's annihilatingly reactionary conclusion?

I am suggesting, of course, that its weakness is precisely the poem's vision of social change as something that occurs from the top down. For Princess Ida's relation to the University and in fact to the whole progress of feminism in the mythical southern kingdom is only an intensification of Sir Walter's relation to "progress" among his tenants: she is the founder, the benefactor, the theorist, the historian, and the beau ideal of a movement whose disinterested purpose is to liberate *them*, to educate *them*, "Disyoke their necks from custom, and assert/None lordlier than themselves. . . ." (II.127–28). Ida's main feeling about actual living women is impatience, a sense of anger and incredulity that she cannot liberate them and their perceptions in a single heroic gesture:

> for women, up till this,
> Cramped under worse than South-sea-isle taboo,
> Dwarfs of the gynaeceum, fail so far
> In high desire, they know not, cannot guess
> How much their welfare is a passion to us.
> If we could give them surer, quicker proof—
> Oh if our end were less achievable
> By slow approaches, than by single act
> Of immolation, any phase of death,
> We were as prompt to spring against the pikes,
> Or down the fiery gulf as talk of it,
> To compass our dear sisters' liberties.
>
> (III.260–71)

In an imaginative world where even a genuinely shared interest can be embodied and institutionalized only in the form of *noblesse oblige*, it is not surprising that a merely personal snag, encountered by the crucial person, succeeds effortlessly in unraveling the entire fabric. A top-down politics of the privileged, sacrificial, enlightened few making decisions for the brutalized, unconscious many will necessarily be an object of manipulation (from inside or outside), of late-blooming self-interest on the part of the leaders, of anomie and sabotage on the part of the led. A feminism based on this particular nostalgia will be without faith or fortitude, a sisterhood waiting to be subverted.

Part of the oddity of Tennyson's poem, however, is that the ideological structure that permits him in the inner narrative to tumble the feminist community down like a house of cards, is the same one whose value and durability for class relations he is blandly asserting, in the frame narrative. It may be this that caused his contemporaries to view the poem as a whole with such unease, an unease which however both he and they persisted in describing as formal or generic.

Tennyson describes the male narrator as being caught between the different *formal* and *tonal* demands of his male and female listeners:

> And I, betwixt them both, to please them both,
> And yet to give the story as it rose,
> I moved as in a strange diagonal,
> And maybe neither pleased myself nor them.
> (Conclusion 25–29)

Indeed, like the slippages of political argument, the formal and generic slippages between frame and inner narratives are very striking, and do catch up and dramatize the issues of class and gender, as well. For instance, the status of the inner narrative as collective myth, as a necessary ideological invention, is underlined by the indeterminacy about its authorship. During the Vivian-place party, the telling of the story, like a woman, is passed from hand to hand among the young men. The identification is directly made between the collectiveness of the male involvement in women and in storytelling: the idea of storytelling had started with an earlier Christmas reading-party of the seven young men from the University, where, Walter tells his sister Lilia,

> Here is proof that you [women] were miss'd: . . .
>   We [men] did but talk you over, pledge you all
> In wassail . . .
>   —play'd
> Charades and riddles as at Christmas here, . . .
> And often told a tale from mouth to mouth.
> (Prologue 175–79)

It is to initiate and place the Vivian-place women in the context of this proceeding that the inner story in *The Princess* is begun. Walter jokes of it as an occasion for making a gift of his sister to his friend—" 'Take Lilia, then, for heroine' clamour'd he,/ . . . 'and be you/The Prince to win her!' " (Prologue 217–19). The story is to be a "Seven-headed monster," of which each male narrator will "be hero in his turn!/Seven and yet one, like shadows in a dream" (Prologue 221–22).

As we have seen, the interior of the "Seven-headed monster" story, the belly of the beast, is no less structured by the male exchange of women than the circumstances of its conception had been. But there is a more unexpected and off-centered, thematic echo between inside and out, as well. The odd comparison of the male narrative communion to that of "shadows in a dream," almost unintelligible in its immediate context, leaps to salience in relation to one of the most notoriously puzzling features of the internal narrative. The Prince inherits from his family, perhaps through a sorcerer's curse, a kind of intermittent catalepsy,

> weird seizures, Heaven knows what:
> On a sudden in the midst of men and day,
> And while I walk'd and talk'd as heretofore,
> I seem'd to move among a world of ghosts,
> And feel myself the shadow of a dream.
>
> (I. 14–18)

This fugue state is described throughout the poem with the words "shadow" and "dream," and most often simply "shadow of a dream."

> While I listen'd, came
> On a sudden the weird seizure and the doubt:
> I seem'd to move among a world of ghosts;
> The Princess with her monstrous woman-guard,
> The jest and earnest working side by side,
> The cataract and the tumult and the kings
> Were shadows; and the long fantastic night
> With all its doings had and had not been,
> And all things were and were not.
>
> (IV.537–45)

The link between the seizures and the "seven and yet one" narrative frame does not disappear from the poem: one of the fugue states, for instance, corresponds to one of the moments when the narrative voice is being passed from one male storyteller to another. Its link to the use of sisters to cement emotional and property relations between men also recurs. Psyche, one of the Princess's companions, is the sister of Florian, a companion of the Prince's whom he considers "my other heart,/And almost my half-self, for still we moved/Together, twinn'd as horse's ear and eye" (I.54–56). Cyril, the Prince's other companion, falls in love with Psyche—and he asks,

> What think you of it, Florian? do I chase
> The substance or the shadow? will it hold?
> I have no sorcerer's malison on me,
> No ghostly hauntings like his Highness. I
> Flatter myself that always everywhere
> I know the substance when I see it. Well,
> Are castles shadows? Three of them? Is she
> The sweet proprietress a shadow? If not,
> Shall those three castles patch my tatter'd coat?
> For dear are those three castles to my wants,
> And dear is sister Psyche to my heart. . . .
>   (II.386–96)

Real estate can give body and substance to the shadowy bonds—of women, of words, of collective though hierarchical identification with a Prince—that link the interests of men.

I have no programmatic reading to offer of the meaning and placement of the Prince's cataleptic seizures. Surely, however, they are best described as a wearing-thin of the enabling veil of opacity that separates the seven male narrators from the one male speaker. The collective and contradictory eros and need of their investment in him—and through him, in each other— seem to fray away at his own illusion of discrete existence. Is the Prince a single person, or merely an arbitrarily chosen chord from the overarching, transhistorical, transindividual circuit of male entitlement and exchange? He himself is incapable of knowing.

In *Great Expectations*, Pip is subject to fuguelike states rather like the Prince's. The most notable is the one that occurs during Orlick's murderous attack on him at the lime-kiln:

> He drank again, and became more ferocious. I saw by his tilting of the bottle that there was no great quantity left in it. I distinctly understood that he was working himself up with its contents, to make an end of me. I knew that every drop it held, was a drop of my life. I knew that when I was changed into a part of the vapour that had crept towards me but a little while before, like my own warning ghost, he would . . . make all haste to the town, and be seen slouching about there, drinking at the ale-houses. My rapid mind pursued him to the town, made a picture of the street with him in it, and contrasted its lights and life with the lonely marsh and the white vapour creeping over it, into which I should have dissolved.
>
> It was not only that I could have summed up years and years and years while he said a dozen words, but that what he did say presented pictures to me, and not mere words. In the excited and exalted state of my brain, I could not think of a place without seeing it, or of persons without seeing them. It

is impossible to over-state the vividness of these images, and yet I was so intent, all the time, upon him himself . . . that I knew of the slightest action of his fingers.[2]

For Pip, as (I am suggesting) for the Prince in Tennyson's poem, the psychologically presented fugue state involves, not an author's overidentification with his character, but a character's momentary inability to extricate himself from his author. Pip's sudden, uncharacteristic power of imagination and psychic investiture—as in his later delirium in which "I was a brick in the house wall, and yet entreating to be released from the giddy place where the builders had set me . . . I was a steel beam of a vast engine, clashing and whirling over a gulf, and yet . . . I implored in my own person to have the engine stopped, and my part in it hammered off" (ch. 57)—is disturbing *to him*, and resembles nothing so much as Dickens' own most characteristic powers, as a personality, as a hypnotist, and of course as a novelist. This abrupt, short-lived, deeply disruptive fusion of authorial consciousness with a character's consciousness occurs in both works under three combined pressures. These are:

First, a difficult *generic* schema of male identifications, narrators, personae;

Second, a stressed *thematic* foregrounding of the male homosocial bond;

Third, undecidable confusions between singular and plural identity.

I have mentioned that the collectiveness of male entitlement is not incompatible with, but in fact inextricable from, its hierarchical structure. This fact, too, has formal as well as political importance in *The Princess*. Even though, among the seven young men, young Walter Vivian is surely the one who is closest to the Prince in power and privilege, it is instead the nameless narrator of the frame narrative—the visiting friend, a young poet—who takes responsibility for having put the Prince's narrative into its final form. Thus some of the political shape of this poem might be attributed to its being an argument on behalf of an aristocratic ideology, aimed at an aristocratic as well as a bourgeois audience, but embodied through a speaker whose relation to patronage is not that of the patron but of the patronized. In addition, the confusion—or division—of genre in *The Princess* has an even more direct and explicit link to the division of gender; for the narrative, feminist content and all, is attributed entirely to the young men, while the ravishing lyrics that intersperse the narrative, often at an odd or even subversive angle to what is manifestly supposed to be going on, are supposed to be entirely the work of women in the group: "the women sang/Between the rougher voices of the men,/Like linnets in the pauses of the wind" (Prologue 236–38). Certainly it is among the ironies of this passionate and confused myth of the sexes, that it has come to be valued and anthologized almost exclusively on the basis of its lyrics, its self-proclaimed "women's work." Perhaps in the eyes of those who actually enjoyed hegemonic privilege, a mere poet could in that age *not* be trusted with the job of articulating a justification for them, however ready he felt himself for the task. Perhaps in their view, if not in Tennyson's, poet's work and women's work fell in the same ornamental, angelic, and negligible class.

Notes

1.   Alfred, Lord Tennyson, *The Princess: A Medley*, in *The Poems of Tennyson*, ed. Christopher Ricks (London: Longmans, 1969), 749 (Prologue, 11. 193–94). Further citations are incorporated in the text, and designated by section and line numbers.

2.   Charles Dickens, *Great Expectations*, ed. Angus Calder (Harmondsworth: Penguin, 1965) 437–38 (ch. 53). Further citations are incorporated in the text and designated by chapter number.

The Collapse of Object and Subject:
In Memoriam

ISOBEL ARMSTRONG

'Lawn Tennyson, gentleman poet'; Tennyson's persistent self-deprecating account of his art as play might be reason enough for endorsing the twice-told joke of Stephen Dedalus and for regarding *In Memoriam* as a delicate, anguished epistemological game. 'And hence, indeed, she sports with words' (XLVIII): 'Or love but play'd with gracious lies': 'A contradiction on the tongue' (CXXV): grief which will 'with symbols play' (LXXXV). His habitual use of the word 'fancy' for imagination, which carries the more restricted, eighteenth-century limitation of meaning and even suggests the idle fancy, a game with poetic artefact, is congruent with the hesitancy which makes him describe the poem as play. But the extraordinarily sophisticated (and daring) version of Catullus, 'O Sorrow, wilt thou live with me?' (LIX), in which sorrow and sexual play are allied—'I'll have leave at times to play/As with the creature of my love', the understanding of the blind man's minute gesture—'He plays with threads' (LXVI)—as a movement of displaced anxiety, should indicate Tennyson's alertness to the complexities of play. So often in the poem a defensively meticulous technical perfectionism carrying an exposed, openly naked poignancy, continues ingenuously with the cadences of pathos, as if oblivious of the irony and contradictions it is dealing with. The gratuitousness of play grants the poem its freedom to be art, and certainly to be artful: it grants it a freedom to experiment, not to 'close grave doubts' but to liberate possibilities unknown to it except in play. Yet a profounder necessity is at work in the need to play. Play *is* a necessity. The poem has to sport with words in order to enable itself to continue, to bring itself *into* play. The sport is willed to rescue language from collapse by enabling it to continue as a game. 'I do but sing because I *must*.' I *must* implies that song is involuntary and imposed as a duty at one and the same time, willed and unwilled. Involuntary song liberates feeling, *'loosens* from the lip' (XLVIII) the pressure of paralysing emotion. The poem is partly, but only partly, about the psychology of expressive language, about the process of naming a 'something', 'clouds' of 'nameless sorrow' (IV) which can only be named with

Reprinted from *Language As Living Form in Nineteenth-Century Poetry* by Isobel Armstrong (1982), by permission. © 1982 by Barnes & Noble (U.S.), Harvester-Wheatsheaf (U.K.), 1982.

difficulty. It is a highly studied study of bereavement. 'And with no language but a cry.' Regression to the inarticulate cry is inevitable when words are not adequate to express emotion. There may be no words to use. In that case the continuance of language can perhaps be enabled by a sport which brings it into play, by inventing it as a game.

There is a fundamental anxiety in *In Memoriam* about the dissolution of language altogether. The breakdown of language is collateral with the obliteration of the regulative 'Type' in the external world. 'So careful of the type? But no . . . a dream,/A discord' (LVI). Discord; the consequence of the collapse of relationships is the absence of agreement and correspondence, the absence of syntax. Nature depends merely on the 'dream' of each solipsist subject for its organisation; nature is 'A hollow echo of my own' (III)—a hollow echo of my *own* hollow echoes. 'For words, like Nature, half-reveal/ And half-conceal the Soul within' (V). The governing analogy between words and Nature is half-concealed in this first poem on language, offered as an aside and interposed almost unnoticed, before the account of the failure of language which occupies it. Half-concealed, perhaps, because nature neces-sarily breaks down as an analogy. Nature is estranged from language, provid-ing no analogies for it and no connections with it except in so far as it is *like* words, which, the poem shows, are external forms, refusing the vital change of meaning, the soul within, which renews the life of language, because they cannot sustain analogy and relationship. They are 'like Nature', empty of self-renewing life, a discord. If there is a 'soul within' language and Nature it is incompletely realised, half concealed, half revealed. The *world* cannot guarantee the structure of language. Relationships are either arbitrary or break down, and it is the same in language. The resilience and intelligence of *In Memoriam* lie in its willingness to confront, however reluctantly, the derangement of idealist language with play, to 'frame' words, to invent them, perhaps even, as the secondary possibilities of 'frame' come into play, with some duplicity. The sport with words enables the poem to keep in existence and ultimately to reconstruct both itself and the 'use' of measured language.

The extremity of idealist language in *In Memoriam* is accompanied by a corresponding intensification of artifice. The poem tries to 'fix itself to form' (XXXIII) like the simple faith of the woman in the Lazarus sequence. The fastidious, carefully compacted units of pairing and parallelism, word with word, phrase with phrase, line and line, the 'stepping stones' (I) by which the poems are built up, express the need to make a form in which matching, concord, correspondence, analogy, are possible. The masking circumlocution of poetic diction, artful personification, insist upon the poem as minutely self-conscious verbal artefact, insist that something can be *made*, even if it is the almost unapproachable patina of surface perfection. But the coexistence of an ambiguous syntax with the formal pattern frequently disrupts the poem from within so that the formal organisation of the poem comes to exist independently of its meanings in a self-enclosed separation and autonomy which severs it from the correspondences it tries to make. 'I scarce could brook the strain and stir': the hiatus after his pairing allows the wild conflation of self and world, psychological strain and the stir of the storm in section XV. Because the stanza breaks after 'strain and stir' the condition can belong to the poet as much to the storm. The archaism, 'brook', enables the language not to be sure whether the poet *allows* or suffers upheaval, just as the meticulously parallel verbs are not sure whether they are active or passive, acting or acted upon—cracked, curled, huddled, dashed. 'And but for fancies . . . And but for fear it is not so.' Parallelism veers apart into contradiction. The poet would disintegrate into the storm unless his fancy insisted upon the calm progress of the boat carrying Hallam's body. But because the words 'it is not so' in this deranged syntax relate immediately to the storm the repetition intended to intensify this fancy—'And but for fear'—reads as a fear of calm, and also wills the strain and stir of the storm upon the dead man, forcing him into an identity with it. The poet would disintegrate except (but) for his fear that it is *not* calm, and but for fear that the 'wild unrest' is *not* so, fear that the strain and stir do not belong to the ship. The construction, 'for fear', carries with it the meaning of expectation, even hope. If the ship *were* calm and the dead man not sharing in the storm's and the poet's strain and stir, then disintegration would follow. The readings of the parallelism are athwart one another, like the movement of the ship placed in strangely obstructive relation to the sea which carries it, '*Athwart* a plane of molten glass'. Either way the poet and the syntax go mad, making no distinction between self and objects. Undifferentiated, internal unrest and external cloud drag 'a labouring breast', and the syntax, the cloud, the poet, 'topples' to disintegration with an unclosed phrase which is not organically part of the sentence—'A looming bastion fringed with fire'. Poet and storm become inseparable.

> To-night the winds begin to rise
> And roar from yonder dropping day:
> The last red leaf is whirl'd away,
> The rooks are blown about the skies;
>
> The forest cracked, the waters curled,
> The cattle huddled on the lea;
> And wildly dashed on tower and tree
> The sunbeam strikes along the world:
>
> And but for fancies, which aver
> That all thy motions gently pass
> Athwart a plane of molten glass,
> I scarce could brook the strain and stir

That makes the barren branches loud;
  And but for fear it is not so,
  The wild unrest that lives in woe
Would dote and pore on yonder cloud

That rises upward always higher,
  And onward drags a labouring breast,
  And topples round the dreary west,
A looming bastion fringed with fire.
                                    (XV)

The derangement of the storm poem ends in dissolution. *In Memoriam* continually threatens itself with termination. 'But that large grief . . . Is given in outline and *no more*' (V). Language allows grief to be expressed in no more than an outline, but the poem also categorically discontinues itself. It can utter grief 'no more'. And it brings itself to a halt. 'I held it truth . . . That men may rise on stepping-stones/Of their dead selves' (I). Each isolated lyric is a precarious stepping-stone which might not lead to another when language breaks down.

Dark house, by which once more I stand
  Here in the long unlovely street,
  Doors, where my heart was used to beat
So quickly, waiting for a hand,

A hand that can be clasp'd no more—
  Behold me, for I cannot sleep,
  And like a guilty thing I creep
At earliest morning to the door.

He is not here; but far away
  The noise of life begins again,
  And ghastly through the drizzling rain
On the bald street breaks the blank day.
                                    (VII)

'On the bald street breaks the blank day.' Again, the poem can go no further. The day dawns or *fragments*, breaking like something brittle on or against the bald street. The poet, not belonging to the dawn, like the ghost in *Hamlet* (but unlike the ghost, guilty of his exile from life and the day rather than death and the night), fusing the 'blank misgivings' of Wordsworth's 'Immortality Ode' with the blank day, moves about in worlds literally not realised, because the day breaks ambiguously out of, or is only seen *through*, the obstructive drizzle of rain. Breaking day and the hard, resistant street exist in unreactive relation to one another, the light failing to transform the street, the street unresponsive to the day. Bald and blank repel the reciprocity the pairing alliteration attempts to assert. Language fails to establish the correspondence it claims, and offers only a mutual exchange of emptiness. The obstruction of rain, the barrier of the door '*where* my heart was used to beat', by which, and against which, *directly* (with extraordinary physical frankness) the heart-beat knocked to gain entrance, are metaphors of a condition expressed in the organisation of the language of *In Memoriam*. It sets up barriers. Like the self-retarding stanza form, it creates obstructions and blocks against itself. Though the poem longs 'to flood a fresher throat with song' (LXXXIII), and constantly remembers the 'Ode to a Nightingale', it rarely achieves Keats' easeful flow of lyric feeling, because it is halted, and sometimes almost disabled, by an ambiguous syntax which says one thing and its opposite simultaneously, a 'contradiction on the tongue' (CXXV), asserting and negating at one and the same time. Two sentences out of the same words. The double, coalescing Romantic grammar seizes up in contradiction. Parallelism subjects the poem to paralysis. The gaps and transitions which are the life of Romantic language make either voids or barriers. 'O sweet, new year delaying long . . . *Delayest* the sorrow in my blood' (LXXXIII). The delaying spring is accused of the continuance of sorrow and yet at the same time is imperatively asked to delay, to keep sorrow in the blood. The paralysing and the creative energies of grief mutually retard one another.

The poem is most immobilised when it is not sure what form or what language to fix itself to, idealist or non-idealist, mind-moulded or 'matter-moulded' (XCV), actively shaped by the self, passively formed by an external world. It is not even certain whether the distinctions themselves are fixed.

> Old Yew, which graspest at the stones
>   That name the under-lying dead,
>   Thy fibres net the dreamless head,
> Thy roots are wrapt about the bones.
>
> The seasons bring the flower again,
>   And bring the firstling to the flock;
>   And in the dusk of thee, the clock
> Beats out the little lives of men.
>
> O not for thee the glow, the bloom,
>   Who changest not in any gale,
>   Nor branding summer suns avail
> To touch thy thousand years of gloom:
>
> And gazing on thee, sullen tree,
>   Sick for thy stubborn hardihood,
>   I seem to fail from out my blood
> And grow incorporate into thee.
>
> (II)

'And grow incorporate into thee': and grow bodiless, as mind or spirit with the 'dusk' of the yew, or become physically embodied in it. Either way lies the loss of distinction. 'And *in the dusk* of thee, the clock/Beats out': external clock, external time, tolls in the shadow of the yew or else, like a heart *in* the dusk of the tree itself, a shadowy, mind-created symbol of unchanging grief, internally registers 'a thousand years of gloom'—darkness and *sadness*. Whether the yew refuses to 'avail' the branding sun of the objective world to touch it, or whether the concrete world itself cannot 'avail' to reach and touch it, are equal and opposite possibilities. The opposites result, not in conflict, but in paralysis.

'To *touch* thy thousand years of gloom'; 'And learns . . . And finds I am not what I see,/And other than the things I *touch*' (XLV). The blocks occur when Tennyson is talking about perception and the relationship between the physical and mental worlds. Consider the connections made between touch and being in sections XLV and XCV: Created out of pronouns, 'I', 'me', the beautifully economical baby poem about the growth of identity uses verbs as stepping-stones to self-consciousness as the baby knows himself as object to himself and discovers the intransigent world of subject and object—'this is I'.

> But as he grows he gathers much,
>   And learns the use of 'I' and 'me',
>   And finds 'I am not what I see,
> And other than the things I touch.'

But as 'he grows he gathers . . . And learns . . . And finds'. 'And learns the use of "I" and "me" ': the baby gathers his growing, takes the knowledge of his growing as a fact of awareness, learns by its 'use' and finds what he uses. The emphasis is on an almost tragic imprisonment in the physical self and in the consciousness—'the frame that *binds* him in'—which is a necessity for the definition of a separate identity which can relate to the world as other, the not-self, and a necessity for the growth of 'clear memory'. Strictly read, however, the ellipsis of the second parallelism reverses the first and becomes an idealist statement or hypothesis—'And finds "I am not what I see,/And other than the things I touch" ': 'And finds "I am *not* what I see, [And I am not] other than the things I touch".' Two possibilities obstruct one another. Isolation, perhaps, grows defined, like an outline, as the self is sealed off from the world, and independent memory evolves. Or perhaps isolation grows defined through an act of mind which includes the other in its definition of self-separation, fusing subject and object in the process of creating relationship. The ambiguous parallelism returns one to the first stanza of the poem. The baby, *pressing* his palm against the breast (pressing himself away from and *into* the breast) has never thought that 'this is I'. This, the pressing palm exerting itself against its first experience of a resistant physical world, the baby's physical entity and consciousness, is 'I' at the first act of awareness and self-consciousness at the breast as the baby comes to understand that it is other to what it feeds upon. On the other hand, the syntax allows that the breast, source of life and literally part of the baby because its milk is taken in by the child, can also be included as 'I': this, the breast, is 'I'. The circle of the breast is outside the suckling child, or baby and breast are included in a circle of interchange and reciprocal being where subject and object are both other to each other and as one.

This, one of the subtlest poems of *In Memoriam*, is perhaps a lyric which finds momentarily a way of transcending the obstructions it creates for itself. But *In Memoriam* is never stable. 'The dead man *touched* me from the past' (XCV): 'I [am not] . . . other than the things I touch' (XLV):

> And strangely on the silence broke
>   The silent-speaking words, and strange
>   Was love's dumb cry defying change
> To test his worth; and strangely spoke
>
> The faith, the vigour, bold to dwell
>   On doubts that drive the coward back,
>   And keen through wordy snares to track
> Suggestion to her inmost cell.
>
> So word by word, and line by line,
>   The dead man touched me from the past,
>   And all at once it seemed at last
> The living soul was flashed on mine . . .
>
> Vague words! but ah, how hard to frame
>   In matter-moulded forms of speech,
>   Or even for intellect to reach
> Through memory that which I became:

The 'silent-speaking words' which broke on the poet are either the silent words of the dead friend's letter, or words silently reiterated in the poet's consciousness. 'Love's *dumb* cry' cannot be differentiated as belonging to the poet or the writer of the letter, just as 'the faith, the vigour', could belong to each, expressed in written words, or generated in the poet's being. Neither speech, nor even intellect can reach 'Through memory that which I became.' Memory is either creative or passive. The intellect cannot recreate through or by means of memory, but the placing of the words allows a reading, 'that which I became through memory, or the creations of memory'—the 'clear memory' of the baby poem, perhaps, the shaping consciousness itself. Transcendental experience may be given from outside the self or it may be a creation of mind. Experience, and words, may be mind-moulded or they may be matter-*moulded*, formed from the material world. And language may be simply moulded by matter, mere printed marks.

'That which I *became*': 'Thy place is changed; thou *art* the same' (CXXI). The 'double' naming of the Hesper/Phosphor poem simultaneously offers an active and a passive self, a living or a static universe:

> Sad Hesper o'er the buried sun
>   And ready, thou, to die with him,
>   Thou watchest all things ever dim
> And dimmer, and a glory done:
>
> The team is loosened from the wain,
>   The boat is drawn upon the shore;
>   Thou listenest to the closing door,
> And life is darkened in the brain.
>
> Bright Phosphor, fresher for the night,
>   By thee the world's great work is heard
>   Beginning, and the wakeful bird;
> Behind thee comes the greater light:
>
> The market boat is on the stream,
>   And voices hail it from the brink;
>   Thou hear'st the village hammer clink,
> And see'st the moving of the team.
>
> Sweet Hesper-Phosphor, double name
>   For what is one, the first, the last,
>   Thou, like my present and my past,
> Thy place is changed; thou art the same.

'Thy place is changed'—by external conditions, fixed and final. Or, with the openness of a continuous present, thy place is continually in a state of change. What 'thou art', what being is, is defined simultaneously in two radically opposed ways. Hesper watches over 'a glory done', a glory over or a glory *being made*, a glory ended or self-creating and perhaps even made by the watching Hesper itself. The poem has a double name and a double structure, of antithetical, linear beginnings and endings or cyclical renewal. The second and fourth stanzas contrasting cessation and movement, night and day, death and life, are locked in equipoise, miniature pastorals which are virtually inverted images of one another—the team of horses, the boat, the closing door (stanza 2); the boat, the sound of activity, the team. Appropriately, the verbs describing activity and movement are passive in the night pastoral, active in the day pastoral. But paradoxically 'listenest' in the night stanza (like 'watchest' in the first), is a sharper, less involuntary perceptual verb than 'hear'st' and 'see'st' in the day stanza. The transforming agent of perception comes into prominence and questions the passivity of experience when it is most subject to necessity. The locked, antithetical opposition is also subverted by the intervening stanza. Phosphor arises 'fresher for the night', fresher for the quietude of night into dawn, and fresher to *encounter* the cyclical renewal of night which follows the 'greater light'. Both structures are subject to necessity—with delicate toughness the cyclical movement of renewal is the renewal of darkness—but one offers a self and a universe capable of transformation while the other does not.

The more fixed to form, the more miniaturist and precise the language of *In Memoriam* seems, the more ambiguous it actually is. The poem discovers the ambiguity of form—solid form, hollow forms, mere form. 'The hills are shadows, and they flow/From form to form' (CXXIII). 'Vague words! but ah, how hard to frame': to frame, to make a solid physical structure like the baby's 'frame' which binds him in, or to invent, to make something new—even with some duplicity. The work of the poem is to overcome the immobility which arises from the discontinuous and uncertain oscillation between an open, reflexive, mind-created world and a binding, subject/object account of experience. It does so by redefining its form. And this redefinition is inextricably bound up with the overcoming of grief, or the acceptance of it, and the liberation of energy. The project the poem discovers is not to recover so much as to construct an idea of death, which is an 'awful *thought*' (XIII)—death to a living man can only be a thought, an act of imagination. This constructing of death can only be done by an act of imagination, defining death against its opposite, life, and creating both anew, redefining 'my present and my past'. Reflexive, idealist language is ultimately the strongest in this project, for all the doubts about it, because it is found to be most capable of keeping words in play and enables the poem to grow. It grows by flowing from form to form, building itself out of itself, contemplating its past, the stepping stones for growth. It arises, above all, out of the collapse of its analogies, out of its dead self, which enables it to find a new account of analogy and metaphor. The struggle of the poem is with discord and concord. The contemplations of analogy finally lead to a redefinition of the idea of form.

Two kinds of poetic form, each a commentary on the other, exist concurrently in the 'fair ship' sequence, often within the same poem. One is linear, narrative, temporal and external, marking the progress of the ship carrying the dead man from Vienna to England. It uses formal, ceremonial 'measured language' of a consciously organised kind more noticeably than any other group in *In Memoriam*. This sequence is the willed, 'sad mechanic exercise' initiated in Section V. The other form is psychological, expressive lyric, non-temporal, marking the vicissitudes of subjective life. Each form criticises the other. Both forms use the barrier of poetic diction as a means almost of neurotic displacement to mask death and the body, the boat, the sea. Conventional, external poetic diction becomes the greatest source of irony, half-revealing and half-concealing the deepest concern of this sequence which is with the collapse of safe and guaranteed order, the dissolving relationship between the internal and external worlds. The kinds of analogy which can be constructed become a crucial preoccupation here. The sequence tries out both the analogy in which objective equivalents for experience are provided by the external world and the analogy in which relationship is constituted by mind. Both fail.

'The Danube to the Severn gave': Section XIX, the last poem in the sequence, is a last attempt to provide a precise and exquisitely fitting image of experience in objective fact which ostensibly matches and illustrates the retarding movement, the ebb and flow of grief which inhibits song. Yet it is a false analogy in spite of the delicate exactitude with which the parallel appears to be made.

> There twice a day the Severn fills;
>   The salt sea-water passes by,
>   And hushes half the babbling Wye,
> And makes a silence in the hills.
>
> The Wye is hushed nor moved along,
>   And hushed my deepest grief of all,
>   When filled with tears that cannot fall,
> I brim with sorrow drowning song.
>
> The tide flows down, the wave again
>   Is vocal in its wooden walls;
>   My deeper anguish also falls,
> And I can speak a little then.

Just as the flow of the brimming Wye is blocked at its fullest and highest point by the movement of the Severn, so the poet's grief rises, but is paralysed: his tears cannot fall even though they 'brim' at the brink of falling; he cannot give utterance to grief. 'I brim with sorrow drowning song.' In movement again, the Wye is 'vocal' (the equivalent of Tennyson's song) and 'My deeper anguish also falls,/And I can speak a little then'. The lie of the analogy turns on the word 'falls': tears overflow, if this 'falls' is to become congruent with the earlier 'fall'—'tears that cannot fall'—but the Wye 'falls', not by overflowing, but by falling back to its natural level. The parallels between tears and Wye deviate just when they seem most to match. Again, the poem says two things at once. Poetry can be made possible by the release or overflow of feeling (this is a perfect account of expressive art) or by letting the 'deeper anguish' fall to a lower level of the consciousness (as the Wye falls to its bed), repressing the most powerful emotions and giving voice only to superficial feeling. The Wye is an 'exercise' which fails, and turns into a game with language, a game in which the rules of analogy are subverted so that contradictions emerge. The rigorous serenity of this poem masks the strain.

The antithetical storm and calm poems (XI, XV) try out the possibility of subjective analogy, another kind of consonance, by seeing how far the external world may be a replication of the self, structured by the subject and returning the forms of his consciousness to him as object to himself. Though the poems seem antithetical they are actually complementary. Different emotions, 'calm despair and wild unrest' (XVI), but the same collapse of relationship. The storm poem, I have suggested, discovers the derangement of idealist language. The storm is an objective analogy for psychological upheaval but becomes identified with it. The fusion of the mind of the perceiver is so complete that they become inseparable. When nothing falls outside the self relationship is dissolved, and distinction becomes meaningless. The extremities of incompatible verbs—'rises' set against 'dropping' in the first stanza, 'looming' set against 'topples' in the last, mark the disappearance of proportion and concord. Everything becomes part of everything else, everything stands for everything else without distinction in the language of the non-objective world—the poem 'Mingles all without a plan' (XVI).

To mingle. This verb is picked up from the calm lyric by section XVI, which attempts to analyse both it and the storm poem—'Calm and still light on yon great plain/That sweeps . . . To mingle with the bounding main'. Plain and main mingle as rhyme words. The calm poem tries out the possibility of finding the world as an attribute of the self, but whereas the storm poem finds a threatening fusion of subject and object, the calm poem finds only the pathetic fallacy. It cannot evolve the external world from its moods.

> Calm is the morn without a sound,
>   Calm as to suit a calmer grief,
>   And only through the faded leaf
> The chestnut pattering to the ground:
>
> Calm and deep peace on this high wold,
>   And on these dews that drench the furze,
>   And all the silvery gossamers
> That twinkle into green and gold:
>
> Calm and still light on yon great plain
>   That sweeps with all its autumn bowers,
>   And crowded farms and lessening towers,
> To mingle with the bounding main:
>
> Calm and deep peace in this wide air,
>   These leaves that redden to the fall;
>   And in my heart, if calm at all,
> If any calm, a calm despair:

Calm on the seas, and silver sleep,
  And waves that sway themselves in rest,
  And dead calm in that noble breast
Which heaves but with the heaving deep.

'Calm is the morn . . . Calm and deep peace . . . Calm on the seas':
each stanza repeats 'calm' like the self-mesmerising incantation of a lullaby
as an exercise in self-induced serenity. 'Calm oscillates between being a noun,
a possession of the landscape, and an adjective, a psychological, affective
state which 'mingles', creates an affinity between inner and outer worlds.
But the calm is not penetrative. It is '*on* this high wold', '*on* yon great
plain' or dissipated '*in* this wide air'. Finally, calm is refused metaphorical
possibilities altogether. 'Dead calm', the customary metaphor for the sea, is
transferred to the dead man and is a literal truth—'And dead calm in that
noble breast'. The euphemisms for death are transferred to the sea—'silver
sleep', 'waves that sway themselves in rest'—ironically pointing the senti-
mentality of attempts at psychological affinity. The dead language of poetic
diction opposes the living, suffering 'heart' of the poet to the 'noble breast'
of the dead man which 'heaves' but only with the mechanical life of the
heaving deep. We normally think of the heaving breast as the sign of
expressive feeling and emotion, heaving with sighs, but it is breathless here,
deprived of anything but the inert physical weight of the body which is a
dead form, appropriately described in a dead form of words—breast.[1] The
psychological adjective, 'deep'—'deep peace'—has been appropriated as a
noun for the sea—'the deep'—space without limit or shape. Calm is death.
The calm lyric is an attempt to impose a psychological reading of the world
but which poignantly recognises its imposture. The activities of the self and
world are neither reciprocal nor fused. The universe, if not dead, continues
its activity in dissociation from the poet, the chestnut 'pattering' where the
poet discovers a morn 'without a sound', the main 'bounding' in independent
life, leaping in the limitlessness of the present participle, but also the agent
of limit and constricting, bounding, the plain. The sea in affinity with calm
becomes death, which resists the understanding of the human imagination.
The only fusion of self and universe occurs in the calm of death. The reiterated
'calm' becomes not soothing but an obliteration of energy. Repetition is
death.

The haunting possibility that idealist analogy has no content is expressed in the extraordinarily analytical lyric (XVI) which follows and is
enabled by the calm and storm poems. Sorrow is a 'changeling', inconsis-
tent but, as the double note of 'changeling' suggests, transforming. Then
follows the negation of transformation in what is probably the most despairing questioning of the non-objective world in the poem. 'Can sorrow such
a changeling be?'

Or doth she only seem to take
   The touch of change in calm or storm;
   But knows no more of transient form
In her deep self, than some dead lake

That holds the shadow of a lark
   Hung in the shadow of a heaven?
   Or has the shock, so harshly given,
Confused me like the unhappy bark

That strikes by night a craggy shelf,
   And staggers blindly ere she sink?
   And stunned me from my power to think
And all my knowledge of myself;

And made me that delirious man
   Whose fancy fuses old and new,
   And flashes into false and true,
And mingles all without a plan?

The deep self, like some dead lake—deep and dead are changeling words, dead self, deep lake—only seems to register the 'touch' of an external world. But the self or lake create, nothing else, and certainly no other, no object, in place of this illusory relationship. It 'knows' nothing of 'transient form', the living but ephemeral forms of the external world, or 'changeling', internally shaped forms of its own. Not to 'know' is not to know the means of creating knowledge. The dead lake simply 'holds the shadow of a lark/Hung in the shadow of a heaven'. 'Hold' is a verb almost as important as 'touch' in *In Memoriam*. Here the dead self, the deep lake, fixes its images and keeps them stationary. Hold and hung balance one another, the lark in virtual death, hung. The lark may be a static reflection held in the reflection of sky and clouds, passively received and replicated by the dead consciousness, or worse, as the lyric asserts, it may simply be a *shadow* on the surface held in the larger shadows of sky and clouds which move about it. In this case it is an indistinct, indirect and secondary form which has none of the suggestion of transference implied in the idea of reflection. These shadows are more like the insubstantial internal forms of consciousness in Section IV which cannot be released from the self and given external being—'Such clouds of nameless trouble cross/All night below the darkened eyes'.

As if to endorse the failure of integration, the final parallelism describing the failure of unintegrated fancy is itself unintegrated. The fancy fuses 'old and new' and 'flashes into false and true'. The metaphor is drawn from gunpowder and chemistry. One disintegrates, the other blends. ('Flashes' is far away from the climactic Section XCV, where the living soul was 'flashed on mine'.) Old and new, false and true, are neither fused as equivalents nor arranged in meaningful opposition as the arrangement of the pairs would ostensibly insist, line above line, the old falsity, the new truth. The arrangement could equally denote the old truth, the new falsity. It is as unstable as the fancy. The statement about the inconsistency of fancy gives no guarantee even to the stability of the parallel it makes, which falls apart intellectually. What is left is a structure without a content which falls into incoherence, 'without a plan'—without a plan, a projection, a model, a metaphor.

The poems which try out self-reflexive metaphor are the most immediately startling and unsettling in this group. The more formal poems on the ship, suggesting the inexorable progress of a journey, a linear narrative, look conventional. The more formal poems, however, are equally if not more subversive and at the same time paradoxically freer than the purely 'subjective' poems. It is as if the mask of poetic diction grants the poem freedom to 'play' with possibilities which are unreachable by the 'subjective' poems because the formal poems are 'false' as consolation or more outrageous than the 'subjective poems' can ever be. The virtuosity of poetic diction in the Fair Ship series is astonishing. The consolatory, generalised forms of diction 'outlining' grief have a prolific inventiveness and ingenuity which revivifies conventional forms. The inertia of the body and mysteriousness of death for instance, are exquisitely suggested by these circumlocutions—'a vanished life', 'dark freight' (X), 'mortal ark', 'A weight of nerves without a mind' (XII), 'the burthen' (XIII). But this masking diction is both ingenuous and disingenuous, half-revealing and half-concealing consolation, and a refusal of consolation. Poetic diction asserts the freedom of mind to create its objects with a liberation and equanimity unknown to the expressive, subjective lyric forms. In this diction, Phosphor, the morning star, really can 'glimmer' unimpeded 'through early light' and find its image returned back to itself on 'the dewy decks' (IX) in contrast with the obstructed, unreactive world of the dark house poem. The world can be a reflection of the subject in unperplexed concord. The mind can be released, with an outward projection of the imagination, 'to dart' and 'play' (XII): the fancies 'rise on wing' (XIII) or glance about the object of grief and bring it into being. The mind is liberated to fulfil that longing of the bereaved person, so shocking to the unbereaved, for the physical return of the dead. The single, continuous sentence of section XIV asserts, almost outrageously, that if the dead man got off the ship alive 'I should not feel it to be strange'.

The poetic diction *wishes*, and its artifice conceals its wishes, but outrage, shock, subversiveness, the reversal of conventional expectation, is also the mode of this elaborately euphemistic language. 'More than my brothers are to me': the anti-social statement flagrantly undermining the conventional family priorities, violates the evenness of earlier more conventional parallelisms in Section IX—'My friend, the brother of my love'. The widower of Section XIII finds in death 'A void where heart on heart reposed': a void in the place of the companion body and heart but, allowably, a void which was always present, unknown to the mourner even when the dead companion was alive. The funeral service and communion are expressed in the more elaborate circumlocutions—'the ritual of the dead', the kneeling hamlet drains 'The chalice of the grapes of God' (X)—as if to indicate the *obsolete* formalism of a consolatory religious act of burial which merely makes us the 'fools of habit'. Most subversive of all, the syntax of this lyric goes on to tangle, expressing the possibility of suicide simultaneously with the act of religious consolation.

> So bring him: we have idle dreams:
>   This look of quiet flatters thus
>   Our home-bred fancies: O to us,
> The fools of habit, sweeter seems
>
> To rest beneath the clover sod,
>   That takes the sunshine and the rains,
>   Or where the kneeling hamlet drains
> The chalice of the grapes of God;
>
> Than if with thee the roaring wells
>   Should gulf him fathom-deep in brine;
>   And hands so often clasped in mine,
> Should toss with tangle and with shells.

For whom, poet or dead man, is it 'sweeter' 'To rest beneath the clover sod'? 'Than if *with thee* the roaring wells/Should gulf him fathom-deep in brine.' The delayed comparative 'than if with thee' strictly refers to the ship carrying the body who is last addressed nearly three stanzas away from this comparative. The delay inextricably tangles and exchanges pronouns, 'with thee', 'him', even 'us' in the search for a relationship less remote and nearer at hand. The pronouns become interchangeably the poet, Hallam. The last line is so severed from its syntactic relationships that it seems to express a preference for remaining dead and unburied. 'Should' becomes an imperative not a subjunctive—'*should* toss with tangle and with shells'. The poet can clasp the hand of the dead again by being dead too, and the syntax tangles to allow him the possibility of doing so.

In Memoriam is one of the last great triumphs of idealist language over itself. It both overcomes and founders upon the coalescing, ambiguous forms of Romantic syntax, using these forms to express the problem of articulation and relationship which they engender. It struggles, as earlier nineteenth-century poems do not, with a psychological account of expressive language and the pathetic fallacy which threatens to undermine the firm epistemological base of Romantic poetry. Repeatedly it builds itself out of its collapse by giving full play to the language which threatens its destruction. Classical elegy coexists with psychological, idealist lyric: pastoral landscape with mind-created images. The coexistence of these 'forms' is employed to expose the contradictions inherent in each. *In Memoriam* is a poem about death trying to be a poem about life. It is 'life', not pain, the expected moral truism, which forms the 'firmer mind' (XVIII). On the other hand, 'Doubt and Death' '*let* the fancy fly' (LXXXVI), let the liberated mind free and *allow* or create its freedom, actually bringing it into being. The poem recognises its need for simple longings and consolation while continually investigating and complicating these desires. And so *In Memoriam* can be described as a poem of great intelligence. Its sporting with words, its attempt to set the possibilities of metaphor in play, reveals the problems of idealist language. It exposes the collapse of relationship inherent in its structure and looks forward beyond the nineteenth century to the problems of language experienced by later poets. It is not surprising that a poem about bereavement, the self without an object, should recognise so acutely the dissolution of idealist language. It is both willing and unwilling to do so, because it is both willing and unwilling to come to terms with death. A world without relationships: to *In Memoriam* to accept idealist language is to accept death.

The nineteenth-century poets I have discussed are in the grip of a series of problems, problems which they were at least partly in possession of, and which extend themselves into the modern period. My intention has been to describe those problems, in which an almost hubristically cognitive account of poetic language slides over into one which is potentially disabling, denying poetry the capacity to create and transform categories virtually in the act of claiming that it does so and suggesting an incipient collapse of relationship. I have proceeded by exploring the connections between epistemology and the structure of poetic language, believing that each implies the other. Questions of epistemology and the structure of poetic language become implicitly elided with or into political and cultural concerns, not because poetic language is forced to reflect some pre-existing ideological pattern in its form, but because it ceaselessly generates complexities and contradictions which, whether directly or by extension and implication, become questions about the word and the world. The configurations of poetic language are thus actively forming and questioning paradigms of relationship and action which are implicitly to do with possibilities and choices, limitations and freedoms, and they play into the extra-linguistic world as much as it plays into them. It must be self-evident that a particular historical period limits the nature and kind of question that can be asked, and that a writer will never be in full possession of his questions or solutions because they themselves are a part of the complex of contradictions he is trying to solve. But it is how these questions are asked in their ceaseless complexity, their mode of existence in poetic discourse through the form and organisation of words, which tells us something about the way in which language and history become part of one another and about the moments at which poetic form and politics intersect. It is a strangely static account of literature (and of ideology) which assumes that a text is caught in a predetermined pattern rather than responding to it and indeed reordering it through the play of language. And if one is prepared to see the language of a text as a play with limit established in and through the ordering of the work itself, one is relieved of the dubious practice of abstracting a fixed set of ideas and procedures from the text and assuming tautologously that they have produced the text.

Note

1.   This point is made by Alan Sinfield, *The Language of Tennyson's 'In Memoriam'*, Oxford, 1971. I have learned much from this study.

"Descend, and Touch, and Enter": Tennyson's Strange Manner of Address

Christopher Craft

In the concluding chapter of *Sexual Inversion*, Havelock Ellis turns with considerable circumspection to the vexing problem of the correction and consolation of the "sexual invert." In the especially vexed case of the presumptively incorrigible "congenital invert"—in the case, that is, of a person who is the "victim of abnormal [homosexual] impulses" that spring ineluctably from "the central core of organic personality"—consolation through sublimation constitutes the only available palliation because the invert's "inborn constitutional abnormality" remains, by definition, nonductile and fundamentally resistant to "psychotherapeutical [and] surgical treatment."[1] Nonetheless, the impossibility of effective medical remediation did not legitimate an active homosexual genitality. Instead, and for reasons less medical than political and practical, Ellis prescribed the difficult consolation of a more than Penelopean patience: "it is the ideal of chastity, rather than normal sexuality, which the congenital invert should hold before his eyes."[2] Yet if the rigors of so sustained a specular meditation upon "the ideal of chastity" were likely to produce an intense ocular strain, then perhaps this difficulty could be mitigated by a practical program of displacement and surrogate satisfaction: a regimen of sublimation, a course of psychosexual exercises, or, as Ellis cheerfully called it, a "method of self-restraint and self-culture, without self-repression."[3] A civilization, it would seem, without the burden of much discontent.

What does Ellis offer as his primary example of this "method of self-treatment," of "how by psychic methods to refine and spiritualize the inverted impulse"? It is nothing less, and nothing other, than a list of books to read and imitate: a prophylactic mimesis. Such remedial homosexual reading, at once consolatory and disciplinary, would serve a double or ambivalent function: the verbal substitution would express the desire it also nonetheless worked to contain, and the text would be at once the home of desire and the site of its exile. (The *Memoirs of John Addington Symonds* narrate a personal history of this agonistic Victorian belief in efficient homosexual sublimation. Early in his literary career, Symonds had hoped that "literary and imaginative

Reprinted by permission from *Genders* 1 (1988). ©1988 by the University of Texas Press.

palliatives" would double as both "the vehicle and the safety valve for [the] tormenting preoccupations" that beset the victims of "this inexorable and incurable disease."[4] Later he would regard such belief as pure—and self-destructive—fantasia.) First among the exemplary texts enlisted by Ellis in his program of literary surrogation are, predictably enough, the dialogues of Plato, which "have frequently been found a source of great help and consolation by inverts." Indeed, the reading of Plato, especially the *Phaedrus* and the *Symposium*, had for nineteenth-century gay males the force of a revelation Symonds' case history in *Sexual Inversion*, transcribed by Ellis into the third person, is representative: "It was in his eighteenth year that an event occurred which he regards as decisive in his development. He read Plato. A new world opened, and he felt that his own nature had been revealed."[5] This topos of self-recognition via Platonic texts is of course a staple in the cultural construction of nineteenth-century male homosexual subjectivity. Second in order of emphasis in Ellis' itinerary of inverted reading is, again predictably, Whitman's *Leaves of Grass*, with "its wholesome and robust ideal" of "manly love," although Whitman's exuberant sensuality and aboriginal stance rendered his poetry "of more doubtful value for general use." Again, Symonds on Whitman has representative value: *Leaves of Grass* "became for me a kind of Bible. Inspired by 'Calamus' I adopted another method of palliative treatment, and tried to invigorate the emotion I could not shake off by absorbing Whitman's conception of comradeship. . . . The immediate result of this study of Walt Whitman was the determination to write the history of paiderastia in Greece [i.e., Symonds' *A Problem in Greek Ethics*] and to attempt a theoretical demonstration of the chivalrous enthusiasm which seemed to me implicit in comradeship."[6] Here, in the translation of desire into sexual discourse, and of sexual discourse into more sexual discourse, we may see a paradigmatic example of Ellis' program of disciplinary reading and writing, itself a striking confirmation of Foucault's assertion that the nineteenth century worked assiduously to put sex into discourse.[7]

But if Ellis felt the rhetorical need to demur at Whitman's anatomical insistence, his barely veiled genital reference, Ellis had the advantage of an absolutely canonical counter-example, a Victorian text whose passionate discursivity and sexual obliquity everywhere marked its submission to the Victorian imperative "to refine and spiritualize" this problematic desire. He turned with confidence to *In Memoriam*: "Various modern poets of high ability have given expression to emotions of exalted or passionate friendship towards individuals of the same sex, whether or not such friendship can properly be termed homosexual. It is scarcely necessary to refer to *In Memoriam*, in which Tennyson enshrined his affection for his early friend, Arthur Hallam, and developed a picture of the universe on the basis of that affection."[8] Ellis' sentences here pivot on an ambivalence that we should recognize as our own: it may be "scarcely necessary" to adduce *In Memoriam* in this homosexual context, so famous is it as a site of exalted friendship and erotic displacement, yet Ellis equivocates, as indeed he must, as to "whether or not such friendship can properly be termed homosexual." Ellis' verbal equipoise here—his dichotomous need to affirm the homosociality of Tennyson's poem while refusing to specify the homosexuality of Tennysonian desire—responds faithfully both to Ellis' own delicate discursive situation as a writer of suspect texts and to a certain strategic equivocation within *In Memoriam* itself, an equivocation accurately identified by Edward Carpenter when he described *In Memoriam* as being "reserved" and "dignified" "in [its] sustained meditation and tender sentiment" but as also "half revealing here and there a more passionate feeling."[9] Exactly this strategic equivocation defines the critical and taxonomic problem of whether *In Memoriam* "can properly be termed homosexual."

This is not to deny but rather to assume and affirm that desire in *In Memoriam* pivots and circulates around Hallam as around "the centre of a world's desire."[10] Or, rather more accurately, around Hallam's absconded presence, for he is, as Carol Christ writes, "the absent center around which the poem moves."[11] But if Hallam is Tennyson's "central warmth diffusing bliss," the elegy negotiates its problematic desire less by a centering of its warmth than by the dispersion of its bliss, less by acts of specific definition than by strategies of deferral, truncation, and displacement: strategies that everywhere work to "refine and spiritualize" what otherwise would be "the wish too strong for words to name" (93). But *In Memoriam* is more than a machine for the sublimation, management, or erasure of male homosexual desire. It is, rather, the site of a continuing problematization: a problematization not merely of desire between men but also of the desire, very urgent in the elegy, to speak it.

A certain anxiety attends the reading of *In Memoriam*, and always has. The first reviews were, of course, largely laudatory, but a palpable disease haunts particular early responses. An anonymous review in the *Times* (November 28, 1851), now usually attributed to Manley Hopkins, father of the Victorian poet, Gerard Manley Hopkins, specifically complained of the elegy's erotic metaphorics, its "strange manner of address to a man, even though he be dead."[12] A "defect," this reviewer noted, "which has painfully come out as often as we take up the volume, is the tone of—may we say so!—amatory tenderness." "Very sweet and plaintive these verses are," Hopkins the elder continued, "but who would not give them a feminine application? Shakespeare may be considered the founder of this style in English." Here the reviewer's palpable gender anxiety, his fear of the unhinged gender within Tennyson's poetic voice, reflects the bewildering ease with which Tennyson employs heterosexual desire and marriage as a trope to represent his passion for lost Hallam: a tropological indiscretion, the reviewer assumes, derived from "floating remembrances of Shakespeare's sonnets," which "present the startling peculiarity of transferring every epithet of womanly endearment to a masculine friend—his master-mistress, as he calls him by a compound epithet, harsh, as it is disagreeable." This homo-erotic linkage of *In Memoriam* to Shakespeare's sonnets is not anomalous. In another anonymous review, Charles Kingsley found in *In Memoriam* a descend-ent of "the old tales of David and Jonathan, Damon and Pythias, Socrates and Alcibiades, Shakespeare and his nameless friend, of 'love passing the love of woman,' " although recently Christopher Ricks has charged Kingsley with "recklessness" and has balked at the allusion to 2 Samuel, calling it "that perilous phrase."[13] By the 1890s, when Tennyson's son Hallam wrote his biography-cum-hagiography *Alfred Lord Tennyson: A Memoir* (1897), the per-ils of what Ricks calls the "homosexual misconstruction" incited Hallam to a prudential pruning of any material that might conduce to equivocal interpretation. For example, as Ricks' biography of Tennyson informs us, when Hallam quoted Benjamin Jowett regarding "the great sorrow of [Ten-nyson's] mind," he carefully elided anything suggesting what Jowett called, with discreet indirection, "a sort of sympathy with Hellenism." Jowett's comment on Tennyson's grief, that "it would not have been manly or natural to have lived in it always," succumbed to Hallam's editorial prudence and was cut from the *Memoir*.[14]

Very much the same critical propensity to keep Tennyson "manly and natural" has governed more recent criticism of *In Memoriam*, although modern evasions of the poem's disturbing sexuality have generally demonstrated more cunning than Hallam Tennyson's. Perhaps the simplest of contemporary critical circumventions of *In Memoriam's* homoerotic discourse are those, like Jerome Buckley's *Tennyson: The Growth of a Poet* (1960), that don't find sexuality pertinent at all to the elegy's recuperative desiring. A more intri-guing strategy for negotiating the problematics of same gender desire can be found in Harold Bloom's early essay "Tennyson, Hallam, and Romantic Tradition" (1966), in which Bloom declares, with a falsifying assurance, that it "need disturb no one any longer . . . that Tennyson's Muse was (and always remained) Hallam."[15] Bloom's poetic/sexual centering of Hallam is of course substantially correct, but his cosmopolitan poise would be more convincing did he not directly exculpate himself from further musing on homoerotic muses by saying, first, that "the sexual longings of a poet *qua* poet appear to have little relation to mere experience anyway" and by saying, second, that "the analytical sophistication in aesthetic realms that would allow a responsible sexual history of English poetry is not available to us." There is therefore very little to say. We may see in Bloom's passing acknowl-edgment of the homosexual subject an ambivalence characteristic of our tradition's reading of this poem. On the one hand he acknowledges the inescapable homoerotics of *In Memoriam's* elegiac desire, while on the other he precludes a sustained and detailed analysis of that desire by foreclosing critical access to either "mere experience" (which in the case of Tennyson and Hallam is unrevealing anyway) or to the "analytical sophistication" that would render such criticism "responsible."[16]

Furthermore, Bloom's blithe assurance that Hallam's erotic centrality in *In Memoriam* "need disturb no one any longer" seems not to have had its pacifying effects; seems indeed to have gone unheeded, for in 1972 (six years after Bloom's essay) Christopher Ricks in his astute critical biography *Tennyson* paused for some ten pages to worry over precisely this issue. "But do we too," Ricks asks, "need to speak bluntly? Is Tennyson's love for Hallam a homosexual one?"[17] Ricks' answer—I doubt that I am betraying any suspense here—is no, although a number of equivocations beset this denial. His discussion of this anxiogenic question opens with a gesture that recalls Bloom's deferral of adequate discussion to that millennial day when analytic sophistication in aesthetic realms will enable intelligent discourse; but whereas Bloom's displacement is temporal, Ricks is spatial. Disclaiming the authority of literary criticism altogether, Ricks invokes another professional discipline, and a predictable one: "the crucial acts of definition will have to be left to the psychologists and psychiatrists, though it should be said that literary historians usually vitiate their arguments by conveniently jumbling the old severely differentiating view with the newer 'something of it in everybody' one." Such recourse to psychiatry and psychology does double duty; in submitting poetry to pathology the literary critic escapes ultimate responsibility for what must remain a *literary* decision about the representational function of *desire in the text*, while simultaneously and inescapably situating that decision within an ideological economy of disease, dysfunction, and presumptively desirable remediation. Implicit in this gesture is the normativizing hope that Tennyson was not "bluntly" "homosexual" or, in Ricks' other locution, "abnormally abnormal." More importantly still, the deferral of literary decision to medical authority quite simply misses the point. The question at issue is not the history of Tennyson's genitalia (which Tennyson's most recent biographer suggests would yield a rather brief and tedious narrative) nor the potentially psychopathic trajectories of an obviously tortured psyche. Rather, as we shall see, the issue that matters here is the function of represented sexual desire within the verbal economy we call *In Memoriam* and within the larger tradition of representation from which the poem arises and to which it continues to direct its strange manner of address.

Ricks' extended "defense (so to speak) of Tennyson" against imputations of homosexuality remains sympathetic to certain Tennysonian notions of an orderly and conventional androgyny, of an androgyny that perhaps mitigates but never subverts the disciplinary bifurcation of gender characteristics, as when Tennyson admonishes that "men should be androgynous and women gynandrous, but men should not be gynandrous nor women androgynous."[18] A transparent ambivalence informs Tennyson's sentence: on the one hand a desire to escape the containments of gender, on the other a desire to contain the escape. Tennyson's precise marshalling of prefixes and suffixes, of fronts and backs, of (to borrow one of Ricks' metaphors) "heads" and "tails," bespeaks an anxiety of gender inversion strong enough to require careful regulation at the level of the signifier. If signifiers can be compelled into remaining "jubilantly straight" (Ricks again), perhaps signifieds will follow suit. The disciplinary punctilio of gender enacted by Tennyson's sentence suggests one reason for the obliquity of sexual representation in *In Memoriam*, and it certainly anticipates the dis-ease circulating throughout Ricks' defense of Tennyson's (hetero)sexuality.

The foregoing reading of our tradition's reading of *In Memoriam*, brief and partial as it is,[19] is intended to suggest the conceptual and imagistic burden suffered by our culture's discourse on same gender eroticism. *In Memoriam* remains a pivotal case in this regard precisely because the problematics of the poem's erotic representations are indistinguishable from readerly problems of interpretation and feeling. To mouth the Tennysonian "I," as the reader of this poem must repeatedly and obsessively do, is to bespeak (for the duration of reading at least) an anxiogenic identification with the poet's fierce reparational desire, a longing that regularly presses to a transgressive homosexual verge. But *In Memoriam* approaches this verge only when compelled by an incommensurate grief. Why, we must now ask, does *In Memoriam* disclose homosexual desire as indissociable from death? As itself a mode of mourning? Why this constitutive linking of desire and death?

In *In Memoriam* death discovers desire, the latter arriving in and as the wake of the former. The linkage between desire and death is not a causal metaphorical articulation; it is rather a causal narrative one. For in the very personal erotic myth that *In Memoriam* so extensively develops, the death of Hallam, when "God's finger touch'd him, and he slept" (LXXXV), initiates in the poet both a recuperational homosexual desire—a desire to restore to its preschismatic unity the "divided hal[ves] of such / A friendship as had master'd Time"—and, what is worse, a desperate need to speak this potentially philosophic "desire and pursuit of the whole" under the aegis of a transgressive erotics.[20] "Descend, and touch, and enter," Tennyson dangerously pleads, and "hear / The wish too strong for words to name" (XCIII). The extremity of such expression, its desperate mode of erotic address, derives from the poet's belated recognition that no other human love will ever be "as pure and whole / As when he loved me here in Time" and from the correlative fear that "love for him [may] have drain'd / My capabilities of love" (XLIII, LXXXV). Thus desire's duration, the temporal and spatial extensions of this very distended text's poetic wooing (cf. LXXXV, "I woo your love"), commences not with Arthur's desirable presence (for when Arthur is present desire and language are redundant media), but rather with its opposite, with the poet's recognition that his "dear friend" has become in death's difference "my lost Arthur's loved remains" (CXXIX, IX). The language of active desiring therefore finds its origin in a death or terminus that retrospectively figures the gap or aporia intervening between the now disjunct members of an ontologically prior wholeness or sameness whose unitary gender remains emphatically, inescapably male. In what we may now correctly call the hom(m)osexual economy of *In Memoriam*, death and not gender is the differential out of which desire is so painfully born.[21]

This structure of desire entrains certain disciplinary relations which are coextensive with, indistinguishable from, the desire itself. The elegiac mode disciplines the desire it also enables: on the one hand the sundering of death instigates an insistent reparational longing, on the other it claustrates the object of this desire on the far side of a divide that interdicts touch even as it incites the desire for touching. An infinite desire is infinitely deferred, subject always to postponement, displacement, diffusion. Death thus inscribes a prophylactic distance, as Tennyson himself suggested in a related context. Commenting on the initial line of poem CXXII ("Oh, wast thou with me, dearest, then"), the poet said: "If anybody thinks I ever called him 'dearest' in his life they are much mistaken, for I never even called him 'dear.' " Ricks finds this statement "naive perhaps, but not tonally suggestive of homosexuality."[22] I would say, rather, that such "naivety" marks Tennyson's perfectly Victorian strategy of linguistic displacement, precisely because it embeds "homosexuality" within an idealizing elegiac register. This is to repeat the elegy's own insistence that the interfiguration of desire and death derives from a tropological necessity: "Let Love clasp Grief lest both be drown'd" (I). What is "saved" in this embrace is a poetic logic that instantiates homosexual desire as already its own distantiation. "My prime passion [is] in the grave," and "so hold I commerce with the dead".

Of course, as Victorian and modern readers have been quick to notice, the formal solution to this problem is Christ. In a way that is so straightforward as to be transparent. Tennyson would master his unconventional desire for Hallam by figuring it as a subspecies of a very conventional desire for "the Strong Son of God" (Prologue). A perfectly conventional trope of typological interpretation enables Tennyson to represent Hallam as a "noble type / Appearing ere the times were ripe" (Epilogue)—as, that is, a medial character whose death repeated the ontologically prior sacrifice of the other "He that died" (LXXXIV) and whose earthly presence had pointed to the superior consummation of a second coming. Yet simply to identify Hallam and Christ as interpenetrated figures of erotic and religious devotion is to repeat what the criticism has already noticed. "*In Memoriam*," Gerhard Joseph writes, "describes the transformation of Hallam into an analogue of Christ; to render this Hallam-Christ accessible Tennyson eroticizes him, giving him female attributes."[23] Joseph's sentence is of course summarily correct (correct, that is, as a summary), but the pages to follow will argue that a more capable understanding of Tennyson's fluent erotics demands that we pause at length to consider how *In Memoriam* articulates the analogy between Hallam and Christ, and how that analogy works to relieve the speaker's desperate erotic distress, a distress that is indistinguishable from his grief. To rush to the Christological or phallologocentric solution—to chant compliantly with Tennyson, "Love is and was my lord and king" (CXXIV)—is to risk another terminological reduction, one that, in its leap to the available comforts of a conventional faith, fails to register the anxious and fluctuant interfusion of sexual desire and religious faith in a poem justly more famous for the quality of its oscillations than for the force of its closural affirmation. *In Memoriam*, Eliot was right to say, "is not religious because of the quality of its faith, but because of the quality of its doubt."[24] If, making explicit what Eliot in his essay leaves implicit, we recognize doubt as a figure of desire, as a mode of suspension poised between the loss of Hallam and the promise of his restoration in a Christological embrace, then we will have begun to trace the homoerotic basis of the elegy's extensive yearning.

In its most orthodox articulation, Tennyson's typological strategy figures Hallam as a quotidian declension, a beautiful but fallen simulacrum of the absolutely perfect and ontologically prior archetype of Christ himself. The disciplinary and transferential trajectory of such a figural strategy is clear: a desire that would seem to begin in Hallam is discovered to begin and end in Christ, whose forgiving body safely absorbs, relays, and completes a fierce homoerotic cathexis. The elegy's sustained appeal to the "conclusive bliss" of its Christological closure identifies apocalyptic death as the site of a deferred but certain erotic restoration. In the closural ecstasis of the "one far-off divine event / To which the whole creation moves," a similifying Christ will "take" the lovers' riven halves and restore them to a "single soul" (LXXXIV). *In Memoriam* thus solves the problem of desire's divisiveness by fantasizing a dissolving incorporation:

> Dear friend, far off, my lost desire,
>   So far, so near in woe and weal;
>   O loved the most, when most I feel
> There is a lower and a higher;
>
> Known and unknown; human, divine;
>   Sweet human hand and lips and eye;
>   Dear heavenly friend that canst not die,
> Mine, mine, for ever, ever mine.
>   (CXXIX)

As is perhaps obvious, the intermediate qualities identified in these quatrains refer equally or indistinguishably to Hallam and to Christ. The blended might of erotic and religious devotion at once mediates and idealizes the poet's indefatigable longing for "that dear friend of mine who lives in God" (Epilogue); in this transfiguration the conventional topoi of a reparational theology subsume and discipline the transgressive force of Tennyson's elegiac desire.

As is consistent with its consolatory structure, *In Memoriam* both begins and ends with an orthodox stress upon this Christological figuration. Begins

31. For more on developmental homophobia, see Sedgwick, *Between Men*, 176–77, where she proposes a "slow, distinctive two-stage progression from schoolboy desire to adult homophobia." Thinking of Dickens, she writes:

> *David Copperfield*, among other books, makes the same point. David's infatuation with his friend Steerforth, who calls him "Daisy" and treats him like a girl, is simply part of David's education—though another, later part is the painful learning of how to triangulate from Steerforth onto women, and finally, although incompletely, to hate Steerforth and grow at the expense of his death. In short, a gentleman will associate the erotic end of the homosocial spectrum, not with dissipation, not with viciousness or violence, but with childishness, as an infantile need, a mark of powerlessness, which, while it may be viewed with shame or scorn or denial, is unlikely to provoke the virulent, accusatory projection that characterizes twentieth-century homophobia.

32. Rosenberg, who also quotes these lines, provides the apposite gloss: "Yet these hands, which Tennyson has sought throughout the poem, are not Hallam's but those of the immortal Love of the Prologue." Rosenberg in *In Memoriam*, 214.

33. Eliot in Hunt, *Casebook*, 133.

34. Sigmund Freud, "Mourning and Melancholia," *The Standard Edition of the Complete Works of Sigmund Freud*, trans. James Strachey (London, 1953–1974), XIV, 244–45.

35. Ricks, *Tennyson*, 216.

36. Irigaray, *This Sex*, 193.

37. Tennyson quoted in Hallam, Lord Tennyson, *Alfred, Lord Tennyson: A Memoir* (London, 1897), 300.

38. Rosenberg, "Two Kingdoms," 216.

39. The present essay is a shortened version of a dissertation chapter that has benefited from a number of readings; for these I want especially to thank Carol Christ, Catherine Gallagher, D. A. Miller, Eve Kosofsky Sedgwick, and Alex Zwerdling.

Maud and the Doom of Culture

HERBERT F. TUCKER

Tennyson was understandably apologetic about *The Princess*, and even about the faith of *In Memoriam* he had twinges of bad conscience. Things were dramatically different with *Maud*. This third panel in the triptych of Tennyson's middle years stayed with him like nothing else he ever wrote, and it invariably stirred his most truculently protective instincts. Tennyson was nettled more by what was harsh in the mixed reviews *Maud* received than by any of the voluminous criticism his career called forth. Although his habitual choice of this text for after-dinner recitation may have had a compensatory motive, there must have been more than a wish for redress behind the way he flourished *Maud* as a test for all comers. The note of obsession remains audible in the bravura performance of "Come into the garden, Maud" that he chanted into a microphone during his very last years, and no fresh reading of its headlong measures will fail to find it in the written text either. Tennyson had little cause to worry about *Maud*'s being, like *In Memoriam*, "too hopeful"—those who disapprove the conclusion, one suspects, are reprehending its grim despair as much as anything else—and he evidently felt that this poem, unlike *The Princess*, was more than "only a medley."[1] Nor did he ever offer much by way of an interpretation. Public recitation, instead, became his defense of poetry; what was required was not to reason why, but to read *Maud* straight through, ideally in polite mixed company.

The poet's insatiable demand for social ratification of this work suggests that he, like the rest of us, found it impossible to endorse *Maud* wholeheartedly. Furthermore, the uniquely social dimension of this text's after-history bears directly on its procedures and themes. For *Maud* is indeed more than a medley: at once love story and social critique, an imperialist tract riddled with anatomies of a sociopathic yet also sociogenic madness, it represents the most complete fusion of private with public codes anywhere in Tennyson. The poem makes the laureate's principal contribution to the Condition of England question, by representing that condition and the condition of its deranged hero as utterly congruent and as reciprocally determined, in a dizzying weave of "cause" with "consequence" (I.x.374) that raises Tenny-

Reprinted from *Tennyson and the Doom of Romanticism*, by Herbert F. Tucker (1988), by permission. © 1988 by Harvard University Press.

son's habitual confusion of active and passive moods to a rare analytic instrumentality.[2] *Maud* elaborates a tragically disabling vision of doom, and it remains a radical, perennially disturbing document.

The composition of the poem began, like so much else in the work of Tennyson's maturity, in 1833–34. The stanzaic fragment "Oh! That 'Twere Possible," which found a place eventually in part II of *Maud*, epitomizes the exploratory work of the ten years' silence between 1832 and 1842, with its tension between impulses of inward and outward reference. The opening stanza hearkens back to the English undefiled of "Westron Wind," an anonymous lyric that for centuries has spurred readers to imagine a narrative context for its pure pathos. *Maud* was written in order to provide its lyric germ with such a context, but the original lyric both does and does not lend itself to narrative explanation. While it suggests that the speaker's "true love" (3) is dead to him, the poem leaves unanswered the question of what happened. It interests itself instead in the mood of frustration that an acknowledged impossibility imposes, and its interest for us lies in the scenic juxtapositions whereby Tennyson rendered this mood. For the alternating stanzas of "Oh! That 'Twere Possible" play conventional images of a rural past against something quite new in the canon of English poetry: hypnotically surreal imagery of a desolate urban present. Tennyson was aware of the novelty of this imagery, if we may judge from the way he capitalizes on it in Trinity Notebook 21. Already in the first draft the bereaved lover is stealing "Through the hubbub of the market" (42), "Through all that crowd, confused and loud" (45); and decades before his successor J. Alfred Prufrock, he loathes "the squares and streets, / And the faces that one meets" (58–59). These stray early images of the modern city Tennyson systematically expands in the Trinity notebook, inserting new stanzas on "the leagues of lights, / And the roaring of the wheels" (21–22), "the yellow-vapours" (37) and "drifts of lurid smoke / On the misty river-tide" (40–41).[3] These revisions show the poet installing a traditional expression of erotic grief within a markedly modern context, and generalizing that grief into a malaise whose cultural specificity, at the level of imagery, widens its appeal beyond the power of narrative explanation.

Tennyson's only significant publication during the ten years' silence—picked out in 1837 from an array of unpublished manuscripts that few poets can ever have matched—"Oh! That 'Twere Possible" at first seems an odd choice for that honor. But if we reflect that this poem uniquely combines a traditional passion with an unprecedented contemporaneity, we may see it as an unerring choice: a dispatch from the field, a telegraphic progress report on the directions in which Tennyson's explorations of genre were leading him. That progress culminates in *Maud*, and it is fitting that this experimental lyric should have found its home there; for what was a lyric germ in "Oh! That 'Twere Possible" becomes in *Maud* the rampant virus of modern life, "the blighting influence," as the poet later named it, "of a recklessly speculative age."[4] The major analytic innovation of *Maud* is its measured and diffusive contamination, by imagery drawn from economic and political life, of a series of lyrical passions that run the Tennysonian gamut from fury to ecstasy to resignation. We could think of the poet's practice here as a kind of inoculation by the jaundiced eye, if only the poem had the strength, or the naiveté, to imagine a cure. But in this text, where the hero at last donates his body and his intellect in military service to the very interests that have crippled him, the cure *is* the disease. The virulent poem Tennyson wrote has force to resist both the antidote of patriotic sublimation, which his own later glosses would prescribe, and the antibody of liberal and humanitarian criticism, which *Maud* has provoked since the year of its publication.[5]

Before inspecting the text, we might first consider the implications of its genre for the eddying dialectic of its public and private motives. The poem was subtitled *A Monodrama* only in 1875, with a term Tennyson borrowed from reviewers trying to label the *sui generis* production he himself had first issued simply as *Maud*, after toying with a title that despaired of generic classification: *Maud, or the Madness*. The new term appealed to the poet as a match for the generic innovation of his favorite brainchild: "No other poem (a monotone with plenty of change and no weariness) has been made into a drama where successive phases of passion in one person take the place of successive persons."[6] Tennyson's career began with drama in *The Devil and the Lady*, and his sad late attempts to write a stageworthy play let us see in retrospect how important the drama remained to him as a genre affording direct contact with the public. Monodrama offered a version of such contact, as A. Dwight Culler has shown in tracing its descent from the parlor "attitudes" in vogue around the turn of the nineteenth century: intimate performances for select audiences of much the same kind that Emily Tennyson would convene for her husband's readings half a century later.[7]

A failure at drama, Tennyson nonetheless could succeed at monodrama because of just the generic difference his comment on *Maud* emphasizes. In a monodrama he could circumvent his constitutional weakness at imagining other minds and concentrate instead on his forte, the depiction of fixed moods or "phases of passion." Tennyson makes these moods public in two ways. In accordance with the use to which he puts cliché in *The Princess* and *In Memoriam*, he keeps the moods stereotypically standard, as in the Regency "attitude" or the Victorian melodrama. Beyond this, and in sharp contrast to his early mood pieces, Tennyson consistently renders his hero's phases of passion as reactions to stock situations drawn from contemporary life. Thus, while on one hand this monodrama parts company with the social interaction that Tennyson the failed dramatist appears to have craved in vain, on the other hand it repeatedly represents its solitary central consciousness as instinct with a largely unacknowledged social content. The highly individualist generic form of monodrama appears to counteract the poet's unmistakable intention to indict the social consequences of laissez-faire values; yet the form as he deploys it carries his indictment into the very stronghold of individualism, planting conspicuous social codes within the supposed confessional sincerity of the lyrically speaking, lyrically overheard self.[8]

It is never easy to know how much awareness of the social weave of his rhetoric to attribute to Tennyson's hero. The pervasive ambiguity of this issue is one of the features that distinguish the monodrama from the dramatic monologue, where undecidability on this scale would soon burst the generic limits of tolerance. In dramatic monologues we require to know more firmly whether and when speakers know what they are talking about; *Maud* very often leaves this question wide open, so as to open its discourse, and its version of the self, as fully as possible to the influence of the "recklessly speculative age" that not only blights but largely constitutes it. Clearly Tennyson's hero is a rather recklessly speculative type himself when it comes to social analysis, as appears from his version of peace in a "Mammonite" culture (I.i.45) as nothing less than an undeclared civil war of each with all. No class struggle here, because no class consciousness; and therefore no witting solidarity, either, to focus the hero's blurry maledictions. He adopts the pose of a nostalgically anarchic satirist, sharpening on one social object after another the tools of an unsteady Romantic irony that implicates him as well: "Sooner or later I too may passively take the print / Of the golden age—why not? I have neither hope nor trust" (I.i.29–30). In referring to "the golden age," the hero yokes idealized and mythical with modern and economic associations, in a satirical counterpoint that chastizes the present with the standard of the past. Within the economic sphere the hero may also be consciously playing the old and forthright order of "gold" against the more dubious "printed" currency he will have to "take" as a citizen in a modern economy. This much is sturdy fulmination of a recognizable sort. How are we to take it, though, when the scion of a fallen family, manifestly feeling bilked of his inheritance, complains that he has no "trust"? The term implies a relation between his legal and his metaphysical situation, which the plot insists we entertain later on: if he marries Maud he will be recouping his family's fortune with justice (and with interest). But this same relation, if apparent to the hero himself, would place his disinterested absorption by the salvific power of love in a peculiar light indeed.

We cannot know with any precision, in this entirely representative passage, how much the hero knows whereof he speaks; and our bafflement arises from Tennyson's monodramatic rendition of the modern self as lunatic, tidally swayed by a cycle of passional phases that fall, in turn, under the influence of the age. When the hero recalls how, upon his father's bankruptcy, "the wind like a broken worldling wailed, / And the flying gold of the ruined woodlands drove through the air" (I.i.11–12), we may assume that the economically pathetic fallacy lies within his control. But is a similar assumption justified when this inhabitant of a world where "only the ledger lives" (35) describes the scene of his father's suicide as a deranged accountant's entry in the red, where "The red-ribbed ledges drip with a silent horror of blood" (3)? Jonathan Wordsworth (1974) and others have noted the sexuality of this primal scene, but the overdetermination of imagery here and through-out *Maud* seems to call for not just a Freudian but also a social psychology, an account of manic boom and depressive bust.[9] To take another example, there is bitter wit in the hero's charges that "a company forges the wine" (36) and that "chalk and alum and plaster are sold to the poor for bread, / And the spirit of murder works in the very means of life" (39–40). In conflating the adulteration of subsistence staples with that of the sacramental elements of eternal life, the hero scores his point with prophetic keenness. Yet when he turns closer to home and the lyrical sphere of personal feelings, his language starts veering out of control and into a social orbit: "Maud with her sweet purse-mouth when my father dangled the grapes" (71). Pursed lips are sweet, but so are purses, especially in a context that includes the bankrupt father. The hero cannot intend such economic associations, yet he cannot avoid them either—least of all, it seems, in passages that touch on the most private parts of his life.

Given this pattern of obsessive return, it is no wonder that he has such difficulty imposing upon his inventory of social and personal ills the explanatory pattern of cause and effect. "Villainy somewhere! whose? One says, we are villains all" (I.i.17). Like Hamlet, to whom Tennyson liked to compare him, the hero of *Maud* wants the comfort of clearly assigned virtue and blame. But this desire is inhibited, first by a Hamlet-like sense of complicity in what he attacks, and more generally by a Dickensian vision of universal implication in an unbeatable system: "We are puppets, Man in his pride, and Beauty fair in her flower; / Do we move ourselves, or are moved by an unseen hand at a game / That pushes us off from the board, and others ever succeed?" (I.iv.126–128). If others ever succeed where we lose, their success is not their doing but that of the invisible hand; worse yet, those who "succeed" figure not as recipients of success but merely as later victims in a blind succession. In sum, the galloping exposition with which *Maud* opens dismantles responsibility and suspends a baffled passion in its place—thus articulating Tennyson's familiar vision of doom, but now with a degree of mimetic realism and cultural specificity that is without parallel in his work.

The hero seeks anesthetic refuge from this condition of passive suffering in the "passionless peace" of an Epicurean "philosopher's life" (I.iv.150–151). Yet his philosophy falters when it comes to explaining his alienation in casual terms: "Do we move ourselves, or are moved?" The explanations the hero produces contradict each other. At times he seems to himself the victim of his history and environment,

Living alone in an empty house,
Here half-hid in the gleaming wood,
Where I hear the dead at midday moan,
And the shrieking rush of the wainscot mouse,
And my own sad name in corners cried,
When the shiver of dancing leaves is thrown
About its echoing chambers wide,
Till a morbid-hate and horror have grown
Of a world in which I have hardly mixt.

(I.vi.257–265)

These circumstances, the hero says, have made him what he is; yet if Tennyson's Mariana of 1830 were to account for herself in this way, as she could with virtually no change of imagery, we should rightly suspect that the conditioning circumstances were fantastic projections from a self less acted upon than active. And indeed, when a few sections later a preaching pacifist has come into town, the hero reverses his behaviorist position and insists on its moral opposite, the purity of inward discipline:

This huckster put down war! can he tell
Whether war be a cause or a consequence?
Put down the passions that make earth Hell!
Down with ambition, avarice, pride,
Jealousy, down! cut off from the mind
The bitter springs of anger and fear;
Down too, down at your own fireside,
With the evil tongue and the evil ear,
For each is at war with mankind.

(I.x.373–381)

The chiastic relation between these two passages—private moods arise from circumstances, whereas the public arena evokes an individualistic morality—illustrates the crossing of social upon personal issues that is the poet's larger theme. Not just the "huckster" but the hero too confuses cause with consequence, in a repeatedly frustrated attempt to grasp, from within, the monodramatic dialectic in which he lives and speaks.

The form of monodrama, as a kind of lyrical narration, lends itself particularly well to Tennyson's rendition of the problematic social and individual reciprocity of cause with consequence. Monodrama is a narrative form in which, within the phenomenology of reading, consequences always precede causes. *Maud* thus situates its hero reactively, his phases of passion having been prompted by some action anterior to the text, usually a social encounter. His speech, which is to say his whole poetic existence, is in this fundamental sense, and with great cumulative force, a product of his social environment.

As we read we learn to ask not what he will do next, but what will have happened to him in the interim. *Maud* thus is a poem not only written backward but inevitably read backward as well, from moment to moment, despite the forward thrust of its plot. This monodramatic retrospection kinks up the chain of cause and effect by compelling us to gather the story by extrapolation from what the hero tells us. Especially given so suspiciously erratic a narrator, this technique emphasizes the arbitrary and inferential nature of the causal linkage involved in understanding any narrative; it lands us, therefore, in uncertainties akin to those that beset the nonplussed hero himself.[10]

It is in representing the pivotal deed, the hero's fatal duel with Maud's brother, that Tennyson exploits the narrative resources of monodrama most brilliantly and makes the question of causality most strikingly problematic:

> "The fault was mine, the fault was mine"—
> Why am I sitting here so stunned and still,
> Plucking the harmless wild-flower on the hill?—
> It is this guilty hand!—
> And there rises ever a passionate cry
> From underneath in the darkening land—
> What is it, that has been done?
>
> (II.i.1–7)

This last question is a version of the one Tennyson's monodrama provokes in its reader throughout, and its passive wording is precisely right. The hero's implication—something uncomprehended has taken its unstoppable course—faithfully reproduces the bewilderment that has suffused his vision since the start. Without dodging responsibility ("It is this guilty hand!"), his narrative of the duel depicts both antagonists as caught up in roles that their high passion assumes by social reflex: roles ordained by "the Christless code" of honor (II.i.26), dated by 1855 but still very much in force, which marshals the vindictive energies of their caste.[11] The doom, and the guilt, that the hero thus shares with his victim are brilliantly presented with the opening line, which is both the most naked admission of responsibility in all of *Maud* and the most resistant to personal attribution. "The fault was mine"; but the words are whose? They repeat what the brother has said, yet obviously they tell the hero's truth too. However the *beau geste* of Maud's brother was intended, his unimpeachably terminal confession is the noble, Christless code's last cunning article, one that will rivet the hero for life to a fugitive and inexpiable guilt. " 'The fault was mine,' he whispered, 'fly!' " (II.i.30). Although winning the duel, the hero has lost by the rules of every code he might stand by: the dictates of human decency, true lovers' faith, the biblical commandment—even, now that Maud's brother has upstaged him forever, the standard of honor underlying this most lethal of aristocratic field sports. And yet the hero has played the game: having done wrong, he cannot say where he has *gone* wrong, because he is finally victimized by the confluence of incompatible cultural imperatives.

In a sense this terrible confluence is just bad luck. Luck is the prosaic underside of the doom Tennyson's poetry envisions ("the shocks of Chance," says section XCV of *In Memoriam*, not "Change"); but it is a side he rarely risks exhibiting so nearly as in *Maud*. If the poem escapes the charge of plot contrivance, it does so principally through the very excess of that contrivance. For while from one perspective the monodrama suspends the connection of cause with effect that binds together more traditional narratives (like Tennyson's idylls), from another it furnishes a surplus of explanations. The hero has not one but every reason to quarrel with Maud's brother, to flee the scene of the duel, to take leave of his senses, to enlist at last in the war effort. This causal overload imparts to the poem much of its driven fatalism; to ask motivational questions about any of its main events is to be stormed by a rush of eligible answers—passional, economic, political, clinical—none of them especially convincing, by reason of their very multiplicity and cooperation. It is this interlock of motives, the whole self-reinforcing and self-perpetuating ideological complex, that Tennyson has taken up in *Maud*; and as the poet pursues its strategy across the phases of passion, the poem raises the etiological stakes from happenstance, through the charisma of personal good or bad fortune, toward an inescapable cultural bondage.

The operation of a cultural complex, and not just an Oedipal one, is nowhere stronger or more poignant than where Tennyson's contemporaries would least have expected to find it: in the hero's love affair with Maud. The erotic sphere notoriously served the Victorians as a stay against the allied forces of selfishness and impersonality that a society founded on the cash nexus had unleashed. The hero of *Maud* certainly regards love in this way, as did his poet when commenting that the hero is "raised to a pure and holy love which elevates his whole nature"; and most criticism has followed suit. [12] Yet when we consider the widespread ideological resistance of Victorian culture to any desecration of its Romantic erotic ideal—a resistance to which Tennyson's comment on "a pure and holy love" shows him also subject—we may surmise that this was the feature of his scandalous poem that aroused the profoundest indignation, as it was also his hardest-won triumph.

The social analysis of love begins where the love story does, as the hero fatally overhears Maud singing by the manorial cedar "an air that is known to me" (I.v.164). In this poem that ends with a decision to enlist, it matters of course that Maud's is "a martial song" (166); but it equally matters that her song is a traditional one, a ballad the hero recognizes at once. Because Maud has not invented the song but found it in the aristocratic past, the hero can deflect his spontaneous devotion from Maud herself onto the nobility that speaks through her: to "adore / Not her, who is neither courtly nor kind, / Not her, not her, but a voice" (187–189).[13] If we compare this passage to Tennyson's lines on the singing bulbul from "Recollections of the Arabian Nights" (1830)—"Not he: but something which possessed / The darkness of the world" (lines 71–72)—we glimpse in little the thoroughness with which in *Maud* the poet has devoted his usual rhetoric of impersonal transcendence to hegemonic conditions of culture. From the beginning the hero loves courtliness, not Maud; and the imagery of stars, flowers, and especially gems in which he consistently represents her, like the singularity of her voice here, points to an imaginative and erotic elitism that is not merely figurative but refers to the constellation of rank and wealth that determines the place of these lovers in the Victorian world.

In view of the events this incident precipitates, it is an awful coincidence for both lovers that he should hear her singing just this song at just this point. And yet, in their time and place, what else should she sing, and how else should he react? This decisive first link in a concatenated plot is already decided before it begins, an entirely natural consequence flowing from who the two principals are, which is to say, from where they are in society and history. A reader who means to condemn the hero in part III for joining troops who "have proved we have hearts in a cause, we are noble still" (III.vi.55) will have to read the judgment backward to this moment of apparently innocuous lyricism, where a song of noble men "in battle array, / Ready in heart" (I.v.169–170), stirs the hero's heart so readily because the codes of nobility are what his heart is ready for.[14] The hero's peroration declares the Crimean War "a cause"; and though his part in it seems less a cause than an irresistible consequence, his declaration rings true. The cause that is "noble still" remains the same cause that has determined the love whose aftermath his soldiering may bring to terminal resolution.

As the love story advances, Maud appears to her lover not a person intrinsically worthy, nor an object of desire, but a sign whose worth arises from the place she holds in a social system. Even physical beauty, the most inalienably personal of possessions, exists in Maud only as it appears to her socially conditioned beholder:

> I kissed her slender hand,
> She took the kiss sedately;
> Maud is not seventeen,
> But she is tall and stately.
> (I.xii.424–427)

Readers have not been kind to this stanza, taking offense at the patronizing decorum of its courtship and its rhyme. But the stiffness of the lovemaking, and of the language that describes it, makes an important point: Maud's beauty *is* her decorum, her school-finished poise a cultural accomplishment for which the semipublic "stately" is just *le mot juste*. Here is a young woman bred to receive a courtly kiss as her due; and the hero's patronizing approval of her breeding includes his awareness that, at seventeen or a little older, she will be able to raise him to her estate as a landed paterfamilias. Not her, not her, but a poise, a prize, a place.

The hero's metaphor of choice in describing Maud is the gem or pearl (I.iii.95, v.175, x.352, xviii.640), with its obvious connotations of wealth. More often, though, he describes her metonymically instead, in tropes focused on the associations that make her such a catch.[15] This metonymic displacement, from Maud's proper self to her properties, often leads the hero to dwell on the other men in her life, who are always described in greater detail than Maud herself, for the simple reason that their opinions, doings, and prospects are of greater account. The "dandy-despot" brother (I.vi.231), the "snowy-banded, dilettante, / Delicate-handed priest" (I.viii.310–311), the "padded shape" and "waxen face" of the new suitor he calls "little King Charley snarling" (I.x.358–359, I.xii.441), fix upon the hero's imagination with the fascination of a social taboo; the trappings of their power represent what, for all his philosophy, he cannot help coveting. He finds a warrant for his courtship in a dream memory of "two men," his father and Maud's, plotting their children's future together, their voices spectrally empowered by dream but also by a patriarchal convention that is nowhere and everywhere, "Somewhere, talking of me; / 'Well, if it prove a girl, my boy / Will have plenty: so let it be' " (I.vii.297–300). Even in rare moments of speculation about Maud's mind, the hero assumes that her marriage choice—the one culturally crucial exercise of a Victorian lady's will—must turn on her estimate of a husband's prospective standing in a gentleman's world: "She would not do herself this great wrong, / To take a wanton dissolute boy / For a man and leader of men" (I.x.386–388).

Metonymy is the rhetorical mode of nineteenth-century realism; and since the real, the Tennysonian "that which is," (*In Memoriam* XCV) appears in *Maud* as the ideological ordinance of culture, it makes perfect sense that his hero's nervous love should crackle at every synapse with the rhetoric of power. The climactic sections of part I take as their subject the empowerment of love; and it is here, in the realm of erotic fantasy, that Tennyson's experimental interfusion of private with public discourse becomes most acute.

> O beautiful creature, what am I
> That I dare to look her way;
> Think that I may hold dominion sweet,
> Lord of the pulse that is lord of her breast,
> And dream of her beauty with tender dread,

From the delicate Arab arch of her feet
To the grace that, bright and light as the crest
Of a peacock, sits on her shining head,
And she knows it not: O, if she knew it,
To know her beauty might half undo it.
I know it the one bright thing to save
My yet young life in the wilds of Time.
(I.xvi.546–557)

A King Arthur of desire, the hero seeks salvation from "the wilds of Time" in the establishment of just the masculine "dominion" that, in his time, the ideology of gender prescribes. Maud must not "know her beauty," because that is her lover's prerogative. It is he who will *own* it when confessing his love ("For I must tell her"; I.xvi.569), while her part is confined to the giving, keeping, or breaking of "her word" (561–565), yes or no, when man proposes—a version of the passivity, the mere responsiveness to social mandates, from which the hero means to carve himself an escape by asserting the claims of male dominion.

The exotic images the hero imports for Maud's beauty (the "Arab arch," the curiously male peacock's crest) suggest that his fantasies of erotic dominion are imperial fantasies as well. The next section bears this suggestion out very fully indeed. Section xvii, though it has not fared well with critics, seems to me one of Tennyson's tours de force, a chaste imagination of erotic triumph to which images of global hegemony come as if unbidden:

Go not, happy day,
　From the shining fields,
Go not, happy day,
　Till the maiden yields.
Rosy is the West,
　Rosy is the South,
Roses are her cheeks,
　And a rose her mouth
When the happy Yes
　Falters from her lips,
Pass and blush the news
　Over glowing ships;
Over blowing seas,
　Over seas at rest,
Pass the happy news,
　Blush it through the West;
Till the red man dance
　By his red cedar-tree,
And the red man's babe
　Leap, beyond the sea.
Blush from West to East,

> Blush from East to West,
> Till the West is East,
> Blush it through the West.
> Rosy is the West,
> Rosy is the South,
> Roses are her cheeks,
> And a rose her mouth.

The form and imagery of this poem speak eloquently to the relation between erotic and cultural power, and about both in relation to language. The lines fall into natural quatrain stanzas (as in sections vii and xii), but here the poet has fused his quatrains into a formal continuity that mirrors the seamlessness of a global vision. The most remarkable fusion occurs at the end of the eighth line, which Tennyson consistently left unpunctuated, I think in order to stress a crucial point about the rhetorical power of his hero's metaphor-making in the rose poem tradition.[16] "Rosy," describing the west and south, is either a straight adjective or a buried simile; "Roses are her cheeks" crosses the rhetorical line into metaphor, but metaphor of a weakly conventional sort that suggests rather too many literary girls with roses in their cheeks.[17] The empowered metaphor of this quatrain is the last, "And a rose her mouth"—an image that is wonderfully erotic in itself and that the unusual punctuation shows to be simply irresistible from the vantage of Tennyson's acculturated hero. For Maud's mouth can not only kiss but speak, and thus can bear the news of a surrender whose import is hyperbolically global because the cultural freight behind it is literally global. Love makes the world go round, for Tennyson's hero, as and because the British empire does. That is why the hero breaks through into original metaphor at the point at which eros and culture form one "dominion sweet." Maud's mouth is a rose when it assents to the authority of patriarchal empire, which her faltering blush of submissive pride also confirms, and which the succeeding images of the westering course of commerce ("glowing ships") and of colonial bliss and fecundity ("the red man's babe") expand upon, until a young man's fancy and the first flush of sexual conquest have utterly merged with the Victorian Englishman's proudest boast: that upon his empire—rosy red on any good Victorian map of the world—the sun never sets.

If the shadow of mortality falls across this text, it does so to signal the death of unconditioned subjectivity, the preemption of lyrical by imperial wealth, the cultural doom of romantic—and Romantic—desire. We can catch this fatal shadow best by comparison to Wordsworth's ode on a germane topic, "Intimations of Immortality." In Wordsworth "the Babe leaps up on his Mother's arm" (49) as a culminating figure of communal joy, which the poet joins only after a singular admonition from "a Tree, of many, one" (51) has exiled him to a state of solitary *thought*; from this state, in turn, a visionary memory that sees "the Children sport upon the shore" (166) effects partial restoration, again only "in thought" (171). Precisely the thought-lessness of *Maud* I.xvii has provoked adverse critical comment; yet it is only its thoughtlessness, its uncritical absorption in a phase of passion, that makes possible its success as an ecstatic lyrical essay in the cultural sublime. The single tree and the leaping babe, which are opposed images for Wordsworth, come back joined in Tennyson's lyric by the rhythm of an imperialist ethnic mythology. With his red babe leaping by his red cedar tree, the red man dances to the rhythm of the white man's burden. Such primitivism locates primal sympathy not in the philosophic mind but in the greater deep of unconscious acculturation, where custom lies upon the self with a weight deep indeed as life.

Insofar as the erotic was the sphere into which Victorian culture most notably domesticated the Romantic ideology of the autonomous self, and insofar as *Maud* deconstructs the self into its cultural constituents, it is appropriately when Tennyson is dwelling on romantic love that he draws most conspicuously on Romantic texts—and draws on them, moreover, as parts of the culture within which he is writing. We have just seen how a revisionist allusion to Wordsworth's ode sharpens the cultural argument of section xvii. Its greater successor, section xviii ("I have led her home"), goes beyond allusion, taking Keats's "Ode to a Nightingale" as a central argumentative and imagistic model. The parallels between Tennyson's eight-stanza meditative lyric and Keats's are striking: high Miltonic syntax and purity of diction; the embalmed darkness of a fragrant setting; starlight playing through verdurous glooms; the opposition of human imagination to misery; a flirtation with and then a rejection of mortality; a valedictory bell. Yet all these parallels set off an essential difference, itself different in kind from Tennyson's frequent earlier revisions of this ode. "Ode to a Nightingale" turns on a dialectical relation between imagination and nature, or between the imagining self and its own mortality. But for Tennyson neither term of the Keatsian dialectic is simple or stable. He has presented each as subject to mediation by the linguistic structures of consciousness since very early in his career; and when he has alluded to the "Nightingale" ode he has always done so with an eye, or an ear, for some transcendent ground that subtends both the created world and the creative mind that confronts it. In *Maud* this transcendent ground stands revealed, with unique force, as *culture*, in its contemporary Victorian incarnation; and this revelation lets Tennyson rewrite Keats's ode with remarkable fidelity to its images and even to their sequence, but with an altogether original purpose that conduces on occasion to poetic effects more Keatsian than those we find in Keats.

The note of section xviii is acceptance, which if not finally Keats's note is certainly the note Tennyson heard when he read Keats. The hero's blissful calm proceeds from his having found, after hundreds of lines of alienation and nostalgia, "the promised good" (I.xviii.604), a rightful place that justifies the world around him. "I have led her home": whatever has or has not happened this day among the wildflowers by his home, it is now the hero's conviction that Maud's home, within whose grounds he reposes as he speaks, will be his; and that "long-wished-for end" (603) provides the social substrate for the sense of erotic arrival—coming rather than consummation—which the poem also lavishly elaborates: "Maud made my Maud by that long loving kiss" (656). Keats's gift for recreating the natural world of generation and death, and finding it good, takes in Tennyson's lyric the form of an acceptance of the cultural world. For both poets a full acceptance entails recognition of what is not easily accepted; but where for Keats the obstacles are such natural facts as pain, illness, and death ("Nightingale," 23–30), for Tennyson they inhere in cultural interpretations of nature, "A sad astrology, the boundless plan" that brands "His nothingness into man" (634–638). The hero, who "would die / To save from some slight shame one simple girl" (642–643), seeks an easeful death that is not Keats's blank mortality but an act in a script indited by nineteenth-century chivalry, which he not only would die for but also will kill for soon enough.

The hero's acceptance of love's "madness" and his gallant death wish both illustrate his acquiescence in a cultural role, as the interpolated seventh stanza, based on the seventh stanza of the "Nightingale" ode, makes clear:

> Not die; but live a life of truest breath,
> And teach true love to fight with mortal wrongs.
> O, why should Love, like men in drinking-songs,
> Spice his fair banquet with the dust of death?
> Make answer, Maud my bliss,
> Maud made my Maud by that long loving kiss,
> Life of my life, wilt thou not answer this?
> "The dusky strand of Death inwoven here
> With dear Love's tie, makes Love himself more dear."
> (I.xviii.651–659)

Dying means living the life of a culture hero, which Tennyson risks spoiling his poem by describing in the virtuous bromides of these first two lines. But the stanza executes a handsome recovery in what follows, which complicates its verbal magic with a suggestion that it is the verbal magic of culturally canonical texts that largely inspires the hero's moral reform. "Like men in drinking songs": we would do the "Ode to a Nightingale" no disservice by calling it the finest-toned drinking song in the canon, and the ode receives something like that compliment here from Keats's great port-loving successor. Tennyson finds his way to a meditation on the Keatsian themes of love and death through meditating on the tradition of which the "Nightingale" ode forms a part, and the quoted answer at which the stanza arrives feels like what the Keats of "When I Have Fears," "Why Did I Laugh?" and "Bright Star" meant but never came out and said.[18]

Just as in its entirety *Maud* treats the Romantic mythology of imaginative immortality as a dusky strand in the fabric of cultural hegemony, so
section xviii welcomes the influence of "Ode to a Nightingale" by presenting
that influence as part of a cultural tradition. Tennyson at once confirms the
ode's Romantic assertion of imaginative priority to natural facts of love and
death, and diminishes the saliency of this particular text against the vast
tapestry of culture with which it is entangled. This is why the Keatsian
tolling bell prompts in Tennyson's hero no anxiety whatsoever: "And hark
the clock within, the silver knell / Of twelve sweet hours that past in bridal
white, / And died to live, long as my pulses play" (662–664). "No more so
all forlorn" (630), he enjoys for the moment the entire idyllic security of a
Victorian man whose love, whose ambition, and whose literary experience
all converge in "the promised good," the behavior-reinforcing reward. Finally
this satisfaction is intimately and expansively physical; no poem is more
sensuous than the "Nightingale" ode, but Tennyson has written one here
that is more *corporeal*, in representation of his no longer disaffected hero's
blissful merger with the body cultural and politic. Hence the fulfilling bodily
imagery that governs the opening and closing stanzas on the "blood" (601),
the "heart" (608), and the "pulses" that swell to cosmic dimension: "Beat,
happy stars, timing with things below, / Beat with my heart more blest than
heart can tell" (679–680).

To be sure, "some dark undercurrent woe" (681) remains to draw the
hero back to unsolved problems that the monodramatic narrative holds in
store. But when his joy revives in the final love lyric, the hero's body language
dances once again to the music of the time, in the appropriately specific form
of a Victorian polka: "And the soul of the rose went into my blood, / As
the music clashed in the hall" (I.xxii.882–883). This pulse resurges most
powerfully in the lines that close part I:

> She is coming, my own, my sweet;
>   Were is ever so airy a tread,
> My heart would hear her and beat,
>   Were it earth in an earthy bed;
> My dust would hear her and beat,
>   Had I lain for a century dead;
> Would start and tremble under her feet,
>   And blossom in purple and red.
>   (I.xxii.916–923)

Well over a century has passed since Tennyson wrote these lines of prophetic
rapture, and it is no accident that their reputation has risen and fallen, and
now rises again, with readers' sympathy for Victorian tastes. There may be
no firmer testimony of Tennyson's intention to explore in *Maud* the perva-

siveness of cultural determinants for behavior and feeling than the fact that in this last, climactic expression of love's ecstasy, from the most personally invested of all his major works, this prosodic adept chose to stake so much on the specifically contemporary beat of a popular fad.

From the start of part II, the cultural determinants are dramatically realigned against the hero they have momentarily and capriciously supported at the end of part I. The ensuing dissonance makes the abandoned hero, "so stunned and still" (II.i.2), begin seeing double. Maud, now irrecoverably lost, becomes a "ghastly Wraith" (II.i.32), a "hard mechanic ghost" (II.ii.82) that the hero explains as "a lying trick of the brain" (II.i.37), or "a juggle born of the brain" (II.ii.90). He is blaming the victim, of course, in the neurophysiological terms of his day.[19] But his ambidexter images of the lie and the juggle point beyond a psychology of self-division to the schism in society that furnishes the germinally twinned imagery of "Oh! That 'Twere Possible." In this long-deferred lyric (now section iv), images of the mutually alien city and country, the "woodland echo" (II.iv.178) and the market "hubbub" (II.iv.208), may meet only in the hero's mind, which is now more plainly than ever a crossroads of contradictory memories and impressions.

The mad scene of section v carries this tendency to its Victorian extreme. Tennyson piqued himself on having drafted the mad scene in twenty minutes, and it is in this most spontaneous poetry that the unreflective mind most forcefully reflects its social victimization. Insanity is a topic, like love, that summons up the deepest privacies, and Tennyson calls upon it in part II in order to practice a sociopathology similar to that whereby he has earlier dissected "the cruel madness of love" (I.iv.156). In describing his passion earlier in the conventional terms of "madness," the hero was surrendering to the beat of his culture; so he must do again now in succumbing to madness itself: "And the hoofs of the horses beat, beat, / The hoofs of the horses beat, / Beat into my scalp and my brain" (II.v.246–248). The rhythms have changed since part I, but it is still the drum of culture that sounds the inevitable tattoo.

The mad hero's *idée fixe*—that he has died but wants proper burial— affords Tennyson occasions to sustain the urban imagery of the preceding section in a vividly necropolitan mode, and also to venture a reprise of the overt social satire that has been blunted by the coming of love in part I. Churchman, lord, statesman, physician all come under the lash (II.v.266–274), principally for sins of linguistic deviancy. "There is none that does his work, not one" (264); and what fills the space of this unperformed work is language, "chatter," "blabbing," and most significantly "idiot gabble" (257, 274, 279). Etymologically *idiocy* is privacy, and what the hero censures as "idiot gabble" is a cross between autism and bad breeding. The maddening thing about the dead men's chatter, from the hero's standpoint, is its violation of the Victorian decorum that segregates public from private spheres. Tennyson has practiced just this violation since the beginning of *Maud*, as a poetic means of confounding a cardinal Victorian prejudice; but now that the hero shares the poet's secret, it is driving him out of his mind. In its methodical madness section v constitutes the hero's new and crippling consciousness of a breakdown between public and private discourses—a breakdown that unleashes a semiotic bedlam from which he seeks protection. Although he defensively calls the chorus of voices mere "babble" (284), what assails him is rather an excess than a dearth of meaning, an overload of confessional secrets he wants neither to hear nor to have heard by anyone else:

> For I never whispered a private affair
> Within the hearing of cat or mouse,
> No, not to myself in the closet alone,
> But I heard it shouted at once from the top of the house;
> Everything came to be known.
> Who told *him* we were there?
>
> (II.v.285–290)

What is the intolerably open secret from which the hero wants burial? The abortive tryst with Maud to which he suddenly recurs has long since suffered its most devastating exposure; yet it offers a clue, for what was exposed in the exposure of his "private affair" with Maud was the notion of privacy itself. The hero's debacle has exacted his recognition of the inevitably corporate nature of language;[20] and this recognition "Is enough to drive one mad" (II.v.258), into an insanity that is also the poem's most comprehensively public gesture. The subjectively incoherent perspectives of the madman regroup themselves at the level of cultural analysis into an irresistible phalanx that serves Tennyson as the monodramatic equivalent of a tragically fatal objectivity. "Prophet, curse me the blabbing lip,/ And curse me the British vermin, the rat" (295–296): simultaneously "prophet" and "vermin"— accuser, criminal, and judge in one breath, as the condensed syntax suggests—the hero can but perpetuate the discourse that entraps him if he is to speak at all.

Placing social invective against the "Wretchedest age, since Time began" (259) in the mouth of a madman serves the poet laureate, of course, as a means of self-defense—a man would have to be crazy to talk about England like that—but it also defends the reader against a too immediate disclosure of a too intimate vision of the pervasive force of culture. The hero requires defense from this vision as well, of course; and since he lacks the dramatic distance available to poet and reader, he pleads insanity. Even this asylum gives no real refuge, however, and he knows it:

O me, why have they not buried me deep enough?
Is it kind to have made me a grave so rough,
Me, that was never a quiet sleeper?
Maybe still I am but half-dead;
Then I cannot be wholly dumb;
I will cry to the steps above my head
And somebody, surely, some kind heart will come
To bury me, bury me
Deeper, ever so little deeper.

(II.v.334–342)

As death represents acculturation in part I, here half-death represents an acculturation tantalizingly unconsummated. The hero "cannot be wholly dumb" until he becomes wholly deaf to the incongruity of the ubiquitous yet personal idiot gabble that circulates around and within him. He cries out for a burial so full, a cultural immersion so total, that he will no longer know that engulfing rite for what it is. More than anything else, the hero wants to lose a mind that he wishes, or suspects, he has never properly possessed. This goal he may achieve only by ceasing to be—or, barring literal suicide, by ceasing to be piercingly aware, as he now is for the only time in the poem, of culture as an otherness that he has internalized, in the tangled nest of public properties that constitutes his private self.

These equivalent modes of oblivion, either of which the hero would prefer to his current torment, come together in the prospect of military self-sacrifice he accepts in part III. Unable to "bury myself in myself" (I.i.75), whether through the cool reason of a philosopher's life or through the irratio-nal escapes of a lunatic's, the hero says at last, "I have felt with my native land, I am one with my kind, / I embrace the purpose of God, and the doom assigned" (III.vi.58–59). With the natural images of "my native land" and "my kind," the politicization of any ostensibly natural substrate below cul-ture is complete; and with the invocation of "the purpose of God" and its Tennysonian synonym "the doom assigned," supernatural options for transcending culture are terminally politicized as well. In answer to the pathetic final prayer of part II, the merciful ground of culture has opened to swallow the hero up. He has fallen into the bliss of the state.

Culture never did betray the heart that loved her, not when she is loved as by Tennyson's hero, with "the unselfishness born of a great passion."[22] But great passion is greatly blind, and in awaking to "the better mind" (III. vi.56) the hero has deadened himself to a mass of inconsistencies—something we have watched him do throughout the poem, to be sure, but not yet on this scale or with this urgency of implicit appeal to the reader's conscience. At earlier phases of his passion our hero would have been torn, at some level of awareness, between his claims of sympathy with his "kind" and his zealously bloody intention to go to war; between his dedication to the business interests behind modern warfare and his hatred of the "wrongs and shames" (III.vi.40) of the commercial *Pax Victoriana*. He is not thus torn now; now his cultural entombment can weather the most Orwellian of contradictions. The abiding horror of part III arises when the hero's defection into lobotomized jingoism leaves us to take up the ethical slack, without a clue to imagining a credible alternative course of events. The hero's unacknowledged contradictions remain, to sear the critical conscience that would free itself of patriotic heroics without falling into step with some other cultural or countercultural troop.

" 'Maud': I leave before the sad part":[23] Emily Tennyson's discreet exit is understandable but unavailing. We crave excuse from the cultural vision of *Maud*, but such excuse comes hard once we recognize that its hero has satisfied precisely this craving, in one fell swoop of moral abdication. We may imagine its poet feeding such a craving, too, in repeatedly indulged yet never quite fulfilling debauches of vicarious abandonment to full acculturation, as he subjected circle after circle of empire's best and brightest to readings of a poem that held up their shared eminence to unforgiving scrutiny. "Only once, as it seems to me, (at the close of 'Maud')," wrote an American culture pilgrim who had undergone the Tennysonian rite, "has he struck the note of irrepressible emotion, and appeared to say the thing that must be said at the moment, at any cost."[24] What struck young Henry James about the close of *Maud* was the reckless extremity of its contemporary commitment: a unique fusion of Tennyson's antinomian, lyrical intensity with the cultural absorption and finish that always seem so smooth in his idylls of the hearth or of the king. *Maud* is an achievement of lethal force, one that Tennyson himself seems not to have understood very well and that his career never repeated. But then he had no cause to repeat this published experiment, because he was able literally to repeat it in public all the time. The experiment was never over: *Maud* remained a rhapsode's work-in-progress at each of those command performances for captive audiences that nobody (Emily Tennyson included) seems to have rationally willed but that nobody (Alfred Tennyson included) seems to have been able to escape. Those evenings at Farringford or London or Aldworth cannot appear more quintessentially Victorian to us than they must have felt to their participants, who, if they wondered what they were doing there and minded the poem with even the least attentiveness, must have received some deeply disquieting answers. Well may the cultural vision of *Maud* sting us still.

Notes

1.   See James Knowles, "A Personal Reminiscence," *Nineteenth Century* 33 (1893): 182 and Hallam Tennyson, *Alfred Lord Tennyson: A Memoir*, 2 vols. (New York: Macmillan, 1897), II, 70–71.

2. The private side of the monodrama came to Tennyson first, in such lyrics as "Oh! That 'Twere Possible" and "Go Not, Happy Day"; and in the manuscripts it is the elaboration of social detail that gives him the most evident trouble. Issues of causality pertinent to *Maud* are treated, with primary reference to *Idylls of the King*, in James R. Kincaid, *Tennyson's Major Poems: The Comic and Ironic Patterns* (New Haven and London: Yale University Press, 1975), 154; and A. Dwight Culler, *The Poetry of Tennyson* (New Haven and London: Yale University Press, 1977), 239. I cite throughout *The Poems of Tennyson*, ed. Christopher Ricks (London: Longman, 1969).

3. Chapter 9 of Charles Kingsley's *Alton Locke* (1850) begins with a paragraph suggesting that Kingsley had felt the new effects in Tennyson's experimental lyric: "the roar of wheels, the ceaseless stream of pale, hard faces . . . beneath a lurid, crushing sky of smoke and mist." Two pages later Alton, himself a proletarian poet, devotes a paragraph to praising Tennyson for "the altogether democratic tendency of his poems . . . his handling of the trivial every-day sights and sounds of nature"; here, however, he clearly has the domestic idyllist in mind. See Tennyson's extemporized metaphor of the city, as recorded in FitzGerald's copy of *Poems* (1842): "One Day with A T in St. Paul's—1842. 'Merely as an enclosed Space in a huge City this is very fine.' And when we got out into the 'central roar'—'This is the Mind: that, a mood of it' " (135; in Trinity College Library).

4. *Poems*, ed. Ricks, 1039.

5. John Killham, "Tennyson and Victorian Social Values," in *Tennyson*, ed. D. J. Palmer (Athens, Ohio: Ohio University Press, 1973), 172.

6. Gordon N. Ray, *Tennyson Reads "Maud"* (Vancouver: University of British Columbia, 1968), 43.

7. A. Dwight Culler, "Monodrama and the Dramatic Monologue,"*PMLA* 90 (1975): 366–85.

8. Jonas Spatz, "Love and Death in Tennyson's *Maud*," *Texas Studies in Literature and Language* 16 (1974): 506.

9. Jonathan Wordsworth, " 'What Is It, That Has Been Done?': The Central Problem of *Maud*," *Essays in Criticism* 24 (1974): 356–62. See also Roy P. Basler, "Tennyson the Psychologist," *South Atlantic Quarterly* 43 (1944): 143–59; F. E. L. Priestley, *Language and Structure in Tennyson's Poetry* (London: Deutsch, 1973), 115; Spatz, "Love and Death."

10. See also Priestley, pp. 107–108, and Alan Sinfield, "Tennyson's Imagery," *Neophilologus* 55 (1976): 476–78. Robert James Mann, the first systematic expositor of *Maud*, found it necessary to stress this feature of the text: "The object of the poet is evidently not to picture these individuals as they are, but to describe them as they appear to the irritable and morose nature to which they are hostile personalities. . . . It must never be forgotten that it is not the poet, but the chief person of the action, who paints them" (*Tennyson's "Maud" Vindicated: An Explanatory Essay* [London: Jarrold, 1856], 25–26). Mann was defending his friend against malicious misprision, but he was also pointing to generic features that puzzled readers because they were new.

11. See John R. Reed, *Victorian Conventions* (Athens, Ohio: Ohio University Press, 1975), 142–45.

12. *Poems*, ed. Ricks, p. 1039.

13. Compare I.xvi.549, "Lord of the pulse that is lord of her breast," with an earlier version in Trinity Notebook 36: "Lord of the pulses that move her breast." The more interesting revised line plays down the biological in favor of what Eve Kosofsky Sedgwick calls the hero's "homosocial" desire: to lord it over the lord by obtaining the lady.

14. See A. S. Byatt, "The Lyric Structure of Tennyson's *Maud*," in *The Major Victorian Poets: Reconsiderations*, ed. Isobel Armstrong (London: Routledge and Kegan Paul, 1969), 81; Philip Drew, "Tennyson and the Dramatic Monologue: A Study of *Maud*," in *Tennyson*, ed. D. J. Palmer (Athens, Ohio: Ohio University Press, 1973), 136.

15. See Pauline Fletcher, "Romantic and Anti-Romantic Gardens in Tennyson and Swinburne," *Studies in Romanticism* 18 (1979): 81–97.

16. In Trinity Notebook 36, fol. 23 there is a period after "mouth" (though none after "yields" four lines above). Evidently the unusual punctuation came to Tennyson late; it occurs in every published edition I have consulted. Compare with Tennyson's lyric Keats's *Hyperion* III.14–22, where a rosy glow passes in the opposite direction, from the rose itself through "the clouds of even and of morn" to culminate in the erotic: "let the maid / Blush keenly, as with some warm kiss surpris'd."

17. See W. David Shaw, *Tennyson's Style* (Ithaca and London: Cornell University Press, 1976), 179.

18. This passage came into existence in one of the most interesting of the Trinity manuscripts. At this point Trinity Notebook 36, fol. 27 moves directly from line 650 to a version of line 660 ("I scarce can think this music but the swell . . ."), which is altered to its final reading on a third try. The curious second version—"What threefold meaning echoes from . . ."—suggests that Tennyson was hearing a reverberant music whose source troubled him. Stanza 7 (which Harvard Notebook 30, fol. 3–4, likewise lack) is first written out on the facing fol. 26v. It is tempting to believe that at this point Tennyson realized his indebtedness to Keats's ode and capitalized upon the debt—"Not die" corresponding to "Thou wast not born for death," and the "drinking-songs" allusion acknowledging, at a higher level, the complexity of the intertextual weave. The writing of stanza 7 then let Tennyson make sense of the "music" that had mystified him before. That music was Keats's enchanted moan: the stanza from the "Nightingale" ode that Tennyson kept uncannily hearing because to that point he had left it out of his brilliant imitation.

19. See Ann C. Colley, *Tennyson and Madness* (Athens, Ga.: University of Georgia Press, 1983), 125, 166.

20. See Samuel E. Schulman, "Mourning and Voice in *Maud*," *Studies in English Literature, 1500–1900* 23 (1983): 645.

21. See Robert G. Stange, "The Frightened Poets," in *The Victorian City: Images and Realities*, ed. H. J. Dyos and Michael Wolff, II (London and Boston: Routledge and Kegan Paul, 1973), 478; and William B. Thesing, "Tennyson and the City: Historical Tremours and Hysterical Tremblings," *Tennyson Research Bulletin* 3 (1977): 20.

22. *Poems*, ed. Ricks, p. 1039.

23. *Lady Tennyson's Journal*, ed. James O. Hoge (Charlottesville: University Press of Virginia, 1981), 82.

24. Henry James, "Tennyson's Drama," in *Views and Reviews*, ed. LeRoy Phillips (Boston: Bell, 1875), 176. See also W. W. Robson, "The Dilemma of Tennyson," rpt. in *Critical Essays on the Poetry of Tennyson*, ed. John Killham (New York: Barnes and Noble, 1960), 159–63.

The Female King:
Tennyson's Arthurian Apocalypse

ELLIOT L. GILBERT

> Yet in the long years liker must they grow;
> The man be more of woman, she of man.
> Tennyson, *The Princess*

> Dr. Schreber believed that he had a mission to redeem the world and to restore
> it to its lost state of bliss. This, however, he could only bring about if he were
> first transformed from a man into a woman.
> Freud, "A Case of Paranoia"

> The happiest women, like the happiest nations, have no history.
> George Eliot, *The Mill on the Floss*

> Queen Victoria, there's a woman . . . when one encounters a toothed vagina
> of such exceptional size. . . .
> Lacan, "Seminar, 11 February 1975"

> La femme est naturelle, c'est-à-dire abominable.
> Baudelaire, *Mon Cœur mis à nu*

Sooner or later, most readers of the *Idylls of the King* find themselves wondering
by what remarkable transformative process the traditionally virile and manly
King Arthur of legend and romance evolved, during the nineteenth century,
into the restrained, almost maidenly Victorian monarch of Alfred Lord Tennyson's most ambitious work. Many of the earliest of these readers of the
Idylls deplored the change, noting in it disquieting evidence of the growing
domestication and even feminization of the age.[1] And more recent critics,
though they may have moderated the emotionalism of that first response,
continue to see in Arthur's striking metamorphosis a key element in any
analysis of the poem. I will argue here, however, that such a metamorphosis
was inevitable, given the nineteenth-century confluence of what Michel Foucault has called "the history of sexuality" with what we may call the history

Reprinted by permission of the Modern Language Association of America from *PMLA* 98 (1983).
© 1983 by the Modern Language Association of America.

of history, and that Tennyson's Arthurian retelling, far from being weakened by its revisionary premise, is in fact all the stronger and more resonant for depicting its hero as a species of female king.

Tennyson was attracted to the legend of King Arthur as a prospective subject for literary treatment almost from the beginning of his career; "the vision of Arthur had come upon me," Hallam Tennyson quotes his father in the *Memoir*, "when, little more than a boy, I first lighted upon Malory."[2] *Poems, Chiefly Lyrical*, published in 1830, when Tennyson was just twenty-one, contains the picturesque fragment "Sir Lancelot and Queen Guinevere," and by 1833, when his next volume appeared, the poet had already written, or was in the process of writing, two of his best-known Arthurian works, "The Lady of Shalott" (1832) and the ambitious rendering of King Arthur's death that, at its first publication ten years later, he called "Morte d'Arthur."

By this time, however, Tennyson had come to question the propriety of a nineteenth-century artist devoting his energies to the reworking of medieval materials. That is, he came to feel that only some contemporary significance in the Arthurian retellings, only "some modern touches here and there" (as he puts it in "The Epic"), could redeem his poetry "from the charge of nothingness," from Thomas Carlyle's characterization of it as "a refuge from life . . . a medieval arras" behind which the poet was hiding "from the horrors of the Industrial Revolution" or from John Sterling's judgment that "the miraculous legend of 'Excalibur' . . . reproduced by any modern writer must be a mere ingenious exercise of fancy."[3]

The idea that nineteenth-century artists ought to concern themselves with nineteenth-century subjects was a pervasive one.[4] When, for example, Matthew Arnold omitted *Empedocles on Etna* from a collection of his poetic works, he found it necessary to explain that he had not done so "because the subject of it was a Sicilian Greek born between two and three thousand years ago, *although many persons would think this a sufficient reason*" (italics mine). In the Preface to *Poems* (1853), Arnold goes on to quote "an intelligent critic" as stating that "the poet who would really fix the public attention must leave the exhausted past, and draw his subjects from matters of present import, and therefore both of interest and novelty."[5] Four years later, in a long discourse on poetics in *Aurora Leigh*, Elizabeth Barrett Browning takes a similar position. "If there's room for poets in this world," Barrett Browning declares in book 5 of her blank-verse novel,

> Their sole work is to represent the age,
> Their age, not Charlemagne's
> . . . .
> To flinch from modern varnish, coat or flounce,
> Cry out for togas and the picturesque,
> Is fatal—foolish too. King Arthur's self
> Was commonplace to Lady Guenevere:

And Camelot to minstrels seemed as flat
As Fleet Street to our poets.[6]

    That Tennyson himself was influenced by such attitudes is plain from the fact that when he published "Morte d'Arthur" in 1842, he set his medieval story in a modern framing poem, "The Epic," whose only partly ironic theme is the irrelevance of such a historical subject to the contemporary world. Edward FitzGerald asserts that Tennyson invented this setting "to give a reason for telling an old-world tale" (quoted in H. Tennyson 1:194). Otherwise, as poet Everard Hall remarks in "The Epic," explaining why he has burned his own long Arthurian poem,

> "Why take the style of those heroic times:
> For nature brings not back the mastodon,
> Nor we those times; and why should any man
> Remodel models?"

The lapse of fifty-five years between the writing of the "Morte d'Arthur" in 1833 and the publication of the complete *Idylls of the King* in 1888 suggests how difficult a time Tennyson had finding the contemporary significance he was looking for in his medieval material. Nevertheless, nearly all readers agree with the poet that "there is an allegorical or perhaps rather a parabolic drift in the poem" that permits the work to be read as "a discussion of problems which are both contemporary and perennial" (H. Tennyson 2:126–27).

    The exact nature of that discussion remains an open question, though a few facts about the allegory do seem clear. The book, proceeding seasonally as it does from spring in "The Coming of Arthur" to winter in "The Passing of Arthur," is certainly about the decline of a community from an original ideal state, about the corruption and nihilism that overtake a once whole and healthy social order. Just as surely, an important agency of this decline is identified by the story as human sexuality and, in particular, female passion. The four idylls published by Tennyson in 1859—"Vivien," "Guinevere," "Enid," and "Elaine"—under the general title *The True and the False* focus on the polar extremes of feminine purity and carnality, and however the author may have altered his plans for the book in the following years, his emphasis on the corrosiveness of female sexuality never changed. "Thou hast spoilt the purpose of my life," Arthur declares grimly in "Guinevere," about to part forever from the queen and plainly placing the whole blame for the decay of the Round Table and the fall of Camelot on his wife's unfaithfulness.

    The association of marital fidelity with the health of the state did not please all the first readers of the *Idylls*. Swinburne, for one, condemned what he felt was the reduction of Sir Thomas Malory's virile tales of chivalry to a sordid domestic quarrel. To him, Victorian King Arthur was a "wittol," or willing cuckold, Guinevere "a woman of intrigue," Lancelot "a co-respondent," and the whole story "rather a case for the divorce court than for poetry." In the same essay, Swinburne refers to the *Idylls* as "the Morte d'Albert," alluding to Tennyson's 1862 dedication of his poem to the recently deceased prince consort but, even more than that, to the royal family's celebrated bourgeois domesticity.[7]

Swinburne was right to see that Tennyson's idylls turn on the issue of domestic relations and specifically on the willingness or unwillingness of men and women to play their traditional social and sexual roles in these relations. He was wrong, however, to think such a subject contemptible. Indeed, his sardonic reference to "the Morte d'Albert" inadvertently calls attention to a major theme in the poem as well as to one of the central problems of Victorian society: the growing assertion of female authority.

In his Dedication of the *Idylls of the King* to Prince Albert, Tennyson describes a relationship between husband and wife that on the surface is entirely conventional. Albert is presented as an active force in national life, as "laborious" for England's poor, as a "summoner of War and Waste to rivalries of peace," as "modest, kindly, all-accomplished, wise," and, most important, as the ultimate pater familias, "noble father" of the country's "kings to be." Victoria, by contrast, appears in the Dedication principally in the role of bereaved and passive wife, whose "woman's heart" is exhorted to "break not but endure" and who is to be "comforted," "encompassed," and "o'ershadowed" by love until God chooses to restore her to her husband's side.

What lies behind this traditional domestic relationship is, of course, a very different reality. In that reality, Victoria is the true holder and wielder of power, the repository of enormous inherited authority, while Albert possesses what influence and significance he does almost solely through his marriage. This reversal of the usual male-female roles, superimposed on the more conventional relationship depicted in Tennyson's Dedication, produces a curious dissonance, much like one that came to sound more and more insistently in the culture as a whole as the nineteenth century progressed and that received powerful expression in the *Idylls of the King*. Indeed, Tennyson's very contemporary poem can be read as an elaborate examination of the advantages and dangers of sexual role reversal, with King Arthur himself playing, in a number of significant ways, the part usually assigned by culture to the woman.

Such revision of the female role in the nineteenth century is closely associated with the period's ambivalent attitude toward history. It was during the nineteenth century that the modern discipline of history first came fully into its own as a truly rigorous inquiry into the past, demanding, as Frederic Harrison puts it, "belief in contemporary documents, exact testing of authorities, scrupulous verification of citations, minute attention to chronology, geography, paleography, and inscriptions."[8] Defined in this new way, history had a distinctly male bias. This was true for a number of reasons. To begin with, its "disavowal of impressionism" in favor of a preoccupation with hard facts permitted it for the first time to rival the natural sciences as a "respectable" career for intellectual young men. Francis Parkman, American student of the Indian Wars, "defiantly chose history," one commentator tells us, "as a protest against what he considered the effeminacy of the liberal church."[9] In addition, as a record of great public events, history had always tended to dwell almost exclusively on the activities of men. "It should not be forgotten," writes Arthur Schlesinger, "that all of our great historians have been men and were likely therefore to be influenced by a sex interpretation of history all the more potent because unconscious."[10] In *Northanger Abbey*, Jane Austen alludes sardonically to this fact when her heroine dismisses history books for being full of "the quarrels of popes and kings, with wars and pestilences in every page; the men all so good for nothing, and hardly any women at all."[11]

But nineteenth-century history was male-oriented in an even deeper and more all-pervasive sense than this; for to the extent that historians were principally concerned with recording the passage of power and authority through the generations, their work necessarily preserved the patrilineal forms and structures of the societies they investigated. "The centuries too are all lineal children of one another," writes Carlyle in *Past and Present*, emphasizing the intimate connection that has always existed between history and genealogy.[12] In *The Elementary Structures of Kinship*, Lévi-Strauss argues that culture, and by extension history, can only come into existence after the concept of kinship has been established.[13] But this means that in those societies where family structure is patrilineal, women must inevitably play a secondary role in history, since they do not have names of their own and therefore do not visibly participate in the passing on of authority from one generation to the next. The rise of "scientific" history in the nineteenth century, then, might have been expected to confirm, among other things, the validity of the traditional male-dominant and female-subordinate roles.

But in fact, those roles came more and more frequently to be questioned during the period, as did the new history itself. Ironically, it was the very success of scientific history at reconstituting the past that provoked this resistance. For what soon became clear was that, seen in too much detail and known too well, the past was growing burdensome and intimidating, was revealing—in Tennyson's metaphor—all the models that could not be remodeled. John Stuart Mill's celebrated dismay, reported in his *Autobiography*, that all the best combinations of musical notes "must already have been discovered" was one contemporary example of this anxiety. Another was George Eliot's declaration, in *Middlemarch*, that "a new Theresa will hardly have the opportunity of reforming a conventual life . . . the medium in which [her] ardent deeds took shape is for ever gone." For a nineteenth-century woman like Dorothea Brooke, George Eliot tells us, it is often better that life be obscure since "the growing good of the world is partly dependent on unhistoric acts."[14] Such a conclusion follows inevitably from the idea that history, simply by existing, exhausts possibilities, leaving its readers with a despairing sense of their own belatedness and impotence. And this despair in turn leads to anxious quests for novelty, to a hectic avant-gardism, and in the end to an inescapable fin de siècle ennui. "The world is weary of the past, / Oh, might it die or rest at last," Shelley declares in *Hellas*, expressing a desire for oblivion, a longing for the end of history. Only through such an apocalypse, the poet suggests, can life be made new and vital again.

The great apocalyptic event for the nineteenth century was the French Revolution, at its most authentic a massive and very deliberate assault on history. To be sure, regicide is the ultimate attack on the authority of the past, but if it is dealt with merely on a political level, its deeper significance is likely to be missed. To be fully understood, it must, rather, be placed in the context of the many other revolutionary acts whose collective intent was to overthrow not only the old historical regime but history itself. Among these acts were laws that abolished the right to make wills and that declared natural children absolutely equal with legitimate offspring. Both struck directly at the power of the past to control the present and, just as important, at the right of patrilineal authority to extend itself indefinitely into the future. Revolutionary calendar reforms were an even more literal attack on history. By decree, official chronology, for example, began at the autumn equinox of 1792; the first day of the new republic thus became the first day of the new world. Even the names of the months were changed in the revolutionary calendar, with the seasons replacing the Caesars—nature replacing history—as the source of the new nomenclature.

From these revolutionary activities two important principles emerged. The first is that wherever intolerable social abuses are the consequence of history, reform is only possible outside of history.[15] The French Revolution sought to incorporate this idea, at least symbolically, into an actual working community, a community for which not history but nature would provide the model. In that new dispensation, each person would be self-authorized, independent of genealogy, and each day would have the freshness of the first day or, rather, of the only day, of *illo tempore*, a moment in the eternal present unqualified and undiminished by an "exhausted past." Such an ambition has never been entirely fanciful. Mircea Eliade, for one, reminds us of "the very considerable period" during which "humanity opposed history by all possible means. . . . The primitive desired to have no "memory," not to record time, to content himself with tolerating it simply as a dimension of his existence, but without interiorizing it, without transforming it into consciousness. . . . That desire felt by the man of traditional societies to refuse history, and to confine himself to an indefinite repetition of archetypes, testifies to his thirst for the real and his terror of losing himself by letting himself be overwhelmed by the meaninglessness of profane existence."[16] The Revolution's famous exchange of "fraternity" for "paternity" makes the same point. The father-child relationship is generational and thus principally a product of history. Brothers, on the other hand, are by their nature contemporaries, and their relationships are therefore more "spatial" than temporal. In *Parsifal,* Wagner describes the realm of the Grail knight brotherhood in just these terms. "Zum Raum," Gurnemanz explains to the at-first uncomprehending Parsifal, "wird hier die Zeit" 'Time changes here to space.' Significantly, James R. Kincaid finds this same idea built into the very structure of Tennyson's *Idylls.* "The overlaid seasonal progress in the [poem]," he writes, "suggests not so much objective, physical time as the spatial representations of time in medieval tapestry or triptychs. This emphasis on space seems to imply the absence of time, the conquest of time."[17] It is a conquest that Ann Douglas believes was, for the nineteenth century, inescapably gender-identified; distinguishing between "scientific" historians and feminine and clerical historians, she remarks that the latter, "in their well-founded fear of historicity . . . substituted space for time as the fundamental dimension of human experience" (199).

As the Douglas comment shows, the second principle established by the Revolution is closely related to the first, asserting that the apocalyptic end of history signals the end of a system in which women are instruments of, and subordinate to, patrilineal continuity. In particular, the revolutionary law making natural children the absolute equals of so-called legitimate offspring had the effect of taking from men their familiar right to direct and subdue female sexuality. In the saturnalia of sexual "misrule" that followed, with its release of aboriginal energy and its invitation to self-discovery and self-assertion, traditional gender roles were radically reexamined. Eliade's study of ceremonial transvestism describes this symbolic sex role reversal as "a coming out of one's self, a transcending of one's own historically controlled situation, a recovering of an original situation . . . which it is important to reconstitute periodically in order to restore, if only for a brief moment, the initial completeness, the intact source of holiness and power . . . that preceded the creation."[18] Interestingly, 1792, the first year of the new French Republic, was also the year in which Mary Wollstonecraft published her *Vindication of the Rights of Woman,* inaugurating the modern era of feminism. Wollstonecraft would later include in her own study of the French Revolution descriptions of the part women played in overturning the monarchy. "Early . . . on the fifth of October," she reports, "a multitude of women by some impulse were collected together; and hastening to the *hôtel de ville,* obliged every female they met to accompany them, even entering many houses to force others to follow in their train." The women are only temporarily delayed by national guardsmen with bayonets. "Uttering a loud and general cry, they hurled a volley of stones at the soldiers, who, unwilling, or ashamed, to fire on women, *though with the appearance of furies,* retreated into the hall and left the passage free."[19]

One can perhaps find in these latter-day Eumenides the originals of Dickens' Madame Defarge and her ferocious female companions of the guillotine. The same image seems to have occurred independently to Edmund Burke, who equated the insurrection on the Continent with the dismemberment of King Peleas of Thessaly by his daughters, an act contrived by the vengeful Medea.[20] Clearly, the nineteenth century perceived the French Revolution as juxtaposing two key contemporary themes, the attack on history and the assertion of female authority. The reading of Tennyson's *Idylls of the King* proposed here focuses precisely on this juxtaposition: on the rich potential for a new society that emerges from the original association of these two themes and on the disaster Tennyson says overtakes such a society once all the implications of the Arthurian apocalypse are revealed.

The coming of Arthur at the beginning of the *Idylls* is plainly an apocalyptic event, recognized as such by the whole society.[21] The advent of a king who proposes to reign without the authorization of patrilineal descent is an extraordinary and threatening phenomenon. "Who is he / That he should rule us?" the great lords and barons of the realm demand. "Who hath proven him King Uther's son?" The community first attempts to see if the situation can be regularized, to see, that is, if some evidence can be found that Arthur is, after all, the legitimate heir of an established line of kings. Leodogran, the king of Cameliard, is particularly anxious for such confirmation since Arthur has asked to marry his daughter, Guinevere. "How should I that am a king," Leodogran asks, "Give my one daughter saving to a king, / And king's son?" In seeking evidence of Arthur's legitimacy, Leodogran, parodying the methodical inquires of a historian, tracks down one source of information after another: an ancient chamberlain, some of Arthur's own closest friends, a putative step-sister. None can supply the absolute assurance the king wants, and over against their only partly convincing stories stands the undoubted truth that, while Arthur's supposed parents, Uther and Ygerne, were dark-haired and dark-eyed, the new monarch is himself "fair / Beyond the race of Britons and of men."

What emerges from all this investigation is the fact that Arthur represents not a continuation and fulfillment of history but rather a decisive break with it. Indeed, the failure of Leodogran's conventional historical research to establish some connection with the past suggests that in Arthur's new dispensation even the traditional methods for acquiring knowledge have become ineffectual. "Sir and my Liege," cries a favorite warrior after one of Arthur's victories, "the fire of God / Descends upon thee in the battle-field. / I know thee for my King!" Here is a way of recognizing authority very different from one requiring the confirmation of genealogy. Arthur's fair coloring also confounds genealogy. Not only does it set him apart from the people most likely to have been his parents, it isolates him as well from all other Britons and even, we are told, from all other men. Radically discontinuous with the past in every one of its aspects, Arthur is like some dramatic mutation in nature, threatening the integrity of the genetic line as the only means of infusing new life into it.

In fact, nature does replace history as the sponsor of the new king. Tennyson affirms this idea both in what he chooses to drop from the traditional account of the coming of Arthur and in what he invents to replace the omission. Perhaps the best known of all legends associated with the identification of Arthur as England's rightful king is the story of the sword in the stone. In Malory, for example, young Arthur wins acceptance as lawful ruler because he is the only person in England capable of removing a magic sword from a marble block on which have been inscribed the words "Whoso pulleth out this sword of his stone and anvil is rightwise king born of all England."

In nearly every retelling of the Arthurian stories down to our own time, this dramatic incident plays a prominent part. Tennyson's omission of the anecdote from his own rendering of the Arthurian material, then, is at least noteworthy and may even be a significant clue to one of the poet's principal intentions in the *Idylls*. For what the phallic incident of the sword in the stone emphasizes is that Arthur, though not as incontrovertibly a descendant of the previous king as the people of England might like, is nevertheless the inheritor of some kind of lawful authority, the recipient of legitimate power legitimately transferred. And the participation in this ritual of the church, with its traditional stake in an orderly, apostolic succession, further ensures that such a transfer is, at least symbolically, patrilineal. Tennyson's rejection of this famous story, therefore, may well suggest that the poet was trying to direct attention away from conventional continuity in the passing of power to Arthur and toward some alternative source of authority for the new king.

What that alternative source of authority might be is hinted at in "Guinevere," the eleventh of the twelve idylls, an unusual work in that, as Jerome Buckley points out in his edition of the poetry, it draws on little "apart from Tennyson's own imagination."[22] This "self-authorized" and so-to-speak "unhistorical" idyll contains a striking description of the early days of Arthur's reign—the account of a magical initiatory journey, invented by Tennyson, we may conjecture, as a substitute for the omitted episode of the sword in the stone. We hear this story from a young novice, who repeats the tale her father had told her of his first trip to Camelot to serve the newly installed king. "The land was full of signs / And wonders," the girl quotes her father's narrative of that trip. By the light of the many beacon fires on the headlands along the coast

> the white mermaiden swam,
> And strong man-breasted things stood from the sea,
> And sent a deep sea-voice thro' all the land,
> To which the little elves of chasm and cleft
> Made answer, sounding like a distant horn.

> So said my father—yea, and furthermore,
> Next morning, while he past the dim-lit woods
> Himself beheld three spirits mad with joy
>
> . . . .
> And still at evenings on before his horse
> The flickering fairy-circle wheel'd and broke
> Flying, and link'd again, and wheel'd and broke
> Flying, for all the land was full of life.
> And when at last he came to Camelot,
> A wreath of airy dancers hand-in-hand
> Swung round the lighted lantern of the hall;
> And in the hall itself was such a feast
> As never man had dream'd; for every knight
> Had whatsoever meat he long'd for served
> By hands unseen; and even as he said
> Down in the cellars merry bloated things
> Shoulder'd the spigot, straddling on the butts
> While the wine ran.

This visionary scene both celebrates and ratifies the coming of Arthur, affirming that the young king's authority over the land proceeds directly from the land itself, from the deepest resources of nature, and that "all genealogies founder," as J. M. Gray puts it, "in that 'great deep.' "[23] Metaphors of depth and interiority are everywhere: seas, woods, chasms, clefts, cellars. All the spirits of nature rejoice in Arthur, seeing in him their rightful heir, the repository of their power. In Tennyson's remarkable vision, radically departing as it does from historical sources, Arthur's coming fulfills that revolutionary law of the French National Convention which declared "natural children absolutely equal with legitimate."

This Romantic idea that the true source of kingly power is natural and internal rather than historical and external is more fully developed in the first of the idylls. There, Arthur's legitimacy is shown to derive from two sources: an inner strength, of which his successful military adventures are symbols, and the depths of nature, themselves metaphors for the young king's potent inwardness. When we first meet Arthur in the *Idylls*, he is a newly fledged warrior, driving the patriarchal Roman Caesars from his land as determinedly as the French would later drive them from the calendar.[24] Later, we see the young monarch receiving the sword Excalibur from the Lady of the Lake, a mystic wielder of subtle magic who "dwells down in a deep" and from whose hand, rising "out of the bosom of the lake," the new king takes the emblem of his authority.

To the extent that such derivation of power from the deep symbolizes access to one's own interior energy, Arthur's kingly mission is ultimately self-authorized; and in particular, it is authorized by that part of himself which, associated with creative, ahistorical nature, is most distinctly female. Tennyson emphasizes this idea not only by assigning the Lady of the Lake a prominent role in the establishment of Arthur's legitimacy but also by introducing the mysterious muselike figures of the "three fair queens" who attend the young king at his coronation: "the friends / Of Arthur, gazing on him, tall, with bright / Sweet faces, who will help him at his need."[25] In his preface to *The Great Mother*, Erich Neumann declares that the "problem of the Feminine [is important] for the psychologist of culture, who realizes that the peril of present-day mankind springs in large part from the one-sidedly patriarchal development of the male intellectual consciousness, which is no longer kept in balance by the matriarchal world of the psyche."[26] Clearly, the new dispensation promised by the coming of Tennyson's nineteenth-century Arthur will involve, as an important part of its program, the freeing of that matriarchal psyche, of feminine energy, from its long subservience to male authority and consciousness. Everything we know about the new king makes this certain. The very manner of his accession directly challenges such authority and consciousness, and his establishment of the community of the Round Table can best be understood as an attempt to assert the wholeness of the human spirit in the face of that sexual fragmentation described by Neumann.

What the dominance of male consciousness over female psyche can lead to in society is made plain in the *Idylls* through Tennyson's description of the all-male community of King Pellam in "Balin and Balan," the last of the books to be written. Pellam, a rival of King Arthur's, determines to outdo the court of Camelot in piety, and as a first step he pushes "aside his faithful wife, nor lets / Or dame or damsel enter at his gates / Lest he should be polluted." As a manifestation of abstract male reason and will, such suppression of the feminine renders the society moribund. The aging Pellam, described by Tennyson as "this gray king," has "quite foregone / All matters of this world" and spends his listless days in a hall "bushed about . . . with gloom," where "cankered boughs . . . whine in the wood." Nature here, rejected as a source of energy and replenishment, takes suitable revenge on its sullen oppressor.

King Pellam is the guardian of a most appropriate relic. The old monarch, who "finds himself descended from the Saint / Arimathaean Joseph," is the proud possessor of "that same spear / Wherewith the Roman pierced the side of Christ" as he hung on the cross. Death-dealing, Roman, phallic, linear, the spear—its ghostly shadow haunting the countryside— symbolizes the dessicated male society of Pellam's court; indeed, it is very literally the male "line" through which Pellam—who, unlike Arthur, is deeply interested in genealogy—traces the source of his authority back to Joseph of Arimathaea. Significantly, as a symbol of the linear and the historical, the spear belies the cyclical promise of the resurrection represented by the Grail, the companion relic from which, in the sexually fragmented culture described both by Neumann and by Tennyson, it has long been separated.[27]

As the country of King Pellam is the land of the spear, so Arthur's Camelot is the court of the Grail. At least, it is from Camelot that the knights of the Round Table, tutored in Arthur's values, set out on their quest for the sacred cup, familiar symbol both of nature and of the female, a womblike emblem of fecundity associated with what, in pagan legend, is the Cauldron of Plenty, an attribute of the Goddess of Fertility.[28] Such female energy is, in traditional mythography, ahistorical, a fact to which the Grail also testifies. The vessel's circular form, like that of the Round Table itself and like the "flickering fairy circles" and "wreaths of airy dancers" associated with the coming of Arthur, mimics the timeless cycles of nature, a timelessness in which the Round Table knights themselves participate. As we noted earlier, fraternal relationships are necessarily contemporaneous ones, expressing themselves in space rather than in time. The whole of Camelot partakes of this anachronistic quality. The young knight Gareth, catching his first glimpse of the sculptured gates of the city, marvels at how intermingled—how contiguous rather than continuous—all the events depicted there seem to be: "New things and old co-twisted, as if Time / Were nothing." His intuition of the ahistorical character of Camelot is confirmed by the "old seer" at the gate, who speaks of the city as a place "never built at all, / And therefore built forever." Significantly, the principal subject of "Gareth and Lynette" is young Gareth's commitment "to fight the brotherhood of Day and Night" in "the war of Time against the soul of man," a war in which, in this early idyll, the soul signally triumphs.[29]

The optimism expressed in the early idylls about the joyous and lively new society that would result from an apocalyptic release of natural and, by extension, female energy into a world heretofore dominated by history and male authority was largely a product of one form of nineteenth-century Romantic ideology. Traditionally, nature has been seen as the enemy of rational and historical human culture. Indeed, it has been argued that culture functions to permit human beings to assert their independence of—and superiority to—nature. In examining the origins of kinship, for example, Lévi-Strauss suggests that the whole elaborate and extended structure of the family can best be understood as a means by which "culture must, under pain of not existing, firmly declare 'Me first,' and tell nature, 'You go no further.' "[30] In this view, nature is dangerous, anarchic, indifferent to human concerns. Its frightening power may have to be placated or invoked on special occasions, but it must always be treated warily, must be controlled and even suppressed.

The Romanticism of the early nineteenth century, as one of its most striking innovations, managed momentarily to suspend the traditional enmity between nature and culture. In the benign natural world of the Wordsworthian vision, for example, breezes are "blessings," vales are "harbors," clouds are "guides," groves are "homes." Where human culture is a burden, it wearies the poet precisely because it is "unnatural." Under such circumstances, Wordsworth attempts to reconcile these traditionally polar opposites, submitting his cultivated sensibility to a sustaining and unthreatening nature in order to receive a new infusion of energy. It is nature in this ameliorative sense that underlies the scene in the *Idylls* in which the coming of Arthur is celebrated by all the mermaidens, elves, fairies, spirits, and merry bloated things we would naturally expect to find inhabiting a land that is "full of life."

The same Romantic optimism that permitted nature to be so readily domesticated in many early nineteenth-century works of art, that allowed nature's powers to be courted so fearlessly, also made possible the hopeful invocation of female energy that is such a striking feature of the *Idylls*. Historically, this benignant view of female power is unusual. Both in history and in myth women have for the most part been associated with the irrational and destructive forces of nature that threaten orderly male culture. As maenads, bacchantes, witches, they express in their frenzied dances and murderous violence an unbridled sexuality analogous to the frightening and sometimes even ruinous fecundity of nature. Indeed, the control of female sexuality is among the commonest metaphors in art for the control of nature (just as the control of nature is a metaphor for the control of women).[31] And as Lévi-Strauss points out, the earliest evidences of culture are nearly always those rules of exchange devised by men to facilitate the ownership and sexual repression of women.

Tennyson's departure, in the early idylls, from this traditional fear of female sexuality coincides with a dramatic development in modern culture history. "Between the seventeenth and the nineteenth centuries," Nancy F. Cott remarks about this change, "the dominant Anglo-American definition of women as especially sexual was reversed and transformed into the view that women were less carnal and lustful than men." Or as Havelock Ellis put it more succinctly in his *Studies in the Psychology of Sex*, one of the most striking creations of the nineteenth century was "woman's sexual anesthesia."[32] Cott substitutes for Ellis' "anesthesia" her own term "passionlessness," linking it with Evangelical Protestantism, which "constantly reiterated the theme that Christianity had elevated women above the weakness of animal nature for the sake of purity for men, the tacit condition for that elevation being the suppression of female sexuality" (227). Plainly, Tennyson's nineteenth-century recreation of Camelot depends to a considerable extent on this contemporary theory of female passionlessness—what another critic calls woman's "more than mortal purity"—and its ameliorative influence on male sensuality.[33] Unlike the society of King Pellam, which preserves the earlier view of women as sexually insatiable and which adopts a grim monasticism as the only defense against feminine corrosiveness, Arthur's court welcomes women for their ennobling and now safely denatured regenerative powers. In this respect, Camelot seems to resemble the many nineteenth-century utopian communities that attempted to experiment with a new and higher order of relationship between the sexes and that Tennyson himself had already commented on obliquely in *The Princess*.[34]

It is in his own "passionlessness" that Arthur most clearly embodies the nineteenth-century feminine ideal on which he seeks to build his new society.[35] "Arthur the blameless, pure as any maid," he is called, sardonically but accurately, in "Balin and Balan," and it is in these terms that he becomes a model for all his knights, urging them "To lead sweet lives in purest chastity,/To love one maiden only, cleave to her,/And worship her by years of noble deeds." Such sexual restraint will, according to Arthur, win for the Round Table knights the moral authority to purify a land "Wherein the beast was ever more and more, / But man was less and less." These lines perfectly express the Evangelical Protestant belief, just noted, that "Christianity had elevated women above the weakness of animal nature for the sake of purity for men," and they confirm that it is on the female ideal of passionlessness that Arthur means to found his new community. Tennyson even goes so far as to alter his sources in order to make this point, rejecting Malory's designation of Modred as Arthur's illegitimate son and instead having the king refer to the usurper as "my sister's son—no kin of mine."

The scene would now appear to be set for the triumph of the Round Table experiment. With the apocalyptic overturning of history and male authority and the substitution for them of a benign nature and a safely contained female energy, Arthur's new society ought certainly to flourish. How, then, are we to account for the famous decline of this ideal community into corruption and nihilism, how explain the fall of Camelot? Tennyson's revision of the story of Modred's origins may offer one answer to these questions. As I have suggested, the point of the poet's departure from Malory is to maintain unblemished the record of Arthur's sexual purity. But the textual change has unexpected ramifications that reveal a serious flaw in the Arthurian vision. For if Modred is not Arthur's son, illegitimate or otherwise, then in the story as we receive it, Arthur has no children at all. He and Guinevere produce no offspring, and even the foundling he brings to his wife to rear as her own dies.

Such sterility, appropriate symbol of a denatured sexuality, means the end of Arthur's dream of a new society; the rejection of history and patriarchy that is the source of the young king's first strength here returns to haunt the older monarch, who now perceives that without the continuity provided by legitimate descent through the male line, his vision cannot survive him.[36] This point has already been made obliquely in the passage from "Guinevere" describing the natural magic that filled the land when Arthur first began to rule. The story, we know, is recounted by a young novice who explains that she is repeating a tale her father had told her. Thus, even this early in

Arthur's reign, the dependence of the king's authority on the preservation of a historical record is recognized, a preservation that in turn—the passage reminds us—requires men capable of begetting children through whom to transmit that record.[37]

It is precisely Arthur's incapacity to propagate his line that renders his new society so vulnerable. In "The Last Tournament," for example, the Red Knight calls tauntingly from the top of a brutally phallic tower: "Lo! art thou not that eunuch-hearted king / Who fain had clipt free manhood from the world—/The woman-worshipper?" The Red Knight's equation of Arthur's sterility with a worship of woman suggests how enfeebling the king's sentimentalizing of nature has become. The female ideal worshiped by Arthur (and scorned by the Red Knight) is tame, disembodied, passionless, itself the product of an abstract male rationalism and no real alternative source of strength. Lancelot, describing to Guinevere, in "Balin and Balan," a dream he has had of "a maiden saint" who carries lilies in her hand, speaks of the flowers as "perfect-pure" and continues:

> As light a flush
> As hardly tints the blossom of the quince
> Would mar their charm of stainless womanhood.

To which Guinevere replies, resenting such an imposition of the ideal on the natural,

> Sweeter to me . . . this garden rose
> Deep-hued and many-folded! sweeter still
> The wild-wood hyacinth and the bloom of May!

In the end, Guinevere's reality triumphs over Arthur's and Lancelot's abstraction in the *Idylls of the King*, just as her irresistible sexual energy at last defeats her husband's passionlessness.

Given the subject and the theme of the *Idylls*, this outcome is inevitable. Indeed, Tennyson's profoundest insight in the poem may be that nature cannot be courted casually, that the id-like energy of the deep must not be invoked without a full knowledge of how devastating and ultimately uncontrollable that energy can be. Again, for the nineteenth century it was the French Revolution that most dramatically embodied this insight. We have already seen how that event, for all its celebration of myth over history, nature over culture, female over male, itself began by trying to contain the outburst of insurrectionary energy it had released within a number of easily manipulated abstractions: new laws governing the inheritance of property, new names for the months of the year. Even regicide was intended as a kind of abstract statement, the removal of a symbol as much as of a man.

But unaccountably, the blood would not stop flowing from the murdered king's decapitated body. It poured into the streets of Paris from the foot of the guillotine and ran there for years, as if newly released from some source deep in the earth. From the first, the bloodstained Terror was associated with female sexuality. The key symbol of the Revolution was the figure Liberty, later memorably depicted by Eugene Delacroix as a bare-breasted bacchante striding triumphantly over the bodies of half-naked dead men. The Dionysian guillotine haunted the imagination of Europe; a mechanical *vagina dentata*, it produced, with its endless emasculations, an unstoppable blood flow, the unhealing menstrual wound curiously like the one suffered by the maimed king in the story of the Grail. In primitive societies, such menstrual bleeding is the ultimate symbol of a polluting female nature, an unbridled sexual destructiveness that the power of patriarchal authority must at all costs contain. In nineteenth-century England, the bloody denouement of the French Revolution produced a similar reaction, a suppression of sex and a repression of women that to this day we disapprovingly call Victorian.

From the beginning of his career, Tennyson had been preoccupied with these issues—with what Gerhard Joseph has called the poet's "notion of woman as cosmic destructive principle"[38]—and in particular with the point at which the themes of nature, blood, and female sexuality converge. An early sonnet, for example, begins:

> She took the dappled partridge fleckt with blood,
>   And in her hands the drooping pheasant bare,
>   And by his feet she held the woolly hare,
>   And like a master-painting where she stood,
> Lookt some new goddess of an English wood.

This powerful figure of female authority, bloody, dangerous, but curiously attractive, springs from the imagination of a young poet already moving toward a post-Wordsworthian view of nature as "red in tooth and claw." In "The Palace of Art," the protagonist, withdrawing too deeply into self, approaching too closely the dark, secret springs of nature, comes "unawares" on "corpses three-months-old . . . that stood against the wall" and on "white-eyed phantasms weeping tears of blood." In the *Idylls*, the doom of the Round Table is sealed at the moment during "The Last Tournament" when, to defeat the bestial Red Knight, Arthur's men give themselves up to the almost erotic appeal of blood lust, when

>   swording right and left
> Men, women, on their sodden faces, [they] hurl'd
> Till all the rafters rang with woman-yells,
> And all the pavement streamed with massacre.

But the dismantling of the brotherhood had begun even earlier, as a direct result of the Grail quest. The blood-filled holy cup, itself a menstrual symbol, first appears in the *Idylls* to Percival's sister, a young nun in whose description the vessel seems almost explicitly a living female organ:

> Down the long beam stole the Holy Grail,
> Rose-red with beatings in it, as if alive,
> Till all the white walls of my cell were dyed
> With rosy colors leaping on the wall.
>
> ("The Holy Grail")

It is when the Round Table knights abandon themselves to the visionary pursuit of this symbol of the "eternal feminine" that Camelot, literally "unmanned," begins to fall into ruin.

"Creator and destroyer," Robert M. Adams comments on the Victorian image of the femme fatale, "but more fascinating in the second capacity than the first, woman for the late nineteenth century . . . is both sacred and obscene, sacred as redeeming man from culture, obscene as content with a merely appetitive existence that declines inevitably from the high fever of Eros to the low fever of dissolution and decay."[39] In the end, Arthur's dream of a natural community is destroyed, Tennyson suggests, by the carnality to which such a dream must necessarily lead, is spoiled by an irrepressible female libidinousness that, once released by the withdrawal of patrilineal authority, can be neither contained nor directed. The second half of the *Idylls* is one long record of licentiousness: the faithless depravity of Gawain and Ettarre, the crass sensuality of Tristram and Isolt, the open adultery of Lancelot and Guinevere. "Thou hast spoilt the purpose of my life" we have already heard Arthur declare bitterly to the queen at their last meeting, a key passage in the long-standing controversy about the psychological and moral sophistication of the *Idylls*. For if Christopher Ricks, among others, is right that in this speech Guinevere is made "too much a scapegoat, [since] the doom of the Round Table seems to antedate her adultery," he is surely wrong to find, in such an attack on her, evidence of "a root confusion in Tennyson."[40] Rather, what the poem preeminently shows is that the confusion here is Arthur's. It is Arthur's naiveté about the dynamics of the human psyche that dooms his ideal community from the start; it is his own well-intentioned but foolish binding of his knights "by vows . . . the which no man can keep" that threatens his dream long before the adultery of Guinevere and Lancelot can precipitate its destruction.[41]

In his isolation from reality, the king resembles other self-authorizing post-Renaissance heroes, from Faust to Frankenstein, who begin by creating the worlds in which they live out of their own private visions and end by succumbing to the dark natural forces they have raised but fail to understand or control. The solipsistic isolation of such figures becomes their fate as well as their failing, their retribution as well as their sin. For where the historical record provides individuals with a context independent of themselves, a past and a future in which they need not participate to believe, a variety of experiences unlike their own but just as real, myth asserts the sovereignty of the eternal moment, which is forever the present, and the ubiquitousness of the representative human, who is always the same, without antecedents or heirs. It is into this reductive timelessness and silence of myth that characters like Merlin and Arthur ultimately fall in the *Idylls* for having cut their connections with patriarchal history.

Merlin, Tennyson tells us in the sixth idyll, derives his power from an ancient volume that is the paradigmatic book of history, passed down through the generations from one male magician to another. The first owner we hear of is a little, shriveled, Pellam-like wizard whose strength comes from his rejection of sensuality in favor of the intensest possible concentration on the text. (The seer's principal use of this text is to help a local king exercise absolute control over his queen.) The book then "comes down" to Merlin, who describes it as

> Writ in a language that has long gone by.
> . . . .
> And every margin scribbled, crost, and cramm'd
> With comment, densest condensation, hard
> . . . .
> And none can read the text, not even I;
> And none can read the comment but myself;
> And in the comment did I find the charm.

Here is the perfect symbol of what we have been calling patrilineal continuity, continuity dependent on a bequeathed historical record that is both the ultimate source of male power and, with its antiquity and its accumulating burden of interpretation, a constant reminder of the belatedness of the present. Shut out of history by her gender, a vengeful Vivien determines to seduce Merlin from the satisfactions of male tradition with the blandishments of female sexuality. For a long while the old magician holds out against the woman, but in the end he yields, revealing to her the secret of the ultimate charm. The next moment, Vivien has turned the spell back on him, robbing him—significantly—of "name and fame," the two best gifts that patrilineal history can bestow on a man, and casting him into the eternal isolation of myth, "Closed in the four walls of a hollow tower / From which was no escape for evermore."[42]

In his final battle, Arthur suffers a fate much like Merlin's. Because he has received authorization from no father and conveyed it to no son, the king is trapped in the reflexiveness of the prophecy that has governed him all his life: "From the great deep to the great deep he goes." That same solipsistic reflexiveness characterizes Arthur's last hallucinatory battle against his sister's son, a war, he tells us,

> against my people and my knights.
> A king who fights his people fights himself.
> . . . .
> I perish by this people that I made.
> ("The Passing of Arthur")

The war is fought in "a death-white mist" in which the solid reality of the world proves an illusion, "For friend and foe were shadows in the mist, / And friend slew friend not knowing whom he slew."

Ironically, the reign that began with the whole world doubting the legitimacy of the king ends with the king himself doubting it. "On my heart," says Arthur,

> hath fallen
> Confusion, till I know not what I am,
> Nor whence I am, nor whether I be king;
> Behold, I seem but king among the dead.

In the end—Tennyson summarizes the central theme of the *Idylls*—all certainty is impossible for a man who rejects the stability of patrilineal descent and seeks instead to derive his authority from himself, to build a community on the idealization of nature and female energy.

The resemblance of this scene, in which "friend slays friend," to the equally confusing struggle of "ignorant armies" on "the darkling plain" in Matthew Arnold's "Dover Beach" reminds us that, in writing the *Idylls of the King*, Tennyson was participating in an elaborate symposium with his fellow Victorians on the troubling state of their world. But where Arnold's poem focuses on a particular moment in the history of that world, Tennyson's *Idylls* provide, in John D. Rosenberg's phrase, "the chronicle . . . of a whole civilization" (34) as it passes from the Romantic optimism of its first days—about which Wordsworth could exult, "Bliss was it in that dawn to be alive"—to the fin de siècle disillusionment of the last hours—which found, in Walter Pater's words, "each man keeping as a solitary prisoner, his own dream of a world." The springtime innocence and eagerness of the first idylls wonderfully convey the excitement of the Romantic rediscovery of nature, and the Arthurian credo of passionlessness embodies the early Victorian belief in the benevolence and controllability of that nature. But just as the Victorians' famous efforts to suppress female sexuality only succeeded in generating a grim and extensive sexual underground, so Arthur's naive manipulations of nature conclude in the society of the Round Table being swept away on a great wave of carnality.

Despite the failure of the Arthurian assault on history, Tennyson persists at the end of the *Idylls*, as he does elsewhere, in seeking a rapprochement with myth. Thus, against the linear and historical implications of the king's

214 ♦ ELLIOT L. GILBERT

famous valedictory, "The old order changeth, yielding place to new," the poet reiterates the traditional cyclical promise of Arthur's eventual return as *rex quondam rexque futurus*. In the same way, at the end of *In Memoriam* Tennyson sets the historical and progressive "one far-off, divine event / To which the whole creation moves" within a cycle of seasons. To be sure, the hero of "Locksley Hall" seems to offer the definitive disavowal of myth when he declares, "Better fifty years of Europe than a cycle of Cathay." But it is significant that the narrator of that poem lives long enough to discover how the inevitable alternation of "chaos and cosmos" in the universe renders even the most intense vision of historical progress trivial.

Such ambivalence about history, our starting point for this consideration of the *Idylls*, marks the history of the poem itself, a history that records the poet's entrapment in a familiar nineteenth-century dilemma, one with its own broader ramifications. Like Merlin, Tennyson is committed—since "first light[ing] upon Malory"—to the authority of a historical text of which he is his generation's principal interpreter. "And none can read the comment but myself; / And in the comment did I find the charm." But no belated expositor such as he, no descendant of patriarchal exegetes, can hope to make the unimaginable backward leap through commentary to the mystery of the text itself. Indeed, it is the very weight of traditional commentary—"densest condensation, hard"—that renders such a leap impossible, precisely that burden of the past that unmans where it means to empower. For in exhausted latter days, as Merlin informs us, "None can read the text, not even I." Yet Tennyson's attempt, in the face of this exhaustion, to reject traditional sources in favor of a contemporary, ahistorical representation of Arthurian materials—his refusal, that is, to "remodel models"—courts another kind of weakness, risking, in the absence of patrilineal resonances, the domesticity and effeminacy of a "Morte d'Albert."

A similar ambivalence toward history characterizes the century for which Tennyson wrote. Already during the early decades Viconian cyclical theory was becoming influential, Thomas Carlyle was denouncing scientific reconstructions of the past as "tombstone history" and time as "a grand anti-magician and wonderhider," and the First Reform Act, Britain's bloodless version of the French Revolution, had dramatically rejected genealogy as society's sole authorizing principle. In the light of such reformist impulses, Tennyson's investigation of a natural community in the *Idylls of the King,* one in which the female energy of myth substitutes for the male energy of history, seems inevitable. Equally inevitable, however, is the failure of that community, given the growing Victorian disillusionment with the Romantic experiment.[43] For Carlyle, for instance, who in his own way shared the fate of Tennyson's Arthur, the magic creativity of *Sartor Resartus* unavoidably declined into the solipsistic self-imprisonment of the *Latter-Day Pamphlets.* Just as inescapably, the First Reform Act led to the Second and toward that "anarchy" which Matthew Arnold prophesied and deplored and of which the developing women's movement was seen by the Victorians as a powerful symbol. And, despite eager celebrations of myth, over this perceived decline brooded a sense of the enervating, irreversible historicity of things. Particularly in the *Idylls*, Tennyson depicts a disintegration of society from which there can be no reasonable expectation of a return. From his long, dark Arthurian speculation, Tennyson seems to be saying, the century can only move inexorably forward through fin de siècle hedonism into the fragmentation and alienation of a modernist waste land.

Notes

1.   See, e.g., George Meredith's description of Arthur as a "crowned curate," quoted in Robert B. Martin, *Tennyson: The Unquiet Heart* (New York: Oxford Univ. Press, 1980), 423–24. "Tennyson was criticized," Mark Girouard writes, "both at the time and later for turning Malory's king and knights into pattern Victorian gentlemen" (*The Return to Camelot* [New Haven: Yale Univ. Press, 1981], 184). Quotations from Tennyson's poetry are drawn from *Poems of Tennyson*, ed. Jerome H. Buckley (Boston: Riverside, 1958).

2.   Hallam Tennyson, *Alfred Lord Tennyson: A Memoir by His Son*, 2 vols. (London, 1897), II, 128.

3.   Carlyle is quoted by F. E. L. Priestley, "Tennyson's *Idylls*," *University of Toronto Quarterly* 19 (1949), 35; John Sterling, review of Tennyson's *Poems* (1842), *Quarterly Review*, Sept. 1842, 385–416. Rpt. in *Tennyson: The Critical Heritage*, ed. John D. Jump (London: Routledge & Kegan Paul, 1967), 19. See also John Ruskin's comment to Tennyson about the *Idylls* in a letter of Sept. 1859: "So great power ought not to be spent on visions of things past but on the living present . . . The intense, masterful and unerring transcript of an actuality . . . seems to me to be the true task of the modern poet" (*The Works of John Ruskin*, ed. E. T. Cook and Alexander Wedderburn, 39 vols. [London: George Allen, 1909], XXXVI, 320–21).

4.   See Margaret Gent, " 'To Flinch from Modern Varnish': The Appeal of the Past to the Victorian Imagination," in *Victorian Poetry*, ed. Malcolm Bradbury and David Palmer, Stratford-upon-Avon Studies 15 (London: Edward Arnold, 1972), 11–35.

5.   Matthew Arnold, Preface to *Poems* (1853), in *On the Classical Tradition*, ed. R. H. Super (Ann Arbor: Univ. of Michigan Press, 1961), 1, 3.

6.   Elizabeth Barrett Browning, *The Poetical Works of Elizabeth Barrett Browning*, ed. Ruth M. Adam (Boston: Houghton, 1974), lines 200–213.

7.   Algernon Charles Swinburne, *Under the Microscope*, in *Swinburne Replies*, ed. Clyde K. Hyder (Syracuse, N.Y.: Syracuse Univ. Press, 1966), 56, 57.

8.   Frederic Harrison, "The History Schools," in his *The Meaning of History* (New York: Macmillan, 1908), 121.

9.   Ann Douglas, *The Feminization of American Culture* (New York: Knopf, 1977), 173–74.

10.   Arthur Schlesinger, "The Role of Women in American History," in his *New Viewpoints in American History* (New York: Macmillan, 1921), 126.

11.   Jane Austen, *Northanger Abbey*, in *The Novels of Jane Austen*, ed. R. W. Chapman, vol. 5 (London: Oxford Univ. Press, 1923), 108.

12.   Thomas Carlyle, *Past and Present*, ed. Richard D. Altick (Boston: Houghton, 1965), 45.

13.   Claude Lévi-Strauss, *The Elementary Structures of Kinship* (Boston: Beacon, 1969).

14.   George Eliot, *Middlemarch*, ed. Gordon S. Haight (Boston: Houghton, 1956),

612; italics mine. The complete passage reads: "[Dorothea's] full nature, like that river of which Cyrus broke the strength, spent itself on channels which had no great name on the earth. But the effect of her being on those around her was incalculably diffusive: for the growing good of the world is partly dependent on unhistoric acts; and that things are not so ill with you and me as they might have been, is half-owing to the number who live faithfully a hidden life, and rest in unvisited tombs" (613). In speaking of Theresa at the end of the novel, George Eliot implies that it is the girl's childish innocence, analogous to the innocence of her time, that made possible her great work. By contrast, the present is so burdened with knowledge of the past that "its strength is broken into channels," and people like Dorothea Brooke are effective precisely because they are "unhistoric." Were they to be historic—that is, memorable—they would only add to the burden of the next generation, become one more influence for the future to be anxious about. Their importance, then, derives from the fact that their lives are "hidden" and their tombs "unvisited." Note that unhistoric people are likelier to be women than men (history remembers more Cyruses than Theresas), women's "hidden" influence being "incalculably diffusive," like nature, rather than immediate and focused, like history. In this connection, consider the puns on Dorothea's "nature" and on her last name, closer in meaning to channel than to river.

15.   See, e.g., National Socialism's twentieth-century exploitation of this nineteenth-century idea in support of its own revolutionary theories. "I, as a politician," Hitler is quoted by Hermann Rauschning, "need a conception that enables the order that has hitherto existed on an historic basis to be abolished and an entirely new and antihistoric order enforced" (*Hitler Speaks*, ed. Hermann Rauschning [London: Butterworth, 1939], 229).

16.   Mircea Eliade, *Cosmos and History* (New York: Harper, 1954), 90–91.

17.   James R. Kincaid, *Tennyson's Major Poems: The Comic and Ironic Patterns* (New Haven: Yale Univ. Press, 1975), 151–52.

18.   Mircea Eliade, *Mephistopheles and the Androgyne*, trans. J. M. Cohen (New York: Sheed & Ward, 1965), 113.

19.   Mary Wollstonecraft, *An Historical and Moral View of the Origin and Progress of the French Revolution and the Effect It Has Produced in Europe*, in *A Wollstonecraft Anthology*, ed. Janet M. Todd (Bloomington: Indiana Univ. Press, 1977), 133; italics mine. "The Revolution," writes Virginia Woolf of Mary Wollstonecraft, "was not merely an event that had happened outside her; it was an active agent in her own blood" (*The Second Common Reader* [New York: Harcourt, 1932], 143.)

20.   Edmund Burke, *Reflections on the Revolution in France*, ed. Thomas H. D. Mahoney (New York: Bobbs-Merrill, 1955), 109. G. P. Gooch, in *History and Historians of the Nineteenth Century* (London: Longmans, 1913), writes that "in combating the French Revolution, Burke emphasized the continuity of historic life and the debt of every age to its predecessors" (9), just those patriarchal values under attack by the apocalyptic female energy Burke associated with the Revolution.

21.   See John D. Rosenberg's discussion of Tennyson's deep interest in apocalyptic subjects, an interest evident as early as the poet's fifteenth year in the fragment "Armageddon," in *The Fall of Camelot: A Study of Tennyson's Idylls of the King* (Cambridge: Belknap-Harvard Univ. Press, 1973), 14–19.

22.   Buckley, *Poems*, 536.

23.   J. M. Gray, *Man and Myth in Victorian England: Tennyson's "The Coming of Arthur"* (Lincoln, Nebr.: Tennyson Society, 1969), 11.

24.   Indeed, the early nineteenth century found victory over Rome a particularly compelling metaphor. When Napoleon seized the crown from Pius VII at Reims and placed it on his own head, he was attacking the most venerable patriarchy in Europe, substituting for an "apostolic" descent of royal power a self-authorizing kingship that may well have influenced Tennyson's depiction of Arthur in the *Idylls*.

25.   Tennyson himself refused to be tied down to a specific identification of the three

queens; he responded to readers who saw them as Faith, Hope, and Charity that "they mean that and they do not . . . They are much more" (H. Tennyson, *Memoir*, II,127).

26.   Erich Neumann, *The Great Mother* (Princeton: Princeton Univ. Press, 1955), xlii.

27.   Some forty years earlier, Tennyson had dealt with this same fragmentation in "Tithonus." In that poem, he sets the Pellam-like figure of the aged male protagonist— unable to die, obliged to move always forward in time burdened more and more by his own past, his own history—against Aurora, the female representation of the dawn, a natural phenomenon who, existing out of time in Eliade's *illo tempore* and always circling back to her beginning, continually renews her youth. In the end, Tithonus' dearest wish is to awake from the nightmare of history, to which he had willfully consigned himself, and to reenter the restorative cycle of nature, even though that change can only be inaugurated by his own death.

28.   That Arthur is himself dismayed at how the embodiment of those values in the Grail quest must necessarily destroy the Round Table brotherhood prefigures the king's later despair at the final collapse of his ideal. See the discussion of the Grail symbol in Jessie L. Weston, *From Ritual to Romance* (New York: Anchor-Doubleday, 1957), 72–76. See also Robert Stephen Hawker's contemporary "Quest of the Sangraal" (1863), where the poet writes about Joseph of Arimathaea, keeper of the Grail, that "His home was like a garner, full of corn / and wind and oil: a granary of God" (in *Cornish Ballads and Other Poems* [Oxford, 1869], 184).

29.   "The timelessness of myth was one of its greatest attractions to the Victorians," writes James Kissane. "It was the realm of myths and legends that came closest to constituting an idealized past that could solace Tennyson's imagination as a kind of eternal presence" ("Tennyson: The Passion of the Past and the Curse of Time," in *Tennyson*, ed. Elizabeth A. Francis [Englewood Cliffs, N.J.: Prentice-Hall, 1980], 129).

30.   Lévi-Strauss, *Kinship*, p. 31. If Lévi-Strauss does not explicitly equate culture and history, he clearly links the two through his association of culture with genealogy.

31.   See, e.g., Henry Nash Smith, *The Virgin Land* (Cambridge: Harvard Univ. Press, 1950); and Annette Kolodny, *The Lay of the Land* (Chapel Hill: Univ. of North Carolina Press, 1975).

32.   Nancy F. Cott, "Passionlessness: An Interpretation of Victorian Sexual Ideology, 1790–1850," *Signs* 4 (1978), 221. Havelock Ellis, *Studies in the Psychology of Sex*, 2nd ed. (Philadelphia: F. A. Davis, 1913), III, 193–94.

33.   Carol Christ, "Victorian Masculinity and the Angel in the House," in *A Widening Sphere*, ed. Martha Vicinus (Bloomington: Indiana Univ. Press, 1977), 146. See also Ward Hellstrom's comment that "if the *Idylls* fail to speak to the modern world, that failure is the result to a great degree of Tennyson's attempt to preserve a lost and perhaps ultimately indefensible ideal of womanhood" (*On the Poems of Tennyson* [Gainesville: Univ. of Florida Press, 1972], 134). As my own essay tries to establish, it is Arthur rather than Tennyson who futilely defends this ideal. I fully agree with Hellstrom, however, that the "woman question is more or less central to all the books of 'The Round Table' " and even with his more daring assertion that it is "perhaps the most significant and revolutionary question of the nineteenth century" (109).

34.   "In the *Idylls*, Tennyson takes up with complete seriousness, although not without irony, the question of woman's role in private and public life—a topic that in *The Princess* he treated half seriously, half satirically" (J. Philip Eggers, *King Arthur's Laureate* [New York: New York Univ. Press, 1971], 144).

35.   Tennyson had also dealt with the issue in *The Princess*, where he dramatizes "a pattern of feminine identification in his portrayal of the Prince" (Carol Christ, "Masculinity," 154). Such mildness would also be appropriate, of course, to the more conventional association of Arthur with Jesus. But the attack on mid-nineteenth-century Christianity for its effeminacy, already noted, suggests that the familiar image of Arthur as Christ and Tennyson's new depiction of him as female king were beginning to coincide.

36. Margaret Homans, in "Tennyson and the Spaces of Life," *ELH* 46 (1979), 693, makes a similar point, speaking of Arthur as "a victim of continuity: his origins, from which he has endeavored all his life to escape, have successfully reasserted the claim that the past makes on the future."

37. Interestingly, Robert B. Martin sees this issue reflected in what he calls the poet's "slackened language" in the *Idylls*, a neglect of grammatical cause and effect that "robs the characters of any appearance of '*real man*' because there is no feeling of behavior resulting from antecedents" (*Unquiet Heart*, 496; italics mine).

38. Gerhard Joseph, *Tennysonian Love: The Strange Diagonal* (Minneapolis: Univ. of Minnesota Press, 1969), 127.

39. Robert M. Adams, "Religion of Man, Religion of Woman," in *Art, Politics, and Will: Essays in Honor of Lionel Trilling*, ed. Quentin Anderson et al. (New York: Basic, 1977), 185.

40. Christopher Ricks, *Tennyson* (New York: Macmillan, 1972), 272.

41. Jerome Buckley comments that Arthur is "ineffective" in dealing with Lancelot and the queen "despite his ideal manhood, or perhaps because of it" (*Tennyson: The Growth of a Poet* [Cambridge: Harvard Univ. Press, 1960], 177).

42. Henry Kozicki, in *Tennyson and Clio: History in the Major Poems* (Baltimore; Johns Hopkins Univ. Press, 1979), describes this passage as portraying "the lotos death of old historical form through its hero's withdrawal into self" (112). Kozicki's study comments usefully on Tennyson's vision of, and attitude toward, history during the course of his career.

43. "With its lesson that the world is irredeemable," writes Clyde de L. Ryals, "the *Idylls of the King* seems to reflect much of the pessimism of nineteenth-century philosophy" (*From the Great Deep: Essays on Idylls of the King* [Athens: Ohio Univ. Press, 1967], 94).

The Contours of Manliness and the Nature of Woman

Marion Shaw

'I didn't roar out a bit, you know,' Tom said. . . . 'It's cowardly to roar.'

But Maggie would have it that when anything hurt you very much, it was quite permissible to cry out . . .

George Eliot, The Mill on the Floss

'You are thinking,' he said, 'that my face is old and tired. You are thinking that I talk of power, and yet I am not able even to prevent the decay of my own body. Can you not understand, Winston, that the individual is only a cell? The weariness of the cell is the vigour of the organism. Do you die when you cut your fingernails?'

George Orwell, Nineteen Eighty-Four

In describing the 'masculine reticence as to the tender emotions' which Tom Tulliver, even as a very youthful 'pink and white bit of masculinity', must display if he is to sustain his role as only son and elder brother, George Eliot was drawing on definitions of manliness which by 1860, the date of *The Mill on the Floss*, had been developed and codified with a self-conscious thoroughness that gave them, at least among the middle classes, gospel status.

'Manliness' and 'masculinity' were by no means identical concepts although they obviously overlapped. 'Masculinity' described a set of beliefs about male sexuality which were, as Jeffrey Weeks has pointed out, 'inextricably linked to concepts of male self-expression and power' 'Manliness', however, was not merely a question of sexual performance. Virility, as William Acton had noted in 1857, may be essential 'to give a man that consciousness of his dignity, of his character as head and ruler, and of his importance,'[1] but as Acton's comment implies, virility had to be consciously translated into social behaviour recognizably manly.

The translation involved a contradiction: the socially acceptable behaviour denoting manliness—being a strong, reliable worker, an authoritative

Reprinted from *Alfred Lord Tennyson* by Marion Shaw (1988), by permission. © Harvester-Wheatsheaf (U.K.), 1988; Humanities Press International (U.S.), 1988.

yet loving husband and father, and a respected public figure—may have been nourished by a man's consciousness of his masculinity but it also disallowed all but the most severely regulated display of that masculinity. Manliness therefore came to mean the exercise of restraint upon the manifestations of male sexuality—the passion, lust, aggression, violence and neediness of the 'pulsing full man' of Tristram's description[2]—and either their suppression or their redirection into sanctioned forms. The extent of a man's mastery and redirection of powerful sexual energies became a measure of the manliness of his character. 'Manliness' implied virility but expressed itself in social terms as courage, capacity for toil, protectiveness towards the weak, self-control and emotional reticence. These qualities were not merely a question of manners but of self-respect and self-definition. As Mr Thornton in *North and South* says, 'when we speak of . . . "a man" we consider him not merely with regard to his fellow-men but in relation to himself,—to life—to time—to eternity'.

There is a marked scarcity of manly men in Tennyson's poetry. In contrast to Browning's characters, who are unmistakably masculine, Tennyson's male figures are, for the most part, vacillating, weak and effeminate and display a vulnerability which belies the patrician image that Tennyson himself presented, particularly throughout his Laureate years. There are exceptions to this generalization: characters in *Idylls*, such as Gareth and Tristram, Enoch Arden perhaps, and a group of old or ageing men who, by reputation at least, are heroic: Ulysses, Tithonus, Tiresias and the Arthur of 'Morte d'Arthur'. This last group are the protagonists of poems written in the immediate aftermath of Arthur Hallam's death. In his grief for Hallam, Tennyson assumed a 'mask of age' and deflected his sorrow and bewilderment into heroic or gnomic figures from myth and legend. But although heroic in gesture, these poems about old men were in some respects an evasion of a 'proper' manly role which should surely have been that of a young man (Tennyson was twenty-four at the time), a David mourning a Jonathan, a successor to the ever-youthful second generation of Romantic poets Hallam so much admired and, more important, an inheritor of an elegiac tradition which in Milton's *Lycidas* and Shelley's *Adonais* had, with most youthful and manly directness, confronted the enormity of early death.

In each case, Tennyson's old men poems enact a scene in which an ageing man finds solace in the contemplation of death: as a last adventure for Ulysses, as release from wearying mortality for Tithonus, as noble self-sacrifice for Tiresias, and as part of a progressive development—'The old order changeth, yielding place to new'—for Arthur. Tennyson seems to be rehearsing four ways of dying: the heroic, the nihilistic, the Christian and the evolutionary. In each exercise, the old men are placed in a triangular relationship with a younger man and a woman: Telemachus and the 'aged wife' in 'Ulysses', Tithonus's younger self and Aurora in 'Tithonus', Menœceus and Pallas Athene in 'Tiresias', and Sir Bedivere and the Lady of the Lake in 'Morte d'Arthur'. The younger men are shadowy observers or companions in the protagonists' journey towards death, mute commentators on the old men's anguish and mortal desire. The women are even more shadowy and distant yet they are all-important points of reference, indeed they *cause* the action in the poems in that they are the locus of anxiety and dissatisfaction which generates the move towards death. Death is proposed as a solution to problems to do with women which cannot be otherwise solved: the impregnability of the 'agèd wife', Aurora's insatiability, Pallas Athene's implacability, and the inexorability of the Lady of the Lake, all these provoke crises not merely of masculinity—the failure in virility of the protagonists is clear—but of manliness also. The roles and functions of manhood which the younger men now fulfil—Telemachus is an efficient governor, Sir Bedivere's voice will 'Rise like a fountain'—are now forever denied the poems' heroes. Impotent to solve the problem created by the women, and consequently powerless to perform the social tasks required of their sex and position—'this useless hand', Tiresias says—Tennyson's old men can find in death their only destiny, a longed-for dissolution into quietude and inanimation. Each poem articulates this longing for rest in terms of an ideal landscape of either pastoral or chivalric convention in which the speaker is passively absorbed into the scene: 'Take me up . . . And lap me deep within the lonely west' (25–27), is Tithonus's cry, and in the inversions of Arthur's departing words—'I am going a long way . . . Where falls not hail, or rain, or any snow, / Nor ever wind blows loudly' (256–61)— is all the sense of distance, fatigue and failure these poems are centred on.

Tennyson's grief for Hallam, his loss of this most dear friend, precipitated an anxiety expressed in these monologue poems about both masculine competence and manly function. This anxiety was narratively developed and concluded, in a manner characteristic of Tennyson's frequent need at a later stage in his life to rework his early themes within an enlarged social context, in a poem of thirty years later, 'Enoch Arden' (1864), the story of a 'strong heroic soul' whose name, like Adam Bede's, suggests an essence of English manhood. The poem employs familiar Tennysonian motifs: childhood sweethearts, a triangle of lovers, and a test of courage and endurance which is also a suicide bid. Additionally, as Ricks points out, the poem 'brings to a climax' another lifelong preoccupation, the return of the dead to see their place as husband, father and man of property taken by others.[3]

In *Adam Bede*, George Eliot was content to leave her triangle of lovers in harmony, albeit slightly ambivalently so, at the end of the novel. 'Enoch Arden' forces a crisis of competition and completion upon a similar situation. In other poems which treat of rivalrous lovers—*The Lover's Tale*, 'Locksley Hall', *Maud, Idylls of the King*, for example—the hero's failure to win and keep the woman he loves is, at least partially, explained by his weakness, particularly by a quality of effeminacy such as Tristram notices in Arthur: 'Man, is he man at all?' ('The Last Tournament', 658). But there are no such doubts about Enoch. His manliness is established early in the poem; he is 'stronger-made' and more aggressive than Philip, with weather-beaten face, a bold and successful fisherman. Unlike Philip, who inherits property, Enoch is a self-made man who in his thrift, resourcefulness and domestic reverence exemplifies all the virtues of mid-Victorian capitalist enterprise:

> Enoch set
> A purpose evermore before his eyes,
> To hoard all savings to the uttermost,
> To purchase his own boat, and make a home
> For Annie.
>
> (44–48)

Naturally, Annie loves him in preference to the effeminate and Seth-like Philip.

There are sufficient external casual factors, including that same spirit of enterprise which made him so proper a man, to account for Enoch's disappearance and eventual death. Trading ventures and the misfortunes that could overtake them were issues sympathetically familiar to the Victorian reading public. Yet the perverseness of Enoch's decision to leave his family, the excess and disproportion of his act, is very evident in the poem. Of course, his stubborn determination is seen as an exercise in rightful husbandly authority, but beyond that is the recognition that in the question of Enoch's identity as a man, his wife, children and home operate more forcefully as an emblem, an image carried in the mind's eye to strengthen the resolve of manliness, than as a reality. Indeed, the reality has become mysteriously burdensome and debilitating. Enoch's investment in his family as an image is powerfully suggested in the description of how he builds and equips Annie's shop before he leaves her:

> [He bought] Annie goods and stores, and set his hand
> To fit their little streetward sitting-room
> With shelf and corner for the goods and stores.
>   . . . and his careful hand,—
> The space was narrow,—having ordered all
> Almost as neat and close as Nature packs
> Her blossom or her seedling, paused; and he,
> Who needs would work for Annie to the last,
> Ascending tired, heavily slept till morn.
>
> (169–81)

The passage emphasizes the connection between his home and the trading enterprise he deserts it for; he colonizes and appropriates the space his absence leaves just as he intends to colonize and impregnate the vacant places he sets sail for. The allusion to Nature's economy and her fecundity—'as neat and close as Nature packs . . . her seedling'—reflects the containment (his family as image) and potential growth (in memory) of his action whilst lending the transaction a softeningly organic yet revealingly sexual colouring. Enoch's attempts to fill Annie with merchandise as surrogate for his sexual presence, to replace with goods what his masculinity can no longer supply, are congruent with the violent urgency of his departure. It is a destructive urge which has some similarity to Leontes' need, in *The Winter's Tale*, to break the ordered pattern of his life and cancel the bonds of husband and father. As with Leontes, this compulsion coincides with the birth of another child; significantly in Enoch's case it is a puny baby boy who will soon die. Annie's Cassandra-like warning, 'well know I / That I shall look upon your face no more' (211–12), is heeded as little as any such woman's cry throughout history by men bent on self-destruction.

Enoch's exile is to a timeless, ahistorical world of nature, an 'eternal summer' reminiscent of the island in 'The Lotos-Eaters' and, like the speakers in that earlier poem, he stands in relation to his former life as both haunted and haunter:

> Dear is the memory of our wedded lives,
> And dear the last embraces of our wives
> And their warm tears: but all hath suffered change:
> . . . our looks are strange:
> And we should come like ghosts to trouble joy.
> ('The Lotos-Eaters', 114–19)

When Enoch does return to the world of manhood responsibilities it is in just such a changed state, as a ghost, effectively absent yet uncannily present. His absent-presence is powerfully captured in two complementary passages describing, firstly, his children's estranged vision of him:

> for Enoch seemed to them
> Uncertain as a vision or a dream,
> Faint as a figure seen in early dawn
> Down at the far end of an avenue,
> Going we know not where:
> (352–56)

and his stranger's vision of them:

> Now when the dead man come to life beheld
> His wife his wife no more, and saw the babe
> Hers, yet not his, upon the father's knee . . .
> And him, that other, reigning in his place,
> Lord of his rights and of his children's love . . .
> (754–60)

But the most important result of Enoch's exile is the prohibition upon speech it imposes, particularly the speech of social intercourse. He can tell Miriam Lane of his solitary experiences on the island but when Miriam tells him 'all the story of his house', it is only her final words about himself that he 'pathetically, / Repeated muttering "cast away and lost;" / Again in deepest inward whispers "lost!" ' (710–12). Above all, since she represents all that he has forsaken, he cannot speak to Annie: 'Not to tell her, never to let her know' (794).

'Enoch Arden' was immensely popular during its own period but has since been much abused as the worst kind of Laureate writing, popularly pious and embarrassingly sentimental. The extreme reactions it has caused seem to point to an excessive discrepancy between the ostensible meaning of the poem and its subterranean obsessions; for 'Enoch Arden' as a story of noble, heroic manhood is also a fascinating dramatization of an anxiety at the heart of male self-esteem: the anxiety that men, even the best and bravest, could fail in masculinity, and therefore in manliness, and that in ways not readily understood this is a failure to be desired. Not only the wilfulness of Enoch's exile but the weighting of the story towards his home-coming (in this it is a significant development from 'The Lotos-Eaters') suggest that the exile represents something of great desirability as well as of fear, and of such enormity that it 'haunts' the story ever afterwards. Enoch's ghost, like any other guilty and unquiet thing, with increasing intensity haunts the scene of his 'crime': as an absence neither living nor dead during his years on the island, as a living ghost on his return to his home village, and then as a legendary ghost after his death. As such a ghost, he is both familiar and strange; he is, in fact, uncanny. As Freud says, 'the uncanny is in reality nothing new or alien, but something which is familiar and old-established in the mind . . . the uncanny [is] something which ought to have remained hidden but has come to light.'[4] Enoch does indeed 'come to light'; in the proper order of things he ought to have perished at sea with his colleagues but as a ghost he returns to take alien and uncanny possession of his familiar landscape. His apparently benign prohibition on Annie not to visit him ('For my dead face would vex her afterlife' (887)) is in effect an unremovable curse; it oddly recalls Kent's words on the dying Lear—'Vex not his ghost. O! Let him pass' (*King Lear* V.iii.312)—, but in Tennyson's poem it will be the ghost of the young Enoch, not the dead man but the younger one who left her at the prime of his manhood, that will trouble the living woman and will not let her pass beyond that far-off moment of his desertion. His final and terrible revenge upon the family and community he transgressed so many years before is the 'token' of his dead baby's hair by which Annie's new baby is illegitimized, her marriage to Philip made bigamous and his children fathered by a corpse: "But if my children care to see me dead,/Who hardly knew me living, let them come,/I am their father" (884–86). If, like Titho-nus, Ulysses and the other 'strong, heroic' men of Tennyson's poems, Enoch wills his own death, it follows that this desired annihilation expresses a revulsion against life, against living the life of a man with the responsibilities of 'head and ruler' (in Acton's words), and perhaps also a revulsion within masculinity itself, a dark and annihilative centre to male sexuality. 'Everything dies for *internal* reasons', says Freud, and 'the aim of all life is death'.[5]

Freud's theory of the death instinct seems to be modelled on a pattern of male sexual activity in which loss and void are implicated in satisfaction; although such a theory ill fits female experience, its very androcentricity offers real insights into Enoch's case. At the point when Enoch seems to have achieved satisfaction in the ways Yeats describes in 'What Then?'—'All his happier dreams come true—/ A small old house, wife, daughter, son, / Grounds where plum and cabbage grew'—, the point when the sexual instinct, Eros, is fulfilled, then the conservative or death instinct, the urge inherent in organic life 'to restore an earlier state of things' asserts itself: "Is it really the case that, *apart from the sexual instincts*, there are no instincts that do not seek to restore an earlier state of things which has never yet been attained? I know of no certain example from the organic world that would contradict the characterization I have thus proposed. . . . The present development of human beings requires, as it seems to me, no different explanation from that of animals."[6] Enoch's weakling child, the surrogacy of his sexual relations with Annie, his fall from his boat, the failure of his business enterprise, imply a slackening of the tension between the life and death instincts, a failure in the masculinity necessary to keep the regressive impulses at bay. The climax of his self-made manhood is reached at the end of 'Seven happy years of health and competence, / And mutual love and honourable toil' (82–3) and what remains beyond this point of optimum drive is the need to escape from social and sexual life into an absorption into landscape, into the inanimate world from which life derives. The only 'desire' Enoch now can have is the desire to die. But this is both so deep an urge and so transgressive a wish that it must be repressed and the only expression it is allowed in the poem is as an interlude, the time on the island, and as a haunting, an uncanny presence, the return of the dead.

The concluding lines of 'Enoch Arden' have always aroused derision: "So past the strong heroic soul away./And when they buried him the little port/Had seldom seen a costlier funeral." Tennyson defended them by saying that 'The costly funeral is all that poor Annie could do for him after he was gone. This is entirely introduced for her sake, and, in my opinion, quite necessary to the perfection of the Poem and the simplicity of the narrative'.[7] Indeed, the ending is a necessary recognition that this has been a poem about a haunting and an exorcism, a costly burial of the repression of Enoch's 'crime' and an attempt to rid Annie of her curse. 'Enoch Arden' is also Tennyson's own burial of his obsession; it is the last of his poems to be concerned with the return of the dead (Arthur's return is a distant hope not a present fear) and the one that most clearly, schematically almost, brings the crime of self-annihilation and its repression face to face. In the future, the problem of manhood will not go away, indeed it will be of paramount concern in *Idylls of the King*, but the crime of admitting its frailty and destructiveness, of speaking the unspeakable truth of its deathward destiny, has been buried with Enoch.

No English poet has written more about women than Tennyson. As a young poet practising his craft, he seems to have turned to portraits of women as another poet might have written of landscape. His youthful gallery of ladies—'Claribel', 'Lilian', 'Madeline', 'Amy', and so on—are both technical exercises of some virtuosity and images of a range of early nineteenth-century female types. They are images, rather than simple descriptions, because of Tennyson's ability to isolate and embellish a stance, a gesture, an outline, so that the form of the woman becomes a perfect and memorable representation of the idea of her:

> She, looking through and through me . . .
>   Smiling, never speaks:
> So innocent-arch, so cunning-simple,
> From beneath her gathered wimple
>   Glancing with black-beaded eyes . . .
>   ('Lilian', 10–15)

Amongst coquettes like Lilian, saints like Isabel and Amy, and spirited and haughty girls like Rosalind and Kate, in Tennyson's early poetry there emerges a group of women who are frustratedly trapped in a situation which has to do with being female, sometimes mysteriously so: 'Mariana', 'Mariana in the South', 'Œnone', 'Fatima', 'A Dream of Fair Women' and, of course, 'The Lady of Shalott', who, as Nina Auerbach has suggested, summarizes the type for all time: 'We may allegorize her into the artist, the poet's anima, a fragile divinity, an heretical anti-divinity . . . but she carries a suggestive resonance beyond these classifications, weaving a myth that belongs to her alone . . . [a] mysterious amalgam of imprisonment and power'.[8] She casts a long shadow into Tennyson's future poetry as the woman who waits to be released by a man from a sterile self-absorption and inactivity into marriage or into death. The heroines of 'The Miller's Daughter', 'The Gardener's Daughter', 'The Sleeping Beauty' and *The Princess* are set free by marriage. Death is the alternative release, either achieved or desired, for those like Fatima, Œnone, Maud and Elaine, whom the lover fails. In either case it is the waiting for deliverance, the suspenseful moment before fulfilment, which yields both romantic and erotic enthralment: 'She is coming, my life, my fate . . . she is near, she is near' (*Maud* I.911–12), and it is the 'coming' of the woman that Tennyson's poetry celebrates. Yet the essence of such coming is that it has to be transformed into an image; fixed and possessed by the poet's technique, its sexual display is available for leisurely surveillance by the reader. And as John Berger has pointed out in his survey of the European nude in painting, 'the spectator in front of the picture . . . is assumed to be a man'; nudes in painting, like Tennyson's women, are 'offering up [their] femininity as the surveyed'.[9]

In 'The Gardener's Daughter' (1842; composed 1833–34) the girl is displayed with loosened hair and arm aloft, and the reader's specular caress in invited through the male touching of her body by the day, and by the poet's acknowledgement that his words make of her an image—'such a breast/As never pencil drew'—which can be hoarded and its erotic and romantic potential savoured in the privacy of the mind's eye:

> One arm aloft—. . .
> Holding the bush, to fix it back, she stood,
> A single stream of all her soft brown hair
> Poured on one side: . . .
> But the full day dwelt on her brows, and sunned
> Her violet eyes, and all her Hebe bloom,
> And doubled his own warmth against her lips,
> And on the bounteous wave of such a breast
> As never pencil drew . . .
> So home I went, but could not sleep for joy,
> Reading her perfect features in the gloom . . .
> And shaping faithful record of the glance
> That graced the giving—
>
> (124–74)

In 'The Miller's Daughter' (1832), with guileful circumstantial precision, the lover-poet positions the girl 'leaning from the [window] ledge above the river', and as in the development of a daguerreotype, her image forms in the water's mirror and the poet's gaze:

> And there a vision caught my eye;
> The reflex of a beauteous form,
> A glowing arm, a gleaming neck . . .
> And when I raised my eyes, above
> They met with two so full and bright—
> Such eyes!
>
> (76–87)

In the oxymoron of the description the eye 'catches' what is transient, what is in the act of becoming, yet the 'vision' of the woman is fixed because, as Jennifer Gribble says of the Lady of Shalott, the woman is 'framed by time and memory, perpetuating her emblematic significance in the stasis of romantic portraiture'.[10]

In some poems, the possession is more complete; the woman's consciousness is invaded and, as in ventriloquism, she speaks the man's possession of her and registers the obsessive erotic spell in which she is held. When Fatima says, 'I will . . . Grow, live, die looking on his face, / Die, dying clasped in his embrace' ('Fatima', 40–2), she holds a mirror to the poet-lover's sight which narcissistically reflects his sexual power. Œnone creates a solipsistic world—'I alone awake'—in which all natural objects are held in a stasis mimetic of her erotic dependency on Paris:

> For now the noonday quiet holds the hill:
> The grasshopper is silent in the grass:
> The lizard, with his shadow on the stone,
> Rests like a shadow, and the winds are dead.
> The purple flower droops: the golden bee
> Is lily-cradled: I alone awake.
>
> ('Œnone', 24–29)

Tennyson's contemporary readers responded excitedly to this kind of poetry. Men of varied political and literary inclinations such as W. J. Fox, Arthur Hallam, Christopher North and J. S. Mill shared a sense of the troubling, intriguing qualities of poems like 'The Ballad of Oriana' and 'Mariana' and found them new: 'Words surely never excited a more vivid feeling', wrote Mill, and 'How wonderful the new world thus created for us, the region between real and unreal', said Hallam. For indeed, this was innovative writing. Sweet virtuous girls, luscious Eastern maidens, coquettes, flirts and noble elusive ladies were present in the work of Tennyson's Romantic predecessors, but the poems which mark Tennyson's distinctive quality of writing and which herald the characteristics of his later poetry, poems like 'Mariana', 'Fatima', 'Œnone' and 'The Lady of Shalott', introduce a new type of woman and describe her in a new way. Only Keats had approached the suspenseful sensuality of such poems and his poetry does not achieve the degree of self-conscious eroticism that Tennyson's female impersonations possess. Such female eroticism, or rather the male fantasy of female eroticism which these poems embody, is, as Tennyson's later poems will show, danger-ous. Although Mariana is powerless and, like Guinevere after her, given entirely into male keeping for her happiness and her status, she is a threat to male power. It is a function of her passive sexuality to be destructive of the very force—male desire—which creates her. She is the new *femme fatale*.

Yet the source of Mariana's power is essentially domestic and familiar; the 'broken shed', the buzzing fly, the 'sparrow's chirrup', the poplar tree, these are the appurtenances of everyday life, particularly the enclosed and shuttered lives of middle-class women: 'I am like Mariana in the moated grange', wrote Elizabeth Barrett in 1845, voicing what many women must have felt, 'and sit listening too often to the mouse in the wainscot'.[11]

In this ordinariness, Mariana differs from the dangerous women in Romantic poetry who are characterized by beauty which is extraordinary, often unearthly. Mario Praz sees the epitome of this beauty in the Medusa of Shelley's poem:

> . . . all the beauty and the terror there—
> A woman's countenance, with serpent-locks,
> Gazing in death on Heaven from those wet rocks.
> ('On the Medusa of Leonardo da Vinci in the Florentine Gallery', 38–40)

'This glass-eyed, severed female head,' says Praz, 'this horrible, fascinating Medusa, was to be the object of the dark loves of the Romantics and the Decadents throughout the whole of the [nineteenth] century'.[12] Yet Praz's prognosis does not fit Tennyson; there are no fatal women of this kind in his poetry. Although there are women who do men harm, none of them has the mystery and terror of Shelley's Medusa or Keats' Belle Dame Sans Merci.

'Eleänore' (1832) provides an example of Tennyson's difference in this respect; in a manner that foreshadows the rose-lily dichotomy in *Maud*, the male speaker in this poem makes a dual response to a woman:

> In thee all passion becomes passionless,
> Touched by thy spirit's mellowness . . .
> Serene Imperial Eleänore . . .
>
> But when I see thee roam, with tresses unconfined,
> . . . then, as in a swoon,
> With dinning sound my ears are rife,
>   My tremulous tongue faltereth,
> I lose my colour, I lose my breath,
> I drink the cup of a costly death,
> Brimmed with delirious draughts of warmest life.
> I die with my delight . . .
>
> (102–40)

Both Gerhard Joseph and Clyde de L. Ryals have seen Eleänore as a type of '*the* fatal woman' for Tennyson, a 'powerful figure who traps the minds of all men who gaze on her'. Joseph sees a development of this response in 'Lady Clara Vere de Vere' of 1842 where for the first time 'the "I" of a Tennyson love poem is actively hostile towards such a woman. . . . After [this] when the fatal woman appears she does so with increasing virulence'.[13]

Certainly throughout his career Tennyson's division of women into good and bad became more pronounced and his conception of the dangerousness of women intensified and darkened. But to call his women 'fatal' seems a misnomer in the context of their Romantic predecessors whose distinguishing quality is summarized in Shelley's line: ' 'Tis the tempestuous loveliness of terror.' In this line, says Praz, 'pleasure and pain are combined in one single impression. The very objects which should induce a shudder—the livid face of the severed head, the squirming mass of vipers, the rigidity of death, the sinister light, the repulsive animals . . . all these give rise to a new sense of beauty, a beauty imperilled and contaminated, a new thrill.'[14] The Gothic features Praz discovers are not to be found in Tennyson's dangerous women; even Vivien, the most obviously wicked of all his women, has none of the terrible splendour of Shelley's Medusa or the sweet corruption of Keats's Lamia. In spite of the imagery of snakes and spiders, Vivien is no more than a coquette:

> And lissome Vivien, holding by his heel,
> Writhed towards him, slided up his knee and sat,
> Behind his ankle twined her hollow feet
> Together, curved an arm about his neck,
> Clung like a snake; and letting her left hand
> Droop from his mighty shoulder as a leaf,
> Made with her right a comb of pearl to part
> The lists of such a beard as youth gone out
>   Had left in ashes . . .   drew
> The vast and shaggy mantle of his beard
> Across her neck and bosom to her knee,
> And called herself a gilded summer fly
> Caught in a great old tyrant spider's web,
> Who meant to eat her up in that wild wood
> Without one word.
>
>   ('Merlin and Vivien', 236–59)

Even though they come from legend and literature, Tennyson's women have no supernatural power in their beauty; it does not horrify by its unnaturalness. It is significant, for example, that Tennyson's interest in the magic Vivien acquires is perfunctory and that he uses the thunderstorm as a rather stagy backdrop to the panic-stricken pleadings of this sexy little gossip and liar rather than as the magical workings of a real enchantress. Fatal or otherwise, Vivien and her like are very earth-bound women who are frequently victims of men's cruelty and neglect, who suffer from their constrained, dependent positions, and, most of all, from their own sexual and psychological needs. Like the fatal women of the Romantics, their danger lies in the harm they do to men; the difference lies in the kind of sexuality they possess which is passive, internalized, obsessive, neurotic, but the neurosis of the ordinary woman, or what the nineteenth century increasingly inclined to think of as ordinary. If Guinevere and her similarly passionate and frustrated predecessors have a demonic effect it is not ostensibly through demonic powers. It is in their womanliness that the danger lies, not in any fabulous quality. The peril of woman has been transferred from the realms of myth to the drawing-room, has been realized in the social and aesthetic delineaments of the period. The 'serpent-locks' and elfin blood of Shelley and Keats have been transformed into Eleänore's 'large eyes' and 'tresses unconfined' or, for that matter, into Vivien's 'vivid smiles, and faintly-venomed points of slander' and Mariana's gasping cry, 'He cometh not'.

Such a sense of the extraordinary power of ordinary female sexuality makes of Tennyson a forceful and early contributor to the explosion of sexual self-consciousness and neurosis characteristic of a period in which, as Michel Foucault has pointed out, it was by no means the case that sex was 'consigned to a shadow existence, but that [the Victorians] dedicated themselves to speaking of it *ad infinitum* while exploiting it as *the* secret'.[15] Foucault reminds us that:

> Sexuality must not be thought of as a kind of natural given which power tries to hold in check, or as an obscure domain which knowledge tries gradually to uncover. It is the name that can be given to a historical construct: not a furtive reality that is difficult to grasp, but a great surface network in which the stimulation of bodies, the intensification of pleasures, the incitement to discourse, the formation of special knowledges, the strengthening of controls and resistances, are linked to one another, in accordance with a few major strategies of knowledge and power.[16]

The 'discovery' of Mariana's sexuality, the sexuality of the ordinary woman she represents, is not, then, a discovery of a hidden truth about women; it is rather a 'speaking of' her sexuality as part of a power strategy to do with women but operated by those to whom power is a possessible commodity, primarily middle-class men. Mariana as woman and 'Mariana' as poem are both examples of what Foucault calls 'a hysterization of women's bodies' whereby the female body was 'analysed—qualified and disqualified—as being thoroughly saturated with sexuality . . . integrated into the sphere of medical practice [and] placed in organic communication with the social body, the family and the life of children'.[17] Whilst certainly previously, in the eighteenth century for example, women were categorized in relation to men, as wife, daughter, widow, and so on, in the nineteenth century this increasingly becomes not merely an economic and legal classification but also a 'hysterical' one. Woman's function and image becomes defined by her sexuality, literally, by the possession of a womb (hystera), and the state of her womb—virgin, senile, replete, menstruating, privately or communally owned—becomes her categorized biological, and even pathological, state of being female. In social terms the state is translated into the recognizable types of the Victorian literacy scene: pure maiden, 'redundant' woman, Madonna and matron, invalid and neurotic, sensualist and fallen woman. Any of Dickens's novels can supply examples of all such types.

Mariana is herself the type of the lovelorn, waiting woman, but she is also more than that. As Millais recognized in his 1857 painting of the poem and as Elizabeth Barrett also sensed when she compared her imprisoned and undecided state to Mariana's, in the suspended and incomplete, and therefore provocative, nature of her predicament Mariana invokes all the other types of woman with which Victorian ideology will be concerned, an ominous and seductive questioner of the fate of womankind: will Angelo deliver her into marriage, will she grow old alone, will she go mad or onto the streets, or will she die as she says she wishes to? Even now, and certainly in 1830 when the poem was written, the problem the poem leaves with its readers is what to do with Mariana's nubility, how to assuage her desperate sexuality. In the Victorian sexual economy, Mariana's 'development' must take place in one of three ways: in motherhood, in prostitution and, as the only alternative to these polarities, in death. Each of these bears a negative and a positive aspect: the good or the bad mother; the prostitute who is a creature of shame and disease or an instrument of redemption; the woman who dies in spiritual and sexual purity or who withers into sterility and hagdom. The link between all three categories is, of course, the instatement of masculinity and the upholding of male power.

Notes

1. See Jeffrey Weeks, *Sex, Politics and Society: The Regulation of Sexuality since 1800* (London: Longmans, 1981), 39.
2. See Tennyson's 'The Last Tournament', lines 685–94 in Christopher Ricks, ed., *The Poems of Tennyson* (London: Longmans, 1969).
3. *Poems*, ed. Ricks, 1129.
4. Sigmund Freud, 'The Uncanny' [1919], in *The Complete Psychological Works of Sigmund Freud* (London: Hogarth Press), XVII, 241.
5. Sigmund Freud, 'Beyond the Pleasure Principle' [1920] and 'Being in Love and Hypnosis' [1921], in op. cit., XVIII, 38.
6. Ibid, 41–42.
7. Quoted in *Poems*, ed. Ricks, 1152.
8. Nina Auerbach, *Woman and the Demon: The Life of a Victorian Myth* (Cambridge, Mass.: Harvard UP, 1982), 11.
9. John Berger, *Ways of Seeing* (London and Harmondsworth: B.B.C. and Penguin Books, 1972), 54–55.
10. Jennifer Gribble, *The Lady of Shalott in the Victorian Novel* (London: Macmillan, 1983), 3.
11. Elizabeth Barrett Barrett, *The Letters of Robert Browning and Elizabeth Barrett Barrett 1845–1846*, 2 vols., ed. Elvan Kintner (Cambridge Mass.: Harvard UP, 1969), I, 87.

12. Mario Praz, *The Romantic Agony* (London and Glasgow: Collins Fontana, 1960), 43.

13. Gerhard Joseph, *Tennysonian Love: The Strange Diagonal* (Minneapolis: University of Minnesota Press, 1969), 124–25.

14. Praz, *Romantic Agony*, 42.

15. Michel Foucault, *The History of Sexuality: Vol. I, an Introduction* (Harmondsworth: Penguin Books, 1984), 35.

16. Ibid., 105–6.

17. Ibid., 140.

"The Mortal Limits of the Self": Language and Subjectivity

ALAN SINFIELD

Central to Victorian poetry was the relationship between the individual consciousness and a supposed ultimate reality. Here the poet might claim a distinctive authority that did not impinge on the business of cotton spinning. If everyday relations and power structures are not his or her province, transcendental experience surely must be. In this domain poetic privilege is surely justified, for here is the purest state of mind, the final frontier of human experience. This theme, and the precise form it took, were fully acceptable to many of Tennyson's contemporaries. Writers since the time of the Reformation had often reflected independently on questions of religion, and Blake, Wordsworth and Shelley, at the peak of their powers, had been profoundly radical. In Tennyson's time religious debate became general, with the spread of education, the growth of scientific knowledge and publishing, and the inability of the Anglican Church to cope with the rate of social and demographic change. Engagement with matters of 'faith and doubt' seemed a responsible move for a poet. It was also temperamentally attractive to Tennyson, perhaps the more so because of disorientating political conditions.

In a letter of 1874, responding to a query about 'revelations through anaesthetics', Tennyson wrote:

A kind of waking trance I have frequently had, quite up from boyhood, when I have been all alone. This has generally come upon me thro' repeating my own name two or three times to myself silently, till all at once, as it were out of the intensity of the consciousness of individuality, the individuality itself seems to dissolve and fade away into boundless being, and this not a confused state, but the clearest of the clearest, and surest of the surest, the weirdest of the weirdest, utterly beyond words, where death was an almost laughable impossibility, the loss of personality (if so it were) seeming no extinction but the only true life.[1]

Increasingly, Tennyson was haunted by the thought that this kind of experience might underwrite something like God and the soul, as they had tradi-

Reprinted from *Alfred Tennyson* by Alan Sinfield (1986), by permission. © 1986 by Basil Blackwood Ltd.

tionally been authorized by the churches and the Bible. In 'The Ancient Sage' (1885), the sage reads from a scroll which he has taken from a young follower and argues against its scepticism. He offers as climactic evidence for the existence of an ultimate reality an experience like Tennyson's:

> And more, my son! for more than once when I
> Sat all alone, revolving in myself
> The word that is the symbol of myself,
> The mortal limit of the Self was loosed,
> And past into the Nameless, as a cloud
> Melts into Heaven. I touched my limbs, the limbs
> Were strange not mine—and yet no shade of doubt,
> But utter clearness, and through such loss of Self
> The gain of such large life as matched with ours
> Were Sun to spark—unshadowable in words,
> Themselves but shadows of a shadow-world.[2]

The preoccupation here with individual identity, and the yearning for an ultimate ground of fullness of being, are related—both as two poles of the one opposition, and as twin attempts to push past language to a reality beyond it. Tennyson's personal anxieties about identity and meaning, fuelled by historical conditions, pick up on a traditional theme. The passage re-enacts the fundamental project of western metaphysics: the attempt to locate a final, secure ground of meaning—in the self, a transcendent other, or, best of all, in a relationship between the two.

Tennyson's account echoes that of Plotinus, the third century Neo-Platonic philosopher: 'Many times it has happened: lifted out of the body into myself; becoming external to all other things and self-encentred; beholding a marvellous beauty; then, more than ever, assured of community with the loftiest order; enacting the noblest life, acquiring identity with the divine.'[3] Tennyson was inclined to take such similarities as evidence of the significance of his trances (*Memoir*, 168). Alternatively, we might view the similarities as evidence that Tennyson has construed his physical experience within the framework of ideas made available by his culture—that the significance that can be ascribed to experience is determined culturally. And from this we might infer, rightly I think, that Tennyson's idea that his trances might point towards a meaning beyond culture is, precisely and inevitably, a chimera.

A major impetus behind recent critical theories has been the thought that experience is constructed culturally, in language. Saussurean structuralism points out that language is always differential—founded in oppositions which say finally that *a* is *a* because it is not *b*. Thus language actually constructs the distinctions which it appears to identify in the world. This theory does not address the question of whether the world is there or not, but, rather, what kinds of things we can say and think about it. Our perceptions, let alone statements, are mediated through the grid of language into which we are born and which arranges sense impressions, abstract concepts and human relationships into schemes of significance.[4]

Jacques Lacan has argued that the self, also, has no essential existence, that it is formed as the infant moves into language, that it identifies itself only in terms of the symbolic system of the society into which it is received.[5]

And Marxists observe, in notions that the world and the self are *essentially* thus or thus, ideological strategies working to persuade men and women that the present order of things is necessarily so.

In the light of this body of theory, Tennyson's concern with his own name, and with the possible existence of 'the Nameless', appears as an anxiety about the constructedness of reality in language, and as an attempt to move beyond it. It is in this sense that his approach is metaphysical. As Jacques Derrida has argued, metaphysics strives always to bridge or efface the gap between language and reality and to control the play of language, in the hope, always just beyond fulfilment, that language can achieve 'full presence, the reassuring foundation, the origin and end of play'.[6] Tennyson's writings are fascinating in relation to the whole issue of the construction of reality in language, for they often encourage specific awareness of its implications, though usually drawing back from the fullest conclusion. His language exhibits the pressures of handling the most problematic and provocative aspects of the metaphysical project. The earnestness of Tennyson's engagement and the precariousness of his resolutions perhaps manifest a certain desperation. Also, they challenge and inform the reader.

Tennyson's poetry is saturated with attempts to name the Nameless. In 'The Two Voices' it is given as a characteristic of 'man' that 'His heart forebodes a mystery:/ He names the name Eternity' (290–91). Tennyson alludes to one of his trances at the turning point of *In Memoriam*, in section XCV: 'And all at once it seemed at last/The living soul was flashed on mine'; in section CXXIV the poet recalls:

> And what I am beheld again
>   What is, and no man understands,
>   And out of darkness came the hands
> That reach through nature, moulding men.

'What is' cannot be given a name, but finally it seems to promise 'In the deep night, that all is well' (section CXXVI).

Tennyson knows that the notion of ultimate being is fundamentally bound up with the inability of language to formulate that notion. In 'The Ancient Sage' words are 'Themselves but shadows of a shadow-world'; in *In Memoriam* they 'half reveal/And half conceal the Soul within' (section V). The assumption is that there is a reality beyond language which may be glimpsed but not expressed; in fact, what actually happens in these instances is that ultimate being is gestured towards precisely *through* the complaint about the inadequacy of language. So in *In Memoriam* (XCV) the reality of the poet's vision is set off against the dulling effect of language. His 'trance' is 'cancelled, stricken through with doubt' (notice the language of writing), and he declares:

> Vague words! but ah, how hard to frame
> In matter-moulded forms of speech,
> Or even for intellect to reach
> Through memory that which I became.

Tennyson is ready to recognize that language is a human construction because he can use this to point beyond it, to a realm which is not to be comprised in language. In 'The Higher Pantheism' he speaks of the physical world as a language *because* it manifests our separation from 'Him who reigns': "Earth, these solid stars, this weight of body and limb,/ Are not they sign and symbol of thy division from him?" Language is of the physical world and it manifests our exile from ultimate reality.

Hence the juxtaposition of the mortal name and 'the Nameless' in 'The Ancient Sage':

> revolving in myself
> The word that is the symbol of myself,
> The mortal limit of the Self was loosed,
> And past into the Nameless.

The sage separates his self from the symbol of his self: he does it by revolving that symbol in himself so that the outer (the name) becomes the inner. But what is then reached is not the self deeper inside, but the Nameless, that which is beyond 'The mortal limit' and the language which demarcates that limit. So the inner is transformed into a new outer. The non-mortal quality of this state is indicated by its lack of a name, for to be in language is to be in the mortal condition. Of course, the sage can only gesture towards this state beyond language, for 'the Nameless' *is a name*. But this is in the nature of the metaphysical project: the ultimate ground is always that which is just beyond reach, and language can only point beyond itself. Browning put this very clearly when Andrea del Sarto exclaims: 'Ah, but a man's reach should exceed his grasp,/Or what's a Heaven for'?[7]

As the sage reaches towards the Nameless, in the passage quoted, language progressively reveals its inadequacy so that a further state, just eluding containment, can be intimated. Initially language names the individual, and its intensive use ('revolving in myself/The word') looses the limits of 'the Self' and affords access to 'the Nameless'. But then the ultimate reality is defined in terms of its inaccessibility to language, and by the end of the passage the adequacy of language even to the human world is in question: words are 'Themselves but shadows of a shadow-world'. Yet the distinction is not allowed to be watertight; it cannot be, for after all there is no final escape from language, and the sage returns to the world:

> . . . And past into the Nameless, as a cloud
> Melts into Heaven. I touched my limbs, the limbs
> Were strange not mine—and yet no shade of doubt,
> But utter clearness, and through such loss of Self
> The gain of such large life as matched with ours
> Were Sun to spark—unshadowable in words,
> Themselves but shadows of a shadow-world.

Concepts and images interlock so that the second term picks up the first and augments it, at the same time seeming to abandon it: the 'cloud/Melts into Heaven', with the capital H turning the physical analogy into a premonition of its own spiritual implications; 'my limbs' become 'the limbs . . . not mine'. The replacements become more definite—though still negatively propounded—as the syntax continues to extend itself, as far as a possible stopping point at 'Sun to spark'; then the play on shadows runs the same effect backwards, depositing the sage back in the 'shadow-world' of the follower and his scroll—'I touch thy world again' (249). The language strives to name the Nameless by undermining progressively its own claim to reference, requiring, as the condition for a return to the 'mortal limit', a recognition that language itself constructs that limit at third remove from ultimate being.

There are two ways of regarding this linguistic strategy. If one is inclined to credit the ultimate reality it seeks to address, one will think that the poet has pointed to it as fully as is possible. If one is disinclined to credit it, one will see it as a suppressed admission of failure behind which may lurk all manner of further doubts and anxieties. The latter was Swinburne's response, who wrote beneath 'The Higher Pantheism': 'God, whom we see not, is; and God, who is not, we see:/Fiddle we know, is diddle: and diddle, we take it, is dee.'[8] These interpretive alternatives are always available: one may accept Tennyson's position or warily read through it, disclosing its strategy.

In 'The Ancient Sage' Tennyson moves boldly to address the major flaw in the kind of binary opposition which the sage, in the manner of the metaphysical tradition, has been constructing. The flaw is that the terms can all too easily be reversed; and so the sceptical scroll reverses the sage's light/dark imagery: 'Night and Shadow rule below/When only Day should reign.' The sage replies by admitting the problem:

Some say, the Light was father of the Night,
And some, the Night was father of the Light.
No night no day!—I touch thy world again—
No ill no good! such counter-terms, my son,
Are border races, holding each its own
By endless war.

(247–52)

The two terms have to fight, which is how each establishes its identity. This insight approaches Derrida's analysis of how such oppositions are secretly parasitic upon each other. Metaphysics imagines that by examining and revealing the terms of such an opposition, it is making progress; but in reality it is merely confirming the initial delimitation of the field, and the exclusion of other factors.[9]

It is bold of Tennyson to confront this issue, for his own thought works continuously through such binaries: language/self, self/ultimate being, inner/outer, shadow/sun, doubt/belief. But the confrontation is not sustained. Tennyson sidesteps it: 'The Ancient Sage' continues: 'but night enough is there/In yon dark city: get thee back . . ./. . . and help thy fellow men.' The light/dark opposition is shifted back into purely mortal terms—what people make of their cities—and its pretensions to point towards ultimate being are set aside for the goal of work in the world. This is perhaps a move we would welcome, but the idea of the Nameless is left as, implicitly, a higher level of experience which somehow ratifies such good work in the city.

Tennyson's willingness to expose his sage to questioning is not uncourageous. If the modern reader has difficulty seeing that, it is because the terms of the debate no longer seem very important, but the reader who ridicules the Victorians' faith and doubt may be far less ready to question his or her own ruling concepts. Although Tennyson seems, in my judgement, to want the sage to win the argument, by permitting questions he allows the reader scope to move, and opens up the possibility that the reader will find what was supposed to be the weaker argument to be the stronger. So T. S. Eliot declared of *In Memoriam*, 'Its faith is a poor thing, but its doubt is a very intense experience'.[10] For all this, faith/doubt constructs a metaphysical opposition, whichever way we tilt it. The point is not how or whether we decide between the two, but the centring of this opposition, so powerfully that other questions seem to be squeezed out. This is apparent when Tennyson himself reverses the terms: 'There lives more faith in honest doubt,/Believe me, than in half the creeds' (*In Memoriam*, XCVI). 'Believe me', redolent with earnestness and authenticity, exposes what is happening here: commitment to doubt is being offered as a new, superior brand of faith (so Eliot said this may 'justly be called a religious poem'). Faith and doubt are mutually supporting constructs: they sustain between them the notion that people

need an authority beyond the human to make sense of their lives, and thus
efface other ways of thinking about the world.

    The individual self is supposed to provide the starting-point for the
vision of the Nameless; it is offered as the first term against which the second
is defined. Modern theory, above all, denies the autonomy of the subjective
self. The idea of individual subjectivity, as a given which is undetermined
and unconstructed and hence a ground of meaning and coherence, is one of
the main tenets of conventional nineteenth and twentieth century thought.
In Literature, from the Romantics onwards, poetry authenticates itself in
terms of the poet's consciousness; and the realist novel, as a framework of
understanding at least, assumes that its characters are the sources of actions
and the place where actions have their principal effects. As a critical notion,
the autonomous self is elaborated conveniently by William Walsh, who
enumerates as the meanings of 'character': 'the source of action and, in
particular, of habitual action'; 'individuality, the incommunicable self'; and
'the person directed towards moral ends'.[11] Of course, as soon as this way of
thinking is established its problems are opened up—not least in the novels
and poems which partly depend upon it; nevertheless, the autonomous human
subject is the starting-point. It is also the critical construct in the faith/
doubt opposition: as ecclesiastical and rationalist authority weakened, belief
became something to be tested and affirmed in the authentic self.
    It is not enough to analyse the autonomous self merely as a philosophical
mistake: its significance is political. The constitution of the idea of the
individual in the eighteenth century was a progressive stage in the sequence
by which the bourgeoisie, spearheaded often by radical intellectuals, repudi-
ated a corrupt aristocratic rule in the name of the rights of each person—or,
at least, of each European male—to pursue legitimate goals without the
interference of arbitrary authority, and to contribute to the good republic on
the basis of individual rational decisions. Nevertheless, the idea of the individual made it all too easy to slide away from political objectives when, as
for instance in the French Revolution, they proved problematic, and to
narrow the range of sympathies to those of like mind (i.e. the same class).
The individual, eventually, was perceived as the opposite of the social and
the political, as a site of essential human values to which those 'public'
discourses could contribute little and from which they might well detract.
In this sequence Tennyson's position is transitional. He addresses political
issues in his poetry, though often by referring them to the individual (in *In
Memoriam*, for instance, confidence in the future of the political order depends
on the poet's sense of a continuing relationship with Hallam). And the
poems which Tennyson probably regarded as his most profound construct the
individual/universal dichotomy which, I have argued, effaces the political
and the historical.

In relation to the discussion so far, the issue of the self is the same as that of ultimate reality: whether there is any such entity, whether the name attached to it has any secure referent. Jacques Lacan has argued in psychoanalytic terms that the self is not innate but acquired: 'When the human baby learns to say "me" and "I" it is only acquiring these designations from someone and somewhere else, from the world which perceives and names it.'[12] The infant's own name is part of the differential system of language which I have already described, and the identity signalled by that name is equally acquired as the child moves into language. The child does not discover and develop a pre-existing identity, it receives an identity constructed in the world. Initially the infant experiences a sense of wholeness and harmony which it derives from the security of the relationship with the mother. The entrance into language and identity is founded in the loss of this imaginary wholeness: the belief that there must be a point of harmony and certainty persists, but attempts to locate it inevitably incorporate the split which they would heal.

By repeating his own name—'revolving in myself/The word that is the symbol of myself'—Tennyson's sage loosens the king-pin of the sense of identity, in a quest for the ideal imaginary wholeness which, Freud and Lacan claim, precedes identity. This might lead to the discovery that the self is a construction which is always in language and so always threatened by language, that it cannot be any essential entity and therefore cannot form the basis for locating ultimate being. But Tennyson veers away from such a conclusion by projecting the wholeness of the imaginary self onto a supposed ultimate reality.

In earlier poems, the instability of the self and the construction of identity as the infant moves into language are matters for confusion and despondency. The Lady of Shalott does not live in the world, but weaves her web from the reflection in a mirror. Her name and 'Camelot' are the twin refrain words, but she cannot relate the two—cannot locate a coherent sense of her self in the world. When she finally decides she is 'half sick of shadows', she writes 'The Lady of Shalott' around the prow of a boat and floats down to Camelot: she claims her name as a necessary prelude to entrance into social life, but the project is doomed. The concluding stanza as Tennyson originally published the poem makes clear the lady's claim to enter language and social identity:

> There lay a parchment on her breast,
> That puzzled more than all the rest,
>   The wellfed wits at Camelot.
> 'The web was woven curiously
> The charm is broken utterly,
> Draw near and fear not—this is I,
>   The Lady of Shalott'.

The Lady acknowledges to the society of Camelot that the coherent web she was weaving in her self-referential isolation has to break, and the illusion with it: thus she can claim 'this is I'. But her claim is disallowed—both in that her communication achieves only puzzlement, and in that she is dead, no longer a 'self' at all.

'Supposed Confessions of a Second-Rate Sensitive Mind' is ostensibly about the loss of religious faith but, as D. J. Palmer has pointed out, it is mainly about 'individuation, when the mind grows to self-awareness and loses its undifferentiated sense of being one with the world-beyond-self.'[13] The speaker's present crisis of identity—'I am void,/Dark, formless, utterly destroyed' (121–2)—is contrasted with 'the infant's dawning year' (67):

> Thrice happy state again to be
> The trustful infant on the knee!
> Who lets his rosy fingers play
> About his mother's neck, and knows
> Nothing beyond his mother's eyes.
> (40–44)

This passage is unclear about the kind of identity it attributes to the infant: he is happy and trustful, but totally dependent on 'his mother's eyes'. This may amount to a Lacanian sense of the constructedness of self. As Jacqueline Rose puts it: 'The mother does not (as in D. W. Winnicott's account) mirror the child to itself; she grants an image *to* the child'.[14] That identity may be to this degree dependent on the mother is again in play when the speaker says he beheld 'Thy mild eyes upraised, that knew/The beauty and repose of faith/And the clear spirit shining through' (74–76). The thought that there is no identity other than that which is imparted may contribute to the speaker's distress and bafflement at the withdrawal of the mother: 'Oh! wherefore do we grow awry/From roots which strike so deep? . . . Myself? Is it thus? Myself?' (77–78, 86). The poem ends in frustration and despondency: "O weary life! O weary death!/O spirit and heart made desolate!/O damnèd vacillating state!"

Tennyson's preoccupation with identity would seem to indicate a particular degree of psychological desperation. In 1923, Harold Nicolson overturned the image of the conventional Victorian laureate with his intuition of Tennyson's psychological state: 'One would prefer not to fall back upon the jargon of the psycho-analysts, but the application of the Freudian system to the case of Tennyson is quite illuminating. For Tennyson was afraid of a great many things: predominantly he was afraid of death, and sex, and God. And in all these matters he endeavoured instinctively to sublimate his terrors by enunciating the beliefs which he desired to feel, by dwelling upon the solutions by which he would like to be convinced.'[15] Since then, successive biographies have displayed Tennyson as a strange, unstable individual, immobilized by depression and haunted by fear of epilepsy, taking hydropathic 'cures' which involved 'rolling the naked patient in a wet sheet laid on two blankets, which were then folded around him until he was powerless to move'. Martin, Tennyson's recent biographer, links the trances with mental illness rather than ultimate being.[16]

In *The Princess* Tennyson himself gives a medical context for the trances: the prince is subject to 'weird seizures':

> On a sudden in the midst of men and day,
> And while I walked and talked as heretofore,
> I seemed to move among a world of ghosts,
> And feel myself the shadow of a dream.
> Our great court-Galen poised his gilt-head cane,
> And pawed his head, and muttered 'catalepsy'.
>
> (I. 15—20)

'And feel myself the shadow of a dream' is the language of the sage's vision, but here it denotes a disability. The 'weird seizures' occur at each main juncture in the action, and in the climactic battle the prince falls into 'some mystic middle state' (VI. 2) such that his survival is doubtful. This condition is recognized as like that of the infant:

> but I,
> Deeper than those weird doubts could reach me, lay
> Quite sundered from the moving Universe,
> Nor knew what eye was on me, nor the hand
> That nursed me, more than infants in their sleep.
>
> (VII. 35—39)

'The moving Universe' could be the ultimate reality of *In Memoriam* (XCV) and 'The Ancient Sage', but here there is no route through to it from the dissolved self. The resolution, instead, is the conventional one of the love of a good woman in the world. The princess, although she suspects that the prince is really seeking the security of the infant's relationship with the mother ('It seems you love to cheat yourself with words:/This mother is your model', VII. 314—15), agrees to marry him, and the trances are dispelled.

All the passages referring to the prince's seizures were added to *The Princess* in 1851, immediately after the publication of *In Memoriam* and Tennyson's marriage. These events seem to have released him to write of the trances as 'catalepsy' and to acknowledge a psycho-sexual dimension to them. If the prince's trajectory indicates Tennyson's belief that his trances, and the anxieties about identity which they provoked might cease, it seems he was mistaken. The Nameless was the alternative solution, and Tennyson had begun to develop it in *In Memoriam*.

The process by which Tennyson came to relate the infant's entrance into language and identity with the idea of ultimate being, and the problem in which this involved him, are apparent in section XLV:

> The baby new to earth and sky,
>   What time his tender palm is prest
>   Against the circle of the breast,
> Has never thought that 'this is I':
>
> But as he grows he gathers much,
>   And learns the use of 'I' and 'me',
>   And finds 'I am not what I see,
> And other than the things I touch'.
>
> So rounds he to a separate mind
>   From whence clear memory may begin,
>   As through the frame that binds him in
> His isolation grows defined.
>
> This use may lie in blood and breath,
>   Which else were fruitless of their due,
>   Had man to learn himself anew
> Beyond the second birth of Death. [17]

The movement of this poem is subtle and significant. The ideal imaginary harmony of the breast precedes the move into language and identity, but this move initially seems quite positive—it is gathering, learning, finding. The third stanza enacts a change of direction. The language of growth continues in the first two lines—'So rounds he', 'clear memory'—but the last two lines shift to ideas of confinement and alienation: 'As through the frame that binds him in/His isolation grows defined'. To be *defined*—determined in form and limits, given a precise and fixed meaning—is to be isolated.

The last stanza leaps suddenly to the thought that the only purpose of earthly individuation is that it sets us up for life after death. What the poet has in mind, in the context of the surrounding sections, is the loss of Hallam and the possibility of renewed intimacy with him. To be a mortal individual is to experience isolation and loss, but identity may have a purpose in an after-life; the 'second birth of Death' will not need to initiate again the entry into language.

This idea might seem to solve all Tennyson's problems at a stroke, but it is not sufficiently comprehensive (let alone credible). Such a projection of mortal identity onto eternity does not afford a conception of ultimate being powerful enough to deal with the full scope of the poet's distress. By remaining within the definition of human life in language, it actually impedes the ascent into the realm of the Nameless. So, two sections later, Tennyson raises the notion that life after death will consist of a merging into a 'general Soul':

> That each, who seems a separate whole,
>   Should move his rounds, and fusing all
>   The skirts of self again, should fall
> Remerging in the general Soul,
>
> Is faith as vague as all unsweet:
>   Eternal form shall still divide
>   The eternal soul from all beside;
> And I shall know him when we meet.
>
> (XLVII)

Division is preferable to ultimate being if it offers personal reunion with Hallam. But ultimate being still has an ineluctable claim: so Tennyson compromises and envisages

> Upon the last and sharpest height,
>   Before the spirits fade away,
>   Some landing-place, to clasp and say,
> 'Farewell! We lose ourselves in light'.

This sequence in *In Memoriam* reveals the fundamentally unsatisfactory implications of the self/Nameless opposition. Immediately Tennyson has described how he induces a trance by repeating his name, he realizes that to relinquish individuality for a sense of ultimate being may be a bad bargain. As he told his son: 'But in a moment, when I come back to my normal state of "sanity", I am ready to fight for *mein liebes Ich* [my beloved self], and hold that it will last for æons of æons' (*Memoir*, 268). The trap in which Tennyson is caught is this: that the more he resorts to ultimate being to validate this mortal life and its meanings, the further he is forced away from life and the human relationships which might help to secure his sense of identity. The Nameless affords an answer only at the expense of abolishing the question. Tennyson's problem is not his inability to believe, but that there is no coherent belief that will cope with all his needs. He has intuited that identity is constructed in language, and that language inevitably holds us at one remove from the reality which is supposed to lie beyond it. But he casts around continually for a position somehow beyond language. It is not to be found.

The idea that poetry is densely structured language derives from the Romantics (as Jonathan Culler points out), and was consolidated during the

Victorian period. Palgrave chose his lyrics for the *Golden Treasury* on the principle, 'above all, that excellence should be looked for rather in the whole than in the parts' and omitted passages 'only when the piece could be thus brought to a closer lyrical unity.'[18] Consequently we may assume that Tennyson composed *with this in mind*, and therefore that many of his short poems may indeed manifest it. ' "Every short poem", he remarked, "should have a definite shape, like the curve, sometimes a single, sometimes a double one, assumed by a severed tress or the rind of an apple when flung on the floor" ' (*Memoir*, 871). At this point it becomes difficult to distinguish the properties of the poem from the conventions of reading, since both are constructed within the same discourse. This fact does not give us what many structuralists have looked for, namely an exclusive definition of poetry, nor does it justify the privileges accorded to poetic language in conventional criticism. Nevertheless, the kind of structural density which Tennyson deploys is one of several features of his writing which invites attention.

This song is read to herself by Ida in *The Princess* at the point where she is reconsidering her rejection of the prince's suit:

> Now sleeps the crimson petal, now the white;
> Nor waves the cypress in the palace walk;
> Nor winks the gold fin in the porphyry font:
> The fire-fly wakens: waken thou with me.
>
> Now droops the milkwhite peacock like a ghost,
> And like a ghost she glimmers on to me.
>
> Now lies the Earth all Danaë to the stars,
> And all thy heart lies open unto me.
>
> Now slides the silent meteor on, and leaves
> A shining furrow, as thy thoughts in me.
>
> Now folds the lily all her sweetness up,
> And slips into the bosom of the lake:
> So fold thyself, my dearest, thou, and slip
> Into my bosom and be lost in me.

There is an obvious shape to this poem. Syntactical structures are in parallel both within and between the divisions marked by the arrangement of the lines, and they point to a systematic relationship between natural objects or creatures and the movements of the two loves, as well as to a sequence in those movements. The structural density admired by Palgrave and Tennyson lies within this shape, in the teasing interplay between positive and negative connections and active and passive roles. The structure is not simple: it arises through an alternation of correspondences and differences which builds only gradually, and with work from the reader, towards a complex outcome.

In the first line, the repeated 'now' may signify either intensity of the present (in this one moment, now) or alternation (at this moment the crimson, at that the white). This uncertain effect is developed into the next two lines by the relationship between 'now' and 'nor': they sound alike but, logically, they are establishing a contrast; yet the contrast is finally a similarity, since the idea in all the first three lines is of absence of movement. And in the fourth line the woman, 'thou', is both like the still features in that she is asleep, and like the fire-fly in that she is to waken. The effect is sustained in lines 5–6, for the peacock seems to be like the lady (both are 'like a ghost') but 'glimmers on to me' sounds more active than 'droops' ('glimmers on' at first seems passive and stationary—she continues to glimmer—but then 'on' becomes 'on to', suggesting movement). Lines 7–10 introduce another model of divergence/convergence: they take us outwards to vastly more distant objects of analogy and inwards to the lovers' consciousness. At the same time, there is a movement of interchange, for whilst the speaker enters the heart of the lady (as Jove's golden rain entered Danaë), it is the lady who corresponds to the meteor, her thoughts which enter the speaker.

This interchange in lines 7–10 proves to be a change of direction and the pivot of the poem, for it establishes the lady as the active one. Although the speaker exhorted her to wake and her heart lies open to him, her thoughts move like a meteor and in the final lines she is like the lily which folds her sweetness up and slips into the lake. This casting of the lady in the active role is relevant to *The Princess*, where conventionally 'feminine' qualities are attributed to the prince. To the modern reader at least, it may seem that implicitly phallic imagery is deployed in a direction which is the opposite of the customary one: it is the lady who 'slips into' the male speaker. Yet despite the lady's active role, the outcome is that the male speaker, without moving, has absorbed her. She began the poem in a state of solitary oblivion, analogous to isolated natural phenomena; she ends it in oblivion once more, 'lost in me', with all her activity used in the process of her incorporation into the man. The indeterminacy—which offers structures, then denies them, and then offers them more complexly—suggests the hesitancy and the final success of the speaker's wooing. Every detail seems to be working so much harder, more purposefully, than in 'ordinary' language.

The quest of structuralist criticism for a systematic density of implication is met by the manifest and self-conscious organization of 'Now sleeps the crimson petal'. Critics have asserted comparable levels of organization in long poems like the Arthurian idylls: J. M. Gray points in 'Balin and Balan' to 'dramatic parallelism, multi-levelled implication and symbolic analogy. . . . By such the poem has an *inner* coherence'.[19] However, this is by no means the sole tendency in Tennyson's writing: it is challenged by the use of conventionally 'poetic' effects apparently for their own sake. In *Idylls of the King*, certainly, the structures which critics have discerned coexist with a powerful countervailing tendency towards dispersal into local effects. Even in 'Now sleeps the crimson petal' it is doubtful how far the intricate patterning of sound can be demonstrated as contributing to a unified whole. With this thought in mind, Northrop Frye quotes from 'Oenone' and observes: 'the repetitions in Tennyson slow down the advance of ideas and narrative, compel the rhythm to return on itself, and elaborate what is essentially a pattern of varied and contrasting sound';[20] and E. L. Epstein quotes from 'Tithonus' to find that 'the vowel patterning seems to operate on its own, and even tends to de-emphasize the specific message.'[21] This tendency towards a self-sufficient sound patterning is finally at odds with a demand for complete structural integration: the effect is there to make the language more dense *in itself* rather than to build towards a significant structure. The underlying conception is illustrated by Tennyson himself when he remarks of *The Princess*: 'In defence of what some have called the too poetical passages, it should be recollected that the poet of the party was requested to "dress the tale up poetically".'[22] Such 'dressing up' pulls against the idea of a structured totality; nevertheless, I will argue in a moment that both tendencies may be viewed as part of the same larger project.

Within the framework I was using in *The Language of Tennyson's 'In Memoriam'*, I had some difficulty in handling the charge that 'Tennyson sought, by disguising his meaning in vague or ornate diction, to give his writing a merely artificial elevation.'[23] I now think that Tennyson cannot be 'defended' on this score, though I would want to consider what is really going on, rather than merely prefer one mode against another. The complaint goes back at least to Walter Bagehot, who responded to the publication of *Enoch Arden* in 1864 with a review which distinguished pure, ornate and grotesque poetry. Wordsworth and Milton are taken as instances of the first, Browning of the third. Ornate poetry is instanced by Tennyson and is defined thus: 'The essence of ornate art is . . . to accumulate round the typical object, everything which can be said about it, every associated thought that can be connected with it, without impairing the essence of the delineation.'[24]

Bagehot quotes the description of the tropical island upon which Enoch is wrecked:

> A shipwrecked sailor, waiting for a sail:
> No sail from day to day, but every day
> The sunrise broken into scarlet shafts
> Among the palms and ferns and precipices;
> The blaze upon the waters to the east;
> The blaze upon his island overhead;
> The blaze upon the waters to the west;
> Then the great stars that globed themselves in Heaven,

The hollower-bellowing ocean, and again
The scarlet shafts of sunrise—but no sail.

(586–95)

The passage manifests structural correspondences such as I discussed in 'Now
sleeps the crimson petal', but tends more towards an accumulation of effect
than the delicate distinctions of that poem; Bagehot identifies 'a mist of
beauty, an excess of fascination, a complication of charm' (355). Within the
principle that the poem should be a highly structured totality, such elaborate
writing has to be defended as relevant to the whole effect. Bagehot denies
that it is, declaring that there is 'a great deal . . . which a rough sailor like
Enoch Arden certainly would not have perceived' (352). A reply is offered
by Martin Dodsworth: 'Tennyson's point, which Bagehot misses, is that
Enoch *feels* nothing of the splendours described; his attention is turned
completely away from them.'[25] This is fair but, as Dodsworth actually suggests, it is not quite enough: he says that the repetitions of words and
phrases and accumulations of physical detail in the passage 'are dramatically
appropriate to the subject-matter', but also that 'the style is consistently
Tennysonian' and the subject-matter 'highly characteristic of the poet' (12).
There is a distinctively Tennysonian excess in the language, which goes
beyond the 'appropriate'.

The second passage Bagehot quotes is even more difficult to deal with
within the canons of structural relevance:

Enoch's white horse, and Enoch's ocean-spoil
In ocean-smelling osier, and his face,
Rough-reddened with a thousand winter gales,
Not only to the market-cross were known,
But in the leafy lanes behind the down,
Far as the portal-warding lion-whelp,
And peacock-yewtree of the lonely Hall,
Whose Friday fare was Enoch's ministering.

(93–100)

The reader may have trouble working out that this is all about the fact that
Enoch sells fish in the market and also supplies the upper classes. Here we
are plainly dealing with a stylistic mannerism. Bagehot's analysis is rather
limited: "Many of the characters of real life, if brought distinctly, promi-
nently, and plainly before the mind, as they really are, if shown in their
inner nature, their actual essence, are doubtless very unpleasant. They would
be horrid to meet and horrid to think of. We fear it must be owned that
Enoch Arden is this kind of person. A dirty sailor who did *not* go home to
his wife is not an agreeable being: a varnish must be put on him to make him
shine (363)." What Bagehot does not remark is that all sorts of Tennysonian

characters are treated in the same way as Enoch; he is actually saying that the manner seems to him absurd when applied to a lower-class person. The point is that Tennyson believed such 'dressing up' proper to poetry, and it has little to do with structural relevance.

What Tennyson cannot be accused of—and the point comprises both ornateness and structural density—is transparency of style. Bagehot attributes transparency to 'pure' poetry: 'The form is sometimes said to be bare, the accessories are sometimes said to be invisible, because the appendages are so choice that the shape only is perceived' (342); so 'to Wordsworth has been vouchsafed the last grace of the self-denying artist; you think neither of him nor his style, but you cannot help thinking of—you *must* recall—the exact phrase, the *very* sentiment he wished' (345). As Antony Easthope has pointed out, this Wordsworthian effect sets aside the whole preceding rhetorical tradition in English poetry. In the Preface to *Lyrical Ballads*, Wordsworth maintains that poetry is 'so wholly transparent to experience that it is virtually identical with it', and in the 1802 Appendix to the Preface he 'gives a polemical history of rhetoric as the "mechanical adoption" of "figures of speech", "a motley masquerade of tricks, quaintnesses, hieroglyphics, and enigmas" '.[26] Such an attempt to efface the process of writing is one way of trying to get past the fact that experience is always constructed in language; a transparent style seems to assert a direct access to reality.

I discussed above Tennyson's yearning to locate an ultimate ground of being and truth beyond language, attributing it both to personal anxiety and to the disorienting political conditions in which poetry was expected to find a role for itself. In Derrida's terms, Tennyson strives within the tradition of western metaphysics to bridge or eradicate the gap between language and reality. One way of pursuing this always-postponed goal is to make language transparent. Richard Rorty has observed that this has been a typical strategy of philosophers, who seem to 'think that writing is a means of representing facts, and that the more "written" writing is—the less transparent to what it represents and the more concerned with its relation to others' writing— the worse it must be'.[27] Tennyson takes an opposite path: he seeks to make his language as dense and substantial as possible. It might be argued, as Easthope does of Modernist poetry, that 'by insisting on itself as production it asserts the subject as made, constituted, relative rather than absolute' (135): that such self-conscious linguistic excess draws attention to the constructedness of what we imagine to be reality. But although Tennyson's verse may be read to this effect (which, indirectly, is what I am doing), to suggest that this was in some sense his project would be to ignore all the other indications that Tennyson wanted desperately to assert an ultimate reality, and to discover a means of apprehending it through poetic language. It seems, rather, that both the structural density and the ornateness which Tennyson cultivated are parts of his strategy for limiting the arbitrariness of the sign and imparting a sense of presence. The elaborate diction, the obtrusive syntax and the intense effects of sound and rhythm all act in the same direction. They offer not an enhanced transparency in the relationship between sign and referent, but an unattributed density *in the sign itself*.

Rather than closing the gap between sign and referent, Tennyson creates, as it were, a plenitude of the sign. Language cannot be brought closer to the world, but it can be made more full and substantial *in itself*. In Tennyson's writing any particular word has, or appears to have, many reasons for being appropriate: it is linked to other words through effects of sound and rhythm, syntactical parallelism, and figurative associations which may extend through a network of images across hundreds of lines; and passages which seem ornate rather than organic also seem to make the word more substantial in itself. Thus the arbitrariness of language seems to be controlled. And it all works in relative independence of reference to the world: significance begins to seem a property of the poem, not of the world. The poem creates an alternative reality which is bounded entirely by its language. Of course a deception, no doubt benign, is involved here: for if the relationship between sign and referent is in principle arbitrary, then to multiply the facets of that relationship will not help. Twenty kinds of arbitrary relationship, however much they interlock, are still arbitrary. There is—can be—only the *impression* of plenitude. Perhaps the distinction between highly structured and ornate poetry amounts to that between those passages where we find this impression achieved, and those where we do not. Through this strategy of 'filling up' the sign, Tennyson sought to locate a ground of truth and ultimate being beyond the unstable constructions of language.

Tennyson's early awareness that the sign lacks the fulness of the real world is powerfully expressed in 'Early Spring', a poem written in 1833 but published only in 1883 and without most of the stanzas I will discuss. The poem celebrates the marvellous budding forth of spring, and after twenty-eight lines of evocative description the idea of language enters:

> My tricksy fancies range,
> And, lightly stirred,
> Ring little bells of change
> From word to word.

But this thought of correspondence between words and reality provokes Tennyson, immediately, to address its inadequacy:

> Ah! lightest words are lead,
> Gross to make plain
> Myriads of hints of things
> That orb and wane.

The poem is forced away from description and into abstraction:

> O fullness of the worlds!
> O termless field,
> Relation, difference,
> Not all concealed,
> Fair feast of every sense
> In part revealed.

The world has a fulness beyond that of language: it is 'termless', not subject to the confines of language. The endless possibilities of meaning in the world—all its relatedness and distinctions—are there, not narrowed into the structures of language but laid out before the viewer. Yet there is a lack: it is *'Not all* concealed . . . *In part* revealed'. The limits of language are, after all, in some measure the limits of consciousness. We may regard this as an acknowledgement of the extent to which consciousness is constructed in language—we see that which language encourages or permits us to see. More likely, Tennyson means that there is a spiritual implication in the landscape which is only partially appreciated through the senses, for the last stanza reads:

> O soul reflecting forms
> Of this wide beach,
> Comparing at thy will
> Each form with each,
> Let tears of wonder fill
> Thy void of speech.

The language here struggles to relate the fullness of the landscape to that of the soul: the lack of a clear grammatical subject for the second two lines enacts Tennyson's difficulty in locating a perceiving self which is free from the inhibitions of language, which can compare 'at . . . will'. The void which speech opens up can be filled only by tears; it is a question for interpretive license whether we should remark that the tears will interrupt the poet's view, making his experience increasingly self-constructed. In 1883 Tennyson withdrew these awkward implications and offered a final stanza which returns to the 'Heavenly Power' of the poem's opening:[28]

> . For now the Heavenly Power
> Makes all things new,
> And thaws the cold, and fills
> The flower with dew;
> The blackbirds have their wills,
> The poets too.

The last line is new. It asserts the poet's harmony with the external world and his achievement, presumably poetic achievement: he has done what he wills, and the poem is finished. A proclamation of success replaces the intensifying problematization of the early version.

That in poetry the defect of words is remedied seems to have been Tennyson's customary assumption (though he would still, as I instanced above, suggest that visionary moments are beyond all language). Hence his emphasis when he wrote to Emily Sellwood in 1839: 'In *letters*, words too often prove a bar of hindrance instead of a bond of union'.[29] Poetry affords a special fulness of significance. Tennyson's view here converges upon a whole movement in European poetry. Gérard Genette finds that for Mallarmé 'the nonmimetic character of language'—its general failure to give transparent access to a secure referent in reality—is 'the opportunity and the condition for poetry to exist', for poetry is the special mode of language which compensates for 'the defect of languages'.[30] Genette uses the term 'Cratylism' (from Plato via Barthes) for 'that great secular myth which wants language to imitate ideas and, contrary to the precisions of linguistic science, wants signs to be motivated' (360). The move of Mallarmé and Valéry, to create not a transparency of the sign but an incantatory, self-sufficient density of language, Genette calls 'secondary Cratylism'—'a Cratylism of the poem. . . . Henceforth there are two languages in language, one of which (everyday language) is left to arbitrariness and convention, while the other (poetic language) is the refuge of mimetic virtue, the locus of the miraculous survival of the primitive verb in all its "incantatory" power' (363).

Hence the cultivation, apparently for their own sake, of 'musical' properties in verse. Valéry's key statement, Genette points out, is that 'the power of verse stems from an *indefinable* harmony between what it *says* and what it *is*' (366): 'music' is needed for its suggestiveness. All this is anticipated in Hallam's review of *Poems, Chiefly Lyrical*, in which he says that great poets like Dante and Petrarch

> produce two-thirds of their effect by *sound*. Not that they sacrifice sense to sound, but that sound conveys their meaning, where words would not. There are innumerable shades of fine emotion in the human heart, especially when the senses are keen and vigilant, which are too subtle and too rapid to admit of corresponding phrases. The understanding takes no definite note of them; how then can they leave signatures in language? Yet they exist; in plenitude of being and beauty they exist; and in music they find a medium through which they pass from heart to heart.
>
> —Armstrong, 96–97

It is all there: the fullness of experience, especially the poet's experience, the inadequacy of ordinary language, the short-circuiting of the usual modes of reference to the world, and the achievement of a marvellously direct communication 'from heart to heart'.

As well as intoning his own name, Tennyson found a strange charm in the words 'Far—Far—Away', and he wrote about it in 1888 in a poem called that:

> What vague world-whisper, mystic pain or joy,
> Through those three words would haunt him when a boy,
> Far—far—away?
>
> A whisper from his dawn of life? a breath
> From some fair dawn beyond the doors of death
> Far—far—away?
>
> Far, far, how far? from o'er the gates of Birth,
> The faint horizons, all the bounds of earth,
> Far—far—away?
>
> What charm in words, a charm no words could give?
> O dying words, can Music make you live
> Far—far—away?

This is a quintessential Tennyson poem: the repeating of the words so that language evaporates and points beyond itself to what the poet takes to be an intuition of an ultimate reality; the location of imaginative experience in remote places and the sense that the horizon recedes ('Far, far, how far?'); the suggestion that words cannot do that which nevertheless is being done by poetical magic. The poem is subtitled '(For Music)', suggesting both that the poem should be set to music because only thus could it fully transcend ordinary language, and that the poem is dedicated to music whose profound power is thus identified as that of the words 'Far—far—away', a power beyond their power as words. So in the last stanza we should understand 'charm' as magic, incantation: it is through the special power of music that these words may be made fully vital—because their effect was always more like that of music than ordinary language. A. Dwight Culler quotes R. H. Horne's comment: 'he will write you a poem with nothing in it except music, and as if its music were everything, it shall charm your soul.'[31]

That literature generally, and poetry in particular, should attain to some such density of effect, constituting through and beyond language a reality which language cannot reach, became a commonplace of literary criticism as it developed within a utilitarian framework. In *Mythologies*, Roland Barthes observes that poetry 'tries to transform the sign back into meaning: its ideal, ultimately, would be to reach not the meaning of words, but the meaning of things themselves. This is why it clouds the language, increases as much as it can the abstractness of the concept and the arbitrariness of the sign and stretches to the limit the link between signifier and signified.'[32] It is through this project—to which Tennyson contributed crucially—that poetry stakes its claim over against utilitarianism, political economy and machinery: it heals the breach between humankind and reality.

Notes

1. Hallam Tennyson, *Alfred Lord Tennyson: A Memoir by His Son*, 1 vol. (London: Macmillan, 1899), 268. Referred to subsequently in the text as *Memoir*.

2. Lines 229–39, in Christopher Ricks, ed., *The Poems of Tennyson* (London: Longmans, 1969). Cf. A. Dwight Culler, *The Poetry of Tennyson* (New Haven and London: Yale Univ. Press, 1977), 1–8.

3. Plotinus, *The Enneads*, trans. Stephen MacKenna, 4th edn., revised B. S. Page (London: Faber, 1969), IV, 8, 357.

4. On Saussure, see Terence Hawkes, *Structuralism and Semiotics* (London: Methuen, 1977).

5. On Lacan, see *Feminine Sexuality: Jacques Lacan and the École Freudienne*, ed. Juliet Mitchell and Jacqueline Rose (London: Macmillan, 1982).

6. Jacques Derrida, *Writing and Difference*, trans. Alan Bass (London: Routledge, 1978), 292.

7. *The Poetical Works of Robert Browning*, 2 vols. (London: Hutchinson, 1906), II, 510.

8. See Kerry McSweeney, *Tennyson and Swinburne as Romantic Naturalists* (Toronto Univ. Press, 1981), 21.

9. Derrida, *Writing and Difference*, p. 19; *Of Grammatology*, trans. Gayatri Chakravorty Spivak (Johns Hopkins Univ. Press, 1976), 315.

10. T. S. Eliot, *Selected Prose*, ed. John Hayward (Harmondsworth: Peregrine, 1963), 172.

11. William Walsh, *The Use of Imagination* (Harmondsworth: Peregrine, 1966), 180. Walsh aims to correct a tendency in this view not to take into account the 'potential and dynamic nature' of character.

12. Juliet Mitchell in *Feminine Sexuality*, 5.

13. In *Tennyson: Writers and their Background*, ed. D. J. Palmer (London: Bell, 1973), 28.

14. Jacqueline Rose in *Feminine Sexuality*, 30.

15. Harold Nicolson, *Tennyson: Aspects of his Life, Character and Poetry* (London: Grey Arrow Books, 1960), 34.

16. Robert Bernard Martin, *Tennyson: The Unquiet Heart* (Oxford Univ. Press, 1980), p. 277; also 27–29, 83–85, 238, 278–80.

17. This section seems to derive from Arthur Hallam's essay 'On Sympathy', in *The Writings of Arthur Hallam*, ed. T. H. Vail Motter (New York: Modern Language Association of America, 1943), 134, 137. Its Lacanian properties are noted by Terry Eagleton in 'Tennyson: Politics and Sexuality in *The Princess* and *In Memoriam*', in *1848: The Sociology of Literature*, ed. Francis Barker et al. (University of Essex, 1978), 104. See also, on infants and language, *In Memoriam* LIV and CXXIV.

18. Jonathan Culler, *Structuralist Poetics* (London: Routledge, 1971), 171; Francis T. Palgrave, ed., *The Golden Treasury*, Complete Edition (London: Macmillan, 1909), viii.

19. J. M. Gray, *Tennyson's Doppelgänger: Balin and Balan* (Lincoln: The Tennyson Society, 1971), 26.

20. *Sound and Poetry*, English Institute Essays, 1956 (Columbia Univ. Press, 1957), p. xiv.

21. E. L. Epstein, *Language and Style* (London: Methuen, 1978), 37.

22.   Quoted in Ricks, ed., *The Poems of Tennyson*, 743, with reference to *The Princess*, Conclusion, line 6.

23.   Alan Sinfield, *The Language of Tennyson's 'In Memoriam'* (Oxford: Blackwell, 1971), 44.

24.   Walter Bagehot, *Literary Studies*, 3 vols. (London: Longmans, Green, 1898), II, 353.

25.   *The Major Victorian Poets: Reconsiderations*, ed. Isobel Armstrong (London: Routledge, 1969), 10.

26.   Anthony Easthope, *Poetry as Discourse* (London: Methuen, 1983), 124–25.

27.   Richard Rorty, 'Philosophy as a Kind of Writing: An Essay on Derrida', *New Literary History* 10 (1978): 146.

28.   For the 1833 version of 'Early Spring' see Ricks, *Poems*, 496–98; for the 1883 version see 1314–16.

29.   *The Letters of Alfred Lord Tennyson*, ed. Cecil Y. Lang and Edgar F. Shannon, Jr., Vol. 1 (Oxford Univ. Press, 1982), 173.

30.   Gérard Genette, 'Valéry and the Poetics of Language', in *Textual Strategies*, ed. Josué V. Harari (London: Methuen, 1980), 364.

31.   Culler, *The Poetry of Tennyson*, p. 5. Horne's essay, of 1844, is in John D. Jump, ed., *Tennyson: The Critical Heritage* (London: Routledge, 1967): see 155.

32.   Roland Barthes, *Mythologies* (St Albans: Paladin, 1973), 133.

INDEX

◆

257

Byatt, A. S., 193n14
Byron, George Gordon, 2, 9, 59

Carlyle, Jane, 18
Carlyle, Thomas, 18, 196, 214; *Latter-Day Pamphlets*, 214; *Past and Present*, 199; *Sartor Resartus*, 214
Carpenter, Edward: Ioläus, 155
Catullus, 136
Cervantes, Miguel de, 9
Chadwick, Joseph, 7, 83–99
Chapin, Chester: *Personification*, 123n25, 123n31
Christ, Carol, 217n33, 217n35; *Victorian and Modern Poetics*, 84, 85, 98n8, 155
Coleridge, Samuel Taylor, 9, 59; "Eolian Harp," 84
Colley, Ann, 194n19
Collins, William, 113; "Ode to Evening," 123n25
Cott, Nancy, 207
Cowper, William: "Negro's Complaint," 118
Crabbe, George, 9
Craft, Christopher, 7, 153–73
Craik, George, 11, 13
Cromwell, Oliver, 12
Culler, A. Dwight, 176; *Poetry of Tennyson*, 64, 81n6, 85, 98n11, 119n1, 121n12, 193n2, 254
Culler, Jonathan: *Structuralist Poetics*, 245–46

Dallas, E. S.: *Gay Science*, 104
Dante Alighieri, 9, 253; *Divina Commedia*, 55, 59, 76, 168
Day, Aidan: *Tennyson Archive*, 8
Delacroix, Eugène, 210
De Man, Paul: *Rhetoric of Romanticism*, 83–84
Derrida, Jacques, 250, 256n27; *Of Grammatology*, 70, 239; *Writing and Difference*, 236, 239
Dickens, Charles, 18, 20, 162, 178, 232; *David Copperfield*, 173n31; *Great Expectations*, 133–34; *Tale of Two Cities*, 202
Dodgson, Charles Lutwidge, 18
Dodsworth, Martin, 46n47, 249
Donohue, Mary Joan, 65, 119n1, 121n12, 121n13, 123n23

Douglas, Ann: *Feminization of American Culture*, 201
Drew, Philip, 193n14
Durkheim, Emile, 117

Eagleton, Terry, 255n17
Easthope, Anthony: *Poetry as Discourse*, 250
Edward III, King, 10
Eggers, J. Philip: *King Arthur's Laureate*, 217n34
Eliade, Mircea, 217n27; *Cosmos and History*, 200; *Mephistopheles*, 201
Eliot, George (Marian Evans), 123n28; 125; *Adam Bede*, 129, 221; *Middlemarch*, 199, 215n14; *The Mill on the Floss*, 195, 219
Eliot, T. S., 125, 239; "*In Memoriam*," 5–6, 27, 37, 160, 164–65; "The Love Song of J. Alfred Prufrock," 175
Elliott, Philip L.: *The Making of the "Memoir,"* 11, 13
Ellis, Havelock: *Sexual Inversion*, 153–55, 170; *Studies in the Psychology of Sex*, 207
Emerson, Ralph Waldo, 67n15
Emma, Queen, 18
Epstein, E. L.: *Language and Style*, 248

FitzGerald, Edward, 11, 18, 21, 24, 26, 197
Fletcher, Angus: *Allegory*, 123n24
Fletcher, Pauline, 194n15
Flynn, Philip, 120n6
Fordyce, David: *Dialogue Concerning Education*, 115, 116
Forster, John, 18
Foucault, Michel, 170, 195, 231
Fox, W. J., 45n6, 228
Francis, Elizabeth: *Critical Essays*, 1
Fraunce, Abraham: *Arcadian Rhetorike*, 45n9
Fredeman, William E., 121n11
Freud, Sigmund, 224, 241, 242; "Being in Love and Hypnosis," 225; "Beyond the Pleasure Principle," 225; "A Case of Paranoia," 195; "Mourning and Melancholia," 165–67; *Totem and Taboo*, 118
Frye, Northrop: *Sound and Poetry*, 248
Fuseli, Henry, 20

Property of
THE HIGH POINT
NEAL F. AUSTIN
PUBLIC LIBRARY

9305681

821.8 Critical essays on Alfred
T312   Lord Tennyson.
T892c

**THE HIGH POINT
NEAL F. AUSTIN
PUBLIC LIBRARY
HIGH POINT NC**

DEMCO